Further Praise for *Globalization and Its Discontents*

"Development and economics are not about statistics. Rather, they are about lives and jobs. Stiglitz never forgets that there are people at the end of these policies, and that the success of a policy should be defined not by how fast international banks are repaid, but by how much people have to eat, and by how much better it makes their lives."

—*Christian Science Monitor*

"[An] urgently important new book." —*Boston Globe*

"Whatever your opinions, you will be engaged by Stiglitz's sharp insights for a provocative reform agenda to reshape globalization. A must read for those concerned about the future, who believe that a world of decent work is possible and want to avert a collision course between the haves and the have nots." —Juan Somavia, director-general of the International Labour Organization

"[Stiglitz's] rare mix of academic achievement and policy experience makes *Globalization and Its Discontents* worth reading. . . . His passion and directness are a breath of fresh air given the usual circumlocutions of economists." —*BusinessWeek*

"This smart, provocative study contributes significantly to the ongoing globalization debate and provides a model of analytical rigor concerning the process of assisting countries facing the challenges of economic development and transformation. . . . Impassioned, balanced and informed. . . . A must-read." —*Publishers Weekly*

"An insightful analysis of why globalization has been failing too many of the world's poorest citizens and how to build and manage a more inclusive global economy. Timely and provocative."

—Mark Malloch Brown, administrator, United Nations Development Program

"A great tour of the complexities of economic policymaking. Getting a top economist to subject the U.S. Treasury and the IMF to withering scrutiny . . . is good for the long-term health of the system."

—*Financial Times*

"Stiglitz has presented, as effectively as it is possible to imagine anyone making it, his side of the argument, including the substantive case for the kind of economic development policies he favors as well as his more specific indictment of what the IMF has done and why. . . . [His] book will surely claim a large place on the public stage."

—*New York Review of Books*

"This book is everyone's guide to the misgovernment of globalization. Joe Stiglitz was there. He knows. And he explains it here in plain and compelling language."

—James K. Galbraith, University of Texas at Austin

"A fresh, much-needed look at how institutions—primarily the International Monetary Fund—affect policy. . . . Stiglitz has done important work by opening a window few of us ever get to look through, into institutions that are, after all, public."   —*San Francisco Chronicle*

"When Joe and I first met in Kenya in 1969, the creativity of his thinking and his deep commitment to development were immediately striking. During more than three decades of friendship I have always found his ideas interesting and incisive. He is one of the most important economists of modern times."   —Nicholas Stern, chief economist and senior vice president, World Bank

"Stiglitz . . . is hardly the first person to accuse the IMF of operating undemocratically and exacerbating Third World poverty. But he is by far the most prominent, and his emergence as a critic marks an important shift in the intellectual landscape."   —*The Nation*

"Gripping. . . . This landmark book . . . shows him to be a worthy successor to Keynes."   —*Independent* (UK)

GLOBALIZATION AND ITS DISCONTENTS REVISITED

Also by Joseph E. Stiglitz

The Euro: How a Common Currency Threatens the Future of Europe

*Rewriting the Rules of the American Economy: An
Agenda for Growth and Shared Prosperity*

The Great Divide: Unequal Societies and What We Can Do about Them

*Creating a Learning Society: A New Approach to Growth,
Development, and Social Progress* (with Bruce C. Greenwald)

The Price of Inequality: How Today's Divided Society Endangers Our Future

Freefall: America, Free Markets, and the Sinking of the World Economy

*The Three Trillion Dollar War: The True Cost of
the Iraq Conflict* (with Linda J. Bilmes)

Making Globalization Work

*Fair Trade for All: How Trade Can Promote
Development* (with Andrew Charlton)

The Roaring Nineties: A New History of the World's Most Prosperous Decade

Globalization and Its Discontents

GLOBALIZATION AND ITS DISCONTENTS REVISITED

Anti-Globalization in the Era of Trump

Joseph E. Stiglitz

W. W. NORTON & COMPANY
Independent Publishers Since 1923
NEW YORK LONDON

For information about permission to reproduce selections from this book, write to
Permissions, W. W. Norton & Company, Inc., 500 Fifth Avenue,
New York, NY 10110

For information about special discounts for bulk purchases, please contact
W. W. Norton Special Sales at specialsales@wwnorton.com or 800-233-4830

Manufacturing by LSC Communications, Harrisonburg
Production manager: Anna Oler

ISBN 978-0-393-35516-1 (pbk.)

W. W. Norton & Company, Inc.
500 Fifth Avenue, New York, N.Y. 10110
www.wwnorton.com

W. W. Norton & Company Ltd.
15 Carlisle Street, London W1D 3BS

1 2 3 4 5 6 7 8 9 0

To my mother and father who taught me to care and reason,
and to Anya who put it all together and more

Contents

GLOBALIZATION AND ITS DISCONTENTS REVISITED

INTRODUCTION TO GLOBALIZATION AND ITS DISCONTENTS REVISITED

DONALD J. TRUMP became president of the United States on January 20, 2017, and threw a hand grenade into the global economic order—the arrangements governing the movement of goods, services, and capital across borders and attempting to ensure stability. The United States was pivotal in the creation of this system in the aftermath of World War II. Partly because of this system, the second half of the twentieth century was markedly different from the first half, which was marred by two world wars and the Great Depression. The smoke has not yet cleared, but the post-Trump world will almost surely be different from what came before. While for three-quarters of a century efforts had focused on creating a more globally integrated world, entailing global supply chains that had enormously lowered the costs of goods, Trump reminded everyone: borders do matter.

In the beginning of this century, I wrote *Globalization and Its Discontents* (which, for brevity, I write as *GAID* going forward) to explain the unhappiness with globalization on display in so many countries in the developing world that I had been able to observe closely from my perch as chief economist of the World Bank. This is the part of the world with 85 percent of the world's population but with 39 percent of the world's income.[1] The unhappiness was greatest in Sub-Saharan Africa, often rightly called a forgotten region, with a burgeoning population expected to reach 2.1 billion by 2050—close to seven times that of the United States today; its rich human and natural resources have been stolen from it for centuries, leaving it today with a per capita income 2.5 percent of that of the United States.[2]

Now, globalization's opponents in the emerging markets and developing countries are joined by those in the middle and lower classes of the advanced industrial countries. Trump took advantage of this discontent, crystallized and amplified it. Trump explicitly blamed the plight of America's Rust Belt workers on globalization—on the signing of the "worst trade deals ever."

On the face of it, this is a remarkable claim. The United States and other advanced countries wrote the rules of globalization, and they run the international organizations that govern it. The complaint of those in the developing world was that the advanced countries had written the rules and managed these international organizations in ways that disadvantaged them. Yet, President Trump claimed—with enormous support from American voters—that the very trade agreements and other institutions that it shaped were unfair to America.

Populists in both emerging markets and advanced countries are giving voice to their citizens' discontent with globalization, but just a few years earlier, establishment politicians promised that globalization would make everyone better off. So too, two and a half centuries of economic research—starting with Adam Smith writing at the end of the eighteenth century and David Ricardo early in the nineteenth—argued that globalization was beneficial to all countries.[3] If what they said is correct, how do we explain why so many people in both the developed and developing world have become so hostile to it? Was it possible that not just the politicians, but also the economists, got it wrong?

One response occasionally heard from neoliberal economists—those economists who believe that the freer the markets the better, and accordingly advocate for "freeing" up trade—is that people *are* better off, but they just don't know it. Their discontent is a matter for psychiatrists, not economists.[4]

ALL IS NOT WELL IN THE ADVANCED COUNTRIES

The fact, though, is that large segments of the population in advanced countries have not been doing well. The New Discontents have taken power in the United States in the form of the Trump presidency partly because the United States does things bigger than others—including having more inequality than elsewhere in the advanced world. But much of what I say for the United States applies in a somewhat diminished form to the rest of the advanced world, apart from a few countries, particularly in Scandinavia; here, and elsewhere in my discussion of the New Discontents in Part I, I use the United States as an illustration.

The Sobering Statistics

The data describing what has been happening in the United States are sobering: for nearly a third of a century the incomes of most Americans have been essentially stagnant. A middle-class life—a decent job with decent wages and a modicum of security, the ability to own a home and to send one's kids to college, with the hope of a reasonably comfortable retirement—has been moving increasingly out of reach for a large proportion of the country. The numbers in poverty have been increasing, as the middle is being eviscerated. The one group doing well has been the top—especially the top 1 percent and even more, the top .1 percent, the richest several hundred thousand Americans.

While moving up the ladder seems increasingly difficult, everyone knows someone who has fallen down: trying to avoid falling down the ladder has put increasing stress on individuals, and not surprisingly, has had health consequences. This stress, combined with increasing inequality and the absence of an adequate health "safety net," has had dramatic consequences: by 2015, the mortality rate (the probability of death) of American middle-age white males was increasing—while elsewhere in the world, it was decreasing.[5] (This is to say nothing of life expectancies of, say, black Americans, which continue to lag far behind those of whites.) This was not because of an AIDS epidemic, Ebola, or the spread of some other virus: the death rate reflected social strains—alcoholism, drugs, and suicide. By 2016, life expectancy for the country as a whole was in decline.[6] Such declines are shocking: they occur in rare circumstances, such as the AIDS epidemic in Sub-Saharan Africa or the United States, or the breakup of the Soviet Union.

It is not just in the United States that the middle class is suffering. My former colleague at the World Bank, economist Branko Milanović, has studied how people in different segments of global income distribution have fared over the past quarter century, and he has found that the middle and working classes in Europe and the United States have experienced near stagnation. There are others that also seem not to have done well—including those at the bottom of the global income distribution (poor farmers in Africa and India, for example). As I explain in *GAID,* they have been among the victims of the "unfair" rules of globalization.

Not surprisingly, there are some who have done well over the past quarter century: the big winners are the global 1 percent—the multimillionaires and billionaires—and the new middle classes in India and China.[7]

The global picture then is this: in most countries around the world there is growing inequality—those that followed the American economic model have typically done worse than countries following other models, though their outcomes have not been as bad as that in the United States. Of concern is not just the disparity between the top and bottom; it's that large parts of the population are not doing well. The economic model that's been sold as the best possible—the "liberalized" and "globalized" free-market economy—has not been delivering for large fractions of the population, even more so in the country that seemed to be the most liberalized, the most globalized, and the most market-oriented: the United States.

This raises three questions: To what extent are these results the consequences of globalization? To what extent are they inevitable? And if due to globalization, to what extent do they occur because the rules of the game for globalization are poorly designed, and to what extent do they come about because individual countries have done a poor job at managing the effects of globalization, *given the rules*?

GAID—both the original book and this new volume—gives clear answers: Globalization has played a central role, even if there were other important forces at play, like changes in technology and the structure of economies. These adverse outcomes are not inevitable—they are a result of policies. Globalization has been mismanaged. The rules governing globalization are partly to blame—they are, for instance, unfair to developing countries and have given free rein to destabilizing capital flows. But, even with these rules, the advanced countries could have prevented what has emerged, with so many in the developing world, and now in the advanced countries as well, counted among the losers from globalization.

So, the short answer to the question of whether the economists and politicians who boasted of the virtues of globalization were correct is this: they were partly wrong, partly right. Globalization, if well managed, could have benefited all. But it was typically not managed well, and globalization has resulted in some—even possibly a majority—of citizens being worse off.

The Benefits of the Global Economic Order

Before beginning our discussion of what has gone wrong with globalization, we should say a few words about its benefits. Given the title of this book—and the mood around the world that inspired it—it is to be expected that I focus on the downsides of globalization, what has gone wrong. But we should not lose sight of its benefits. In spite of all the discontent, for all the inequities which are real, the world has benefited enormously from the post–World War II global economic order, of which globalization is a part. I alluded to these benefits earlier. It has contributed to creating the fastest rate of global economic growth ever, and the successes of emerging markets in particular, with hundreds of millions moving out of poverty—more than 800 million in China alone[8]—and the creation of a new global middle class.

The second half of the twentieth century was in many ways a vast improvement on the first half, when millions died in two devastating world wars. Part of that improvement may be attributed to the economic successes associated with the global economic order, in the creation of which the United States was central. Modern economics has shown that the rule of law has been an important ingredient in the success of the advanced countries. But the same arguments for why the rule of law has economic benefits *within* a country hold internationally: a rules-based system is infinitely better than the law of the jungle.

As I look back at my critique of globalization today—distanced by two decades from the controversies that I was embroiled in at the World Bank and the IMF—I feel that I should have celebrated the successes more. The UN has succeeded in reducing conflict and protecting children and refugees. Global diseases have been effectively attacked—including HIV/AIDS, the avian flu, and Ebola. Life expectancies have increased in many countries through the efforts of international organizations. Cancer-causing ozone holes, a result of the use of chlorofluorocarbon gases, are being repaired. These are remarkable achievements in a relatively short period, achievements which should be recognized and in which globalization has played a key role. The right way to read *GAID* is that, given the importance of globalization and the global order that had been established in the aftermath of World War II, it was essential that we make that system as equitable and efficient as possible. *GAID* was written out of the conviction that we could improve it; indeed, that we *had* to improve it.

THE MISMANAGEMENT OF TRADE GLOBALIZATION

How we have managed one of the most important aspects of globalization—the freer movement of goods and services across borders, sometimes called "trade globalization"—illustrates the mismanagement of globalization more generally.

Trade Agreements: Unfair to Whom?

Global trade has increased enormously, some 50 percent faster than global growth since 1980.[9] In the United States, imports went from 10 percent of GDP to 15 percent over the same period.[10] This increase in trade results partly from the lowering of transportation costs, but even more important have been changes in the rules of the game, the reductions in tariffs (the taxes imposed on imports) and other man-made barriers to trade. These reductions typically occur through trade agreements, in which there is a mutual reduction of trade barriers.

Trump's claim that in negotiating these agreements U.S. trade negotiators got snookered is simply false. American negotiators got most of what they wanted. Anyone who has watched these trade negotiations, as I have for years, would view Trump's charges as laughable. The problem was with *what* they wanted: From the perspective of America as a whole, they wanted the wrong thing. What they asked for was essentially what American corporations wanted. American corporations wanted access to cheap labor, without environmental and labor protections. The corporations also liked the fact that threats to move their factories abroad weakened workers' bargaining power. This enriched their coffers, as wages were driven down. They were pleased that trade agreements helped ensure the property rights of investments made in developing countries, for this made their threats to relocate their plants in these cheap-labor countries more credible. When they drafted the provisions concerning intellectual property rights, they weren't thinking about what would be good for the advancement of science in the United States, let alone the world. They were thinking about what would increase the profits of America's big corporations, and especially its large drug and entertainment companies—even if it increased the prices that American consumers had to pay and even if it resulted in a slowing down of the overall pace of innovation.[11]

Trade Globalization: Benefiting Some at the Expense of Others

Thus, the real problem with trade globalization was simple: even if globalization *was* good for the country as a whole, as its boosters claimed—in the sense that overall national income went up—it was not good for everyone in the country. The trade agreements were unfair, but they were unfair in favor of America and other advanced countries—the developing countries were justified in their complaints. But the agreements were also unfair in favor of corporations, and against workers whether in the advanced countries or the poorer ones. So the workers in America were also right to complain.

Within each country, there were winners and losers. Those at the top got more than 100 percent of the gains, meaning that the rest—and unskilled workers in particular—were worse off. The gains went to those who were already doing well, the losses to those who were already suffering. I will explain in Part I on the New Discontents how all of this came to be.

Could Everyone Have Been a Winner?

If the advocates of globalization were correct about the magnitude of the gains, then in principle, it would have been possible to take some of the gains away from the winners, having them share their gains with the losers, and everyone could have been better off.

But to put it bluntly, the winners as a group were selfish: politics in the era of globalization's rapid advance concentrated globalization's gains ever more in the hands of the winners, especially in the United States, where money has so much influence in determining political outcomes. There were successive tax cuts (for instance, in 1997, 2001, and 2003) under both major political parties[12]— aimed at the top, the groups that were benefiting the most from globalization.

Had the advocates of globalization in the United States and other advanced countries been more enlightened and less shortsighted, they would have recognized the threat to workingmen and -women posed by globalization and they would have done something about it—just as they would have recognized the threat to economic stability posed by unbridled financial market deregulation. They should have known that in a democracy, policies that, year after year, leave significant groups of the population worse off are likely not politically sustainable.

Destroying Communities

Globalization not only exacerbated the already too-high level of inequality among individuals[13] but also deeply weakened many communities.

In the decades well before Ronald Reagan's presidency, when a company grew, the executives and workers prospered together and so did the communities in which they lived and worked together.[14] But increasing inequality split management, workers, and the communities in which they lived. Increasingly, as economic segregation grew apace, the executives making key decisions lived in separate neighborhoods from ordinary workers.[15] They didn't have to bear the consequences of living in dying communities; they could pretend they didn't exist. Corporations often rotated managers among different locations—enabling the executives to get to know the company better, but distancing them from the community in which they lived. The community that is important to the executive is that of his or her fellow executives—very different from a hundred years ago, when the business leaders lived in the community where their businesses were located and were part of it and its leadership. The care for the community was born partly out of true social responsibility—a kind of noblesse oblige—and partly out of enlightened self-interest—well-functioning communities meant happier and more productive workers.

Globalization worsened trends that were already underway. With outsourcing, the separation grew even greater—workers and management didn't even have to live in the same country. In this new era, labor was commodified—getting labor power was just like buying coal; one looked for the cheapest source. Never mind the consequences.

Some communities prospered—those in which the well-educated and well-off lived; but others, especially those relying on manufacturing, decayed. Gary, Indiana, the steel-mill town in which I grew up, was part of the "scorched earth" that followed. Its history represented that of globalization. Founded in 1906 by U.S. Steel—and named after its chairman of the board—to host the largest integrated steel mill in the world, it reached its peak in the mid-1950s when I was growing up. The steel mills today produce the same amount of steel that they ever have, but with one-sixth the labor force. Without enough good jobs, the city decayed and the well-educated left.[16] (The ultimate irony of globalization was that it was an Indian steel company that finally saved one of the plants in the region from closing.)

When I went back to my fifty-fifth high school reunion in 2015, I got a glimpse of what globalization, deindustrialization, and the failure of America to deal adequately with these trends meant. When I was a student there in the 1950s, the students at Gary's Horace Mann High School came from a wide swath of society—from the children of superintendents and executives in the steel mills and local businessmen to those of ordinary steelworkers, both skilled and unskilled. The school—and much of the dream for which it stood, a society which is economically integrated if not racially integrated—has now been abandoned.[17] Some had wanted to get one of the jobs in the steel mill upon graduation, but the country was going into one of its episodic downturns. Many had aspired to go to college, but while America had provided college education for all who had fought in World War II under the GI Bill, that sense of generosity had waned by the time of the Vietnam War. There was among many a sense of bitterness. They saw others passing them up on the ladder of life. They had a feeling that the system was unfair, rigged. Even before Trump had appeared on the scene, it was clear that they could be prey to a demagogue. There was a smattering of teachers who had had rewarding careers, and they were among the few that did not seem angry and disgruntled. I saw in my former classmates in Gary what the statistics had been telling me for years.

COMMON THEMES IN THE DISCONTENT WITH GLOBALIZATION

Rereading *GAID,* it appears that the answers to the questions being posed about globalization today—and how we can reconcile the seeming benefits with the widespread discontent—were largely anticipated by my analysis nearly two decades ago. While in *GAID* I focused on the developing world, most of what I said was equally applicable to the developed countries. There are eight related themes in *GAID*:

1. While globalization has benefits, the benefits were less than the advocates claimed. The advocates used simplistic models, which did not appropriately capture either the benefits or the costs. In some cases, for certain countries, the costs could even exceed the benefits, unless offsetting actions were taken—and the advocates of globalization typically did nothing to counter these adverse effects. If globalization is not managed well, it could thus lead to lower growth and more instability, with large fractions of the population worse off.
2. Because globalization has been oversold, when reality differed from the promises—when there were job losses instead of job creation—confidence in globalization, the elites, and the institutions that had advocated it waned.
3. Globalization has huge distributive effects on income and wealth—with large groups being worse off unless countervailing measures were taken to share the gains, but these measures were seldom undertaken.
4. We must see the failures of globalization in part as arising from deficiencies in the governance of globalization—in the way that the crucial decisions about globalization are made, including whose

voices are heard.[18] That implies that if we are to hope for well-managed globalization, we have to reform global governance, giving more weight, for instance, to the newly emerging economies. *GAID* notes, for instance, the distorting effects arising from the fact that one country and only one country—the United States—has effective veto power in the IMF.

5. But the problems of governance are deeper: the positions taken by, say, the United States reflect the special interests and the particular ideology of only a small part of the country, the financial and corporate interests. Thus, globalization was run, to too large an extent, by and for large multinational corporations and financial institutions in the large advanced countries. They were the winners. And much collateral damage occurred as they sought to maximize their winnings. Even if the United States as a whole was among the winners, many groups of American workers and workers in other advanced countries could be among the losers.

6. The positions taken typically reflected the interests of these groups; but in some cases, they reflected as much the ideology—sets of beliefs that are not always perfectly congruent with interests. The zeal for deregulation and liberalization was central in bringing on the global financial crisis, which imposed enormous costs even on many of those who had been the advocates of these policies.

7. Globalization can have and has had large effects on the distribution of power, both within and between countries. Some countries (poor developing countries) can become effectively dependent on the goodwill of others. Actions that could and should have been taken to prevent these changes in power relations were not taken. As globalization led to more inequality, in countries in which money matters a lot in politics—like the United States—the winners from globalization had increased power to shape globalization to benefit themselves, at the expense of others. There was a vicious circle—broken only by the popular uprising of the "new protectionism."

8. Globalization has put a greater burden on governments to offset its adverse effects on so many at the bottom. But at the same time, it reduced their capacity to deal with the problems; globalization set off a race to the bottom among countries offering low taxes to corporations and individuals. As if that weren't bad enough, rich

individuals and corporations then took advantage of globalization to avoid paying taxes—even corporations that prided themselves on being good citizens with a strong sense of corporate responsibility couldn't resist. Clever firms like Apple avoided billions of dollars in taxes. The failure to stop the use of globalization for tax avoidance is itself a manifestation of the mismanagement of globalization and an illustration of the power relations underlying writing the rules of globalization. It would have been no more difficult to have international agreements circumscribing global tax avoidance than to have international agreements over trade. But it was in the interests of corporations to have global trade agreements, and so we had them; and it was in the interests of multinational corporations to avoid taxation, and so we didn't have agreements to circumscribe tax avoidance. In the end, in the United States, corporate tax receipts fell from 5 percent of GDP in the 1950s to 2 percent today.

Even with all of these constraints, even with the rules of globalization that were far from ideal, globalization could have been managed better, especially by the advanced countries. It could have been managed in ways that could have prevented large segments of the population from suffering from the effects of globalization—ways which simultaneously could have led to more growth, stability and equality. Most of the advanced countries (including the United States) didn't do so—and for much the same reason that the rules of globalization were "distorted." Corporate interests that had shaped globalization in a way which led to lower wages were not interested in "correcting" this problem: they liked the lower wages, and they disliked the taxes that would have to be imposed to prevent workers from having significant income losses.

If one grasps these eight ideas, one understands the discontent with globalization, and one even has some notion about what should be done. But this analysis also provides some insights into why it's so difficult to make changes, to make the changes that would enable globalization to work: the corporate forces that have created a globalization that works for them, but not for the rest, are not going to easily and willingly give up their power.

The Failures of Globalization Are Not Inevitable

There is one underlying theme I want to emphasize: *The failures of globalization were not inevitable.* These failures were not, for the most part,[19] failures of economic science. The adverse effects were predictable— and predicted. Economists had explained that, without government assistance, trade liberalization would result in unskilled workers in the advanced countries actually being worse off.

Of course, some economists forgot their role as analysts and became cheerleaders of globalization, emphasizing the potential benefits but not mentioning the downsides. Too many economists used simplistic models that led them to overestimate the benefits and underestimate the costs. And, of course, politicians turned to economists who said what they wanted to hear.

But still, the economics literature provided clear warnings. The fault lay with our politicians, who were responding to where the money was: finance and corporate America, in particular, were pushing a self-interested form of globalization through both political parties. It was called "free trade," but it was really managed trade—managed for corporate and financial interests. Under these agreements, knowledge moved less freely, but short-term capital more freely. Agricultural subsidies for rich farmers were allowed in the developed countries, but subsidies to help the poor developing countries to catch up with the advanced countries were frowned upon.

So the problem was not with globalization itself, but with the way we managed it. The story of globalization could have been written differently—and in a few places, it was. The Scandinavian countries realized that as small countries they had to be open—they could only survive if they were globalized. But they understood too that market forces alone might result in there being winners and losers; and if the losers were too numerous, opposition to globalization would grow. So they created a system that provided a modicum of protection—they showed that there could be social protection without protectionism.[20] They put in place policies that reduced inequalities in both market income and in income after tax and transfers: they have shown that inequality is not just a result of the laws of economics, but of the policies that countries put in place to respond to economic forces, including globalization, that have been pulling countries apart.

As a result, the Scandinavian countries enjoy the highest living standards in the world—and shared prosperity.[21] Of course, these are relatively small countries, with a certain degree of homogeneity (though immigrants still make up 15 percent of the population in Norway and 17 percent in Sweden), but there is nothing about the policies that they used to achieve these outcomes that makes them inapplicable elsewhere. The problem is not the policies, it's the politics. These countries understood what was in the collective interest of their people. Other countries, most notably the United States, seemingly have not. Their experience shows that inequality is a matter of choice, and that if globalization has detrimental effects, those effects are not inevitable or immutable. It is the wrong choices made in the United States and most of the other advanced countries that have fed the discontent with globalization.[22]

Had domestic policies been more attentive to the effects of globalization and the growing inequality within their borders, countries could have undertaken policies that would have prevented there being so many losers. Had globalization been better managed globally, the outcomes too would have been better—indeed, the positive outcomes asserted by its advocates could have been achieved. But the kind of globalization that would have worked is markedly different from that foisted on developing countries by the IMF and the World Bank back in the earlier era of globalization described in *GAID*. This collection of policies is referred to as the "Washington Consensus" because it emerged in the 1980s as a consensus between 15th Street (home of the U.S. Treasury) and 19th Street (home of the IMF) in Washington, DC.[23] While it was supposed to be a consensus of what constituted good development policies, in fact it was not a consensus forged *in* the developing countries—among those that were living through the consequences of those policies. It was only a consensus among those who imposed the policies, not among those who experienced the bulk of their effects, especially the negative ones.

Those policies, for instance, restricted government assistance in helping firms adapt to globalization, helping new industries develop through what are called "industrial policies."[24] They proscribed interventions in financial markets that would have made it more likely that firms in expanding export sectors got access to credit. They paid no attention to the danger of excessive risk taking by banks. After all, it was argued, private firms know better than government. By the same token, the policies' backers argued for opening up markets to volatile short-term capital flows—of the kind that wreaked havoc during the East Asia crisis, plunging the countries into deep recessions and depressions as hot money suddenly left. Education was emphasized—but only primary education, not the kind of education that could have closed the knowledge gap separating advanced countries and developing countries. They paid little or no attention to inequality—the effects of which have proven to be the major political impediment to the sustainability of globalization itself.[25]

While the Washington Consensus policies were directed at developing countries, the same economic philosophy predominated the response to globalization among the elites in the developed countries. At Davos, in January 2017, as these elites finally had to confront the mounting opposition to globalization and the growing inequality, the policy responses still—remarkably—focused on lowering corporate income taxes and deregulation, accompanied by a dose of better retraining. Their belief in trickle-down economics was unshaken: the best way to deal with the discontent was to get the economy to grow faster, the best way to do that was another dose of deregulation and tax cuts for the rich. If we could only make the economy grow faster, the disgruntled laid-off Rust Belt workers' problems would be solved.

Key Differences of Globalization's Impacts
on Developed and Developing Countries
While the eight themes are relevant to both developed and developing countries, there are two fundamental differences between globalization as it affects a country like the United States and how it affects, say, a small African country. The first is, as I have noted, that the rules of the game have been largely set by the United States and other advanced countries. This means that globalization should be of benefit to these countries—or at least to certain influential groups within them. By contrast, developing countries may face an impossible choice: agree to the terms of globalization as they've been set, or be ostracized, excommunicated. And even the latter is often not really a choice: many of the developing countries have large amounts of debt. They are effectively in a debtor's prison. The creditors can demand what they will as a condition for the country getting the funds it needs to function. For some

of the developing countries in Africa, globalization has been at best of ambiguous benefit—no matter how they handle their internal affairs.

Indeed, for some of the poorest countries, globalization as it has been managed may be—and as *GAID* points out, often is—a raw deal. For instance, U.S. cotton subsidies have driven down the global prices of cotton significantly, pushing those in India and Africa already near the point of starvation closer to the verge of it. Tariff structures were designed to encourage African countries to produce raw materials—and not to produce the higher value-added products, which were supposed to be the province of the developed countries.[26]

The second is that the advanced countries have the resources and capabilities to ensure that almost all within their borders benefit. The developing countries typically have less capacity to raise taxes, to generate the revenues necessary to compensate those who are hurt by globalization. They also have less institutional capacity; for instance, developed countries have stronger financial institutions that can provide finance to export industries that benefit as a result of a trade agreement, putting them in a better position to create new jobs even as jobs in import-competing sectors are destroyed.

CHANGES IN GLOBALIZATION IN THE TWENTY-FIRST CENTURY

I wrote *GAID* just at the dawn of the new millennium. We live in a fast-changing world. In the last quarter century we've had the Argentine crisis, the Russian crisis, the East Asia crisis, the global financial crisis, and the euro crisis. We've had wars in Iraq, Syria, and Afghanistan. Many countries have already begun to feel the consequences of climate change. Confidence in globalization and the market economy has been volatile. There have even been wide swings in economists' views of the world. While the standard model a quarter century ago was based on rational households and firms interacting in competitive markets in ways that achieved efficiency and stability, each of the underlying assumptions has come to be questioned: firms and households often act in a far-from-rational manner;[27] markets are often not competitive; and the outcomes often seem far from efficient or stable.

Not surprisingly, globalization today is different from what it was like when I wrote *GAID*. In the afterword, I describe how the changes have affected developing countries. Here, I want to provide a broad overview, with a simple message: While globalization has changed over the past quarter century, giving more voice, for instance, to emerging markets, the changes are less than one might have hoped. Corporate and financial interests of the advanced countries still predominate. The conflict is not so much between workers in developing countries and those in developed countries, but between workers around the world and corporate interests. The backlash against globalization that the world is now experiencing should not, accordingly, come as a surprise. Globalization can be a positive-sum game, with workers in both developed and developing countries gaining. As it is, corporate and financial interests in the advanced countries have been the big winners. But the "reforms" proposed by Trump and the other protectionists are negative-sum: everyone is likely to lose, including the workers in the advanced countries whom Trump and his likes *supposedly* speak for. There are other ways of reforming globalization that can ensure that all, or at least most, citizens benefit. But these reforms will only be successful if they are part of broader progressive reforms, which achieve shared prosperity and inclusive growth.

The Historical Context

In *GAID* I tried to put globalization, as it existed at the time of publication, in historical context.[28] Before the collapse of the Berlin Wall, there was competition for the hearts and minds and loyalty of those in the developing world between communism and the West. That competition prevented the United States from abusing its enormous economic power. The end of the Cold War gave the United States almost free rein in shaping globalization. It could have used that power to reflect its values and principles—to support governments that showed a commitment to human rights, provide assistance to end poverty, create systems of social protection, and ensure that young people had access to education. It did so, but only to a very limited extent; but it simultaneously tried to change the rules of international commerce in ways that would entrench the advantages of the advanced countries, and particularly their corporate and financial interests. Bill Clinton was elected on a platform of "Jobs, Jobs, Jobs!" and "It's the economy, stupid." He decided to focus trade policy on advancing U.S. economic interests— but that turned out to mean U.S. corporate interests. In doing so, the United States lost an important opportunity to redefine globalization.

Globalization in the New Millennium

There was but a decade of relative calm after the fall of the Berlin Wall before a series of storms hit. First, in December 1999, came the Seattle anti-globalization protests, which were focused against a new round of trade talks. They brought together those worried about the effect of trade agreements on jobs, about the inequities imposed on developing countries, and about the environment. Protesters felt they knew where the talks would go: to another trade agreement advancing corporate interests in the advanced countries. The protestors won the day: the talks did not begin.

Shortly before *GAID* was published, the global war on terrorism began with the 2001 attack of 9/11. It became clear that not only did good things move more easily across borders in the era of globalization, but so did bad things. In the moment of solidarity that followed, a new round of trade talks, called the Development Round, began with a promise to rectify the imbalances of previous trade agreements that were very tilted against the developing countries. As I discuss in the afterword, that spirit of unity was short-lived; the United States and Europe reneged on their promise to reform trade rules to help the less developed countries grow, and fourteen years later, the Development Round was formally abandoned. By then, the larger emerging markets had shown that they could stand up to the United States; and the United States had not learned how to navigate negotiations in this new world—it could not tame the special agricultural interests, which, as I have noted, were powerful enough to ensure the continuation of massive subsidies for themselves.

But the real storm came in 2008, with the global financial crisis— globalization had enabled America to sell its toxic mortgages around the world, and globalization meant that an economic crisis originating in America spread quickly around the world, inflicting enormous pain to hundreds of millions. Ironically, as the United States sought to recover, with its forceful monetary policies (quantitative easing), it imposed still more instability on others: a rush of liquidity led to asset price bubbles in the emerging markets, and an increase in their exchange rates led to decreases in exports and surges of imports.

The Rise of Trump

All of this has given unfettered globalization a bad name, or at least given rise to skepticism about globalization in much of the world. But almost surely, nothing will have done as much to undermine faith in globalization as Trump.[29] Trump and his supporters seemed to be saying to the world, if we can't win in the game of globalization, we'll take our marbles and go home. America had thought it had created a globalization that served its interests; and when that didn't seem to be the case, it decided that the rules had to be changed, *or else*.

But the world of the twenty-first century is very different from that of the years immediately after World War II, when much of the developing world didn't even have its freedom. By the first decade of the twenty-first century, the United States–led wars in Vietnam, Afghanistan, and Iraq had shown the limits of military power. America couldn't even decisively win against small, poor countries. Its soft power—the influence exerted by its moral values and culture—had been diminished by the way it conducted the Iraq War, how it treated the poor in its own country, by the hypocrisy it demonstrated in its international trade negotiations, and by the power of money in its elections. Again, the election of a president so untethered to the truth—who is totally unfazed by lying—has simply compounded matters. In short, with the diminution of its soft power, with a new global balance of economic power, and with the limits of military power so evident, the United States is unlikely to be able to unilaterally rewrite the rules of globalization.

Trump, for instance, has complained about trade agreements like the North American Free Trade Agreement (NAFTA), which allows for the free movement of goods between Canada, Mexico, and the United States. There will be changes—agreements made close to a quarter of a century ago or more will have to be updated (NAFTA went into effect in 1994)—but they will be changes that will be mutually agreed to. The United States has the power to exit agreements—often, though, only with the consent of Congress—but that is a far cry from getting a new agreement. Many of the trade agreements (such as that with Korea) faced strong opposition not only in the United States but in the other signatory nations. Any significant change that disturbed the balance of benefits and costs within and between the signatories would ensure the death of the agreement: citizens now realize that no agreement is better than a bad agreement.

There is thus considerable uncertainty about what globalization in a post-Trump world might look like—and this uncertainty itself will impede trade and economic integration. Trump is likely to fail to carry out many of his campaign promises, since many of them require unlikely congressional support, while others have been struck down by courts. Within months of taking office, he was equivocating on his promises. The 45 percent across-the-board tax on Chinese imports quickly became forgotten, replaced by the standard duties imposed in previous administrations on goods that China sells below costs. Even as negotiations on NAFTA began, the administration had no serious proposals on how to reverse the trade deficit with Mexico. Indeed, chapter 3 explains that Trump's policies are likely to increase America's overall trade deficit. America's voters are used to there being a gap between campaign rhetoric and what follows; but just as Trump's campaign rhetoric was outsized, so too has been the gap. Even so, because Trump has shown that borders matter, firms will now be more cautious in creating global supply chains.

Even without Trump, it is likely that globalization would have changed. The collapse of the Development Round of trade negotiations in 2015 meant that, for the foreseeable future, there would be no more global agreements. The opposition to the United States–driven trade agreements across the Pacific (the Trans-Pacific Partnership, or TPP) and across the Atlantic (the Transatlantic Trade and Investment Partnership, or TTIP) suggested it would be increasingly difficult to push forward the corporate-driven agreements that had marked the past.[30] On the other hand, South-South agreements—among developing countries and emerging markets—were expanding: Trump's "America First" rhetoric gave a big spur to a trend that was already under way. For instance, the Pacific Alliance, which since 2011 has brought together Peru, Mexico, Colombia, and Chile, enjoyed a major boost to its relevancy in the wake of the U.S. election. And there are a number of regional agreements moving forward in Asia.

A New Global Economy

In *GAID* I discuss some of the inequities between the North and the South. Several changes in the last fifteen years have only heightened the sense of injustice. The first is the heightened awareness of climate change—with most of the increases in the atmospheric concentration of greenhouse gases which give rise to it coming from the advanced countries,[31] and most of the costs being borne by the developing countries. The United States, with its refusal to go along with any agreement with fair burden sharing—and with so many Americans, including Trump, even claiming that it's a hoax—generates particular resentment in this arena.[32]

A second change was an unforeseen consequence of the East Asia crisis and the way it was mismanaged by the IMF. Countries around the world, but especially in East Asia, said "never again." They understood the benefits of globalization, but they also realized that openness exposed them to risks beyond their control. To manage these risks they needed reserves, usually dollars, that they held against a rainy day—and especially against a storm like the crisis of 1997. They knew, though, that they didn't have enough to weather such a storm. Reserves increased by trillions of dollars.

The real irony is this: while it was the U.S. Treasury that was largely responsible for these policies which imposed such enormous costs on the East Asian countries, the U.S. Treasury has also been the big beneficiary. Countries typically hold reserves in the form of U.S. T-bills, which means that they are lending to the United States. However, they are lending at a low rate (in the years after the global crisis, at close to zero interest rate, which means in *real* terms, taking account of inflation, they are getting a negative return), but often borrowing from the United States at much higher rates. It was, in effect, a massive transfer of money from these poorer countries to the United States. The developing and emerging markets thus paid a high price to protect their loss of sovereignty.

There was a ready solution: the creation of a global reserve system. China, Russia, and France supported such a system, and the UN voted to have it studied.[33] But the United States opposed such a system, or even the study of its feasibility—after all, under current arrangements, the United States could borrow from others at an interest rate close to zero, and they liked this. Given U.S. opposition, nothing happened.[34]

A third change was the increasing importance of intellectual property and the payments associated with it. As the world moved more to a knowledge economy, these payments increased, and with most of the patents held by the North, there was a substantial flow of money from the South to the North. Again, rather than money flowing from rich countries to poor countries to help them grow, it seemed as if the global economic system was designed to make the money flow the other way, seemingly defying gravity.

A fourth change is that the model of export-led manufacturing growth that had been the basis of the success of East Asia may well be coming to an end. Even if all the manufacturing jobs in China were to go to Africa, it would provide just a fraction of the needed jobs for the new entrants into the labor force, given the large increase in that continent's labor force expected in coming decades.[35] Without jobs, immigration pressures, especially in Europe, will continue unabated.

Perhaps the biggest change, at least from the perspective of the management of globalization—a change well underway before Trump—was the increasing economic power of the emerging markets. Their relative share in global GDP has grown enormously. Hardly a surprise: China, for instance, grew at nearly 10 percent per year, for a third of a century, doubling its economy every seven years. It grew even faster in some of the years after the global financial crisis, a period in which Europe and the United States performed particularly badly.

Rebalancing the Global System

As the disconnect has grown larger between the voice of the emerging markets in globalization and in global financial institutions like the World Bank and the IMF, established at the end of World War II, and the economic realities, the need for a rebalancing has become more pronounced.

Of course, there have been changes, for instance, small adjustments in voting shares at the IMF and the World Bank, which seem to have had no observable consequences. The global financial crisis made it evident that global problems need to be addressed globally—and not just by the club of the rich countries, the G-7. The G-20 brought in China, India, Turkey, Saudi Arabia, Argentina, and eight other emerging markets and became the key global meeting. But as the global financial crisis faded, disagreements about the direction the global economy should take prevented much progress in redefining globalization. Perhaps the most important achievement was in climate change, with the Paris Agreement signed by 195 countries and entering into effect on November 4, 2016. The strength of the agreement was demonstrated in the aftermath of President Trump's announcement of the U.S. withdrawal[36] from the accord. The rest of the world stood firm in solidarity in support of the agreement, and many businesses and states within the United States reaffirmed their commitment to achieving its ambitions. Trump was mocked everywhere. Rome's City Hall displayed a huge banner: "The Planet First" (making fun of Trump's slogan, "America First"); and President Emmanuel Macron of France used the slogan "Make Our Planet Great Again" (making fun of Trump's slogan, "Make America Great Again").

Not surprisingly, given the slow progress in rebalancing globalization, in giving voice to emerging markets commensurate with their economic power, these countries have taken matters into their own hands, setting up their own institutions—sometimes over the futile opposition of the United States, which made efforts to retain its influence. The United States has had a hard time adapting itself to this world in which its relative economic power is diminished—and I suspect matters will only get worse under Trump.

Rebalancing globalization to give more voice to developing countries and emerging markets will not be easy. It will require a kind of cooperation that will be hard to attain so long as the United States maintains an "America First" position.

THREE WAYS FORWARD

The discontent with globalization is evident both in developing and developed countries. The question, then, is where does globalization go from here?

Doubling Down on the Washington Consensus

One approach is some variant of the Washington Consensus: a continuation of the structure of globalization much as it has been, with rules set by and for the large corporations and big finance in the advanced countries. This would be a doubling down on the Washington Consensus policies that failed in so much of the developing world. I wrote *GAID* to explain why that was not the way the world *should* go. Still, at the time I wrote it, I was very much afraid that that was the direction in which the world *would* go.

If the world took this approach, I felt I knew how things would play out. In *GAID,* I describe IMF policies as being like dropping bombs from 50,000 feet. One couldn't see the human suffering down below. The IMF focused on cold numbers like the unemployment rate. But behind a 10 percent unemployment rate are millions of families without a job. For those families, a change in policy leading to an 8 percent unemployment rate makes a world of difference—a human difference that simply can't be captured in that small change in the statistic. But the disconnect between what advocates of globalization thought and what was happening was even greater. They had a theory that globalization would lead to faster economic growth—but they didn't even look at statistics about how globalization was affecting ordinary people.

Failing to Make Globalization Sustainable

At the time I wrote *GAID,* it seemed to me that globalization, as it was then being structured, was unsustainable. What happened in the ensuing years, as I've described, only made matters worse.

At the national level, somehow, the politics has not worked in a way which would have led to the changes to make globalization sustainable. Those on the right who have been the strongest advocates of globalization have not been willing to push policies that would have protected those who have been hurt by it. To the contrary, they have even resisted assistance to those who have lost their jobs as a result of globalization.

More surprising has been the behavior of the center-left—such as the Democrats in the United States. They should have been the defenders of the interests of the workers who are displaced by globalization—and opposed globalization if those interests weren't protected. In practice, though, they were cognitively captured by the arguments for the benefits of globalization—perhaps attracted a little by the campaign contributions that came from the financial sector for those who supported their view of globalization. Perhaps some even came to believe in trickle-down economics. Finally, as the disillusionment of so many of their "base"—or what should have been their base—became clear, there was a shift, led most forcefully by Bernie Sanders, behind whom rallied not only many workers, but a huge proportion of the young; and eventually, even by Hillary Clinton, who was forced to distance herself from the globalization policies of her husband. Even she came out against TPP.

The New Protectionism

One of my predecessors as chairman of the U.S. Council of Economic Advisers once said: that which is unsustainable won't be sustained. But while I had worried that globalization that paid so little attention to ordinary workers was unsustainable and would come under attack from protectionism, the attack came faster than I expected, with greater vigor and success, with the election of Donald Trump on an explicitly protectionist platform.

A retreat into protectionism is the second way of responding to the challenges of globalization. This "New Protectionism"—actually, little different from old-style protectionism—entails creating a wall between Mexico and the United States to stop the migration across the border (never mind that such immigration had already plummeted),[37] taxes of 45 percent against China, and the castigation of firms that shift production out of the United States.

Trump sought to put workers in the United States and other advanced countries in conflict with workers in developing countries and emerging markets. He suggests that the low-wage workers in China, Mexico, and elsewhere are effectively "stealing" American jobs. The real conflict is elsewhere: on one side, workers and consumers—the 99 percent—in both developed and developing countries, versus corporate interests on the other.

The prospects of New Protectionism working are no better than the first approach, doubling down on the Washington Consensus. The New Protectionist policies—the wholesale destruction of globalization that Trump and other anti-globalizers seem hell-bent on—will only lower the living standards of those who they profess to be helping. The newly discontented have every reason to be unhappy. But the snake oil that Trump and the New Protectionists elsewhere are selling will only worsen the plight of those who are already suffering. In chapter 3, I explain why this is so.

Doubling down on the Washington Consensus was a policy inspired by the special interests that it served, but the belief in the efficacy of these policies was supported by "market fundamentalist" ideologies— the notion that free, unregulated markets were the best way to organize a society. (Ironically, by the time these ideas had become fashionable under Reagan and Thatcher, economic theory had long shown the limitations of these theories. The actual policies pushed were markedly different than one would have thought based on free-market ideology— trade agreements were not free trade agreements, but managed trade agreements, and even the bankers who believed in small government enthusiastically endorsed the trillion-dollar bank bailout.)[38]

By contrast, the belief in this protectionism is not so much based on corporate interests or a realistic analysis of the future as much as a simple nostalgia for the past, a nostalgia which appeared to have enormous appeal to large numbers of voters.

Nostalgia for a World That Will Never Return
Some Americans—especially those who have not been doing well—look back with nostalgia at those years of American dominance after World War II, when their manufacturing jobs seemed secure, their wages were high, and they could attain a middle-class lifestyle that was beyond anything that they, their parents, or their grandparents had dreamed of when they immigrated to the United States. Now, many families struggle to make ends meet even with both parents working; then, a single breadwinner could comfortably support a family. It is this long-gone period—never to return—that Trump recalls, promising to bring it back along with the confidence and the social structures that accompanied it. That won't happen. One can't reverse the arrow of time.

There are many reasons that we can't reshape our world back into the *Leave It to Beaver* era of American dominance that the Make America Great Again campaign fetishized. That period after World War II was unusual in many ways. The war had brought people from all walks of life together to fight the common enemy. There was an unprecedented level of social cohesion and solidarity. It seemed wrong to exploit those who had risked their lives for the sake of the country. In the United

States and many European countries, the period after the war was one of rapid growth, but with shared prosperity: every group saw their incomes grow, but those at the bottom saw their incomes grow faster than those at the top.

Trump promises to bring manufacturing back. This is one among many promises that will be broken. At the end of the war we were completing the transition from agriculture to manufacturing. In the nineteenth century, some 70 percent of workers were in agriculture. Now, in the United States, for instance, less than 3 percent of the workforce grows more food than even an obese society can consume. Now, the advanced countries are in the process of completing the transition from manufacturing to a service-based economy. Of course, just as agriculture still plays a role in our economy, manufacturing will continue to have a part. But it won't employ as many people as it once did—those jobs aren't coming back any more than will the farm jobs that were erased a hundred-odd years ago.

The period after World War II had other distinctive characteristics, especially in the United States. High-paying manufacturing jobs went disproportionately to white males, and put them at the top of a social pyramid among workers, almost always above women and people of color. This was true even though it was nearly a century since the emancipation of slaves and a quarter of a century since women got the right to vote. Civil rights laws reflected and propelled civil society movements attempting to reduce the scope of this kind of discrimination,[39] sometimes with explicit affirmative action programs, sometimes with just greater sensitivity to implicit biases. Once discrimination was reduced, in many arenas—including college graduation, with the access to further advancement that followed—women did better than men. Large numbers of men, who in the old order would have been the "alpha males"—often by dint of unearned social advantage—found themselves being surpassed. To them, it was *as if* they were climbing the ladder of life in the way that they had come to expect, and suddenly, someone was given the green light to pass them up.

Several studies have suggested that a longing for those "good old days"[40]—good in the eyes of the privileged if not in the view of those who were oppressed—has played a role in the discontent of the white males. No wonder their call to take the country back, and becoming drawn to politicians promising to bring back that old order—a promise which they will not be able to fulfill.

The Third Approach: Fair Globalization with Shared Prosperity

If going back to the past—to old protectionism in a new guise—won't work; if doubling down on the Washington Consensus won't work; what will? The third approach has two parts: (a) managing the consequences of globalization within each country to ensure that fewer lose as a result, and (b) rewriting the rules of globalization in ways that are fairer to developing countries and less dominated by the corporate and financial interests.

Making Globalization Work for Each
Country through Inclusive Globalization
GAID strongly criticizes globalization as it has evolved, but its critique begins from exactly the opposite perspective of Trump. As I noted, he is under the delusion that our trade negotiators were snookered. The reality is that, for anyone looking at globalization from the perspective of global social justice, it is the poor countries and ordinary workers that got the short end of the stick. The great achievement of the emerging markets was that even with this "unfair" globalization, they managed to make globalization work for them and for much of their populations. That's why a global middle class has emerged—in China, in India, and even in some African countries.[41] For those concerned with the long-term stability of these parts of the world, nothing could be better news. The global economy is not a zero-sum game, with their gains coming at the expense of the United States or Europe. Rather, if others prosper, demand for the goods and services of the advanced countries *overall* can increase, and so too their GDP.

But there were losers: workers in developed countries, especially those with fewer skills, and the poorest in the poor countries who are near-subsistence farmers whose cash crops, like cotton, have depressed prices because of U.S. subsidies, further impoverishing millions in Sub-Saharan Africa and India. These farmers suffered too in another way from the actions of the United States, Europe, and China: massive pollution (greenhouse gas emissions) from the developed countries has contributed to desertification in Africa and India, further lowering their incomes.

There are other ways that globalization has not worked well at the global level. The world has been marked by repeated crises since the beginning of the era of liberalization—the worse being that of 2008. A failure of American regulators combined with excessive greed and a total absence of moral standards by America's financial system[42] brought the entire globe into crisis. Since the crisis, the world has struggled to impose a set of rules on the financial sector that would prevent another such crisis. Matters are better today than they were in 2008, but few think that the problem has been "fixed."

Domestic Policies for Marking Globalization Work for All

As most countries, and especially smaller ones, begin thinking about globalization's impacts, they don't begin with the grandiose question of how they can change the global rules. They begin with the more modest question: how should they design their economic policies, given the rules of the game and the particular economic situation in which they find themselves.

Advanced countries have to adopt two core sets of policies: an overall economic framework that allows for a modicum of shared prosperity, and social protection for those hurt by globalization because no matter how well our economic system functions, some will be left behind. Those who fall off the ladder of success shouldn't go into an economic abyss. What is required is a progressive agenda, one that recognizes the respective roles that the market, the state, and civil society must play; that recognizes that markets often don't work well, and even when they are efficient, the distribution of income which they result in is often socially unacceptable; an agenda that realizes that markets don't exist in a vacuum, and have to be structured.

Over the past third of a century, there have been marked changes in the "rules of the game." Earlier, I described the Washington Consensus policies. They had their counterpart within most of the advanced countries. The notion was that by freeing up markets—stripping away the regulations that constrained the economy—and incentivizing individuals and firms, through lower tax rates, the power of markets would be unleashed. Economies would grow, and even if those at the top got a larger share of the pie, everyone, even those at the bottom, would prosper. Better to have a smaller share of a much bigger pie than a larger share of a small pie. The results of this experiment, tried in countries around the world, are now in: it has been a dismal failure. Inequality grew even more than expected, but growth slowed, with the result that in countries such as the United States, the vast majority have seen incomes virtually stagnate. The new rules led to excessive financialization and short-termism, with corporate executives focusing on quarterly returns, and on their own compensation, rather than on the long-term well-being of the companies that were entrusted to their care. The rules of the game now have to be rewritten, once again, for the twenty-first century.

We've learned a lot from the failed experiment of the past third of a century: about the need to curb abuses of corporate governance (the ability of CEOs to get a larger and larger share of corporate income), of the financial sector (including the predatory lending, market manipulation, and abusive credit card practices that became so evident in the 2008 crisis), and of market power generally. Workers' productivity has grown, but workers' compensation has not kept pace, partly because of the weakening of workers' bargaining power, and that's partly because of changes in labor legislation, but also partly because of globalization. The world has changed—there are no longer lifetime jobs. But systems of social protection have not kept pace.

Most importantly for purposes of this book, the laws governing globalization need to be rewritten—but not in the protectionist ways advocated by Le Pen and Trump. Here, for insights, I turn to Scandinavia. These countries were too small to dictate the rules of globalization, as Trump wrongly believes he can do. To manage globalization, they had to turn inward, designing policies based on principles of openness with inclusive growth—ensuring that the benefits of globalization are sufficiently shared so that no one, or at least no significant group, is left behind.[43]

The failures and promises of globalization over the past third of a century have one more implication: politicians won't be able just to promise to help those left behind, to provide them with a safety net, perhaps a little job training here or there. Workers who see globalization as threatening their future want more than a bare safety net, something to hold on to when they are drowning. And even such threadbare promises no longer seem credible. What is required is real commitment; many will be reassured only if there is an economic and social system that works for all—and works whether they lose their job as a result of trade or an advance of technology or a change in the structure of the economy.

In chapter 4, I sketch the outlines of this alternative globalization as seen from the perspective of an advanced country like the United States.

Structure of the Book

Globalization and Its Discontents Revisited consists of three parts. In the first, I describe "Globalization's New Discontents," those in the advanced countries who have joined those in the developing world in their antipathy to globalization. I explain in detail why the benefits of globalization have been less than its advocates claimed and why so many have been made worse off by globalization—why there is so much anger toward globalization. I then explain why the new protectionism of Trump will only make matters worse, and describe the alternative policies that will deliver the promise of a globalization that will benefit all.

In the second part, the original text is reprinted, largely unchanged. The original book focused, as I have noted, on the discontents in the developing world. To understand where globalization is today, one has to understand how we got here—and to a large extent *GAID,* written at this early crucial stage of the evolution of globalization when there was such optimism about it, helps us understand globalization as it is today.[44]

The final section, the afterword, picks up where *GAID* ends: it describes the evolution of the battles over globalization over the subsequent fifteen years, and how the global landscape looks so different today than it did then. When *GAID* was first published, there were many battlefields in which the struggle over globalization was going on. There is a natural curiosity: How did these play out? Who, in the long run, won? Who lost? This afterword answers this question and looks toward the New Globalization that may emerge in the post-Trump world.

ACKNOWLEDGMENTS TO GLOBALIZATION AND ITS DISCONTENTS REVISITED

THE ACKNOWLEDGMENTS TO *Globalization and Its Discontents* described the many people who helped shape my thinking on globalization at the time. Over the past fifteen years, I have continued to be engaged in the great globalization debates that have emerged. I have learned much from the participants in those discussions, including the political leaders who drew me into them, and there is now an even longer list of debts.

In 2009, in response to the financial crisis confronting the world, the president of the United Nations General Assembly, Father Miguel d'Escoto Brockmann, asked me to chair an international Commission of Experts on Reforms of the International Monetary and Financial System, to review the causes of the global crisis, what might be done to contain it, and what should be done to prevent a recurrence. That commission provided a unique opportunity to understand especially the workings of financial globalization, and some of these insights are reflected in the discussions in this book.[1] I am deeply indebted to the commissioners and to all of those who helped with the work of the commission.

The global financial crisis (sometimes called the North Atlantic crisis, since it was mainly a crisis in the United States and Europe) spurred many other efforts at rethinking globalization, along with other aspects of our capitalist system. Globalization had led to the rapid transmission of the consequences of America's failures to manage its financial system to the rest of the world. Among the most important responses was the creation of the Institute of New Economic Thinking (INET), where I headed a task force focusing on financial contagion. I would like to acknowledge not just their financial support in bringing together economists to discuss these issues, but also the intellectual support, including from Rob Johnson (who has headed INET from its inception), George Soros, Andy Haldane (chief economist and the executive director of monetary analysis and statistics at the Bank of England), Stefano Battiston (University of Zurich),[2] Mauro Gallegati (at the Polytechnic University of Marche, Ancona), Domenico Delli Gatti (at Catholic University, Milan), Tarik Roukny (at the MIT Media Lab), and Anton Korinek (at Johns Hopkins University).

A third effort was undertaken by the Initiative for Policy Dialogue (IPD), a small think tank I set up after I returned to academia from the World Bank to encourage a rethinking of development strategies and globalization, and to translate some of the insights into changes in policy, bringing together academic and policy economists from both the developed and developing countries. I am particularly indebted to Stephany Griffith-Jones (financial markets program director for IPD) and José Antonio Ocampo (formerly under-secretary-general for economic and social affairs at the United Nations, now on leave from Columbia University, and on the Board of Directors of the Central Bank of Colombia), who coedited with me the proceedings of our conference, *Time for a Visible Hand: Lessons from the 2008 World Financial Crisis*.[3]

Not surprisingly, dissatisfaction with and angst about globalization have given rise to numerous other commissions attempting to understand and reform it. In the early years of this century, the International Labor Organization (ILO) under Juan Somavía created the World Commission on the Social Dimension of Globalization. Membership in that unusual commission, which brought together people from government, business, labor, and civil society from both developed and developing countries, furthered my understandings of the multiplicity of perspectives on globalization.[4]

Another commission on globalization, whose deliberations are just beginning, has been set up by INET, cochaired by Michael Spence (who shared the 2001 Nobel Memorial Prize in Economics) and me. Even at this early stage, I should acknowledge the insights from Spence and Andrew Sheng, who, after working with me at the World Bank, went on to become chairman of the Hong Kong Securities and Futures Commission (SFC) and chief adviser to the China Banking Regulatory Commission.

I should mention some other international commissions, whose deliberations have shaped my thinking and which I cochaired. The first is the Commission on the Measurement of Economic Performance and Social Progress (cochaired by Jean-Paul Fitoussi of the Institut d'Études Politiques de Paris, with Amartya Sen of Harvard University serving as chief advisor) and its successor, the High-Level Expert Group on the Measurement of Economic Performance and Social Progress at the OECD (the official think tank for advanced countries). Though its deliberations focused on measurement issues, by identifying what was not being measured by GDP—such as the growing sense of insecurity—we identified some of the reasons that globalization could simultaneously have increased GDP and decreased the well-being of large fractions of society.[5] A second group centered around a topic to which I devote too little attention in this book—global warming. With Nick Stern, I cochaired the High-Level Commission on Carbon Pricing, identifying the level of pricing of carbon necessary to achieve the ambitions of the world in curtailing climate change set forth in the Paris Agreement of December 2015.[6]

One of the darker sides of globalization has been the opportunities it affords for individuals and corporations to avoid taxation. I have served as a member the Independent Commission for the Reform of International Corporate Taxation (ICRICT), trying to ensure that multinationals pay their taxes fairly, especially in developing countries. The commission was chaired by José Antonio Ocampo, and among its members was Winnie Byanyima, the head of Oxfam (where I serve as an honorary adviser), from whom I have learned a great deal.

The Panama Papers showed an even darker side of globalization, and when, in response, Panama asked me to cochair a committee to give guidance on how they could best reform to become a good global citizen, I thought it would both give me insights into how the global system of tax avoidance works and provide an opportunity to outline a framework to deal with it. But when Panama refused to even be transparent in its seeming drive for transparency, Mark Pieth and I resigned and wrote our own report.[7] I am deeply indebted to Mark for his legal and economic insights into these issues, and I suppose I should be indebted to Panama, and especially its vice president, Isabel Saint Malo, for the opportunities they provided for me to delve deeply into these aspects of globalization.

I am deeply indebted to all the members of these commissions whose active engagement and willingness to share their perspectives helped shape mine, as articulated in this book.

In the early years of this century, many political leaders were deeply engaged in the task of making our global system work better, and my service as chief economist of the World Bank, and *GAID* itself, gave me unusual opportunities to interact with them and see globalization from the perspectives of the leaders of both developed and developing countries. Of the long list of those from who I learned so much, I should mention a few in particular: I repeatedly interacted with Gordon Brown, former prime minister of the UK, as he tried to guide the G-20 in developing a coordinated response to the Great Recession; Nicolas Sarkozy, former president of France when that country chaired the G-20, as he tried to push for a more stable global financial system; and also Kevin Rudd, Australia's prime minister (2007–10, 2013), George Papandreou (Greece's prime minister, 2009–11); Ricardo Lagos (Chile's president, 2000–2006), Cristina Fernández de Kirchner (Argentine president, 2007–15), Nestor Kirchner (Argentine president, 2003–7), Manmohan Singh (India's prime minister, 2004–14), Zhu Rongji (China's premier, 1998–2003), Wen Jiabao (China's premier, 2003–13), Li Keqiang (China's premier 2013 to present), Kemal Derviş (former head of the UNDP, 2005–9, and minister of economic affairs of Turkey, 2001–2), and Fernando Henrique Cardoso (president of Brazil, 1995–2002). More recently, I have benefited from extensive discussions with Canada's current foreign minister, Chrystia Freeland (previously its trade minister), and four of the U.S. trade representatives (equivalent to U.S. trade minister; I did not always agree with them), Mickey Kantor and Charlene Barshefsky (both of whom served with me in the Clinton administration), Robert Zoellick (who later became president of the World Bank), and Michael Froman (Obama's trade representative).

There is no one in the Obama administration that I am more indebted to than Jason Furman, who had worked with me when I was chair of the Council of Economic Advisers (CEA), and who later became chair of Obama's CEA. Central to his concerns were the changing American economy, in which globalization inevitably played an important role.

I owe an especial debt to Leif Pagrotsky, Sweden's former trade minister, and to Kalle Moene of the University of Oslo for providing me insights into the Nordic model, and how they have maintained an open economy without experiencing the adverse effects experienced by so many others.

I was fortunate to be followed as chief economist of the World Bank by a sequence of chief economists who broadly shared my views—Nick Stern, François Bourguignon (now at the Paris School of Economics), Justin Yifu Lin (now at Peking University and founding director of the Center for New Structural Economics), and Kaushik Basu (now at Cornell). Stern established an advisory council, continued by his successors, which provided an opportunity to periodically reassess developments in globalization and development. Each of these people—and the other members of the advisory council, including Nobel Prize economist Angus Deaton (at Princeton University)—in different ways has contributed greatly to my understandings of globalization.

As I note especially in the afterword, the last two decades have been a period of rapid change at the World Bank's sister institution, the IMF (International Monetary Fund), and I am particularly indebted to discussions with Christine Lagarde and Dominique Strauss-Kahn (the current and the previous managing director, respectively, 2007–11); Olivier Blanchard (the previous chief economist, who asked me to work with him to organize two conferences at the IMF trying to absorb the lessons of the global financial crisis);[8] Tharman Shanmugaratnam, Singapore's deputy prime minister since 2011, who served as chair of the IMF's policy committee, called the International Monetary and Financial Committee, from 2011 to 2015; Jonathan Ostry, who served as deputy director of research and was instrumental in the research that led to rethinking the role of inequality and capital controls; Sergio Chodos, the IMF's executive director from Argentina, who was especially engaged in issues of debt restructuring; and Zhu Min, who served as one of the deputy managing directors from 2011 to 2016, and is now president at the National Institute of Financial Research at Tsinghua University.

Given all the concerns about globalization, it is not surprising that there are frequent conferences to enhance understanding of what is going on, many with an annual cycle, and interactions with the participants of these too have given me insights into globalization that I might not otherwise have had. These include the World Economic Forum in Davos, Switzerland, every January, the China Development Forum in Beijing every March, and meetings surrounding the General Assembly of the UN every September and surrounding the biannual meetings of the World Bank and IMF every spring and fall.

Globalization, as *Globalization and Its Discontents* and this sequel make clear, has many dimensions, and in each of them I have had the benefit of discussions and insights from colleagues and coauthors over the past two decades. In trade globalization, I should single out Andrew Charlton (now director at AlphaBeta Advisors), with whom I coauthored *Fair Trade for All*.[9]

On the investment agreements which have taken on an increasing role in trade negotiations, I should mention Todd Tucker at the Roosevelt Institute, Lisa Sachs Johnson and Karl P. Sauvant at Columbia, Richard Kozul-Wright at UNCTAD, Kevin Gallagher of Boston University, and Lori Wallach, director and founder of Global Trade Watch.

Another issue that has been at the center of debate in globalization is intellectual property. Here, I should note again my indebtedness to coauthors Dean Baker (codirector of the Center for Economic and Policy Research), Arjun Jayadev (at Azim Premji University and the University of Massachusetts Boston), Claude Henry (at Sciences Po Paris and Columbia University),[10] Ugo Pagano (at the University of Siena), and Giovanni Dosi (at the Scuola Superiore Sant'Anna in Pisa), among others.[11]

A third issue I touch upon is sovereign debt crises and their resolution. Here (as in many other areas in this book) I need to express a special acknowledgment to Martin Guzman, at Columbia, who has coedited a volume[12] and coauthored several papers on the subject; to the Centre for International Governance Innovation, with whom we collaborated extensively, including Domenico Lombardi (director of the Global Economy program) and Paul Martin (Canada's prime minister, 2003–6), who showed a special interest in this aspect of globalization; to Mike Soto-Class (founder and president of Puerto Rico's Center for a New Economy, CNE) and to other members of CNE and their Growth Commission, who worked diligently to contain the economic effects of the island's debt crisis. Brad Setser, formerly at the U.S. Treasury and now at the Council on Foreign Relations, also provided important insights.

Contrary to Trump, it is not the United States but Africa in which globalization has had perhaps the most ambiguous effects. Over the past fifteen years, I have kept close links especially with Ethiopia—the first country in the continent which I visited when I became chief economist of the World Bank in 1997 and the last before my departure; and with South Africa. I owe an especial gratitude to Meles Zenawi, Ethiopia's president from the overthrow of the despotic Mengistu regime in 1991 until 1995, and its prime minister from then until his premature death in 2012, who spent days with me discussing that country's economy and history, and development strategies in general, and helped me see so much of what was going on there. South Africa has been lucky in having a strong economics team, many of whom I have come to know well and who have shared with me their insights into globalization—in particular Trevor Manuel (finance minister, 1996–2009); Pravin Gordhan (finance minister, 2009–14), Rob Davies (trade minister from 2009 to the present), and Ebrahim Patel (economic development minister from 2009 on).[13]

As I tried to understand better the ongoing effects of globalization on Africa, it was often in small countries that one can best see the whole picture, and a visit to Namibia in 2015 was particularly instructive. I should acknowledge the valuable interchanges both before, then, and after with Calle Schlettwein, its finance minister (from 2015; previously, he had been its trade minister); Hage Gottfried Geingob, its president since 2015, and David Smuts, a member of its High Court since 2010.

Above all, I should acknowledge the influence in my understanding Sub-Saharan Africa of Akbar Norman, my Columbia colleague, who previously worked with me at the World Bank.[14]

As I explain in my book *The Euro*, many of the issues raised by globalization arise, with even greater intensity, in the economic integration that has been occurring in Europe. The Greek crisis in particular provided an opportunity to see what can happen when economic integration goes awry. There is a long list of those to whom I am indebted for insights into that crisis, but the list would include Yanis Varoufakis (a Greek economist, academic and politician, who served as the Greek minister of finance from January to July 2015), Jamie Galbraith (at the University of Texas), and Richard Parker (at the Harvard Kennedy School).

Earlier, I acknowledged my indebtedness to the Initiative for Policy Dialogue (IPD) for its work exploring how the 2008 crisis changed our understandings of globalization. IPD's work has gone into every area of globalization, including in trade and investment agreements, intellectual property, and sovereign debt. The more than thirty volumes of research and proceedings of the conferences we have sponsored has, I hoped, helped move the dial a little bit in creating a better globalization. I would be remiss if I failed to mention a few others who have been particularly influential in my thinking on globalization, including those who have headed some of IPD's taskforces or been active in them. These include Ravi Kanbur of Cornell University (who served as my chief adviser while I was at the World Bank); Dani Rodrik of Harvard; Erik Berglöf of LSE (formerly chief economist of the European Bank for Reconstruction and Development, EBRD); Célestin Monga, now chief economist of the African Development Bank; Narcís Serra, who coedited a book with me on global governance;[15] Jomo Kwame Sundaram, who served as assistant secretary-general for Economic Development in the United Nations Department of Economic and Social Affairs and assistant director-general and coordinator for economic and social development at the UN's Food and Agricultural Organization (FAO); and Shari Spiegel, who served as the executive director of IPD and now is chief of the Policy Analysis and Development Branch in the Financing for Development Office of the Department of Economic and Social Affairs at the United Nations (UN DESA).

IPD is only one of several Columbia University organizations focusing on globalization, and I have benefited enormously from my colleagues at the Committee on Global Thought, CGT (of which I served as founding chair), and at the Center on Global Economic Governance, chaired by Jan Švejnar, to whom I am particularly indebted. One of the projects of CGT was a conference on security and globalization, conducted jointly with Mary Kaldor of LSE.[16] Some of the ideas developed there are reflected in the following discussion.

For almost two decades, Columbia University, and especially its Graduate School of Business, along with its School of International and Public Affairs and the Department of Economics, has provided me an intellectual home, with stimulating colleagues and students, from which I have benefited greatly. Its intellectual liveliness is especially evident in areas touched upon in this book.

And for the last several years, I have been especially engaged with the Roosevelt Institute, a think tank growing out of the Presidential Library of Franklin Delano Roosevelt, and dedicated to advancing the ideas and ideals for which he and his wife stood. We have been especially concerned about the growth of inequality, and the role that globalization has played in the increase in inequality. Grants from the Ford Foundation, Bernard L. Schwartz, and the MacArthur Foundation that have helped support work in this area are gratefully acknowledged, as is the encouragement and vision of Darren Walker, the Ford Foundation's president. Thanks also for the intellectual support of Felicia Wong, president and CEO of the Roosevelt Institute; Nell Abernathy, vice president, Research and Policy; and the many other fellows of the Institute.

As always, I owe my greatest indebtedness in my understanding of globalization to my coauthor and Columbia colleague, Bruce Greenwald, with whom I have taught a graduate course on globalization for seventeen years.

The production of any book such as this requires enormous efforts on the part of a large number of individuals. The team at Norton once again worked with me, from the inception of the project with discussions with Drake McFeely, to Jeff Shreve, who edited it; to Nathaniel Dennett, for his editorial assistance; to Fred Wiemer, who did the copyediting. My UK editor, Stuart Proffitt, once again provided insightful comments.

In my office, I am indebted to Debarati Ghosh and Eamon Kircher-Allen for editorial assistance; to Paul Bouscasse, Matthieu Teachout, and Andrew Kosenko for research assistance; to Gabriela Plump for the management of IPD; to Caleb Oldham for administrative support; and to Sarah Thomas for overall management.

Seventeen years ago, I had a rough manuscript describing some of my reflections on globalization as I left the World Bank. My wife, Anya Schiffrin, now director of the Technology, Media, and Communications program at Columbia University's School of International and Public Affairs, helped me convert that manuscript into a global bestseller, inspiring and teaching me in so many ways in the process. She has continued to be an intellectual companion and a soulmate, for which I am ever grateful.

Part I

Globalization and the New Discontents

WHEN I WROTE *Globalization and Its Discontents (GAID)* in the beginning of this century, I was writing about the discontents in the developing world. But now discontent with globalization has gone global. Even as I wrote *GAID*, one of the striking aspects of globalization was the globalization of the anti-globalization protests and of civil society protesting globalization. In 2002, the protestors were mainly those worried about what globalization would do to the environment, how it would affect the poorest people in the poorest countries, or how it was interfering with access to life-saving medicines. There was ample room for grievance. But the newly discontented are not just student activists and environmentalists. They are the middle and working classes throughout the advanced countries. They are expressing their discontent in the ballot box. And a host of populist leaders—Trump in the United States, Farage in the UK, Le Pen in France, Wilders in the Netherlands, the list goes on—are giving voice to and exploiting this discontent.

There is much that those in the middle and working classes have to be unhappy about. The market economy has not been working for them. But they have turned their ire not on the market economy, not on capitalism, but on a particular aspect of today's market economy—globalization. Opinion polls show that trade is among the major sources of discontent for a large share of Americans. In one careful study done right before the 2016 election, 59 percent of those polled said that they were in favor of trade reform—by which they meant some form of protectionism.[1] Similar views are apparent in Europe. These discontented citizens have translated their views into political action. The UK voted to leave the European Union, and Donald Trump—running on an anti-globalization platform, promising to bring manufacturing jobs back to America, build a wall with Mexico, and impose massive 45 percent tariffs against China—was elected president of the United States.[2]

Here, I explain why there is such discontent about globalization in the advanced countries. The indictment includes several "bills of particulars":

- Globalization, as it has been managed, has contributed to growing inequality—including the evisceration of the middle class—even if it is not the only, or most important, force giving rise to this inequality.
- Globalization has contributed to the frequent crises that have marked the era of globalization—dramatized by the 2008 crisis, originating in the United States, which quickly became global.
- Globalization has contributed to the growth of powerful multinational corporations (MNC)—as powerful, in some ways, as nation-states—some of which have in turn contributed to environmental destruction.
- The intellectual property rules of globalization today have led to higher drug prices and reduced access to knowledge, favoring large multinational enterprises over smaller firms. Particular MNCs have pushed policies that, while they increase their profits and market power, may be adverse to the interests of society more generally, and because of their enormous power, the MNCs have often been successful, for instance, in trampling on rights to privacy, the rights of individuals to own their own data, or even their right to know whether the food they are eating contains genetically modified organisms (GMOs).[3]

Globalization, as it has been managed, will be shown to be guilty on each of these counts. But later, I argue that there are other ways of managing globalization, of shaping and responding to it, which avoid these serious pitfalls.

While the policies advocated by Trump and the other protectionists are deeply flawed—they are likely to make those that are suffering even worse off—it is important to understand why their message has had such resonance. Globalization was oversold, with the benefits exaggerated, the costs underestimated. The benefits to growth were smaller, the loss of employment and the increase in inequality greater. We can make globalization work. But that entails not just rewriting the rules of globalization. It entails making our market economy as a whole work for ordinary citizens. If the market economy is working mostly for the 1 percent, globalization will be too.

Chapter 1 describes the overselling of globalization in trade and chapter 2 in its other dimensions—not just the opening of markets to goods from abroad, but also the global integration of financial markets and the development of multinational corporations. It connects the dots, showing the role globalization has had in the evisceration of the middle class. There is thus more than a little truth in the criticisms of globalization *as it has been managed*. Chapter 3 explains why nostrums provided by Trump and other protectionists will fail. Finally, chapter 4 describes what it will take to ameliorate the discontent with globalization—how we can reconstruct globalization so that most citizens benefit.

Chapter 1

The Failures of Globalization

T HE DISCONTENT WITH globalization in the advanced countries is palpable. As I noted in the introduction, large segments of society feel that their lives are not improving, and those perceptions are accurate: in many countries, such as the United States, even a majority have been experiencing near stagnation for more than a quarter century. Here, I explain the role that globalization has played. It is not the only force, but it is such a powerful force that even if there were no changes in technology—no advances, for instance, that enabled employers to replace unskilled workers with machines—globalization by itself could, and probably would, have led large numbers of unskilled workers to be worse off.

Globalization is about more than trade—it is also about the movement of capital, people, and ideas across borders. But because trade is at the center of current controversies—and because it illustrates so forcefully the issues at play—I begin the discussion focusing on trade.

OVERSELLING TRADE GLOBALIZATION

Economists' belief in the virtues of free trade has been so deep and so long-standing that any economist who expressed skepticism was at risk of losing his "union card"—or at least his credibility as a serious economist. One of the earliest contributions of my thesis supervisor, Paul Samuelson, was to show that the country as a whole was better off as a result of trade liberalization—that is, overall national income was increased.[1] This expanded on the earlier argument of David Ricardo about the gains from trade that arise when each country increases production in what it does *relatively* well; and that of Adam Smith, about the gains from trade that arise when each country specializes, so that it can get better and better at what it does.[2]

A Little White Lie: Trade Creates Jobs

The problem is that the story I've just told about the virtues of trade was not understood by most politicians, and those that did understand it thought it was too complicated. So, sometimes with the help of some economists, they told what they thought was a white lie—trade creates jobs. And when the evidence showed the contrary, they lost their credibility—and so did globalization.

The objective of trade policy is not to increase jobs—maintaining the economy at full employment is the responsibility of monetary policy (the Federal Reserve in the United States, the Bank of England in the UK)[3] and fiscal policy (the setting of taxes and expenditure). The objective of trade policy is to increase standards of living, by increasing productivity.

If exports create jobs, as claimed by the U.S. trade representative (USTR—the U.S. "trade minister," whose job is to design and sell trade policies), then imports destroy jobs. Over the long term, trade is roughly balanced; that is, on average, exports expand with imports. The goods that advanced countries export use less labor than what they import. The advanced countries import textiles and apparel, which require a lot of labor, and export advanced products like aircraft. But this means that if the United States, say, expands exports and imports by $100 million, the new imports destroy more jobs than are created by the new exports.

Hence, on net, trade by itself destroys jobs. But if monetary and fiscal policy do their jobs, this isn't a problem: the economy expands, creating new jobs to offset the jobs that are lost. The new export-sector jobs pay higher wages than the jobs in the import-competing sector that are lost.

Trade increases productivity, and it is this increase in productivity that leads to higher living standards.

Thus, the standard theory recognized that the opening up of trade to cheap imports would result in the loss of jobs in the import-competing sectors; but, it *assumed* that new jobs would be created in the export sectors and that the economy would be able to stay at full employment.[4] But this hasn't always happened.

The True Story: Smaller Benefits Than Promised

Lower Growth, Increased Unemployment
The fact that globalization is seen as contributing to unemployment is perhaps the most important source of opposition to globalization. What went wrong is simple. Sometimes job destruction outpaces job creation, in which case globalization will be associated with an *increase* in the level of unemployment. Moving people from low-paid jobs in, say, textiles or apparel to unemployment lowers GDP. It doesn't help growth. This problem of job loss becomes particularly salient when there is already high unemployment.

This is often the case in developing countries, as I pointed out in *GAID,* but is also true in advanced countries like the United States when monetary and fiscal policy aren't working as they should, and there is thus a scarcity of jobs. This happens episodically when economies go into a recession. But typically, recessions are short-lived. Those who lose their jobs in the downturn get new jobs (though often at lower pay) in the recovery. Some European countries, however, have been plagued with long-term unemployment.

The Great Recession—beginning with the global financial crisis of 2008 which, in Europe, morphed into the euro crisis—has undermined faith in markets, in both their efficiency and their stability. The crisis came at a time that countries on both sides of the Atlantic were already struggling with the loss of manufacturing jobs. The crisis then exacerbated the problem: there were massive job losses. The slow recovery from that crisis meant, for instance, that Americans were particularly sensitive to the job destruction that had followed the surge of imports from China after its admission to the WTO.[5] Not only were jobs in industries competing with these imports destroyed, but as this happened, others in the community were affected, as housing prices fell and demand for nontraded goods and services (like haircuts, restaurant meals, car repairs, legal services, that are bought locally)[6] decreased. As real estate prices fell, small businesses that used real estate as collateral for their loans were hit. Banks in these communities were also hit, and they responded by cutting lending, in a downward vicious circle.

Increased Risk

Advocates of globalization ignored other problems with globalization as well. Many of these "mistakes" were the result of the use of oversimplified models of the economy to guide policy. Oversimplified models, for instance, assumed markets worked so well that there was never a problem with unemployment—hence, they ignored a critical source of opposition to globalization. Oversimplified models led some economists to ignore too the many other ways in which markets differ markedly from the textbook stories, which assume perfect information and perfect competition. In these mythical worlds, markets work so well that there is never any reason for governments to intervene in the economy—there are, for instance, neither bubbles nor recessions. But it should be obvious that it is nonsensical to base any serious policy analysis on models making assumptions that depart so far from reality.[7]

The 2008 crisis brought home how globalization can increase the risks faced by firms and individuals. Indeed, most of the macroeconomic risks facing developing countries come from *outside* of the country—such as a sudden decline in the price of what they export, a sudden increase in the price of what they import, or a sudden increase in the global interest rate. Making matters worse, individuals and firms cannot insure themselves against many of these risks, nor can the risks be shared across society. These shortcomings have profound consequences. Consumers are worse off when they have to bear the consequent risks. Workers too may face greater insecurity. And firms, without insurance protection, may shift production toward safer activities with lower average returns and productivity. The result is that *with imperfect risk markets all individuals may be worse off* as a result of globalization.[8]

One particular risk relates to a country's energy security. Gung-ho globalizers pretended that in the post–World War II era, borders don't matter, and because they don't matter, countries shouldn't mind becoming dependent on others for energy (or food or any other essential item). But borders do matter, and for anyone who has forgotten, Trump has provided a powerful reminder.

Mexico has become heavily dependent on U.S. gas. The North American Free Trade Agreement (NAFTA), the pact between Canada, Mexico, and the United States, assured Mexico of the free flow of gas across the border. Trump, with his virulent and irrational anti-Mexican stance, is planning to build a very expensive wall, and some Mexicans worry that he could take actions that would interrupt the supply of gas; at the very least, it could be an important bargaining chip as he tries to force Mexico to pay for his ill-conceived wall.

So too Germany believed that with the collapse of the Berlin Wall, borders with the East would not matter. It has, as a result, become heavily dependent on Russian gas—a dependence with economic and political consequences. If Russia should suddenly shut off the gas, it could have disastrous effects for Germany's economy. This scenario is not just a remote possibility or an economist's nightmare; Russia did cut off the supply of gas to Ukraine in 2014. Germany might reason that it wouldn't be in Russia's *economic* interests to do this. But Russia (and its leader, Vladimir Putin) might have other concerns—such as inducing the West to remove sanctions imposed as a result of its blatant violation of international law with the invasion of Ukraine and the accession of Crimea. And of course, economists' presumption that humans are always and everywhere fully rational is obviously wrong.

Markets don't appropriately "price" the cost to society of an interruption in the gas supply, and thus German firms, looking for the cheapest source of energy, turned to Russia. The failure to price this risk is an example of a market failure—one with consequences in the short run as serious as the failure to "price" the risk of global warming in the long run.[9]

Imperfect Competition

The standard models also assumed perfect competition—all firms were small—in spite of the fact that much trade is conducted by corporate behemoths which are larger than many countries and which often have marked market power. Walmart may use its market power in China to drive down producer prices, and then, when it enters other countries, like India or South Africa, use the benefits of this market power—the low prices at which it can acquire goods—to effectively drive small producers out of business.[10] Standard results on the unambiguous desirability of free trade do not hold when there is imperfect competition.[11] And yet, policy analysts have tended to ignore these effects, worried that it would open up a Pandora's Box of special-interest claimants for protection.[12]

Dynamic Comparative Advantage

Perhaps the biggest mistake that globalizers made was that they paid too little attention to the long run (as is the case for most firms in our economy). They asked, what is the comparative advantage, the relative strength, of the economy *today*? Cheap labor in China meant that it had a comparative advantage in labor-intensive manufacturing. So, firms shifted their production from the United States to China.

In the past, this shift would have happened slowly. China simply wouldn't have had the initial technological capacities: labor might have been cheap, but not cheap enough to compensate for the technology gap. But China invited American firms in, and these firms were able to couple their advanced technology with China's cheap but often well-trained and disciplined labor. And of course, access to the potentially huge Chinese market made it even more attractive for foreign firms to set up shop there.

What happened next changed the course of globalization: China and other countries in East Asia *learned,* and they learned quickly. They developed their own technological capacities, which meant they still had a comparative advantage in labor-intensive industries even as their wages started to rise.

In manufacturing and many other sectors of the economy, firms learn how to increase productivity by *doing,* by actually producing. But there is an unappreciated converse of this proposition: if firms don't produce, they quickly fall behind. As America shifted production of, say, thermos bottles to China, China learned how to produce even better thermos bottles at a lower cost. And thus, America, as it stopped producing, lost some of its technological advantage.

In essence, globalization's advocates forgot about "spillovers": the ways that learning in one firm spills over to another firm in the area.[13] These spillovers also help to explain "clusters," those dense groupings of high-tech firms in Silicon Valley today, or the new manufacturing enterprises in Ohio and Michigan at the beginning of the twentieth century.

History matters: twenty or thirty years later, after production has shifted to China, we can't just say, let's bring manufacturing back to the United States or Europe. While overall, America has a high level of technology and very skilled workers, in many specific areas we have neither the technology nor the skilled workers required. Of course, America and Europe could also learn. They could train a new coterie of workers. But that would require a concerted effort—beyond the ambit of any single firm. More likely, if production were to return, it would be based on new and different technology—in particular, the use of robots. These are areas where the advanced countries probably do have a comparative advantage. But—and this is key—bringing production back with these new technologies will not resuscitate the old manufacturing jobs; indeed, it is unlikely to create many jobs at all, and the jobs created will be mostly highly skilled jobs and in different places from where the jobs were lost. This doesn't mean that the advanced countries shouldn't try to recover manufacturing jobs, but only that they should have realistic expectations of the results.[14] And bringing back manufacturing jobs can't be at the core of any agenda to "make America great again,"[15] or even a less nationalistic agenda of restoring shared prosperity.

Impact of the Exchange Rate:
Currency Manipulation or Market Forces

A key factor in the changing competitive-advantage landscape is the exchange rate, which determines the relative value of one currency to another. The relatively high value of the dollar as compared to the Chinese renminbi (rmb, also known as the yuan) made competition with China especially difficult. As a result, China's goods can be sold very cheaply in the United States.

A couple of factors led to a high value of the dollar. First, and most important, was the macro-economy in the United States. Beginning with Reagan and his tax cuts of 1981, the country ran large fiscal deficits—that is, the government was spending more than its income; and this was not offset by an increase in private savings within the country.[16] So, to finance the increased deficit, the United States had to borrow from abroad; that is, there was a flow of capital into the country to finance the deficiency between what the United States was investing and its total national savings. But the flip side of this capital inflow is the trade deficit—imports exceed exports.

This is a basic truism of international macroeconomics: the current account deficit—which includes not just the difference between imports and exports of goods, but also of services[17]—equals the difference between domestic investment and savings. I'll return to this several times in this chapter. Economists differ about many things; but they cannot and do not disagree about a truism such as this.

For a third of a century, the entire period of modern globalization, U.S. macroeconomic policy has created and sustained huge trade deficits. The inflow of funds, in turn, leads to a strong dollar.[18] The strong dollar helped make U.S. manufacturing uncompetitive, especially as advanced technology was flowing so freely toward China.[19]

Second, China discovered that by managing its exchange rate, keeping it slightly lower than it otherwise would be, it expanded exports, providing jobs for its burgeoning population and enabling China to industrialize and raise the standard of living for its people very rapidly. The United States accused China of *manipulating* its exchange rate. In practice, all countries engage in policies which affect the exchange rate. When the United States lowered its interest rates in response to the Great Recession, one of the main ways it helped the U.S. economy was that it led to a lower exchange rate, increasing exports and reducing imports—a kind of beggar-thy-neighbor policy that helped the United States' recovery at the expense of that in Europe.[20] Ironically, by the time Trump began accusing China of exchange rate manipulation, China had reversed course, and was actually intervening to *increase* its exchange rate, to strengthen its currency, responding to a flow of money out of the country—between 2014 and the beginning of 2017, China lost about $1 trillion in foreign reserves[21]—which had depressed the exchange rate *too far*.[22]

In no country is the exchange rate *just* a matter of market forces. The most important factor determining movements in a country's exchange rate is the interest rate set by the central bank—by a public institution, not by the market. The United States has gone around the world trying to persuade governments that they should not intervene in their exchange rate, that it should be determined by market forces. In practice, what that means is that it should be determined by the Federal Reserve, America's central bank, but not by their own central banks.

In China, matters are even more complicated. China restricts its citizens putting their money abroad. If China removed this restriction, but then let the exchange rate be determined by "market forces," the exchange rate would plummet as Chinese citizens sought to diversify their portfolios and invest money in other countries. And of course, the United States would complain. What the United States wants is not a market-determined exchange rate for China, but a high exchange rate. Indeed, in the East Asia crisis, the United States put pressure on China to ensure that its exchange rate did not plummet as the other East Asian currencies plummeted. Then, it didn't want China to let the market determine the exchange rate, for if it had, their exchange rate would have fallen in tandem with that of other countries in the region.

SOME BASIC PRINCIPLES OF TRADE

But the most important point is that any one country's exchange rate, even that of China, has little effect on the overall U.S. trade deficit. The overall trade deficit is determined by the balance of domestic savings and investment, which is little affected by any particular country's exchange rate. The value of the renminbi affects the bilateral trade deficit—the difference between exports and imports to China. But that itself is of little relevance. If the United States imported less apparel or shoes from China (because the renminbi strengthened), it would import more from some other developing country like Bangladesh or Vietnam; it wouldn't produce much more inside its own borders.

Bilateral trade deficits only matter in a barter economy. The reason that money was such an important invention is that it avoids barter— it allows multilateral exchange. We buy more from China than we sell. But China may buy more from Australia than it sells there. And Australia may buy more from the United States than it sells to it. We would all be worse off if each of these three trade accounts had to balance individually.

There are, perhaps, a few people who think that because the United

States is better at everything than everybody else we should only be exporting: by definition, in this logic, if someone is undercutting our firms, they must be playing unfair. That's the kind of mercantilist reasoning that Smith railed against more than two hundred years ago. The citizens of a country benefit from consuming, from enjoying the fruits of their labor. It makes no sense for them just to sell to other countries everything that they produce. We export in order to import. A country exports things that it's *relatively* good at, importing things that it's *relatively* bad at. And being relatively bad at something doesn't require ineptitude—it just means someone else can do it at least a little better. It's not a matter of "unfair play." We don't need to export—or to prevent imports—to remain at full employment. As we emphasized earlier, the task of maintaining the economy at full employment is the responsibility of monetary authorities (the Federal Reserve) and fiscal policy. It is not the responsibility of trade policy.

Competing with Cheap Labor and Low Labor and Environmental Standards
The same kind of fallacy arises with complaints about trading partners that have low wages. How can the United States compete? Of course, in competitive markets, the reason that wages are low is that productivity is low—and that translates in turn into lower living standards. It's unfortunate to have low wages and productivity, but not unfair. These low-wage economies could similarly complain, how could they compete with American technology? Or with an economy where the Federal Reserve sets interest rates at near zero? The theory of comparative advantage describes the benefits that arise from trade whenever countries differ in their relative productivities in doing different things: we are relatively more productive in making airplanes, our trading partners are relatively more productive in making clothes.[23] Our trading partner could be far less productive overall—and thus have far lower wages. In the case of trade with poor countries, it should be obvious that there are typically huge differences in relative productivities, and hence huge gains from trade.

This principle of comparative advantage applies as well no matter how different countries decide to spend whatever income they get, or for that matter how they organize various parts of their economy. They could spend, for instance, more money on preventive health care (as our European trading partners do), and less money on emergency room treatment.[24]

There are, however, some important instances where there are large market distortions, which mean that observed patterns of trade may not correspond to those of the underlying comparative advantages. Most obviously, a government could provide subsidies to a firm. As simple as this sounds, in practice, going beyond direct subsidies, it is complex. Some complain that when a country (like the United States) sets interest rates at zero, or bails out banks, so that they can in effect charge their customers lower interest rates than otherwise would be the case, there is a subsidy.

So too there is a real societal cost when a firm imposes environmental damage, and not to charge the firm for the costs it imposes is *de facto* a subsidy. The 2015 Paris Agreement on climate change committed countries to reduce their climate emissions. Many will implement their commitments by imposing charges for carbon emissions. There is a large societal cost to such emissions—the costs arising from climate change. Not charging for such costs is as much a subsidy as having an arrangement by which firms could have free access to labor. Many countries are worried that if some country—say the United States—refuses to impose such a charge, it distorts the pattern of trade. America might produce an emissions-intensive good, like steel, more cheaply not because it is relatively more efficient, but because of the implicit subsidy. Trade based on advantages arising from an absence of environmental regulations or charges for greenhouse gas emissions is "unfair"—or at the very least distorted.

I also noted that imperfections in competition can give rise to distorted patterns of trade. Of particular concern is market power in the labor market—where firms are able to so exploit workers that they provide substandard working conditions.

Trade agreements over the past quarter century have included provisions intended to deal with some of these distortions. When a country provides a subsidy, its trading partners can impose a "countervailing duty" to offset the effects. Some believe that this provision extends to implicit subsidies, such as not charging for environmental damage, including not imposing a carbon price.[25] Recent agreements also include provisions relating to labor and environmental standards, though the evidence is that even the limited conditions are often not enforced effectively.[26]

It is important to realize, however, that most bilateral trade deficits have little to do with these distortions. Thus, the United States has a trade surplus with the Netherlands (of some $24 billion in 2016). But that doesn't mean that America is engaging in some unfair trade policies vis-à-vis the Netherlands, and the imbalance cannot be blamed on the United States having worse labor or environmental laws than the Dutch.

And it is also important to go back to the underlying macroeconomic fundamentals: none of this matters for the overall trade deficit, which is a matter of the imbalance between domestic savings and investment.

Winners and Losers: The Distributive Consequences of Trade

Some of the discontent with globalization arises from the fact it didn't deliver on the promise either of jobs or growth. More apparent than the jobs created were the jobs destroyed. And growth in the era of globalization was slower than in the decades before. But the real discontent arises from the fact that so many people were actually worse off as a result of globalization. That the corporations got more than 100 percent of the gains—all of the growth, and then some of the existing economic pie that had belonged to others—made globalization that much more attractive for them, but that much less attractive to the rest of society.

In fact, honest academics always pointed out that there would be winners and losers in globalization. When globalization worked well, the standard theory arguing for globalization went, the winners gained enough so that they could compensate the losers and everyone would be better off. But the theory said that they *could* compensate the losers, not that they *would*. And typically they didn't. And because they didn't, many—even a majority of citizens—may be worse off. These are inconvenient truths, which were not widely explained in the heyday of globalization, when the advocates seemed to claim that everyone would win.

With perfectly free trade and well-functioning markets, unskilled workers everywhere in the world would get the same wages[27]—and moving *toward* free trade results in unskilled wages in advanced countries going down.[28] The argument was simple: trade in goods was a substitute for the movement of the factors of production, the unskilled and skilled labor and capital that go into making the goods. If the United

States imports more unskilled-labor-intensive goods from China, there is less of a need to produce those goods in America, and that lowers the demand for unskilled labor in the United States, and hence the wage of unskilled labor decreases.

These insights were never highlighted—indeed never mentioned—by the advocates of globalization. Was it a matter of willful deception, ignorance, or because *somehow* many politicians, even Democrats, continued to believe in trickle-down economics? Ever since President Kennedy claimed that "a rising tide lifts all boats,"[29] the idea of trickle-down economics has persisted without theory or evidence backing it. The last quarter of a century has simply provided more evidence against the idea.[30]

Weaker Bargaining Power

Workers' wages were lowered as a result of another force: a weakening of their bargaining power. This had, of course, already been greatly weakened by the attack on unions and changes in labor legislation that began in the United States under President Reagan and in the UK under Prime Minister Margaret Thatcher.[31] But now corporations had another tool. They could threaten to move their factory elsewhere, to China or Mexico, where there was cheaper labor. Trade agreements then gave them the right to bring the goods thus made back to the United States—in the case of Mexico, with no duties, in the case of China, typically with very low duties. Workers felt forced to accept lower wages and worse working conditions. There was nothing the unions could do to stop this outsourcing of jobs and the lowering of wages—and with their power thus diminished, so was their membership, in a vicious downward spiral.

And then there was no one to speak up for what was happening to America's working people. That had also been the role of the Democratic Party. But as elections increased in cost (each party had to spend about a billion dollars in the 2016 election), the Democratic Party had to move increasingly close to the sources of the money—the bankers and the new tech entrepreneurs of Silicon Valley—and increasingly distant from their traditional base. Even when I served in the Clinton administration, when either I or Robert Reich, the secretary of labor, spoke out against the regressivity of our tax system (very rich people actually pay a much smaller fraction of their income than those who are not so rich) or the unwarranted subsidies to our banks and corporations, which we derisively referred to as corporate welfare, we were put down as fomenting class warfare.[32]

Of course, many politicians simply didn't care whether trickle-down economics worked or not: as long as enough of their constituents—or enough of those who financially supported their politics—were doing well, that was all that mattered. And the top 1 percent has been doing very well.

Given this, our politicians didn't want to think about the consequences of their policies for ordinary Americans; they didn't want to hear the voices of those economists who warned of the large potential consequences for America's and Europe's middle class.[33] They listened only to what they wanted to hear.

Balancing Interests under Managed Trade

The globalization which emerged at the end of the twentieth century and the beginning of the twenty-first was not based on "free trade," but on managed trade—managed for special corporate interests in the United States and other advanced countries, balancing those interests even as the agreements put little weight on the interests of others— either workers in advance countries or those elsewhere.

One of the lessons that students in public policy schools take to heart is that a new law should have a name that is the opposite of what it actually does. Thus, a free trade agreement is actually not about free trade. If it were about free trade, it would be short, a few pages—each country gives up its tariffs, its nontariff barriers to trade, and its subsidies. The Trans-Pacific Partnership (see introduction), ran upward of 6,000 pages. I was once asked by a South American president whether he should sign a so-called free trade agreement with the United States. I suggested he propose a true free trade agreement: if he did, almost surely, the United States would refuse. It has consistently refused to do away, for instance, with its agricultural subsidies.[34]

To see that these "managed trade" agreements represent a balancing out of special interests within the advanced countries, imagine, say, congressional reactions to alternative rules. As I have noted, it is almost unimaginable that Congress would have supported a true free trade agreement that would have eliminated both the overt agricultural subsidies and the more covert subsidies for fossil fuels (some of which are hidden in the tax system). In the Uruguay Round of trade negotiations completed in 1994, the United States demanded, and got, a ten-year delay in the elimination of protection for textiles. Given the shortsightedness of the corporate sector, ten years is an infinity. Of course, when the ten years expired, the industry wanted an extension of its protection.

Technology or Globalization

Defenders of globalization argue that globalization is only one of several forces contributing to the growing inequalities and the decline in incomes of unskilled workers. It is (in this view) unjustly being treated as if it is the only, or the major, contributor to inequality.[35] Technical change is more important—advances in technology have made Rust Belt jobs obsolete and reduced the demand for unskilled workers. In a market economy, lowering wages is the inevitable result.

Most of the job loss in manufacturing is in fact due to technology. Even if there were no globalization, the fact that productivity growth in manufacturing is so much greater than the growth in demand would have led to major reductions in manufacturing jobs. By some reckoning, one can explain some 65 to 80 percent of job losses in manufacturing in the United States in this way.[36]

So too Trump has made much of the loss of jobs in coal mining—this time blaming regulations. But the real reason is simple: advances in technology resulted in a massive increase in the supply of natural gas, making coal uncompetitive. The United States exports coal to Europe—depressing coal prices and production there. If the Europeans had the same "protectionist" mentality that the Americans are assuming, they would, of course, keep American coal out. (Trump, like most protectionists, seldom thinks of what would happen if everyone acted as he does.)[37]

Perceptions of ordinary citizens toward technical progress and globalization differ—partly, but only partly, because of how certain politicians have made globalization the villain. To oppose technical change is to be antediluvian. No one wants to wear that label. Moreover, it is hard for individuals to think of what one might do to stop technological progress. There's no activism disposed to smashing machines, as in the nineteenth century Luddite movement.

Besides, optimistic Americans as well as workers elsewhere in advanced countries believe that they can respond to technical progress. They see it as increasing living standards—there is a clear link between that and the new products they love. Moreover, embracing progress is part of the American identity. The ability to innovate and to adapt is part of the success of the country. Many in other countries feel similarly.

Globalization, though, is shaped by politicians at home and abroad. And so it's easy to think of what one could do to stop imports: impose trade restrictions. Those "others" are engaged in *unfair* competition. When I was chairman of the Council of Economic Advisers, I frequently heard pleadings from those in the business community who were resolutely in favor of competition and against subsidies for others. But they were eloquent in explaining how *at that moment* and *in their industry* competition was unfair and destructive, and a little government help—sometimes in the form of subsidies, often by protecting them from "unfair" competition from abroad—would be of enormous benefit, not to themselves personally, but to their workers and their communities. When those who seem to be outcompeting oneself are foreigners, the inclination to say that they are engaging in unfair competition is irresistible: to argue otherwise is to suggest that one simply doesn't measure up.

In short, people feel that at least some of their travails are due to globalization—the way it's been shaped by our political system. They feel they don't have to put up with it, and they shouldn't put up with it.

Besides, whether true or not, it gives little comfort to those in the middle who have seen their incomes stagnate to say that only part of their suffering is due to globalization, or even that most of the decline of the middle class is due to technological change. That this may be so only increases their resolve to do what they can to preserve their standards of living through "reforming" globalization.

There are politicians who are willing to give voice to their anger, to tell those people what they want to hear: America can and should use its economic power; on its own, with protectionism, it would be stronger than it is now. Their jobs would be restored and their wages returned to levels they haven't seen in years. This is the promise—a promise that will inevitably be broken, as I show in chapter 3.

A Thought Experiment

In short, even if globalization is only part of the reason for the decline of the middle class, if citizens feel that it is something they can do something about, then it is natural for them to want to take action. It might not "solve" their problems, but it could make things better.

In fact, technology and globalization are inextricably linked. Without advances in communication and transportation, the kind of globalization we have today would not have been feasible. We couldn't have had outsourcing to the extent that we do.

Nonetheless, it's instructive to engage in a thought experiment. What would have happened if there had been no changes in technology, but globalization had gone forward apace, with the stripping away of barriers to the movement of goods, services, and firms. The standard theory to which I have already alluded gives a clear answer. Wages of unskilled workers would have plummeted, converging toward levels in the emerging markets. Of course, markets never work quite as perfectly as they do in economists' models, so the decline would not be instantaneous. Yet, no one believing in markets and globalization has provided a cogent reason why these wages wouldn't have fallen and by a great deal.[38]

THE ROLE OF TRADE AGREEMENTS

The discontent with globalization has focused on trade agreements, like NAFTA. In exploiting the discontent with globalization as much as he could, Trump called NAFTA the "worst deal ever," blaming America's trade negotiators, even though it was negotiated by former president George H. W. Bush of his own party.[39] In the negotiations, Mexico brought down its tariffs, on average, by 10 percentage points, the United States by only 4 percentage points—and the United States was allowed to keep in place its corn subsidies, which by some accounts did damage to the poorest in Mexico, its corn farmers. American corn farmers receive a substantial portion of their income from Washington rather than from the soil. Mexican farmers might be able to compete against American farmers, but it's hard to compete against Washington—against such subsidies.[40]

Today, the American and Mexican economies are intertwined. While America lost jobs as factories moved to Mexico, jobs were also created; and the new export-related jobs typically paid more than the jobs that were lost. An estimated 5 to 6 million American jobs depend on exports to Mexico.[41]

While the U.S. trade deficit with Mexico (the gap between U.S. exports to Mexico and its imports) is large, $63 billion in 2016, it is small compared to that with China ($347 billion) and roughly the same as that with Germany ($65 billion).[42] The fact that Germany has not experienced Trump's wrath to the same extent as Mexico has never been adequately explained—it may be just racism and bigotry.

In any case, as I've explained, one shouldn't really look at the deficits or surpluses between two countries—the focus should be on the multilateral trade deficit. The United States has a trade deficit with Mexico but a trade surplus—when we include services—with Canada.[43] Selling education, health, or tourist services creates jobs just as selling automobiles does. It appears that some in the Trump administration are enamored with the idea of selling goods but not services. There is no economic basis for this. The fact that the United States has a surplus with Canada does not mean that the country has been engaging in "unfair trade" with Canada, or that NAFTA is unfair.

A Loss of Sovereignty?

Trade agreements do mean that a country gives up certain rights—a free trade agreement means that the country gives up the right to impose a tariff. But it's a reciprocal action: the other country makes a similar agreement. The benefits of this slight loss of sovereignty, through such reciprocity, can be large relative to the cost. And it means that when there are disputes about one party or the other honoring the agreement, both sides agree to respect the outcome of the dispute resolution mechanism. The world is far short of an international government, but these are small steps toward creating an international rule of law. In the absence of such an international rule of law, there is a jungle, with might making right.[44]

Economists have long noted the importance of the rule of law for growth and efficiency—the modern market economy couldn't exist without a modicum of the rule of law.[45] As the world has globalized, there is an imperative for creating an international rule of law. So far, we've fallen short. But our international trade agreements are a step in the right direction. This is especially important for smaller countries. The United States, the EU, and China might be able to bash it out, as each struggles to do better for its exporters but keep out imports. The rest of the world—some 38 percent of global GDP—would especially suffer as collateral damage. Interestingly, with Trump announcing a U.S. retreat from globalization and the global rule of law, China has stepped forward as its defender.[46] China has every reason to do so: its remarkable growth would not have been possible without globalization. It has been explicit that it will defend a rules-based system, which is of such importance to developing countries and emerging markets. It's not just about cutting deals that are of benefit to itself, even though that kind of negotiating is precisely what Trump loves.

The World Trade Organization (WTO), created in 1995, was the critical step forward in creating a global rules-based system. It not only provided for a set of principles, including the most favored nation principle, ensuring that countries wouldn't engage in discrimination against each other,[47] but it also provided for a kind of international tribunal for adjudicating disputes. Its enforcement mechanism was limited— if a country violated its obligations, for instance, if the United States imposed a 45 percent tariff against China—then the injured country could impose duties in an equivalent amount on the offending country. The offending country could, of course, choose to continue to impose the tariffs. But there would be consequences. So far, this system has proven remarkably effective. It has, for instance, prevented, or at least limited, trade wars. There was considerable worry in the aftermath of the 2008 crisis that countries would attempt to reignite their economies by beggar-thy-neighbor policies, shifting demand away from imports and toward their own economy, as happened in the Great Depression.[48] It didn't happen, and the WTO is generally given credit.

Trump has announced that he intends to upend this system, and that he will not honor adverse rulings. If he does as he says, the United States will pay a high price. If it ignites a trade war, the whole world will pay a high price.

Other Goals beyond Promoting Growth

Trade and other economic agreements are about trade, but they are also about other objectives. They are often an instrument of foreign policy—trying to bind countries together. When the United States signed a free trade agreement with Jordan in 2000, no one thought that it would have any significant effect on U.S. growth. The hope was that it would help one of America's closest allies in the Middle East. When Obama argued for the Trans-Pacific Partnership (TPP) agreement, he often did so on the basis of extending U.S. influence in Asia. In his State of the Union address on January 20, 2015, he said, "But as we speak, China wants to write the rules for the world's fastest-growing region. That would put our workers and our businesses at a disadvantage. Why would we let that happen? We should write those rules." Though he talked about the TPP's impact on the U.S. economy, it was clear that he saw it as an instrument to advance our political interests in Asia and the Pacific vis-à-vis China.[49] But in suggesting that the United States would write the rules, he failed to state who *within* the United States would do so. In the secretive process that the USTR employed to negotiate the TPP, corporations were effectively at the table, but not ordinary citizens or civil society groups concerned about health or the environment. And so it was not a surprise that what emerged was an agreement that served corporate interests, with negligible benefits for the U.S. economy as a whole.[50]

These non-trade-related goals of trade agreements are often coincident with the more traditional goals. NAFTA was intended to increase incomes in both Mexico and the United States; and one of the ancillary benefits would be that higher incomes in Mexico would reduce immigration pressure. As I have noted, that has in fact happened, though NAFTA may have played only a minor role in migration from Mexico diminishing to but a trickle.[51]

If, on the other hand, the trade agreements are not well-designed, they may be counterproductive. Thus, the 2004 agreement with Morocco, again intended to help one of the more progressive countries of the Middle East and North Africa, actually had an adverse effect: restrictions in the agreement on access to generic drugs, so important for AIDS patients, gave rise to massive protests in the country.

The New Trade Agreements: A Regulatory Race to the Bottom
Globalization is as badly managed and untempered as it was when I wrote *GAID*, and in some ways it has become worse since then. Until this century, trade agreements entailed pitting producers of one country in one sector against those of another in another sector; the agreement would entail lowering tariffs on one good in one country in return for the lowering of tariffs against another good in another country. Consumers were the unambiguous winners. But this is not so for the new trade agreements of the last decade and a half. With tariffs very low, the focus of trade agreements has been on regulations. Now, producers in one country say that they could sell more in another country if the government only got rid of some regulation, for instance, on emissions of pollutants or safety. The producers of both countries can easily agree: let's get rid of the regulations in both of our countries; and the trade ministers (in the case of the United States, the U.S. trade representative) can quickly agree too—these ministries are typically "captured" by producer interests. But while consumers in both countries gained when tariffs—and prices—were lowered, in this case, citizens in both countries lose from the weakening of important protective regulations, and the corporations gain. International trade becomes their ally in arguing for the kind of world that they, the corporations, had sought, but couldn't get because domestically, within each country's legislature, society balances the cost and benefits of these regulations. Provisions in recent trade agreements (going back to NAFTA) are designed to make it difficult if not impossible for new regulations to be imposed, no matter what the social benefit.[52]

With only producers at the international "bargaining" table, only the costs of regulations are weighed. The TPP, advocated by the Obama administration but subsequently killed by Trump in one of his first acts, serves as a good illustration of this point. It was hailed by Obama as the largest trade agreement ever, embracing 40 percent of global GDP and one third of global trade, involving twelve countries around the Pacific Rim. Yet its *economic* impact was estimated *by the government itself*, after full implementation in, say, fifteen years, to be .15 percent of GDP—that is, its growth impact was negligible.[53] Other studies, more independent, argued that even this small number was a gross exaggeration.[54]

(This didn't stop Obama and other TPP backers from promoting it with language that suggested it would be a major boon to the growth of jobs and the economy. But the real objective, as suggested earlier, may have been in foreign policy: the role of the United States vs. China.) The corporations offer a weak justification for what they ask. They have said it is important to *harmonize* regulations, and that different regulations act as *nontariff barriers to trade*. But in fact, what they wanted was not harmonization itself, but the elimination, or at least weakening, of regulations. In most sectors, we simply don't need to have *full* harmonization of regulations. Indeed, different states within the United States have different regulations. Within Europe, the notion that responsibility for setting regulations should be assigned to the lowest possible level of government—the level closest to the people—is called subsidiarity.[55]

For example, regulation is not needed to set the percentage of heavy cream in ice cream. If different countries want to regulate this, it should be up to them. Of course, consumers should have the right to know the percentage in the product they are purchasing. Thus, what is important, in this case, is a regulation about information.

Different countries may weigh different costs and benefits differently. Some countries may not care much that their citizens are torn to shreds in an accident by shards of glass; Americans may find this particularly distasteful, and so create regulations requiring shatterproof windshields. Just as cars can be ordered with different colors, so too they can be ordered with different kinds of windshields. The additional costs from lack of harmonization are negligible.

We should be asking for the minimal level of harmonization required to make the global system work, not for the minimal level of regulation—the level of regulation that maximizes corporate profits.

Though recent trade agreements have been designed to reduce prospects of future regulations and, where possible, to engineer regulatory rollbacks under the guise of harmonization, there was a broader, more invidious agenda: to develop a system of globalization under which countries competed in every way possible to attract business—lower wages, weaker regulations, and reduced taxation. Of course, corporations love this kind of competition. Globalization has become a race to the bottom, where corporations are the only winners and the rest of society, in both the developed and developing worlds, is the loser.

But corporations do not exist in a vacuum. They have shareholders and executives, who, try as they might, cannot insulate themselves from what is going on. If our environment is polluted, if climate change accelerates, they too will suffer—though perhaps not as much as the rest of society, since the rich are usually more capable of finding ways to insulate themselves from problems. And if our democracies and societies are undermined by populist extremists—as seems to be happening now—even they, their families, their children and grandchildren will be touched.

Chapter 2

The Multiple
Dimensions of
Globalization

TRADE GLOBALIZATION WAS problematic, but other forms of globalization—affecting the flows of capital, people, and knowledge across borders—were equally questionable. In each of these areas, the argument for globalization was simple: for instance, free capital markets would ensure that capital would go to where it was most productive. But often, freeing up capital markets doesn't lead to higher output and faster growth. To the contrary, it can, if not well managed, lead to greater instability and more inequality.

And there has been much hypocrisy in the position of the United States and in that of other advanced countries: even though the American government was telling other countries about the benefits of the globalization of finance—allowing big U.S. banks to open up in their countries, even if the consequence was squeezing out local banks—it was not until 1994 that the United States allowed American banks to open up branches freely anywhere they wanted within the country.[1]

In each of these arenas, the criticisms of globalization have paralleled those of trade globalization—including that the advanced countries benefited at the expense of the developed countries and emerging markets. *GAID* discussed these issues largely from the perspective of the developing countries. This part of *Globalization and Its Discontents Revisited*, however, is about the *new discontents*—those in the advanced countries, such as the United States. But here too the arguments are parallel: the advocates of globalization had overestimated the benefits, underestimated the costs, and paid little attention to how globalization affected people—with the corporations getting a disproportionate share of the benefits and ordinary citizens bearing a disproportionate share of the costs—so much so that many, in some cases a majority, were worse off.

In the following sections I describe how unbalanced and mismanaged globalization in these other arenas, such as in investment and in ideas, has contributed to the new discontent with globalization.

INVESTMENT

Some of the same principles that govern trade relate to investment.

Foreign Direct Investment

The investment of, say, an American firm in China is referred to as foreign direct investment. Different firms have different competencies. If an American firm has a comparative advantage in making, say, earthmoving equipment, it should be able to do that not just in the United States, but elsewhere. Similarly, if a foreign firm has a comparative advantage in making certain kinds of electronic equipment, it should be able to do so in other countries.

Increasingly, the knowledge that is the basis of these competencies is created by and held within a firm; it moves freely within the firm—wherever the firm operates.[2] Thus, allowing firms to invest across borders is part of allowing knowledge to move across borders.

Undermining the Rule of Law
Trump has forcefully illustrated the dangers of poorly thought through government interventions affecting cross-border investment. Should American firms be compelled to invest in the United States? There is, of course, the manner in which he attempts to do so—at the threat of an unfavorable tweet or the loss of government contracts. This is deeply disturbing, for it represents an abrogation of the rule of law, which, as

I've just noted, is part of the foundation of our democracy and is critical to economic growth and well-being.

When a government believes that what individuals or firms are doing is imposing harms on others—when it wants firms or individuals to do something different—it creates incentives, for instance through the tax system, to do what is wanted and not to do what is unwanted; regulations are passed that proscribe antisocial behavior. But to pick on individual firms is the way of despots and demagogues.

Spillovers

An argument can be made that the country benefits from those who invest in the country. In a well-functioning market economy, it is the pursuit of profits that is supposed to incentivize firms to do this, and the private and social returns to investing are supposed to coincide. That this is so is the basic insight of Adam Smith and his "invisible hand theorem," the idea that firms, in the pursuit of their own self-interest, are led to do what is in the interests of society as if by an invisible hand.

Over the past third of a century, though, we have learned that Smith was often wrong, though many conservatives seem to still be back in the eighteenth century when Smith wrote.[3] When firms pollute, for instance, private profits exceed social returns. When there is a high level of unemployment—evidence by itself that markets are not working in the way they should—social returns to job-creating investments exceed private returns. At such times, government should further incentivize investment, through for instance an investment tax credit—an effective reduction in tax liabilities for those firms who engage in job creation. (This is markedly different from an across-the-board tax cut.)[4] When unemployment is especially high in a particular region, it may be desirable to provide such incentives targeted to the afflicted locations.

In general, though, it doesn't make a difference whether the investor is American or foreign—so long as they pay the taxes they should on the profits generated in America. Indeed, to try to force American companies to invest in the United States provides them with an incentive to locate their headquarters abroad; it gives foreign firms, not constrained by the threat of a tweet, an advantage over American firms.

Reciprocity

Trump's "new protectionist" view of investment, like that of trade, doesn't ever ask what would happen if others behaved in a way similar to how we do, that is, if they too discouraged their firms from investing abroad. America has a lot of inward investment—some $373 billion in new foreign direct investments in 2016.[5] Foreign firms produce in the United States for a variety of reasons; for instance, by producing close to their customers, they reduce transportation costs. If these foreign governments discouraged their firms from investing in America, job creation would slow. In short, just as New Protectionist trade policies lower standards of living, but will not deliver on their promised job creation, so too for New Protectionist investment policies.

Making American Goods Less Competitive

Of course, what Trump is really concerned about is outsourcing, when American firms choose to produce abroad because it's cheaper to do so. But that means that if American firms were not allowed to outsource, their prices would have to increase; they would be put at a competitive disadvantage. To offset this within the United States, Trump could raise tariffs—violating WTO rules, and subjecting America to costly penalties. But only by providing subsidies could he offset the disadvantages the firms would have in export markets—still another violation of international trade rules. In short, were Trump and other New Protectionists to think through the full consequences of what they are demanding, they would realize that the net result would be exactly the opposite of what they want.[6]

Short-Term Capital

There is a big difference between the real investment that I've just described, and the short-term financial flows that can go in and out of a country in a nanosecond. The free mobility of short-term capital, so loved by American banks, was indeed a source of profits for them; but it was a source of problems for the rest of the world. When money flowed into a country, the country's exchange rate appreciated, its export businesses found it impossible to compete, and many businesses struggled to compete against cheaper imports. Furthermore, firms couldn't build factories on the basis of money that was here today but gone tomorrow. And inevitably, that tomorrow came, and as the money flowed out, exchange rates plummeted, countries were thrown into crisis, and economic havoc ensued. Jobs were destroyed as money flowed in; jobs were destroyed as money flowed out. Rather than the win-win situation that the advocates of financial globalization claimed, it was a situation in which the recipients of the short-term flows were almost guaranteed to be worse off.

The East Asia crisis of 1997–98 (see chapter 8), caused by a sudden change in sentiment, a loss of confidence in East Asia, illustrated the dangers. Money had flowed into these countries when it was allowed to do so, in the years before the crisis. But the irrational exuberance turned to fear beginning in May 1997, and capital flowed out. And Korea, Malaysia, Thailand, and Indonesia went into deep crises.

But even advanced countries like the United States and those in Europe are not immune from suffering the vagaries of capital flows. The exchange rate between the dollar and the euro has fluctuated between 1.60 and 1.04 between 2008 and 2016. These fluctuations are not due to sudden changes in differences in inflation or productivity rates; they are due to fickle changes in sentiment in financial markets that lead to changes in financial flows, and those financial flows change the demand for dollars relative to euros—and thus the exchange rate. The pro-globalization mantra is that the market should set the exchange rate. But put yourself in the position of a small firm in Indiana making optical equipment that it exports to Europe. Assume it sets its price in dollars. The price in Europe could go up some 50 percent as a result of this fluctuation in the exchange rate. It would be hard for that small firm to retain its customers, and there is no way it could increase its productivity enough to offset the effect of the exchange rate change.

The speculators and financiers who move massive amounts of money across borders aren't thinking about this firm and the effects of their actions (via the exchange rate) on it and its workers. They're only thinking about the short-term profits they make from these speculative moves. These effects are another example of "externalities"—just as, when chasing profits, firms might pollute the air or water and bankers pollute global capital markets with their toxic mortgages, firms that engage in these speculative cross-border activities impose large costs on others, which they don't take into account.[7] And the presence of these large externalities is one of the major costs of unfettered globalization, and provides a rationale for the kinds of intervention I will describe.

Short-Term Capital Encourages Short-Termism and Shortchanges Long-Term Needs

There is another fundamental concern with short-term capital: it encourages short-term thinking, a malady sometimes referred to as short-termism. The managers of most firms, given their short-term tenure (usually around five years), are naturally focused on the performance of the firm over the term in which they hold office. This too gives rise to short-term thinking. "Incentive" compensation schemes have made matters worse. Managers are increasingly rewarded based on how the firm's stock performs *now*, and they have learned how shortsighted investors are. An increase in dividends and stock buybacks drives up prices—even if those payments come at the expense of investments in people, technology, and machinery that would have increased long-run profits. And so they ruthlessly pursue the short-run—part of the explanation for the slowing down of economic growth since around 1980.[8]

At the global level, this short-termism has some major consequences: in the developing world, there is an enormous need for long-term investments. Around the world, there is a large supply of long-term savings by individuals and institutions (such as sovereign wealth funds and pension funds) focusing not on tomorrow, but on the world decades into the future. Yet sitting between the two, supposedly "intermediating," that is, matching suppliers of funds with demanders, are short-term financial markets. No wonder the global economy is not functioning as well as it should.[9]

Rewriting the Rules of the Market Economy through Investment Agreements

Accompanying the increase in cross-border investment and capital flows has been a growth in investment agreements, agreements between countries about how investors from abroad are to be treated. Investment agreements were "sold" based on the idea that they were just protecting against the nationalization of assets—and such protection was a win-win: the investor gained, but the increased investor confidence that ensued meant that the developing country also gained.[10] Such claims, like so many others, were at best deceptive—and more accurately, just lies, not even the kind of white lies that were used to push trade globalization.[11] Furthermore, these agreements weren't even necessary—if expropriation was really what they were about: the World Bank and most governments provide insurance to investors against the risk of expropriation.[12]

The defenders of investment agreements respond by suggesting another justification: the agreements prevent discrimination against foreign investors. But if that were the case, the agreements could simply say that foreign investors would get "national treatment," which means being treated neither better nor worse than domestic firms. Instead, most investment agreements go much further than that; they give foreign firms the right to sue the government if the government passes a regulation that has an adverse effect on the profits of the firm—no matter how justified the regulation. Foreign firms are treated more favorably than domestic firms!

Thus, in a famous case, Philip Morris, the cigarette manufacturer, sued Uruguay in 2010 because the country passed a regulation which required the company to disclose possible harmful effects of cigarettes on health.[13] The regulation had the effect that the government desired—smoking was reduced. But this meant Philip Morris's profits decreased, and it responded by suing—in private arbitration where it appointed one of the three judges (and the judge it appointed had a crucial role in the appointment of a second judge). The arbitration is biased toward corporations. And it is *very* expensive. In the Uruguay case, the judges themselves got paid hundreds of thousands of dollars, and the costs to Uruguay were $7 million.[14] Uruguay eventually won the case and those costs were eventually paid by Philip Morris, as part of the judgment. But the South American country might not have been able to prevail without outside financial help during the arbitration: New York City mayor Michael Bloomberg and other wealthy Americans helped the country defend itself.

Canada has lost multiple such investor-state suits and settled others under NAFTA, mostly over the environment. Other countries have been sued under a variety of investment agreements with similar provisions over matters ranging from the minimum wage to restricting toxic waste dumps to affirmative action statutes attempting to attain racial and social justice.

The intent of these investment agreements is clearly not to prevent discrimination against foreign corporations. They are really an attempt by corporations to write the rules of the economic game in their favor through trade agreements negotiated behind closed doors, with corporate interests at the table, in ways that would not pass muster in an ordinary legislative process. In particular, their intent is to discourage governments from taking actions like passing regulations that would hurt corporate profits, period.[15] There is no weighing of costs and benefits—the costs to society, for instance, of asbestos or smoking. It is a totally one-sided calculus. These provisions have profound consequences. In the absence of these provisions, if a company, like the manufacturer of asbestos or cigarettes, sells a product that imposes damages on others, it can be sued. There is, for instance, in the area of the environment the principle of "polluters pay"—polluters have to pay for the damage they inflict on the environment. These investment agreements reverse this: with these provisions, if government passes a new regulation because there has been a discovery that a product causes harm to health or the environment, the firm sues the government to recover its lost profits. Such agreements embrace a principle that profits are as important as lives, and even if the regulation saves lives, the firm must be compensated for its lost profits.[16] (Well, one might ask, why do countries agree to these deals? The agreements are typically negotiated in secret, so ordinary citizens don't have a chance to express their views as the agreements get developed—and then they're confronted with a take-it-or-leave-it proposition. The United States threatens loss of assistance or other retaliatory measures if the agreement is not signed. And ever-hopeful citizens center their attention on promises of jobs and investment—typically never even noting detailed provisions such as those under discussion here.)

And the investment agreements may have played a role in compounding the problems of workers. One of the big advantages of locating firms in the United States and Europe had been their "rule of law"—the protection they give to property rights—but these new trade agreements, in their investment provisions, effectively encourage corporations to invest abroad, because they have more rights there than they enjoy at home.

Thus, while the investment agreements seem like they just affect developing countries where the rule of law is weak, they affect those in the developed countries and feed into the New Discontents. They are an essential part of the framework encouraging outsourcing of jobs, and of the corporate global race to the bottom—low wages, low taxes, and low regulations—all in the objective of higher corporate profits. Sometimes the effects are obvious—as Canada has already learned. Sometimes, as in the United States, the effects are more subtle, and will be fully realized only gradually over time.

FISCAL PARADISES AND TAX COMPETITION: STEALING YOUR TAX DOLLARS

There are other aspects of globalization in which the costs are even more apparent—and the benefits less so. Globalization has made it possible for corporations to avoid the taxes that they should pay—and corporations have induced competition among jurisdictions around the world to lower taxes, in a destructive race to the bottom. Corporations enjoy the benefit of a trained labor force, good infrastructure, and a rule of law that a country provides—but they want a free ride. They assume an air of corporate responsibility, even as they use all the ingenuity at their disposal to avoid paying taxes—but the first responsibility of any corporation should be to pay its fair share of taxes.

"Fiscal paradises"—places where individuals and corporations can avoid or evade taxes—have cropped up around the world, from Macau and Singapore to Panama, the Cayman Islands, Luxembourg, Ireland, and the Channel Islands. We often think of these as "offshore financial centers," but some jurisdictions in the United States (Nevada, Delaware) and the City of London, the hub of the UK's financial market, have also flourished on the basis of these nefarious activities. We might not have known about the full range of activities of these fiscal paradises—given their success in maintaining secrecy—had it not been for some huge leaks and some impressive investigative reporting. This included the LuxLeaks, which showed the role of Ireland and Luxembourg in tax evasion and avoidance in Europe, and the Panama papers, which showed the global pervasiveness of not only tax evasion and avoidance, but also other antisocial activities, the profits from which were laundered in these fiscal paradises.[17] The prime minister of Iceland and the president of Russia were among those implicated by the Panama Papers. (Iceland's prime minister was forced to resign.)

A congressional hearing in 2013 alerted European officials to one of the most egregious cases of using globalization for tax avoidance: Apple, perhaps the world's most profitable company, had made secret deals with Ireland to get its tax rate down to 0.005 percent.[18]

It was obvious that globalization expanded opportunities for tax avoidance and even made tax evasion easier.[19] Companies could more easily locate production in a low-taxed jurisdiction and sell their goods anywhere in the world. A company could locate its intellectual property in a low-taxed jurisdiction, and claim that most of its profits were attributable to its intellectual property; then, not even the country where the goods were being produced would get much tax revenue. With so much freedom to locate production and to decide where the locus of profits would be, tax competition and the race to the bottom became even worse.

None of this was inevitable. It would have been possible to negotiate as part of trade and investment agreements tax provisions ensuring that corporations paid their fair share of taxes overall, and that there was a fair allocation of taxes among the signatories. But just about the only tax agreements that have been made are to avoid double taxation (which occurs when two jurisdictions attempt to tax the same income)—which in practice often result in no taxation. That this is so says something about globalization: as I have repeatedly noted, it has been a corporate-driven agenda; and corporations were interested in keeping opportunities for tax avoidance open. And they liked the race to the bottom, which lowered their overall tax rates.

We have seen how globalization increased the need for government assistance: large numbers of workers needed help, some form of social protection or assistance in retraining. But just when governments needed more money to cope with the effects of globalization, globalization made raising revenues more difficult. Taxation under globalization compounded insult with injury—American firms didn't have to pay taxes on profits earned abroad until they were "repatriated" (brought back home).[20] Tax laws enabled them to manipulate the numbers, so that they could claim that most of their profits originated abroad—in the case of Apple, the satellite offices in Ireland were supposedly responsible for much of that firm's immense profits. Then they figured out how to borrow to pay dividends, and the escape was complete: now there was in fact no reason to ever repatriate profits.

As part of this race to the bottom, firms threatened to leave the country unless taxes were lower: there was no patriotism among these multinationals.[21]

The promise of globalization had been corrupted. In the absence of cooperation among countries in taxation, the burden of taxation has to be shifted to those that are immobile, who can't take advantage of globalization to move to where they pay little or no taxes—and unskilled workers are the least mobile. They thus suffered thrice—from lower wages, from the shift of the relative burden of taxation onto them,[22] and from the cutback in government services that results when corporations escape paying their fair share of taxation. It is no wonder that many workers are less than enthusiastic about globalization.

INTELLECTUAL PROPERTY RIGHTS: WHO OWNS YOUR GENES?

So far, I have discussed two of the critical aspects of globalization—the movement of goods and services and of capital across borders. But there are two more—the movement of ideas and people. While the globalizers were pushing for freer movement of goods and capital, there was much less enthusiasm for the free movement of ideas and people.

Indeed, a major global effort of the United States and other advanced countries has been to restrict the free movement of ideas—or at least to make sure that those who make use of ideas generated in the advanced countries pay the advanced countries. While in the years after World War II the focus was on how to increase the flow of capital from developed to developing countries, this new focus has had exactly the opposite effect. Royalties for the use of intellectual property rights received by high-income countries from low- and middle-income countries were very high. The United States alone obtained over $20 billion in 2012,[23] which is about the same amount that America gave in economic assistance to poor countries through its development agency, USAID (approximately $18.2 billion in fiscal year 2012).[24]

Not surprisingly, as we move toward a knowledge economy, intellectual property rights have become more important since *GAID* was first published in 2002. The debate is not whether there should be intellectual property rights, but about the *design* of those rights. Intellectual property rights are a *social construction,* and we should try to construct them to encourage innovation by protecting the fruits of such innovation. But we also want to ensure that those who might engage in follow-on innovation are not stymied. We want the rules of the game to be designed so that small and medium-sized firms can easily get patents—not just large corporations. We want knowledge to be constructively used and not wielded in ways that increase monopoly power, as another instrument for rent-seeking in grabbing a larger share of the economic pie.[25]

The economic rules of the game—whether regulation or, as here, intellectual property rights—are increasingly being determined not so much within the country itself but globally, and especially through what are called trade agreements but are in fact agreements that go well beyond trade. One might ask: why are intellectual property rights (IPR) being determined in *trade* agreements? And especially so since there is already an international body concerned with intellectual property, the World Intellectual Property Organization (WIPO), established in 1967 and headquartered in Geneva. Besides, what do trade ministers know about research and innovation? The answer is simple: they know very little. In designing the provisions governing IPR under the WTO, the USTR did consult the Office of Science and Technology Policy in the White House—but paid little attention to what it said. The USTR was not concerned with maximizing innovation, with what would be good for the progress of science and technology. The USTR had one objective: to maximize the profits of the large American firms which had so much influence over it. The reason that IPR are in trade agreements is that these agreements give the governments of the advanced countries a sledgehammer to enforce their rights: the ability to impose trade sanctions.

Thus, globalization pushed a particular set of views on IPR—that what is good for large corporations is good for innovation and society, that the stronger the IPR the better, and that there was a one-size-fits-all set of rules—the rules that worked for the United States were those that were appropriate for a developing country trying to catch up. All three of these propositions have been shown to be wrong, in ways which are particularly harmful to developing countries.[26] But increasingly, it has become clear that ordinary citizens in the United States and other advanced countries also suffer as a result of this corporate-driven agenda, sometimes in ways that are dramatic, sometimes less so.

Consider, for instance, the idea that the stronger the IPR the better. Patents can be a matter of life and death. While a global effort was underway to decode the human genome, a Utah firm named Myriad Genetics rushed to get a patent on two specific genes (called the BRCA genes), and then developed a test to see if a woman has these genes. If a woman has these genes, she has a very high probability of getting breast cancer—hence the interest in having an affordable and accurate test. Meanwhile, Yale University developed a far better test, and through the generosity of those concerned with public health, it was made available at low or no cost. Myriad blocked it in an effort to maintain its monopoly; it knew the value of the data that it was gathering. So what if many women might die as a result? It was a matter of profits *above all*. A coalition of forces including the American Civil Liberties Union sued[27] and eventually prevailed in the Supreme Court (reaching a decision similar to the views on intellectual property in some other countries): naturally existing genes cannot be patented.

More broadly, a key issue in recent trade agreements has been access to generic medicines and other provisions that have the effect of raising drug prices. Americans without adequate insurance may find they simply can't afford drugs they need for their very survival. In countries where the public picks up the tab, with more money going to the drug companies, there is less left around for everything else.

Not surprisingly, the corporate-driven IPR agenda benefits large corporations at the expense of small firms—which was why the former president of BlackBerry, which began as a small Canadian firm, turned against the IPR provisions of TPP, the aborted trade agreement that Obama pushed so hard for.

In the long run, ordinary citizens will be the loser from any IPR system that makes follow-on research more difficult, which fosters the strengthening of firms with market power, like Microsoft, which leads to higher prices and less competition. Higher prices lower their *real* income just as much as the lower wages that result from the weakening of their bargaining power in labor markets.

IMMIGRATION

Both in Europe and America, immigration—the movement of people across borders—has proven to be the most controversial aspect of globalization, more controversial even than trade. Much of this is due to the gap between facts and perception, between reality and Trump's "alternative facts." In America, Trump has painted a picture of a tsunami of Mexicans crossing the border. The reality is that in recent years, the net flow from Mexico into the United States has turned negative.[28] Clearly, Trump and like-minded people in other countries are exploiting latent racism and fears—a long-established tradition of dividing people by turning "us" against "them."

Here, I discuss only the economic aspects of the issue, which are themselves complicated and somewhat controversial. Like other aspects of globalization, immigration has effects on the national economy as well as on income distribution. And as with other aspects of globalization, it is not immediately clear what the right economic model might be to best analyze immigration's effects. The standard "perfect markets" model—which has proven so influential in economics—may again provide uncertain guidance.

In a world in which knowledge and goods moved freely across borders—in which everyone had the same technology, and countries differed only with respect to resources like skilled and unskilled labor and capital—there would be only limited need for immigration.[29] Wages of unskilled workers would, as I noted, be equalized.[30]

In the real world, trade moves wages in the direction predicted, but it doesn't ever equalize wages. This is partly because knowledge doesn't move freely, but it's also partly because institutions matter—having, for instance, good legal institutions enables businesses to execute contracts that can actually be enforced. Even with a clear vision for what makes good institutions, it's not easy to create them. As a result, those living in some countries—whatever their skill level—may enjoy a higher income than someone with the same skill in other countries. There is an income premium associated with citizenship (or more accurately, residency—but citizenship gives rights of residency). Naturally, individuals would want to live in a location with a higher wage, and this gives rise to immigration pressure.[31]

But typically, there are diminishing returns. That is, if more unskilled workers move into a country in which there is an unskilled worker premium, unskilled wages fall and immigration pressure decreases. Sometimes, migration occurs so vigorously and markets adjust sufficiently slowly that there is an increase in unemployment. In either case, the original unskilled residents of the country feel that that they are bearing a cost to migration: lower wages or a harder time getting a job.

Of course, in many cases, the migrants are accepting jobs that others would not have accepted. In other cases, the migrants come with skills that those who are unemployed within the country don't have. The skilled programmer from India is not taking away a job from an auto worker who is unemployed. Indeed, the extra taxes paid by the skilled worker immigrant may help pay for the public services drawn upon by the displaced auto worker. But whether rational or not, resentments arise. And when there are linguistic and cultural differences, these differences reinforce economic arguments against migration.

When we consider the costs of, say, immigration by any category of workers, however, we also need to consider the benefits to *other* groups in society. Take the case of immigration of unskilled workers. The lower wages of unskilled workers lower the costs of nontraded goods that require these unskilled workers. Taxes on immigrants and the profits they generate for those for whom they work help defray the costs of public goods.[32] In short, even if unskilled workers are worse off as a result of the immigration of competitive unskilled workers, other groups may be better off. So different groups in society may have different views of whether such immigration is desirable. If we only consider the aggregate view of the country's existing inhabitants, we could simply ask, "Are they better off?" There is a broad consensus that the

United States—a country based on immigration—is unambiguously better off. Indeed, it could not function without the many hardworking immigrants who have come to the country to seek a better future. The Trumpian vision of American immigrants is totally wrong. But in recognizing that the country as a whole is better off, we must simultaneously recognize that there are groups or locales that may suffer from immigration, and just as in trade, some of the benefits that the country as a whole receives from immigration should be channeled to help those who are adversely affected.

The United States (and many other countries) face an additional immigration problem: what to do with the undocumented workers, including those who entered as children—who know no other home—but whose parents entered illegally. These young people, inhabiting a kind of limbo, face enormous barriers to pursuing the American dream. It is easy for unscrupulous employers to exploit undocumented workers, paying them below-minimum wages or providing unsafe and unsanitary working conditions, knowing that these individuals cannot appeal to the legal system for protection. And the fact that they can be so easily exploited drives down wages and worsens working conditions for other workers. There has to be a quick path to full citizenship for these individuals.[33]

THE FAILURE TO MAKE GLOBALIZATION WORK

In this and the preceding chapter, I've tried to explain why globalization, in each of its aspects, has led to so many new discontents, including in advanced countries like the United States and those in Europe. We've explained why there may well be many losers in globalization—perhaps a majority of the population.

The Political Economy of Globalization

In the standard narrative of globalization, the recognition that there may be so many losers in globalization is something that came only recently. And these "harms" were merely the unintended collateral damage to a globalization that was supposed to make everyone better off. But here I want to suggest that this narrative may be fiction.

Focusing on trade, that narrative has exporters valiantly fighting protectionists in the import-competing sector to ensure that the country's true comparative advantage is realized, in global deals that benefit citizens in all countries. It is the battle of the enlightened reformers against vested interests, in which trade ministries (in the case of the United States, the USTR) are firmly on the side of the reformers. But for more than a quarter century, I've watched these battles up close, and they don't look anything like this battle portrayed as one between good and evil. Indeed, it's never even clear that the USTR knows what the *undistorted* comparative advantage of the United States might be. America is a big exporter of agricultural products, like cotton; but without massive subsidies, the country probably wouldn't export cotton at all. Some agricultural products benefit from hidden subsidies, including for water—rice would probably not even be grown in the Sacramento Valley of northern California, for example, without massive engineering interventions. Another big export is aircraft, a beneficiary (as Europe rightly points out) of help from the U.S. Defense Department.[34] The U.S. auto industry was helped by a large bailout. America's high-tech/Internet sector got its start with government research programs, even to the point that the first browser was largely financed by the U.S. government.[35]

One of the big fights in recent trade negotiations has been over access to generic medicines. One of the reasons that the United States has done so well in pharmaceuticals is the large government support provided to research in this industry. The role of U.S. trade negotiators in this area may be emblematic. It is not about creating jobs in America. Much of the drug production of U.S. companies occurs outside the United States, and there is nothing in the trade agreements that encourages U.S. production. It is not about increasing U.S. tax revenues. The drug companies are notorious for their prowess in tax avoidance. The agreements could have been used to ensure that the drug companies pay taxes on the intellectual property for which the USTR was fighting so hard. But on this they were silent. The USTR was simply enriching the coffers of the drug companies, with no benefit to America's workers, and at considerable cost to its consumers and taxpayers (because the U.S. government picks up about 10 percent of the tab for drugs,[36] and the USTR's trade agreements drive up the prices).[37] The explanation for these provisions is simple—it is testimony to the political clout of the industry, with key congressmen threatening to vote against any trade agreement that provides less than what the pharmaceutical industry demands.[38]

There is, I think, an alternative narrative that places what I characterized earlier as "collateral damage" at the core of the trade liberalization agenda. Adam Smith in his 1776 *Wealth of Nations* provides some insights concerning this alternative interpretation: "People of the same trade seldom meet together, even for merriment and diversion, but the conversation ends in a conspiracy against the public, or in some contrivance to raise prices." Elsewhere in that book, he wrote:

> Masters are always and everywhere in a sort of tacit, but constant and uniform, combination, not to raise the wages of labour above their actual rate. [. . .] Masters, too, sometimes enter into particular combinations to sink the wages of labour even below this rate. These are always conducted with the utmost silence and secrecy.

The quotes remind us that when our business leaders get together urging a particular policy (as they did in the case of globalization) it would be foolish to think that they had not thought of the consequences—including the impacts on the cost of labor. Globalization provided a powerful indirect means to accomplish this long-sought end. The lowering of wages was thus not an "accidental" and unfortunate collateral consequence—it was the *objective*. Besides the widely touted benefits of opening up new markets, employers benefited doubly, from outsourcing to cheap foreign labor, and from the lowering of wages at home. Thus, the advocates of globalization included not so much exporters seeking to be able to exploit their comparative advantage as retailers, like Walmart, seeking to source what they sold at as low a price as possible, and manufacturers looking to outsource as much of their production to low-cost producers abroad as possible. In short, trade agreements are *not* about expanding the production of goods in the United States in which the United States has a "natural" comparative advantage.

Conviction that this is right is bolstered by the efforts business leaders were making at the same time to weaken workers' bargaining power through changes in the rules governing unions, and the resistance of the Republican Party, closely allied with the business community, to efforts to provide assistance to workers displaced by trade, repeatedly voting down provisions to provide such support or, when such support is given, curtailing its size and scope. Knowing that the government will help them should they lose their job would increase workers' resolve in bargaining.[39]

So too the other contentious aspect of recent trade agreements concerns the investment agreements discussed earlier, sometimes embedded within a trade agreement (for example, chapter 11 of NAFTA), sometimes an explicit agreement between two countries. I noted that though the agreements are sold on the notion that they just protect property rights—ensuring that one country doesn't expropriate the assets of a foreign corporation—they really do far more. They have had, for instance, a chilling effect on regulations. Such agreements have been high on the agenda of the leaders of the multinational corporations— and, with the risk of expropriation virtually disappearing, it is precisely these broader benefits that they sought. Early on in the Obama administration there was an effort to redesign these agreements in ways that would satisfy the multinational corporations and representatives of civil society concerned about health, the environment, or other important arenas affecting society. As I noted, it would be easy to rewrite these provisions in ways that address the *alleged* business concerns, such as discrimination against foreign firms, without inhibiting necessary regulations, and that would have a fairer system of adjudicating disputes than the current arbitration system, in which the corporations play a central role in appointing judges. But the business leaders would have none of this, making it clear that their real intent indeed was discouraging environmental, health, safety, and economic regulations.

In short, the kind of globalization that we got—hurting workers and helping multinational corporations—was the kind of globalization the corporations wanted. It was not an accident. This shouldn't come as a surprise, once one understands who was at the table as the rules of the game were being made, and who was not.

The Failure of the Left

The right's opposition to aiding those hurt by globalization was consistent with the influence of these large corporations on the parties of the right and with an agenda of keeping government small. Helping those hurt by globalization would have entailed raising taxes, something to which they are deeply allergic.

The puzzle was why the parties of the center-left, which simultaneously believed in markets and in social equity, didn't take a more active stance against this unbalanced globalization. Too many on both sides of the Atlantic succumbed to market ideology—influenced no doubt by the easy flow of funds from those whom these ideologies served so well. This led them to almost blindly follow the globalization agenda of the right. It seemed like there was a national consensus, at least among the elites—but it was a consensus from which a large number of those that were being left out were excluded. The progressives asked for trade assistance. They worried about what was happening to those in the middle. With muted voices, they even sometimes talked about what was happening at the bottom—but they didn't talk too loudly, lest the middle think they were too focused on the poor.

With no one seemingly defending the interests of the working class, a vacuum was created. But nature abhors a vacuum. And so demagogues and would-be despots, the New Protectionists—Trump in the United States, Marine Le Pen in France—rushed in to fill the vacuum. If the establishment parties support globalization without compensation, leaving large segments of the population worse off, we should expect those hurt by globalization to look for alternatives to defend their interests.[40] In the end, as I have already explained, it doesn't really matter if the source of the problem is technology, or globalization, or something else: if there are large numbers of people who are not doing well and are being left behind—as we saw was the case in the advanced countries— those that have lost their jobs or have had their wages decline will support someone who shows empathy with their plight and promises to do something about it. And it's especially attractive if the diagnosis entails shifting the blame to outsiders, to foreigners who are mistreating "us" and taking advantage of "us." Indeed, such distinctions between "us" and "them" are a traditional part of the toolkit of demagogues.

Interestingly, some political analysts suggest that it's not even important that the policies advocated by the anti-globalization parties work. Voters—especially in countries where the government has been berated for years—don't really expect the government to be able to solve society's problems. They want to be convinced that the government has their interests in heart, and, when the time comes for critical decisions, it will make the decisions that move things in the right way. The establishment parties, so closely associated with the elites and with much of their financial support coming from banks and other corporate interests, have been losing their credibility. And the disparity between the promises of globalization and the reality has been part of this loss of credibility.

If globalization is to be preserved, its advocates must be able to explain not only why the protectionism that Trump, Le Pen, and others on that side of the debate will only make them worse off, but how globalization can be reformed in ways in which all will benefit. But to do that, we have to understand why globalization, as it has been managed, has failed.

Markets on their own won't ensure that globalization will increase the size of the national pie—it won't do so, for instance, if job destruction outpaces job creation, because financial markets are dysfunctional and don't provide the finance required for those who want to take advantage of the opportunities afforded by globalization. And even when it increases the size of the national pie, markets on their own won't ensure that there aren't large numbers who are worse off. And if globalization is not managed well—and it has not been well managed—the losses of the losers will be all the greater.

Under these circumstances, to avoid a backlash against globalization, government must come forward with macroeconomic policies that push the economy toward full employment, adjustment policies to help workers and firms adapt to the new circumstances, and social protection policies to protect them against losses to the standards of living that they may face in the process of adjustment. I discuss these policies in chapter 4, but first, I take a closer look at the alternative: what I call "the New Protectionism," being advocated around the world by Trump, Le Pen, and politicians in other countries taking advantage of the "New Discontents."

Chapter 3

The New Protectionism

THE DISPARITY BETWEEN what was promised from globalization and what was delivered has angered many and led
to a growing distrust of the elites—in politics, in the media,
and in academia. Some of this criticism is misguided, some deserved.
Economic theory did explain that globalization would hurt unskilled
workers in the advanced countries. The dishonesty arose not from
the academics, but from the politicians and those in the corporate and
financial world who benefited from globalization but didn't want to
face up to its darker sides and didn't want to do anything about its
adverse effects.

Most worrying is the collateral damage: because the statements of
some of the elite—the advocates of globalization, for instance—turned
out to be so wrong, some in the Trump camp are claiming that anyone
can just make up his own theory, make his own assertions about what is
true. Everyone even gets to pick his "alternative facts."

We may not know anything for certain, but we know something.
We may not *precisely* know the number of people who turned up for
Trump's inauguration, but we can be almost certain that the number he
alleged was wrong.[1] All scientific findings are tentative, held only with
a certain degree of confidence, open for refutation—science is an open
quest for truth. But this complicated message does not open the door to

a world where all beliefs are of equal weight. Some can be refuted by the evidence with almost a 100 percent degree of confidence.

The irony, of course, is that what has made possible the enormous increases in standards of living over the past two and a half centuries is the advances in science and technology—and none of this would be possible without the Enlightenment and the scientific method, which Trump and his followers have been attacking so fiercely and effectively.

We take our current standards of living so much for granted that we forget that for centuries standards of living stagnated. It was not until the mid to late eighteenth century, less than 250 years ago, that they began to rise. What happened? There is a broad consensus among historians and economists about the answer: it was the scientific revolution of the seventeenth and eighteenth centuries, the origin of the modern rational frame of mind, bound up with the Enlightenment. The new frame of mind brought with it not only the idea of progress and that change was possible, but also the scientific method, of how we go about learning the "truth." Science has progressed enormously since then, and so too have the benefits, with standards of living today that would have been unimaginable then. Life expectancies have been greatly increased by advances in our knowledge of health.[2]

As demagogues like Trump question science and how we distinguish truth from fiction, they threaten the basis of our continued progress.

THE GLOBAL GROWTH OF THE NEW PROTECTIONISM

The high level of inequality, the low level of equality of opportunity, and the struggles facing those in the middle class, evident in the United States and so many other countries, have contributed to a sense that the economic and political system isn't serving the interests of large swaths of society; that the system is unfair; that democratically elected governments cannot be trusted to serve the interests of those who elect them; that the so-called wisdom and knowledge of the "elites" (including academics) cannot be trusted; and that the media, in particular, should be questioned.

The precise unfolding of events that gave rise to these doubts differs across countries, and though there are still many countries in which faith in democratic institutions and appropriately regulated markets remains strong, in a disturbingly large number of countries, Trump-like politicians have been faring well.[3]

The strengthening of this distrust in the aftermath of the 2008 financial crisis is not an accident. The crisis was caused by the excesses of the financial sector. But then the U.S. government—and what happened in other countries was not much different—appointed the very people who were responsible for the crisis to sort it out.[4] Not surprisingly, they put the bankers' interests ahead of the rest of society—ahead of those losing their jobs and homes. They claimed, falsely, that the only way to save ordinary citizens was to save the bankers. The "recovery" was focused on the bankers, not on ordinary citizens: in the first three years of the so-called recovery, 91 percent of the gains went to the top 1 percent;[5] and this happened in a Democratic administration supposedly representing the interests of working individuals.

The economic and political system seemed rigged. And among the focal points of the attacks against the establishment is the establishment's belief in globalization. The distrust for globalization had long been simmering beneath the surface. In the 1992 presidential campaign, a third-party candidate, Ross Perot, criticized NAFTA by saying it would take jobs from the United States: there would be a "giant sucking sound." Even if globalization is only a part of the distress in which so many people find themselves, electoral politics means that they may be able to do something about this source of their travails—by electing politicians committing to changing the rules of globalization.

Protectionist and nativist demagogues have arisen around the world and met with considerable success—including attaining the presidency of the United States. They now have the power to follow up their protectionist rhetoric with protectionist policy.

Listening to Reason

While the elites—including those economists who claimed too much for globalization—clearly don't have all the answers, they can explain with some degree of confidence why certain policies are likely to fail. Trump probably doesn't want to hear why the protectionist policies that he's put forward almost surely won't work. That's perhaps why Trump has decided not to have *any* economists in his cabinet and to rely instead on businessmen who purportedly know how things really work. But businessmen know how to do business and make deals, and in the case of people like Trump, how to take advantage of others. Their business experience doesn't give them a clue about how a complex system like the economy works.[6]

Before turning to what Trump would hear from almost any economist—were he to ask—about why the new protectionism is likely to fail, I should pause to note one of the important lessons that emerges from the overselling of globalization: economists as public servants have, of course, a responsibility to tell those that they advise of the consequences of alternative policies. But their responsibility goes further: they have to understand and explain the limits of their models and of our knowledge; to articulate what we know and what we don't know. Economists might, in the end, decide that the distributive effects are outweighed by or outweigh the aggregative effects, that is, the impact of total output. But it would have been wrong not to explain the potentially large distributive effects, the potential effects on employment in certain locales, the consequences of imperfect risk markets and imperfections in competition, the implications for dynamic comparative advantage. And when economists oversell—as globalization has been oversold—they put at risk both their own reputation and the well-being of those whom they, as public servants, are supposed to serve.

And when politicians oversell—even if they believe that what they're saying is just a white lie to ensure that what they know is good policy is undertaken—they put at risk their credibility and that of the democratic political process.

America will pay a price for the deglobalization which Trump and his protectionism are instigating. In pursuing his America First policies— in not pursuing a set of policies entailing an *enlightened American self-interest*—Trump is actually putting America second, behind the fulfillment of his narcissistic needs. In the following pages, I explain why this New Protectionism will fail—it will even worsen the plight of the Trump supporters who have been left behind by globalization.

WHY THE NEW PROTECTIONISM WILL FAIL

Before Trump arrived on the scene, capturing and enflaming anti-globalization sentiment in the United States, the major worry about globalization was about its mindless, unmanaged advance, with corporate interests prevailing over the well-being of society. My concern, and that of most other serious critics of globalization, was to reform globalization to make it better serve all citizens. It was almost inconceivable that the pendulum would swing too far the other way, with anti-globalization forces so prevailing that there might be a threat of a mindless, unmanaged retreat from globalization.

Trump has, however, redefined the globalization debate, arguing for bilateral agreements and threatening that unless we get a "better deal," he'll slap high tariffs against Mexico (20 percent) and China (45 percent).[7] He even has considerable support from many billionaires and their companies, especially those that compete with imports. Everything the government does has distributive consequences, and there are many firms (and their owners) that would benefit from protectionism—even if others, including exporters, would lose. Of course, the businesses that would be helped seldom ask for protectionism on the grounds that it would increase their profits. They always claim to be selfless entrepreneurs, asking for government assistance to protect them against unfair competition on behalf of their workers—even as they do everything they can, in other forums, to oppose measures like unionization and regulations ensuring basic working conditions that would really make a difference for their workers.

Trump sees trade through the lens of a zero-sum game in which one country's gain comes at the expense of another's loss. Trade, however, is not a zero-sum game—it was never the case that the developing countries were the only winners, the only ones to benefit, as their increased exports of manufactured goods not only created jobs, but also helped transform their economies and societies through industrialization. Their growth thus fueled more demand for goods in developed countries, and their inexpensive products raised living standards. We should have expected the advanced countries to have gained too. After all, it was the United States along with its partners in Europe that designed the game.

They wouldn't have designed a game in which they would lose. The problem was that there were losers *within* the advanced countries, and the corporate winners had no interest in sharing the gains: they liked it that their workers had lost all bargaining power.

Turning the Clock Back Won't Work

The New Protectionism is an attempt to turn back the clock—one of the reasons that it's the wrong solution for dealing with the New Discontents, and impossible to do in any case.

The Glory Days of Manufacturing Are Over

No matter what Trump promises, American manufacturing jobs are not coming back. Global employment in manufacturing is on the decline—a hallmark of our achievement in increasing productivity at a faster pace than increases in demand. This means that if each country's share in that global employment were to be unchanged, U.S. manufacturing employment would be decreasing. In fact, however, the U.S. share is likely to decline. Thus, with a decreasing share of the decreasing global manufacturing employment, the number of U.S. manufacturing jobs will fall.

The emerging markets have become an increasingly effective competitor in making even complex manufactured goods. Even high-end niche manufacturing jobs look increasingly precarious. Countries like Korea not only learned, they learned how to learn: in some areas, they joined the ranks of the innovators.

While those abroad have become more competitive, some of the advanced countries, and especially the United States, have become, in some ways, less competitive. The increase in social diseases—alcoholism, obesity, opioid addiction, and suicide—has its counterpart in a reduction in productivity.

The manufacturing export-led growth model, arguing that the best way to grow and develop was to adopt policies promoting exports, especially in manufacturing, has had a good run—bringing enormous benefits to large numbers of those in the developing world that adopted it. That model was the basis of the success of the East Asian countries, whose growth was so rapid that it was widely described as a "miracle."[8] But with the shrinking of global manufacturing jobs, the export-led model may be reaching the end of its usefulness, and developing countries (such as those in Africa) that had not taken advantage of it earlier will, in part, have to look elsewhere for growth strategies.

There is no way to go back to these earlier eras, just as there is no way of putting the genie of technological advancements back in the bottle; and it's not clear we would want to, to give up our iPhones, computers, or inexpensive clothing. True, had we managed globalization better, had we done a better job of equitably sharing the fruits of globalization, we would be in a different place than we are today. We probably wouldn't be talking about the New Protectionism. But history moves on, and each generation's task is to play with the hand they've been dealt.

Even if some manufacturing production were to come back (as well it may), I noted in chapter 1 that that production will likely entail robots and other automated equipment, requiring different skill sets than those of the many workers who lost their jobs one or two decades ago. The returning firms may well return to different locations as well. The textile industry which decades ago moved from New England to the U.S. South, where labor was cheap, has been moving on from there to elsewhere—to China, for instance. As China's wages have risen, the industry has moved again to other countries where labor is still cheaper—Bangladesh, Sri Lanka, Vietnam, and elsewhere. But with unskilled labor of diminishing importance, wages of unskilled labor will become less of a focus. The quality of schools and the environment becomes paramount—areas in which the United States does not at present excel.[9]

America has become a widely diversified economy: manufacturing constitutes only 8 percent of employment, services some 80 percent.[10] All the rhetoric about manufacturing seems to have forgotten this. There are more people now employed by sports teams and clubs than in mining. The United States derives significant amounts of foreign revenues from service sectors like tourism, telecommunications, financial services, and education and health. The fixation on manufacturing and coal mining reflects a country with a mind-set stuck in a world gone by. By one estimate, the U.S. solar industry already supports about twice as many jobs as the coal industry.[11]

To see the absurdity of the obsession with manufacturing, reflect back on what a conversation about the challenges facing the U.S. economy might have been like a century ago. Those with their heads looking back would be worrying about the decline in agricultural employment. It used to be that 70 percent of the labor force was engaged in farming or providing services to farmers. An economy without farming playing a dominant role was unimaginable. But the decline in farm employment was good news: increased productivity meant that fewer workers were needed to produce the food we needed to survive. The advanced countries managed the consequences: new jobs were created in manufacturing. Now, there is a parallel process under way: the transition from manufacturing to the service sector. The government should be facilitating that transition, for instance with job retraining, not trying to engineer a fruitless return to the past.[12]

Global Power Has Become Dispersed

Trump and his supporters look back toward the past in another way: to the years after World War II when the United States was the only superpower. The bloody conflagration had destroyed Europe and left the United States in a position so dominant that it could effectively write, by itself, the international rules of the game. In the decades following the war, the United States could, with its European allies, still do so— in ways that enabled them to exploit the developing countries, which had so recently been their colonial subjects. Indeed, for some European countries, it proved an even better deal than colonialism: they got much of the economic returns without a pretense of assuming the burdens of imperial responsibility.

While the period after World War II was unusual, the last two hundred years have been a historical anomaly. Since the eighteenth century, an enormous disparity opened up between incomes per capita in China and India, on the one hand, and Europe and North America on the other. In 1820, China and India had between them some 45 percent of global GDP. Because of colonialism, unfair trade agreements, and a host of other factors, that share declined to under 10 percent. It was at this moment of weakness that the West began writing the rules of the game, regulating the rules-based international order. Not surprisingly, the rules were typically written from their perspective, to advance their interests.[13] With the rise of the emerging markets and the end of colonialism, however, that historical anomaly is now rapidly being corrected: China is currently the largest economy in the world, not only in purchasing power parity (the standard that economists use in comparing costs of living across countries, taking account of the different prices of goods in different countries), but also in goods traded[14] and gross savings—in the latter, by more than 50 percent.[15] One cannot now return to a world in which the rules of globalization are set by a few countries—or one country—for their own benefit, and especially for their corporations. We live in a multipolar world.

Those looking back at how the global economy has changed over the past third of a century too often take for granted that it was "right" then, and somehow, since then, things have gotten "unbalanced." The global economy has, in fact, been "unbalanced" for two hundred years: those in Asia and Africa have suffered through two centuries of colonialism, neocolonialism, and then economic colonialism.

At the end of the colonial period, western powers discovered that they could get many of the economic advantages of colonialism by keeping the developing countries under their thumb through debt. The ex-colonies then suffered from the Washington Consensus, the set of policies based on Western interests and free-market ideology that served corporate interests so well.[16] The West could continue to take resources out of Africa, and impose a set of policies that led to its deindustrialization.[17] Their indebtedness—and threats about what might happen if they defaulted—enabled the West to impose these onerous conditions on developing countries.

But there were a set of countries that took a different course—that didn't succumb to the dictates of the Washington Consensus or the neocolonial models.[18] The countries in East Asia took advantage of a particular moment in history, a particular opening. Firms from America and Europe had made a discovery: workers in these countries were even more disciplined (and lower-paid relative to their productivity) than Western workers. Even if they were not as fully efficient, the wage difference more than made up for the discrepancy. East Asia became the factory to the world. And that, simply put, implied a declining role for the Western workers. The East Asian export-led growth model brought increasing standards of living to hundreds of millions of people, many of whom previously seemed to be condemned to a life of poverty.[19]

And then other countries, in different ways, followed that model—

including India, and now, even Ethiopia (see the discussion in the afterword). All of these developing countries also benefited from globalization—it sparked their growth. They didn't benefit as much from globalization as they might have had the rules not been set by corporate and financial interests in the advanced countries—but they benefited nonetheless.

There were many unintended results of this globalization designed by the United States and other advanced countries. No one had intended that some 800 million would move out of poverty in China. Nor did the Western powers intend that their share of global GDP would shrink as it has—that the United States would no longer be the largest economy (in terms of purchasing power parity), the largest trading economy, the largest saver, or the largest investor.

Especially after the crisis of 2008, the global balance of geopolitical and geoeconomic power changed. The United States was still powerful. But it couldn't, on its own, set the rules of the game. Trump may have a nostalgia for that world, but it won't be coming back.[20]

HOW TRUMPIAN POLICIES WILL HURT THOSE WHO ARE NOW STRUGGLING

GAID, and what has happened since its publication, has made it abundantly clear that the benefits of globalization were far from what they were touted to be. But that doesn't mean Trump's answer, a wholesale pulling back—a New Protectionism, a rapid deglobalization—will actually improve the plight of those that he pretends to speak for. Quite the contrary. There are several reasons for this.

History Matters

First, history matters. We described earlier how, in the process of globalization, unemployment often increased as job destruction outpaced job creation. This is actually the story not just for globalization, but for the adjustment of the economy to any major change. And deglobalization—protectionism—is such a change. Just as in the process of globalization itself, so too for deglobalization: job destruction (in sectors losing their

competitive advantage) often occurs faster than job creation in the benefiting sectors. Global supply chains have been created, with each country
in the supply chain making its contribution at the point where it has the
greatest comparative advantage, thereby driving down the overall cost
of production—and "uncreating" them cannot be done overnight, and
doing so will entail great costs.

Consider America's auto industry. Today, it depends heavily on
imported auto parts, from Mexico and elsewhere. If those parts were
produced in the United States, the price of American cars would have
to increase. But that would make America's cars less competitive. The
United States could, of course, respond by increasing tariffs against Japanese and German cars. But that would open up new fronts in a global
trade war—more fronts than even General Trump might think he could
simultaneously command. And the higher tariffs won't help GM sell
more American cars abroad. High tariffs just feed into a less competitive
American car industry.

The Trade Deficit Is Determined by Macroeconomics— and Trump Will Worsen the Trade Deficit

Most important, as we explained in chapter 1, the trade deficit—what
Trump is really complaining about—is not driven by trade policy,
but by macroeconomics. This is something we teach in our introduc-
tory economics courses, but it is something that he seemingly has not
grasped.[21] The trade deficit is equal to the difference between domestic
(national) savings and domestic investment.

Assume Trump succeeded in imposing his protectionist agenda. What
then? The answer is simple: because it would likely have little effect on
either national savings or investment, the trade deficit wouldn't change,
and the dollar would adjust to make sure that that is the case.[22] If the
United States can't import as much from China and Mexico, we will
import more from some other country. A stronger dollar will make
these countries more "competitive." It is not that they are manipulating
their exchange rate. It is that Trump is monkeying around with U.S.
trade policy in ways that have these unintended consequences.

But matters are worse. Because Trump has called for a tax cut for the
rich and increased infrastructure investment, the trade deficit will actually

increase. As this book goes to press, it is not clear how much of what he had originally promised in his campaign will be actually enacted. Even if he got only a fraction of this agenda through Congress, it would still increase the national fiscal deficit—that is, government savings would become even more negative, and so national savings (the sum of government, household, and firm savings) would go down. With national savings down and domestic investment up, our trade deficit would increase—again, brought about through an increase in the value of the dollar.

Trump has finally grasped the role of the dollar in the trade deficit and has responded (like many a politician before him) by thinking that he can talk the dollar down. (Others, believing in a strong dollar, have believed that they can talk the dollar up. Both are equally foolish.) *Sometimes,* a secretary of treasury, or even a president, can do this—rarely for more than a few days and normally not for more than a few minutes.

Standards of Living Will Go Down
While the overall trade deficit won't change for all of Trump's protectionism, Americans' standard of living will go down because of the distortions in trade. The United States won't be buying its imports from countries where it costs the least to produce, but from the low-cost countries toward which, for some reason, Trump has not (yet) expressed an animus. In the end, higher costs of cars means a lower standard of living for Americans. And this is true for the thousands of other items that the United States buys from Mexico, China, Japan, Germany, or anywhere else. Indeed, middle- and lower-income Americans—who spend such a large fraction of their incomes on imported goods, bought at Walmart and Target, not at Gucci and Bloomingdale's—would suffer the most from Trump's protectionism focused on China and Mexico.[23]

Protectionism will drive up prices; the increased inflation may induce the Fed to increase interest rates, which will have two further effects: it will slow down the economy and it will strengthen the dollar further.

ON THE ROAD TO A TRADE WAR?

Trump—if he gets his way—seems determined to start a trade war, unless he can be headed off. The world faced such a trade war once before, in the aftermath of the United States' passing of the Smoot-Hawley Tariff Act in 1930. Much of the effort in creating a global rules-based system for trade after World War II was to avoid another such trade war, which is widely credited with having contributed to the Great Depression. These efforts have paid off: there have been skirmishes, but not outright war.[24] Trump, who seems to love confrontation, may push the world to the brink.[25] In fact, his bark may be worse than his bite, especially since the Republican Congress is unlikely to give him the powers he would need for full-scale combat. The Republicans have been pushing trade liberalization for decades—it has been the Democrats that have been skeptical. It would be the height of hypocrisy—not unheard of in the realm of politics—for them now to turn to a full-scale endorsement of protectionism. Everybody would be the loser from such a war—including America itself, as I shall shortly explain.

Checks and Balances: Limitations in the Powers of the President

There is considerable debate about what exactly the president could do on his own. To see what he can do, one has to understand the nature of the obligations of the United States under the trade agreements it has signed.

The WTO
The most important trade agreement is the United States' membership in the World Trade Organization (WTO). Under the WTO, a country binds itself in a variety of ways, for instance, that its tariffs will not exceed certain levels (the bound levels) and it will not discriminate against any country (called the most favored nation principle, MFN). It also agrees to the WTO adjudication of disputes. When a country engages in a practice in violation of its obligations under WTO, the injured country can sue before the WTO, and if it wins, it can impose retaliatory tariffs or other trade sanctions. These can be finely targeted—where they hurt the most economically and politically. Countries have learned how to do this well.

The president cannot on his own withdraw from the WTO. He must get majority support from both houses of Congress—which is unlikely.

NAFTA

NAFTA, which allows free trade between the United States, Canada, and Mexico, is the trade agreement that Trump has vilified the most, even though in signing it, Mexico made far larger concessions than the United States. Because no one really contemplated the idea of a breakup, the negotiators left more ambiguity than perhaps they should have on the procedures of a breakup. But the critical point, according to some trade economists, is that what is called the implementing legislation—the legislation, for instance, that specified the zero tariff levels for Mexican and Canadian goods—remains on the U.S. books until it is repealed. Thus, without both houses of Congress repealing that legislation, the zero tariff levels remain—whether NAFTA exists or not.

Even if the United States left NAFTA, and even if Congress repealed the implementing legislation, Mexico would be confronted with the "WTO tariffs," which, under the most favored nation provision, would on average be at most just a few percent.

Thus, for Trump to impose 20 percent tariffs against Mexico, he would have to get a majority in both houses of Congress to vote to leave NAFTA and rescind the implementing legislation, and then get them to vote to leave the WTO—or at least impose these tariffs in violation of WTO obligations, knowing full well the serious consequences. Almost surely, Trump was either delusional or uninformed when he made the threats against Mexico.

In a Trade War, Everyone Loses

It appears that some in the Trump administration—and perhaps some in Congress—would like to start a trade war. Nationalists think that wars provide an opportunity for demonstrating their patriotism and the superiority of their country. The pro-war camp looks at our "assets" and that of our opponent, and confidently predicts victory. Every war has begun thus. In the case of trade, they look at China's large exports to the United States—were these cut off, China's economy (in this calculation) would sink. They are more dependent on exports to the United States than the United States is on exports to China, so they reason. But in practice, matters are more complex. China has been moving from export-led and -dependent growth to domestically driven growth.

A trade war with the United States would simply hasten the pace of change. The U.S. economy is only about 24 percent of global output:[26] China could sell much of what it doesn't sell in America to other countries. That might drive down prices in those markets—hurting U.S. exports there and encouraging those countries to try to export more to the United States. Further, China is sitting on a war chest, some $3 trillion of reserves.[27] China has much more control over its vast economy—making it easier for it to adjust to the change. And China is holding as hostage vast amounts of investment by U.S. firms inside China. Not surprisingly, China has exuded confidence: it believes it would win any trade war, and it has warned the United States of that.

Think for a moment how the trade war would play out. The first-round effect would entail a 45 percent price increase or so for clothes, televisions, and everything else the United States buys from China. The already-suffering Trump Rust Belt voter suddenly sees his standard of living plummet. Trump might retort: "I gave you fair warning. I told you that I was going to do this." But they would naturally reply: "We thought you were just strutting, grandstanding. We thought you might use that as a threat, to get our jobs back." At the next stage, the jobs don't come back. Rather, Walmart starts buying more apparel from Indonesia and Vietnam. Walmart's prices will rise because Walmart will not be sourcing its goods from the lowest-price provider; consumers will be worse off, but nonetheless there will be no jobs added, and no real change in the trade deficit.

But the story doesn't end here. China wouldn't be happy with the American tariffs that violate its commitments to the WTO. China believes in globalization and the rules-based system, and wants to show all the other countries of the world the difference between China, a good citizen playing by the rule, and America, at least under Trump, where promises aren't worth the paper they're written on.

China, the fastest-growing aviation market in the world, is not committed to buying airplanes from the United States, and so one would see a sudden collapse in sales of airplanes. Chinese students and tourists have been flocking to America—helping our balance of payments, and in terms of universities, providing the tuition revenues that they need so badly. With the bad mood—not toward the United States in general, but toward a Trump-led America—they may collectively decide not to come. China hasn't been able to grow enough food to feed its 1.3 billion mouths, and America has made up a large part of the deficit. But China can buy much of its food elsewhere, and another major group of Red States (states voting for Trump) may find that life under Trump is more difficult.

Finally, while America and China have been discussing an agreement to provide protection for each other's investment in the other country, that agreement is far from being signed. Already, China is a master in making life difficult for a company that it believes is not behaving correctly—permits are delayed, construction is slowed, inspections become more frequent, laws against corruption (reportedly pervasive) are more vigorously enforced. The huge amounts American firms have invested in China—a major source of their profitability—can be thought of as a potential hostage in an out-and-out trade war. In real wars, governments often seize (temporarily) assets of the countries with which they are in conflict. This would be more subtle. My conjecture is that China would play strictly within the rule of law but would engage in actions which mirrored any actions the United States took, simultaneously taking full advantage of the many tools in their tool kit to disadvantage American firms.

The business establishment—especially the huge array of firms that derive substantial profits from their activities in China—would be very, very unhappy and put enormous pressure on Trump and Congress to end the trade war. They might join the chorus saying China is unfair, but their voices would be especially loud when it came to the refrain: we have to respond intelligently, with engagement, not with war.

DOING MISCHIEF: TRADE SKIRMISHES

It's hard to conceive that a Republican-controlled U.S. Congress would initiate a full-scale trade war, or leave the WTO, or allow Trump to do so. More likely, whether he scales down his protectionist rhetoric or not, Trump is more likely to engage Mexico, China, the EU, and others in trade skirmishes—a more limited engagement than all-out war.

Trade laws give the president the right to initiate certain suits—when a country sells its products at below cost (called dumping) or subsidizes them. The United States is the prosecutor, judge, and jury, and it has written the law not based on principles of "fair trade." Rather, the laws are biased in favor of the American firms bringing the case. During my time in the Council of Economic Advisers, I was frequently involved, and typically opposed the actions. The actions were blatantly trying to protect uncompetitive American firms from competition, driving up prices to consumers. But they did save jobs—though typically at the expense of jobs elsewhere, and often at great costs. The Council's position was that noted earlier—the job of maintaining the economy at full employment was that of the Federal Reserve, and in the era when I served as chair, it did that job well, with unemployment falling to 4.7 percent in 1997. Later, it fell even more.

Dumping

Dumping provides an example of these trade skirmishes. The basic principle of economics is that in a competitive market, price should be equal to the (marginal) cost of production—the extra cost of producing an extra unit. In heavy industry, the major cost is the construction of the factory, so marginal cost can be much less than average cost. When there is a steel shortage, price rises above average cost; when there is a surplus, it falls below. If firms on average make predictions correctly, the periods in which price is above average cost balance out with the periods in which it is below, and the factory breaks even, giving a return on capital just enough to compensate for the risk of the industry. (That is, competition is supposed to drive down profits, taking into account a risk-based return on capital, to zero.) But there is nothing wrong or unfair in having an extended period of price below average costs. If, of course, producers make a mistake and build too much capacity, then the factory loses money. Consumers are the winners from this mistake, the factory owners the losers. In competitive markets, one doesn't shut down the factory unless the total losses going forward from running the factory are greater than the cost of shutting it down. In China, with its historically unprecedented growth, excess capacity today can be quickly converted into a shortage. The construction of cities requires large amounts of steel, and hundreds of millions of people will be moving into those cities. Thus, it is not unreasonable for them to assume that some of the excess capacity is only temporary.

America's dumping duties don't recognize these subtleties, and a company that is selling below average costs can be charged with dumping under WTO rules. Of course, it would make no sense for a firm to permanently sell below its average costs. It defies rationality.

But there is another, less benign scenario. A company might sell below costs in order to drive its rivals out of business, thereby establishing a monopoly position, and with that market power, more than recoup the loss. This kind of "dumping" is called predatory pricing. For it to be profitable to engage in predation, there has to be some large barrier to entry. (Normally, as soon as the price rises above costs, there will be entry. There is then no benefit to driving firms out of the market by charging a low price because one simply can't sustain a monopoly position.) Predatory pricing violates U.S. competition laws, and a company that has been "unfairly" driven out of business can sue. But the courts have frowned on such suits. To win such a case of "unfair pricing," the complainant has a heavy burden—to show not only that the price is low, below costs, but that the market barriers are sufficiently high that the defendant would have a reasonable chance of recouping the losses. Not surprisingly, there are few successful cases.

While trade and antitrust dumping (predatory pricing) deal with similar situations of a firm selling below cost, the standards set in the two are markedly different. If the antitrust standard was applied to trade cases, in almost no cases would there be a finding of an unfair trade practice. By contrast, if the trade standard were used in the U.S. antitrust cases, there would be large numbers found guilty of "predation" or dumping—rather than the very few who are. The explanation is simple: the dumping provisions are protectionist—they were designed to protect American industries and they do that.

There are a few other provisions of the trade agreements that give the United States the right to impose duties as protectionist measures.[28] And these are the things that Trump and his team will almost surely take advantage of. They can be outrageous—but at the same time they are of limited scope. China will challenge the application of these provisions before the WTO, with considerable prospects of winning.

Nonmarket Status and "Surrogate Countries"

One especially peculiar provision that is likely to be challenged by China is called "nonmarket status." In a Communist country, prices can be "made up," so there is no basis of being sure whether a good is being dumped. So a clever alternative system was devised: look for a country that is similar (called the surrogate country), ask what it would have cost to produce the good in that country, and when the good is sold below that number, it can be called dumping. It was clever, in part, because it was so open to abuse. In one famous case, in the late 1970s, when Poland was still a Communist country, the United States alleged that Canada was the market economy most similar to Poland. Never mind the huge disparities in income and wages. Poland was accused of dumping golf carts. The problem was that though one Canadian firm had produced golf carts, it was no longer doing so, perhaps because it wasn't profitable. So the United States calculated what it would have cost Canada to produce golf carts, if it had. Not surprisingly, the price was far higher than what Poland was charging, and a huge duty was imposed.

The agreement signed by China when it became a member of the WTO provided that after fifteen years, China would no longer be subject to this special "nonmarket status." Now, Europe and the United States appear to be trying to wriggle out of this commitment—and this issue too is now being litigated within the WTO.

Tit-for-Tat

Protectionists like Trump fail to remember that other countries can play the same games—and have every incentive to do so. Their citizens would expect no less of their government. Trump's America First policies may be good for some parts of American politics, but it plays badly globally.[29]

China (or any other country against which the U.S. takes protectionist measures) may not wait until a final WTO judgment is rendered—China has grounds for bringing similar actions against the United States. The emerging markets, including China, have been good students: they have learned from America how to take protectionist actions within the constraints of the global rules-based system that was intended to circumscribe protectionism.

There are many easy cases: America's bailout of the auto and banking sector entailed massive subsidies, giving countries the right to impose offsetting countervailing duties, perhaps even on those borrowing from these banks, on the argument that the interest rates charged are lower than they would have been without the subsidy. Almost surely, there will be tit-for-tat. The United States will gain little, and the world will lose a lot, in this process of partial deglobalization.

The hope is that, as the Trump administration debates how and whether to implement the protectionist policies, the grown-ups in the room will persuade Trump of the folly of going down the trade war route. Even if the United States simply acts consistently with WTO rules—but moves aggressively using the latitude that those rules allow for imposing trade restrictions in certain limited cases—the grown-ups will explain that others too can act more aggressively.

Trade wars have something in common with real wars: almost always, everybody—all countries engaged in the war—lose. Even the threat of a trade war has a depressing effect on investment and, therefore, the overall level of economic activity. Earlier, I referred to the painfully constructed global supply chains; a trade war would wreak havoc with such supply chains. The increased costs—and the increased risks—will be shifted onto consumers.

RENEGOTIATING TRADE AGREEMENTS

Trump has expressed enormous confidence in his negotiating skills. He has said the United States must renegotiate its trade agreements. There is much to be said for doing so: the design of agreements like NAFTA paid too little attention to the ever-changing nature of the economy, and to the fact that an agreement that might be "right" in 1992 when it was signed, might need updating a quarter century later. Remarkably, for all the criticism, as this book goes to press, he hasn't laid out what he means by a "good" trade agreement. In his fixation on bilateral trade deficits (which, I explained earlier, simply don't matter) he presumably would like to do something that would reduce Mexico's surplus with the United States but not reduce the U.S. surplus with Canada. It's not easy to see how there's much he could do about either.

There are a few minor things, like changes in the rules of origin—

what percentage of a good that is called "NAFTA-produced" must be produced in one of the NAFTA countries. Before pulling out of the TPP, the United States agreed to loosen the rules of origins—effectively allowing a car with 90 percent Chinese content to be called Japanese. American auto manufacturers would like to go the other way—giving them a little advantage over Japanese or Korean cars that might have more Chinese parts. That would improve the trade balance with the rest of the world but might even lead to a greater bilateral trade deficit between Mexico and the United States.

Earlier, I discussed the investment agreements that are embedded in trade agreements. (In the case of NAFTA, it's called "chapter 11.") I suspect Mexico and Canada would readily agree to redoing, or eliminating, these provisions. The problem is that America's big multinationals love these provisions dearly—simply because they believe it may help ward off increases in regulation or taxation, and it increases their bargaining power with workers, driving down wages.

In short, not only was NAFTA far from being the worst trade deal ever, but in any case, Trump will struggle to significantly improve it. There are, of course, new areas of commerce, not covered by NAFTA, like high tech and data, which a new agreement would deal with. Ironically, the position of the United States is likely to be similar to that in the TPP agreement which he scuttled.

STRATEGIES FOR COUNTERING
THE NEW PROTECTIONISM

Trump, with his protectionism and America First policies, has put the world on notice: countries have to look after themselves and their interests. Borders matter, treaties don't, and America is not to be trusted—it will do what is in its *shortsighted* interests. Trump's extremism may have had a particularly adverse effect on American soft power, because it had already been eroding—as a result of the Iraq War and the way it was conducted, Guantanamo, and other factors discussed in the introduction.

The economy only works because of trust: if every contract had to be litigated, the market economic system would break down. Fortunately, the kind of businessperson that Trump has shown himself to be is rare.

Indeed, the response to such people is typically one of shunning and ostracism. We raise our children to be trustworthy; their word is their honor. We celebrate those who live by their ideals, and we castigate those who break their word, even when they get away with it.

International relations are more complicated. Still, the basis of most diplomacy consists of leaders of one country meeting with those of another, in an attempt to develop understanding and trust. American diplomacy has been based on trying to enhance trust in the United States, to increase confidence that the United States will not abuse its economic and military power. Trump has gone in exactly the opposite direction, announcing that we may not honor our treaties, what matters is power, and America will exercise that power in (what he perceives to be) its own shortsighted interest. For countries without power, the natural question is, what can and should they do? A set of precepts is evolving:

1. Diversify. Don't be dependent on any single country, and particularly, don't be too dependent on the United States, either for exports or for imports. Latin America, for example, will strengthen its ties with Europe and China. Most countries are already reasonably diversified. Mexico is the exception, with some 80 percent of its exports going to the United States in 2016.[30] And Mexico is also highly dependent on the United States for meeting its gas needs. Countries like Mexico had always reasoned: for the United States to cut off gas supplies would hurt America as much or more than it hurts Mexico. But there was an underlying assumption of rationality. That assumption—certainly as it applies to the United States—is now being questioned. The United States would, of course, be hurt by retaliation for its New Protectionist policies. It is not clear whether more reasoned heads will prevail.

2. Redo the global architecture *without* the United States. Part of the new diversification strategy will entail a new set of trade agreements. While the United States has played a pivotal role in the creation of the current global architecture, it has occasionally been an impediment to reaching agreements. One of the reasons that the world couldn't agree on what was called the Development Round

of trade negotiations—negotiations that began in 2001 and were finally abandoned in 2015—was that the United States refused to remove its agricultural subsidies, including and especially on cotton. The United States also played an important role in stopping the creation of the Asian Monetary Fund, which would have helped fight the East Asia crisis, and tried to stop the Asian Infrastructure Investment Bank. Some countries are beginning to realize that with the United States out of the picture, this is the time to strike, to create trade or other agreements that might not otherwise be possible. Countries are likely to be wary in general of agreements in which there is an imbalance of power—there is always the risk of a Trumpian leader who will attempt to take advantage of others through the exercise of power. Thus, countries are likely to explore more South-South agreements and strengthen existing ones. Chile, Colombia, Mexico, and Peru have created what is called the Pacific Alliance. They are seeing the New Protectionism in the United States as providing the imperative to push it further.

3. Grow more through internal demand. All cross-border trade represents a risk, because borders matter. Thus, countries should bias their economies toward internal demand. We saw earlier that markets don't correctly price "border risk." This bias can be thought of as just offsetting this market failure. One element of growing internal demand is improving the distribution of income—when income is skewed toward the top, internal demand will be weak.

There will be high costs to moving from a world striving to reduce the impact of borders—working to facilitate the easier movement of goods, services, and capital across countries—to a world where borders matter and new walls are being constructed. There will be a cost to the inward-looking policies described above. But because in this new world borders can matter, there are grave risks confronting any country that does not take this into account and becomes excessively dependent on others.

Economists had long castigated countries that sought energy or food security—attempting to rely on their own supplies for these vital items was costly and wasteful. But in a world where borders matter, countries that followed that advice, allowing themselves to become dependent on others for food or energy, may rethink their policies.

It is thus likely that the world will be localizing in response to Trump. But for the world as a whole, deglobalization will be very costly, and it will be a kind of deglobalization from which the United States itself will not benefit.

CONCLUDING REMARKS

Chapters 1 and 2 explained that those in the advanced countries have many legitimate grievances against globalization. But I argued that the central problem with globalization was that it reflected an agenda driven by multinational corporations. One shouldn't have expected that a "reform" agenda coming from an administration dominated by plutocrats, where the most responsible individuals with the greatest understanding of globalization come from the multinational corporations, and especially its financial institutions, would devise a reform of globalization that would work for ordinary individuals. And they haven't.

America is one of the few countries which, on its own, can try to change the rules of the game. I have explained why protectionism won't work for the United States. Other countries which go down the protectionist route on their own are likely to fare even worse.

But there are alternative ways of reforming globalization which hold out the promise of improving the lot of all, or at least most, citizens. The next chapter lays out what this kind of globalization might look like.

Chapter 4

Can Globalization Be Saved?

An Agenda for Equitable Globalization with Shared Prosperity

C AN GLOBALIZATION BE "saved"? Can it be managed in ways which redound to the benefit of most citizens in both the developing and the advanced countries?

The question itself is not well stated: there is no way that we can be fully "unglobalized"; no way that we can be just reliant on what we produce within our own countries. Just as it is inconceivable that any of us individually could be completely reliant on ourselves.

When we ask "What is the future of globalization?" what we are really asking is: *What will be the rules governing globalization? Will it be the kind of unfettered trade toward which we seemed to be moving over the past quarter century, or a more regulated system? And who will make the regulations, and on whose behalf?*

In the early days of capitalism, we saw the ugly face of unfettered markets, portrayed for instance in the novels of Charles Dickens and chronicled in the writings of the global muckrakers, like Upton Sinclair. Gradually, we learned how to "temper" the market economy, without going to the extremes of the Soviet Union. Around the world, this became "bipartisan." Under Richard Nixon, for instance, America passed strong environmental laws. Sometimes, it took a Great Recession or a Great Depression to curb the worst abuses, such as those of the financial sector (the passage of the Glass-Steagall Act, separating investment and commercial banking, in 1933, and of the Dodd-Frank Financial Reform Act in 2010). We painfully came to recognize that businesses could increase their profits by exploiting others—rather than through inventing better products or providing better services to their customers. As a response, we passed antitrust laws and consumer protection legislation.[1]

To me, it seems clear: now we need to learn how to temper globalization. The era of idolization of globalization, where every president and prime minister sees as one of his great achievements signing a new free trade agreement with one or more of his country's partners, allowing for the ever-freer flow of goods and services, is over. I think we can temper globalization, but it won't be done if we begin with a Panglossian view that markets, always and everywhere, are efficient, and even less so if we think that the distribution of income that emerges out of market processes is necessarily socially acceptable. And it won't happen if we have the kind of globalization we've had—not really based on free-market principles, but rather managed for the well-being of large corporations and the finance industry of the advanced countries. And it won't happen if we pretend that households and firms can instantaneously adjust on their own to a change in regimes—such as resulted when we admitted China into the global trading system.

Globalization is not an end in itself, but, *possibly,* if it's made to work right, a means to an end—higher living standards for all, with the benefits of globalization equitably shared. Too often, the advocates of globalization confuse ends and means. They continue to glorify globalization, even when it appears to harm a majority of the citizenry, or at least a large portion of it.

The Underlying Problem: Global Governance
At the global level, the reason globalization has not worked out well—whether it's creating a stable global financial system or a global trading regime that's fair to the poorest countries—has to do with governance, how the rules of the game are set and enforced. We live in a world in which countries are heavily interdependent. When the U.S. Federal Reserve lowers its interest rate, it can cause money to rush into emerging markets, setting off asset price bubbles; and when it then raises its interest rates, it can cause those bubbles to break. Yet there is no way to

encourage one country to do things that might benefit others, or to adequately prevent one country—especially a large country like the United States—from harming others. It is not fully the law of the jungle, where might makes right, but neither is it a world marked by fairness or social justice. The poor countries, and the poor within each country, have only limited power to affect globalization. The poorer the country, the less its influence. Thus, in spite of our interdependence, there is no global government to ensure fair and efficient outcomes. Sometimes we work together as a global community, as when we dealt with the hole in the ozone layer. Often we don't. We have a system of global governance without global government.

A central message of *GAID* is that the way the rules of the globalization game are set has enormous distributive consequences, both between and within countries. Globalization has in part been a vehicle for the rich to get richer at the expense of the poor. Finance ministers and central bank governors make the key decisions concerning the global financial architecture; and when they do, they are typically thinking more of multinational enterprises, the firms in the financial sector, the banks and the hedge funds, than they are of the workers and other citizens that are affected by the policies. The siloed structure of international governance exacerbates the problem—finance ministers and central bank officials meet with each other, but seldom with the labor ministers who deal with the labor market consequences of financial sector instability. And of course, making matters worse is the fact that developed countries have disproportionate influence in the bodies in which the rules are made, such as the IMF.

It is not economics that is stopping us from achieving win-win globalization, from rewriting the rule of the global economy—we largely know what to do—but politics, and the shortsightedness on the part of some of the national politicians, and the corporate and financial elites with whom they work. This is perhaps not a surprise: the big critique of our corporate and financial sector is that in every sphere they are shortsighted, unable to make the long-term investments that would enhance long-term growth; and with politicians on two- or four-year election cycles, we can't expect much long-term thinking from them.

The world is changing rapidly, as I have already noted. The five BRICS countries (Brazil, Russia, India, China, and South Africa) alone are now larger than were all the advanced countries at the end of World War II. So the United States can't dominate anymore. Nor does announcing that one is pursuing a policy of "America First," making all other interests and all principles secondary, help much in persuading others to follow American leadership.

If, as Trump seems to be proposing, the United States disengages from the global economy unless the rest of the world agrees to its terms, others will step forward to fill the gap, and there will be a New Globalization, one that the United States will have an even smaller role in shaping.

An Alternative Globalization Is Possible

As this book goes to press, we face a new world. The United States worked hard for more than three-quarters of a century to create a global economic and political order—a rules-based system, an order with the United States at the center. Goods, services, and capital now move more easily across borders. No one had any doubts that America was putting its interests first, but it was a relatively *enlightened* self-interest, which took into account the benefits that the United States itself would receive from the peace, growth, and stability it engendered. The United States' leadership was only possible because other countries recognized America's pursuit of its enlightened self-interest. It was a world of multilateralism—where there was an attempt to understand and improve the workings of the *system as a whole.*

Unfortunately, while the United States pursued an enlightened self-interest, it was not as enlightened as it should have been. It was not entirely selfish, but neither was it fully altruistic. The United States used its leadership to create a globalization that advanced corporate and financial interests in America and other rich countries; the interests of workers, consumers, and those in emerging markets and developing countries were only of secondary concern. The (admittedly questionable) assumption was that if the rich countries' corporate interests were well served, all would benefit.

An alternative world is possible, not that of the New Protectionism being pushed by Trump nor globalization as it has been in recent decades—the managed globalization, managed for various vested interests in advanced countries. We can have social protection without protectionism—

helping protect individuals, especially the most vulnerable, against the shocks they face, without cutting ourselves off, partially or fully, from the rest of the world.

PRINCIPLES OF A REFORMED GLOBALIZATION

It is obviously impossible to summarize in a few pages a set of principles that should guide such a *reformed* globalization. The following ten provide guidelines for the future—and indirectly, a good summary of my critique of globalization as it has been managed.

1. *Globalization is a means to an end, not an end in itself.* The end is improving the living standards of people in all the countries of the world. Too often, ends and means are confused, when, for instance, citizens are asked to lower their wages and accept cutbacks in job protections and government services in order to compete in the global economy.

2. *Global rules are needed where there are cross-border externalities.* When what one country does affects others in a significant way, we need rules and referees, to prevent countries from harming others, and to encourage countries to take actions that benefit others. Of course, matters are not usually black and white; there will often be *some* cross-border externalities. But global governance is difficult, so there should be a focus on those areas where cross-border externalities are particularly significant. The problem, as I've noted, is that too little attention has been paid to those areas, like tax competition—the infamous race to the bottom—fiscal paradises, and short-term capital flows where there are significant adverse externalities; and too much attention on areas—like regulatory harmonization—where cross-border externalities are not as significant. The costs of short-term capital flows can be especially great for developing countries; and there are a variety of measures that they can take to stabilize capital flows, preventing surges of short-term money into or out of a country.[2]

3. *Global action will become increasingly important as we become more interdependent and as we recognize our interdependencies.* We now

recognize, for instance, the importance of what are called global public goods—goods from which everyone in the world benefits (global security, global health, and knowledge) or suffers—as in the case of climate change or global pandemics. The carbon dioxide molecules don't know about visas and passports: pollution generated in the United States easily goes across borders. So too for the viruses associated with bird flu, or the Zika virus. The global climate represents the quintessential global public good. We all share the same atmosphere. Increased concentration of global warming gasses results in global climate change: no one in the world can protect himself. Only through collective global action—working together, cooperatively—can climate change be addressed. Similarly, if we don't act in concert to contain highly contagious diseases, we risk facing global epidemics.

4. ***Governance matters.*** Who makes the rules and enforces them—that is, who makes the decisions concerning globalization—matters. Good governance has to be based on a few simple principles of representativeness, legitimacy, transparency, and accountability. We've argued that globalization will only work if we move away from the law of the jungle to a rule of international law. But it has to be a "rule of law" that is not written by and for corporations. One of the reasons for the failures of globalization is how decisions have been made—who was in the room and who was not. When politicians and governments are not held accountable for the consequences of their actions, they obviously will not have the incentive to do the "right" thing. And they can't be held accountable in the absence of transparency.

5. ***Government and civil society will both have to be part of the system regulating, and tempering, globalization.*** There has been excessive faith in markets and the private sector.[3] The private sector, on its own, created many of the central problems facing national economies and global society: inequality, environmental degradation, and instability. The private sector, on its own, won't solve these problems.

6. ***Large economies are different from small economies.*** Economies like the United States, China, and the EU must be sensitive to the effects of what they do on others in ways that smaller countries don't.

Thus, when the United States began its policy of quantitative easing in 2008, it led to massive capital inflows into many emerging markets, a sharp appreciation in their exchange rates, and a loss of competitiveness of their export industries, among other effects. In short, the United States caused global havoc. Also, in the early 1980s, when the Fed raised interest rates massively to fight inflation in the United States, it brought on the Latin American debt crisis. The difference between the global consequences of Hugo Chávez or Nicolás Maduro in Venezuela and Trump in America also illustrates the point.

7. *One-size-fits-all policies don't work—and one must be especially careful in applying the same policies and rules to both developed and developing countries: developing countries are different from developed countries.* They are poorer, and they need to close the resource and knowledge gap that separates them from more advanced countries. Our trade laws, for instance, have tried to provide for excessive harmonization of intellectual property regimes. The IPR regimes appropriate for developing countries—or the climate change policies—may differ from those appropriate for a developed country.

8. *Any change in the rules of the game involves winners and losers. Change itself is costly and difficult, and households and firms, especially those at the bottom, may need assistance in making changes imposed by globalization.* The antipathy being expressed toward globalization has more to do with the failure to take into account its distributional consequences than with anything else—and especially so when the losers from globalization are those in the middle and bottom, and the winners are those at the top—the same people who keep winning. It adds to the view that our whole system is unfair, rigged, and that the government—which after all is making the rules—can't be trusted. We should be particularly skeptical of reforms in which the winners are corporations—many such reforms are negative sum, with the losses of ordinary citizens even outweighing the gains of the corporations. Governments need to be particularly mindful of the losers when they are at the bottom of the economic pyramid since they are less able to fend for themselves. If, as the advocates of

globalization claim, there are net benefits from globalization, then the winners can be taxed to help the losers. If the winners can't or won't compensate the losers, it should be questioned whether the change is desirable.

9. *There are social dimensions of globalization—effects that extend beyond just economics—and reforms to globalization need to be particularly mindful of them.* Provisions of international trade agreements that have denied access to life-saving generic medicines to the poor have in effect put drug company profits above the value of life.[4] The attempts by overly zealous globalists to curb the ability of countries to subsidize their movie industries provides another illustration. Hollywood has put enormous pressure on the U.S. government to demand that other countries not provide such help. Every country views culture as part of their national identity, and films are one of the ways they maintain this identity. *Rambo 17, Transformers 17,* or *Fast & Furious 17* are not going to be harmed significantly if France decides to subsidize an artistic movie about the life of André Gide—and if France decides that doing so is a good use of its public funds, it should be allowed to do so, without being held in violation of WTO or other trade rules.

10. *The economic consequences of reforms must be evaluated using models that reflect economic realities*—that is, that do not assume that the market is competitive, efficient, and stable. We know that there are massive market imperfections—of competition, information, and risk markets—and pervasive and persistent unemployment. Models that attempt to estimate the costs and benefits of any reform (including any trade agreement) that assume these imperfections away are likely to give very misleading results. We know, for instance, that unregulated and underregulated financial markets can be highly unstable and were largely responsible for the global financial crisis; and so too for unregulated and underregulated cross-border capital flows. The kinds of massive shifts of funds that brought on the East Asia crisis have caused crises around the world. The champions of unfettered globalization partially based their analysis on models with perfect information and perfectly working financial markets—a total fiction. (Truth be told: deregulation, and especially financial market deregulation, was not really based on economic models; it was motivated by greed, pure and

simple. The bankers realized that deregulation would allow them to increase their profits. Deregulation was just another instance of special-interest legislation.)

Moreover, any economic system is complex, and can't be well analyzed using simplistic models. Global rules have global consequences, and can't be analyzed using models that ignore induced changes in behavior, patterns of trade, and prices. Many of the models used, say, by the IMF, before the crisis, highlighted the benefits of diversification of risks, as funds were spread around the world; but after the onset of the crisis, they highlighted the risks of contagion—effects which arose precisely because of the cross-border capital flows that they had trumpeted just shortly before the crisis.[5]

THE WAY FORWARD: WHAT IS TO BE DONE?

The above principles provide some guidance in shaping policies that would make globalization work, or at least work better, in the future. But workers in the advanced countries who have lost their jobs are not interested in principles. They want their jobs back, and they want higher wages. What should we do *today?*

The market, on its own, won't give workers what they want. It didn't smoothly manage the transition from an agriculture-based economy to one resting on manufacturing—the Great Depression can be viewed as one of the big bumps that was part of that transformation. The advanced countries are going through multiple transitions—from a manufacturing economy to a service sector economy, with a slowdown of population growth within their countries. The global geopolitical and geoeconomic order too is changing rapidly. The market is unlikely to manage any of these transitions smoothly on its own.

At this book goes to press, a decade after the breaking of the housing bubble that set off the global financial crisis, the global economy is not fully back to normal. Growth remains anemic. In the United States, while the official unemployment rate remains low, labor force participation is the lowest it's been since women entered the labor force. A weak labor market has contributed to the high levels of inequality. Families worry about falling down the ladder of opportunity—many see this as more likely than going up. This atmosphere of fear feeds into the protectionist spirit that Trump has so ruthlessly exploited.

An essential part of the story of today's discontent with globalization is that untempered globalization has made worse a number of serious ongoing problems—most notably, growing inequality. As I noted, the defenders of globalization have pointed out the role of technology or other changes in our society: true, but such statements are not helpful. The critics of globalization believe it is the one thing about which something can be done.

Hence, anyone serious about advancing globalization—and the benefits which it might bring, if well managed—must see globalization policy within a broader economic framework. What is needed is stronger government actions: macroeconomic policies that push the economy toward full employment; adjustment policies to help worker, firms, and communities adapt to the new circumstances; social protection policies to protect them against losses to the standards of living that they may face in the process of adjustment; and policies that reduce inequalities in market incomes and incomes after tax and transfer.

The following brief sections outline some of the elements of each of these components.

Reducing Inequalities in Market Income

The big drivers of the anger toward globalization are inequality, the lack of jobs, and stagnant and declining wages. Many are finding it hard to get jobs, or at least jobs anywhere near what they had come to expect. While after World War II in the United States and European countries there was a widespread aspiration of joining the middle class, for many today a middle-class life seems out of reach to increasing portions of the population. How to reverse these trends is a big question, but there are a couple of precepts that go a long way.

The analysis begins with an enquiry into why there has been such an increase in inequality. Because the United States has the largest level of inequality among advanced countries, it provides the best case to see what happened. Until the mid-1970s, workers' productivity and compensation moved together, while after that, productivity growth continued, albeit at a slightly slower pace, while compensation virtually came to a standstill. It wasn't that, almost overnight, the technology of the economy changed. But what did happen, rather quickly, is the rules of the game and how they were implemented changed, and especially after the ascendancy of Margaret Thatcher in Great Britain and Ronald Reagan in the United States. There began a process of rewriting the rules of the economy in ways that favored those at the top and hurt the rest.[6] Regulations, such as those on the financial sector, were stripped away and taxes at the top and corporations were reduced with pervasive effects. Unions were weakened, and monetary policy focused more on inflation and less on ensuring full employment.

One of the important consequences is that there has been a marked increase in the concentration of market power—especially as antitrust enforcement and legislation didn't keep pace with the increase in market power resulting from changes in the structure of the economy.

Firms like Microsoft and Google came to dominate the fastest-growing sectors of the economy. Most consumers had a choice of only a few Internet providers and telecom companies. As the economy shifted to a service-based economy, the importance of local service monopolies increased. One important implication: monopolies face downward-sloping demand curves for their products; they can only sell more by lowering prices. Thus, even when their activities are very profitable, they may limit investment—the marginal return is less than the average return. And that is precisely what we are seeing in recent years. Large corporations sitting on hordes of cash, but not willing to reinvest—weakening overall economic performance.

The rules of corporate governance were rewritten, enhancing the power of CEOs to take more of the corporate revenues for their own purposes—leaving less for wages for workers and less to be invested in the future of the company. While before, those in charge of corporations had a duty to look at the long-run interests of all stakeholders—the community in which the company operated, the workers, and the shareholders—now their duty was interpreted more narrowly to look after just shareholders, and that in turn was interpreted to mean shareholders *now*, not over the long run. This encouraged short-term thinking—undermining long-run investments in people, technology, and capital.

The financial sector reflected these changes—and helped bring them about; and the consequences were seen most dramatically in the 2008 financial crisis.

Of course, among the important rules of the economy are those governing globalization, and we've seen how the rules of globalization worked for rich corporations—as the rules increased their bargaining power to drive down wages. But the rules didn't work for the rest.

The result of all of this is that there has been a longer-term erosion of the fundamentals of the economy, including a disinvestment in the economy. The ratio of wealth to income may go up, but that increase has to do with rents—the increase in land values or stock markets, reflecting, for instance, the greater market power of firms and their greater ability to suppress wages.[7] In many countries, including the United States, the ratio of capital to output seems actually to be in decline; real investment has not kept pace.

If this diagnosis is correct, the response is straightforward: rewriting the rules once again, this time curbing market power and abuses of corporate governance, making the financial sector perform the functions it's supposed to perform, and strengthening unions' and workers' bargaining rights.[8]

One of the reasons that the United States and other economies have such limited upward mobility is that, in spite of our equalitarian ideals, those at the top give enormous advantages to their children. I jokingly tell my students that the most important decision you can make in life is choosing the right parents. Reducing the intergenerational transmission of advantage and disadvantage entails strengthening public education—including universal access to preschool and college education. (By contrast, in recent years in the United States, access to higher education has become even more difficult for those in the middle, and there is more inequality in access to quality elementary and secondary schools. The country's education system is managed locally and there has been increasing geographic segregation, with the poor living in poor communities, the rich in rich ones.)[9]

Any agenda attempting to reduce the intergenerational transmission of advantage at the top needs to also include increased estate taxes, but the Republican Party in the United States has been pushing for the opposite reform.

Finally, one of the most important ways to increase equality of market income is to run the economy more tightly. Gains from lower unemployment far outweigh risks of moderate inflation. This is the only proven way to bring marginalized groups into the economy. And a tight macroeconomy not only leads to less unemployment; it increases wages. Had the American economy been run much more tightly for the last six years—had the recovery from the Great Recession been managed differently—arguably the anti-globalization sentiment would have been much weaker.

Some say the Fed has done all it could. I disagree. Fed policies need to be oriented toward increasing the flow of credit, especially to small and medium-sized enterprises (SMEs). Most new regulation of the financial sector has been aimed at preventing the financial sector from doing what it shouldn't—preventing abuses and preventing instability (the costs of which are borne disproportionately by the poor and those in the middle). There should have been more attention on getting the financial sector to do what it should, and that includes providing credit to those who have been excluded, such as young and female entrepreneurs. Another of the striking aspects of the U.S. economy in recent years is the decline in new startups—contrary to America's image of itself as an entrepreneurial economy providing opportunities for all.

But most important, there are many other ways beyond monetary policy that the government could have ensured a tighter economy, which I discuss later in this chapter.

Improving Equality of After-Tax Distribution of Income

This agenda is even more straightforward than that discussed in the previous section, and again, the United States provides the best examples of what not to do. The agenda begins with replacing the current system of regressive taxation with progressive taxation. Those at the top actually pay lower taxes (as a percent of their income) than those with lower incomes. One of the reasons for this is that the returns to capital, and especially capital gains, are taxed at lower rates than wages. At the very least, capital should be taxed at the same rate as labor.

At the bottom, there needs to be a stronger earned income tax credit,[10] effectively complementing the wages paid by corporations to ensure that those who work full-time have at least a livable income.

We need to make corporations and high-income individuals pay their fair share of taxes—what their taxes would have been had they not taken advantage of the myriad of loopholes and special provisions that politicians have put into the tax code on their behalf. As I noted earlier, globalization, as it has been managed, plays a role here too: it has provided individuals and firms ample opportunities not to pay the taxes that they should.[11] Taxation is not just a matter of fairness: carrying out other parts of a successful government program to combat the adverse effects of globalization will require more revenues.

Helping Restructure the Economy

We have to accept that in the future the share of workers working in manufacturing will be lower than what it is today. This is true whether we are speaking of the United States, where it is 13.4 percent, or Germany, where it is about 18 percent.[12] As I have said, global manufacturing employment is declining because the pace of productivity growth exceeds the pace of output growth; and the advanced countries will get a small share of this shrinking number. Advanced countries could slow the pace of decline, for instance, by investing more in advanced manufacturing capabilities. But at best, that would be a stopgap.

Instead, the United States and other advanced countries need a structural transformation—the new economy will have to be based on services, and it will be increasingly knowledge-based.

Markets, as I noted, typically handle such transformations poorly. We saw that in America when we went from agriculture to manufacturing. A part of the story of the Great Depression was that as productivity in agriculture increased, wages and prices in that sector dropped dramatically. With asset values plummeting, those in the rural sector couldn't afford to migrate. World War II actually brought on the required transformation: people had to move to the urban areas for the manufacturing required to produce the bombs, tanks, and other things necessary to win the war. The GI Bill then financed the education that was required for a successful transformation.

My own hometown, Gary, Indiana, exemplifies what has happened in the current transformation. I returned a few years ago to make a film about globalization. With a population half of what it was when I was growing up, it looked like and had the feeling of a war zone, though without quite the same level of danger. And indeed, one of Gary's "growth" areas was serving the movie industry with sets to mimic places like Somalia. Contrast this with what happens in some other countries, where there is assistance in regional transformation: Manchester—England's old textile capital—has become an educational and cultural center. (The beginning of such a transformation, it should be noted, is finally happening to the old U.S. auto capital, Detroit.)

Two of the service sectors that should be a source of growth in jobs in that transition from manufacturing to the service economy are education and health—sectors in which the government understandably plays a large role. The demand for these services is not based on ordinary market forces—it is based on how we as a society value the services they provide, how much we care about those who care for our children, our sick, and our elderly. If we value these services highly, if we value how our children get educated or how our elderly get taken care of, we can tax and pay highly for those services—wages in these sectors would rise and with it the respect given to our teachers, nurses, and care providers.

We also need industrial[13] and educational policies to facilitate structural transformation, just as the government played a central role in the earlier transformation. This will be especially important as we move to the knowledge economy—the government needs to play a central role in creating a learning society.[14]

While government (admittedly somewhat inadvertently) played the central role in the transformation from agriculture to manufacturing, this time, when the need is so much greater, the government has been AWOL: conservatives have demanded cutbacks in government spending in education and health and castigated job retraining programs. The market transformation has devastated large parts of the United States, but without resources from the federal government, these localities can't restructure themselves, and so they become wastelands.

Providing Social Protection

No matter how good a job we do in restructuring the economy, there will be some workers who will be left behind. There will be those who, in their fifties, are unable or unwilling to be trained for the new jobs that are available, jobs that they sometimes believe are unacceptable. A just society must have some system of social protection.

One of the important insights of the past century is that the market provides inadequate insurance for many risks. That's why we have social insurance—annuities for the aged, unemployment insurance, and health insurance for the aged in the United States and for all in most other countries. We need systems to help those who lose their jobs, whether it's because of globalization or technology—job retraining programs are key, part of the structural transformation; but we also need some system of social protection for those who still aren't successful in getting a job.

The answer provided by the anti-globalization advocates—protectionism—won't work, as I explain in chapter 3. What we need is "protection without protectionism," to borrow from the title of another recent book.[15] We need ways of providing greater protection both for workers and for communities that are adversely affected, perhaps through some form of insurance against shocks.

Maintaining Full Employment

Our earlier analysis makes it clear, though, that more than just industrial, education, and retraining programs will be required. There must be better macroeconomic policies. As I argued earlier in this chapter, we need to maintain the economy at close to full employment—and especially to avoid the high levels of unemployment Europe and America have experienced in recent decades. (In the United States, unemployment was almost 11 percent in 1982—its highest point since the Great Depression—and 10 percent during the Great Recession; in some European countries, during the euro crisis unemployment exceeded 25 percent, with youth unemployment in excess of 50 percent).[16] Simultaneously managing the trade deficit, fiscal deficit, and full employment is obviously difficult—beyond the capabilities of America's political processes in recent years—but possible.[17] (Among the main reasons that the United States has not been able to do this is "deficit fetishism," the excessive focus on the fiscal deficit. If the government borrows money, especially if it can do so at the kinds of low interest rates that prevailed in the years after the 2008 crisis, and invests in infrastructure or R&D, the country's balance sheet improves—the value of the increase in assets exceeds the increase in liabilities. Output today increases, and future output also increases.)

While protectionism won't solve the problems posed by globalization—they'll get even worse—there are many policies that can be used systematically to achieve both lower fiscal and trade deficits, sustain the economy at full employment, and reduce the volatility in trade deficits that has contributed to the hardships facing workers in the manufacturing and other traded-goods sectors. Here are some examples.

- Expansionary fiscal policy—with spending used for investments in people, infrastructure, and technology and to facilitate the restructuring of the economy. The 2008 crisis made clear the limitations of monetary policy. For countries like the United States that can borrow at a low interest rate (negative in real terms), the failure to borrow funds to make these investments was a lost opportunity.
- Balanced budget expansions—where taxes are increased in tandem with expenditures. Even in countries that cannot borrow at low interest rates, there is a role for expansionary fiscal policy. By increasing spending and taxes together, the economy expands. This is called the balanced budget multiplier, and if the taxes and expenditures are chosen carefully (say a tax on land or on the very rich and expenditures on education), the impetus to the economy can be very large.
- Encourage domestic savings, especially through programs that "nudge" individuals to save for the future by having retirement programs with high savings rates. If aggregate demand is sustained so the economy remains at full employment, the effect is to change the *structure* of the economy in ways which advantage export industries, including manufacturers.[18]
- Create a global reserve currency. U.S. dollars are held in reserves around the world. This drives up the value of the dollar. A global reserve system would accordingly lower the value of the dollar, implying that, at any level of income, both consumption and investment would be shifted toward domestic content and American exports of goods and services would increase. To maintain full employment, government expenditures could then be reduced. Hence, both fiscal and trade balances would improve.[19]
- Implement the "Buffett" plan to improve the trade balance through trade chits. Much of the volatility associated with the exchange rate arises from volatile cross-border capital flows, as I noted earlier in the chapter. Warren Buffett has proposed an ingenious way to

attain stability in trade flows while maintaining freedom of capital flows, while still relying on market mechanisms.[20] Whenever a firm exports a dollar's worth of goods or services, it would get a trade chit; whenever a firm wants to import a dollar of goods, it would need to buy a trade chit. There would be a market for trade chits. By definition, this system would result in exports equaling imports. (Variants of this proposal can be used to keep the trade deficit within any desired set of bounds.)[21]

In short, if the government makes use of the full panoply of instruments at its disposal, it can smooth the transition from the manufacturing economy to the service sector economy, maintaining full or close to full employment along the way, and enhance macrostability. It is important, though, to see these government interventions as part of a strategy to facilitate the transition, not to block it. Large adjustments in economic systems can be costly and typically occur slowly. This makes it especially important not to succumb to ideologies, such as the "deficit fetishism" described earlier.[22]

The process of globalization sometimes does have a depressing effect on the economy, as I note in chapter 1, with job destruction far outpacing job creation. While there is a variety of ways to offset these effects, a quick remedy is to run a temporary fiscal deficit. The problem is that the ideologues of globalization denied or ignored the adverse short-run effects of globalization and simultaneously tried to circumscribe the ability of governments to respond. It was not just globalization itself that was to be blamed: the fault really lay with the constraints that were imposed on how countries could respond.

Some of the constraints countries face today, though, are themselves the result of globalization, or in any case, are deeply affected by globalization. In the nineteenth century, military might gave the European powers the ability to enforce their rules of the game over the rest of the world. There weren't then (and still are not now) rules governing what happens when a country can't pay back what is owed. The creditor countries decided what happens—often simply by sending troops and taking over the country. In the twentieth and twenty-first centuries, rich countries have figured out how to get what they want in more subtle ways. They have the bargaining power when it comes to global trade rules: developing countries and emerging markets desperately need (or want) access to the markets of the advanced countries, and they need the technology that comes with investments of the multinational corporations. This power—combined with the lack of unity among the developing and emerging countries—has resulted in rules that advantage the rich countries.

But even the advanced countries have had their hands tied by the rules of globalization: a commitment to full capital market liberalization (allowing money to flow freely in or out of the country—see chapter 2) means that any country that goes against the will of the financial markets may find itself buffeted, its exchange rate hammered, its interest rates soaring. Political leaders may well ask themselves: under this rampant globalization, where are decisions really being made: In their capital? Or on Wall Street? Luiz Inácio Lula da Silva ran for president of Brazil three times in the 1980s and 1990s; he was the leading candidate in two of the elections. But he was too far to the left for Wall Street, so they hammered the country, taking their money out. The exchange rate fell, and voters panicked just as investors did—and Wall Street's will was done. Voters decided it was simply too risky to elect him. Of course, while Wall Street may act as if it has 50 percent of the votes, it really doesn't, and sometimes voters rise up against financial markets. On Lula's fourth try, in 2002, he succeeded—and during his eight-year tenure he helped Brazil reduce poverty (the poverty head count ratio fell from 23 percent in 2002 to 11 percent in 2011)[23] and economic growth occurred at a robust 4 percent annually. Wall Street's fear had been unfounded.

Globalization constrains what governments can do in other ways. Global agreements restrict the kinds of help countries can give to firms and industries as they seek to advance the structural transformation I've described as being at the heart of responding to the challenges of globalization.[24]

But there is much that they can do within those constraints to make globalization work. This section has argued that, to paraphrase Shakespeare's famous line, the fault lies not in globalization, but in ourselves—that is, in the domestic policies. In the case of the United States, the problem is with its tax and expenditure programs, its monetary policies and legal systems, all too often designed to benefit corporations and the 1 percent at the expense of the rest, to benefit the winners of globalization and to do little to help the losers.[25]

CONCLUDING REMARKS

Things are changing. As I noted, China is now, by some measures, the largest economy. It is the largest trading economy. It is inevitable not only that the rules of the game will change, but also the system under which the rules are made. China will have more influence. America less. The Obama administration recognized this, but stated that, though China might be the largest trading country, especially in Asia, the United States should continue to write the rules of trade, even for trade in Asia, for the twenty-first century. But in practice, China was already writing the rules, with trade agreements with fifteen countries in Asia alone.

Citizens in the advanced countries may well ask themselves, how will these changes affect them? They didn't fare so well even when the rules were made by the United States and other advanced countries. In some ways, matters could get worse: some worry that China will be just as domineering, just as much devoted to pursuing its "corporate" interests as the old colonial powers, but perhaps even less concerned with environmental and labor standards than the West. The Western rules of globalization at least made concessions here and there to concerns about the environment and labor. The worry is that in the future, even less attention will be paid to these important dimensions of globalization. In Western democracies, civil society has played some role in tempering commercialism, though far less than one would have hoped.

The prospects of America's workers, though, could get better as the developing countries and emerging markets grow. They will want to buy more services from the United States and Europe—send their children to their schools, send their sick (who can afford it) to their hospitals, and take vacations in their cities and national parks. The growth of the emerging markets has also led to their wages increasing faster than those in the advanced countries, so the relative advantage they have in labor costs will diminish. Moreover, improvements in technology have meant that cheap unskilled labor is less important than it was before. This doesn't, of course, solve the problem of those in the advanced countries without skills.

The ultimate irony of globalization, as it has been managed, is that the New Discontents that I have discussed in this part of the book come from the advanced countries—the countries that had written the rules for their own benefit. But as I have repeatedly explained, the rules weren't written on behalf of the ordinary citizens in the United States or other advanced countries, but on behalf of large corporate and financial interests. The adverse effects on workers may not even have been just collateral damage—weakening workers' bargaining power, and thus their wages, was an anticipated part of what would happen and from the perspective of the 1 percent, it was one of the benefits of globalization. When I wrote *GAID* fifteen years ago, most citizens in America had not realized this. In Europe, many had, which helps explain how the book became a best seller in so many countries outside the United States. Indeed, on issues of trade, there was (and is) in France and many other countries an anti-globalization movement whose central message was that another world was possible. We could restructure our economy and our society in ways consonant with our values, with social justice, with protecting the environment, and even with increasing standards of living.

The big change is that now, fifteen years on, these anti-globalists have been joined by the New Discontents in the United States and other advanced countries. There is a big difference, though, between the "New" Discontents and the Old. Many of the New Discontents are nativists, who emphasize the distinction between *us* and *them*. They are not concerned with social justice or the environment.

Don't be fooled by the frequent use of slogans like "free but fair trade," suggesting that all they want is a fair agreement. I have emphasized that in the ordinary use of language, the trade agreements were not fair, but were rather tilted markedly toward the interests of the United States and other advanced countries. The New Discontents in America want an even more tilted managed trade regime.

For now, the New Discontents have put their faith in the Trump administration, dominated by plutocrats and those from global finance, to rewrite the rules of globalization.

I have on several occasions written that if the 1 percent pursues its self-interest too narrowly, there is a risk of a backlash. For the moment in the United States, under Trump, the 1 percent is—in the short term—winning again, through tax cuts and deregulation which benefit them at the expense of the rest of society. But when the New Discontents realize that they have been betrayed, that they are in fact even worse off with Trump policies, they may turn to even more extreme leaders. The growing inequalities are simply not politically or socially sustainable. And besides, the wealth of the 1 percent depends on a healthy economy—and as the IMF keeps reminding the world, economies with high inequality perform more poorly.[26] At the very least, the selfish strategy which ignores the discontent, or even worse, takes advantage of it for its own purposes, is extraordinarily risky, even for the 1 percent.[27]

If the 1 percent must pursue its own self-interest, it should at least be an enlightened self-interest.[28] And an enlightened self-interest means that not only must globalization be tempered, but domestic policies must also be formulated in ways that ensure a modicum of social protection for those left behind and a modicum of shared prosperity as the economy moves forward.

The themes I stressed in *GAID* seem as relevant today as when I wrote the book fifteen years ago—in spite of all the changes in globalization and in our understanding of it. As we've become more interdependent, there is greater need for us to work together. And in democratic societies, that means working together *democratically*.

Governance matters, because economics and politics can't really be separated. Poor governance leads to poor rules. As I've repeatedly written, markets don't exist in a vacuum. They have to be structured. The rules of the game matter. And who writes the rules drives what the rules are.

There is now more widespread awareness of the deficiencies in our system of global governance. Global governance had been moving in the direction that *GAID* suggested would be desirable. In the afterword, I describe the enormous changes that have occurred, for instance, at the IMF. But now globalization's New Discontents—those in the developed countries—have arrived. These New Discontents are different from the old ones. The old discontents, those in the developing world, could identify the precise aspects of globalization that had harmed them and to which they objected: the inequities, the hypocrisies, the inconsistencies with the insights of modern economic theory, the sources of the democratic deficits—by now, this is well-known territory.

The New Discontents in the advanced countries, as we have seen, observe the growth of globalization and the decline in their well-being. There must be, in their simplistic view, a *causal* relationship; and if so, reversing globalization must lead to an increase in the well-being of those middle-income workers in Europe and America. This "reasoning" has been seized upon by the populists (perhaps more accurately described as the extremists and nativists) of the right. I've explained why this is nonsense, and why the kind of deglobalization that these populists argue for not only won't work, but will make many of those who have been injured by globalization worse off.

I've outlined a set of principles that should guide the reform of globalization. But without reforms *within* the countries themselves—including the set of policies that I've laid out here—there is no reform of globalization that will succeed in restoring prosperity to those that have been left behind.

This is true for both developed and developing countries. The impacts of globalization have to be seen in the context of domestic policies. With the right domestic policies, focusing on shared prosperity, globalization can lead to the kind of sustainable and equitable development to which countries aspire.

Part II

Globalization and Its Discontents

(2002 edition)

CHAPTER 5

THE PROMISE
OF GLOBAL
INSTITUTIONS

INTERNATIONAL BUREAUCRATS—THE faceless symbols of the world economic order—are under attack everywhere. Formerly uneventful meetings of obscure technocrats discussing mundane subjects such as concessional loans and trade quotas have now become the scene of raging street battles and huge demonstrations. The protests at the Seattle meeting of the World Trade Organization in 1999 were a shock. Since then, the movement has grown stronger and the fury has spread. Virtually every major meeting of the International Monetary Fund, the World Bank, and the World Trade Organization is now the scene of conflict and turmoil. The death of a protestor in Genoa in 2001 was just the beginning of what may be many more casualties in the war against globalization.

Riots and protests against the policies of and actions by institutions of globalization are hardly new. For decades, people in the developing world have rioted when the austerity programs imposed on their countries proved to be too harsh, but their protests were largely unheard in the West. What is new is the wave of protests in the developed countries.

It used to be that subjects such as structural adjustment loans (the programs that were designed to help countries adjust to and weather crises) and banana quotas (the limits that some European countries impose on the importing of bananas from countries other than their former colonies) were of interest to only a few. Now sixteen-year-old kids from the suburbs have strong opinions on such esoteric treaties as GATT (the General Agreement on Tariffs and Trade) and NAFTA (the North American Free Trade Area, the agreement signed in 1992 between Mexico, United States, and Canada that allows for the freer movement of goods, services, and investment—but not people—among those countries). These protests have provoked an enormous amount of soul-searching from those in power. Even conservative politicians such as France's president, Jacques Chirac, have expressed concern that globalization is not making life better for those most in need of its promised benefits.[1] It is clear to almost everyone that something has gone horribly wrong. Almost overnight, globalization has become the most pressing issue of our time, something debated from boardrooms to op-ed pages and in schools all over the world.

WHY HAS GLOBALIZATION—a force that has brought so much good—become so controversial? Opening up to international trade has helped many countries grow far more quickly than they would otherwise have done. International trade helps economic development when a country's exports drive its economic growth. Export-led growth was the centerpiece of the industrial policy that enriched much of Asia and left millions of people there far better off. Because of globalization many people in the world now live longer than before and their standard of living is far better. People in the West may regard low-paying jobs at Nike as exploitation, but for many people in the developing world, working in a factory is a far better option than staying down on the farm and growing rice.

Globalization has reduced the sense of isolation felt in much of the developing world and has given many people in the developing countries access to knowledge well beyond the reach of even the wealthiest in any country a century ago. The anti-globalization protests themselves are a result of this connectedness. Links between activists in different parts of the world, particularly those links forged through Internet communication, brought about the pressure that resulted in the international landmines treaty—despite the opposition of many powerful governments. Signed by 121 countries as of 1997, it reduces the likelihood that children and other innocent victims will be maimed by mines. Similar, well-orchestrated public pressure forced the international community to forgive the debts of some of the poorest countries. Even when there are negative sides to globalization, there are often benefits. Opening up the Jamaican milk market to U.S. imports in 1992 may have hurt local dairy farmers but it also meant poor children could get milk more cheaply. New foreign firms may hurt protected state-owned enterprises but they can also lead to the introduction of new technologies, access to new markets, and the creation of new industries.

Foreign aid, another aspect of the globalized world, for all its faults still has brought benefits to millions, often in ways that have almost gone unnoticed: guerrillas in the Philippines were provided jobs by a World Bank–financed project as they laid down their arms; irrigation projects have more than doubled the incomes of farmers lucky enough to get water; education projects have brought literacy to the rural areas; in a few countries AIDS projects have helped contain the spread of this deadly disease.

Those who vilify globalization too often overlook its benefits. But the proponents of globalization have been, if anything, even more unbalanced. To them, globalization (which typically is associated with accepting triumphant capitalism, American style) *is* progress; developing countries must accept it, if they are to grow and to fight poverty effectively. But to many in the developing world, globalization has not brought the promised economic benefits.

A growing divide between the haves and the have-nots has left increasing numbers in the Third World in dire poverty, living on less than a dollar a day. Despite repeated promises of poverty reduction made over the last decade of the twentieth century, the actual number of people living in poverty has actually increased by almost 100 million.[2]

This occurred at the same time that total world income increased by an average of 2.5 percent annually.

In Africa, the high aspirations following colonial independence have been largely unfulfilled. Instead, the continent plunges deeper into misery, as incomes fall and standards of living decline. The hard-won improvements in life expectancy gained in the past few decades have begun to reverse. While the scourge of AIDS is at the center of this decline, poverty is also a killer. Even countries that have abandoned African socialism, managed to install reasonably honest governments, balanced their budgets, and kept inflation down find that they simply cannot attract private investors. Without this investment, they cannot have sustainable growth.

If globalization has not succeeded in reducing poverty, neither has it succeeded in ensuring stability. Crises in Asia and in Latin America have threatened the economies and the stability of all developing countries. There are fears of financial contagion spreading around the world, that the collapse of one emerging market currency will mean that others fall as well. For a while, in 1997 and 1998, the Asian crisis appeared to pose a threat to the entire world economy.

Globalization and the introduction of a market economy has not produced the promised results in Russia and most of the other economies making the transition from communism to the market. These countries were told by the West that the new economic system would bring them unprecedented prosperity. Instead, it brought unprecedented poverty: in many respects, for most of the people, the market economy proved even worse than their Communist leaders had predicted. The contrast between Russia's transition, as engineered by the international economic institutions, and that of China, designed by itself, could not be greater: While in 1990 China's gross domestic product (GDP) was 60 percent that of Russia, by the end of the decade the numbers had been reversed. While Russia saw an unprecedented increase in poverty, China saw an unprecedented decrease.

The critics of globalization accuse Western countries of hypocrisy, and the critics are right. The Western countries have pushed poor countries to eliminate trade barriers, but kept up their own barriers, preventing developing countries from exporting their agricultural products and so depriving them of desperately needed export income. The

United States was, of course, one of the prime culprits, and this was an issue about which I felt intensely. When I was chairman of the Council of Economic Advisers, I fought hard against this hypocrisy, as had my predecessors at the Council from both parties. It not only hurt the developing countries; it also cost Americans billions of dollars, both as consumers, in the higher prices they paid, and as taxpayers, to finance the huge agricultural subsidies. The struggles were, all too often, less than fully successful. Special commercial and financial interests prevailed—and when I moved over to the World Bank, I saw the consequences to the developing countries all too clearly.

But even when not guilty of hypocrisy, the West has driven the globalization agenda, ensuring that it garners a disproportionate share of the benefits, at the expense of the developing world. It was not just that the more advanced industrial countries declined to open up their markets to the goods of the developing countries—for instance, keeping their quotas on a multitude of goods from textiles to sugar—while insisting that those countries open up their markets to the goods of the wealthier countries; it was not just that the more advanced industrial countries continued to subsidize agriculture, making it difficult for the developing countries to compete, while insisting that the developing countries eliminate their subsidies on industrial goods. Looking at the "terms of trade"—the prices which developed and less developed countries get for the products they produce—after the last trade agreement in 1995 (the eighth), the *net* effect was to lower the prices some of the poorest countries in the world received relative to what they paid for their imports.* The result was that some of the poorest countries in the world were actually made worse off.

Western banks benefited from the loosening of capital market controls in Latin America and Asia, but those regions suffered when inflows of speculative hot money (money that comes into and out of

---

* This eighth agreement was the result of negotiations called the *Uruguay Round* because the negotiations began in 1986 in Punta del Este, Uruguay. The round was concluded in Marrakech on December 15, 1993, when 117 countries joined in this trade liberalization agreement. The agreement was finally signed for the United States by President Clinton on December 8, 1994. The World Trade Organization came into formal effect on January 1, 1995, and over 100 nations had signed on by July. One provision of the agreement entailed converting the GATT into the WTO.

a country, often overnight, often little more than betting on whether a currency is going to appreciate or depreciate) that had poured into countries suddenly reversed. The abrupt outflow of money left behind collapsed currencies, weakened banking systems and wrecked economies. The Uruguay Round also strengthened intellectual property rights. American and other Western drug companies could now stop drug companies in India and Brazil from "stealing" their intellectual property. But these drug companies in the developing world were making these life-saving drugs available to their citizens at a fraction of the price at which the drugs were sold by the Western drug companies. There were thus two sides to the decisions made in the Uruguay Round. Profits of the Western drug companies would go up. Advocates said this would provide them more incentive to innovate; but the increased profits from sales in the developing world were small, since few could afford the drugs, and hence the incentive effect, at best, might be limited. The other side was that thousands were effectively condemned to death, because governments and individuals in developing countries could no longer pay the high prices demanded. In the case of AIDS, the international outrage was so great that the drug companies had to back down, eventually agreeing to lower their prices, to sell the drugs at cost in late 2001. But the underlying problems—the fact that the intellectual property regime established under the Uruguay Round was not balanced, that it overwhelmingly reflected the interests and perspectives of the producers, as opposed to the users, whether in developed or developing countries—remain.

Not only in trade liberalization but in every other aspect of globalization even seemingly well-intentioned efforts have often backfired. When projects, whether agriculture or infrastructure, recommended by the West, designed with the advice of Western advisers, and financed by the World Bank or others have failed, unless there is some form of debt forgiveness, the poor people in the developing world still must repay the loans.

If, in too many instances, the benefits of globalization have been less than its advocates claim, the price paid has been greater, as the environment has been destroyed, as political processes have been corrupted, and as the rapid pace of change has not allowed countries time for cultural adaptation. The crises that have brought in their wake massive unemployment have, in turn, been followed by longer-term problems of social dissolution—from urban violence in Latin America to ethnic conflicts in other parts of the world, such as Indonesia.

These problems are hardly new—but the increasingly vehement worldwide reaction against the policies that drive globalization is a significant change. For decades, the cries of the poor in Africa and in developing countries in other parts of the world have been largely unheard in the West. Those who labored in the developing countries knew something was wrong when they saw financial crises becoming more commonplace and little progress in reducing the numbers of poor people. But they had no way to change the rules or to influence the international financial institutions that wrote them. Those who valued democratic processes saw how "conditionality"—the conditions that international lenders imposed in return for their assistance—undermined national sovereignty. But until the protestors came along there was little hope for change and no outlets for complaint. *Some* of the protestors went to excesses; *some* of the protestors were arguing for higher protectionist barriers against the developing countries, which would have made their plight even worse. But despite these problems, it is the trade unionists, students, environmentalists—ordinary citizens—marching in the streets of Prague, Seattle, Washington, and Genoa who have put the need for reform on the agenda of the developed world.

Protestors see globalization in a very different light than the treasury secretary of the United States, or the finance and trade ministers of most of the advanced industrial countries. The differences in views are so great that one wonders, are the protestors and the policy makers talking about the same phenomena? Are they looking at the same data? Are the visions of those in power so clouded by special and particular interests?

What is this phenomenon of globalization that has been subject, at the same time, to such vilification and such praise? Fundamentally, it is the closer integration of the countries and peoples of the world which has been brought about by the enormous reduction of costs of transportation and communication, and the breaking down of artificial barriers to the flows of goods, services, capital, knowledge, and (to a lesser extent) people across borders. Globalization has been accompanied by the creation of new institutions that have joined with existing ones to work across borders. In the arena of international civil society, new groups, like the Jubilee movement pushing for debt reduction for the poorest countries, have joined long-established organizations like the International Red Cross. Globalization is powerfully driven by international corporations, which move not only capital and goods across borders but also technology. Globalization has also led to renewed attention to long-established international *intergovernmental* institutions: the United Nations, which attempts to maintain peace; the International Labor Organization (ILO), originally created in 1919, which promotes its agenda around the world under its slogan "decent work"; and the World Health Organization (WHO), which has been especially concerned with improving health conditions in the developing world.

Many, perhaps most, of these aspects of globalization have been welcomed everywhere. No one wants to see their child die, when knowledge and medicines are available somewhere else in the world. It is the more narrowly defined *economic* aspects of globalization that have been the subject of controversy, and the international institutions that have written the rules, which mandate or push things like liberalization of capital markets (the elimination of the rules and regulations in many developing countries that are designed to stabilize the flows of volatile money into and out of the country).

To understand what went wrong, it's important to look at the three main institutions that govern globalization: the IMF, the World Bank, and the WTO. There are, in addition, a host of other institutions that play a role in the international economic system—a number of regional banks, smaller and younger sisters to the World Bank, and a large number of UN organizations, such as the UN Development Program or the UN Conference on Trade and Development (UNCTAD). These organizations often have views that are markedly different from the IMF and the World Bank. The ILO, for example, worries that the IMF pays too little attention to workers' rights, while the Asian Development Bank argues for "competitive pluralism," whereby developing countries will be provided with alternative views of development strategies, including the "Asian model"—in which governments, while relying on markets, have taken an active role in creating, shaping, and guiding markets, including promoting new technologies, and in which firms take considerable responsibility for the social welfare of their employees—which the Asian Development Bank sees as distinctly different from the American model pushed by the Washington-based institutions.

In this book, I focus mostly on the IMF and the World Bank, largely because they have been at the center of the major economic issues of the last two decades, including the financial crises and the transition of the former Communist countries to market economies. The IMF and the World Bank both originated in World War II as a result of the UN Monetary and Financial Conference at Bretton Woods, New Hampshire, in July 1944, part of a concerted effort to finance the rebuilding of Europe after the devastation of World War II and to save the world from future economic depressions. The proper name of the World Bank—the International Bank for Reconstruction and Development—reflects its original mission; the last part, "Development," was added almost as an afterthought. At the time, most of the countries in the developing world were still colonies, and what meager economic development efforts could or would be undertaken were considered the responsibility of their European masters.

The more difficult task of ensuring global economic stability was assigned to the IMF. Those who convened at Bretton Woods had the global depression of the 1930s very much on their minds. Almost three-quarters of a century ago, capitalism faced its most severe crisis to date. The Great Depression enveloped the whole world and led to unprecedented increases in unemployment. At the worst point, a quarter of America's workforce was unemployed. The British economist John Maynard Keynes, who would later be a key participant at Bretton Woods, put forward a simple explanation, and a correspondingly simple set of prescriptions: lack of sufficient aggregate demand explained economic downturns; government policies could help stimulate aggregate demand. In cases where monetary policy is ineffective, governments could rely on fiscal policies, either by increasing expenditures or cutting taxes. While the models underlying Keynes's analysis have subsequently been criticized and refined, bringing a deeper understanding of why market forces do not work quickly to adjust the economy to full employment, the basic lessons remain valid.

The International Monetary Fund was charged with preventing another global depression. It would do this by putting international pressure on countries that were not doing their fair share to maintain global aggregate demand, by allowing their own economies to go into a slump. When necessary it would also provide liquidity in the form of loans to those countries facing an economic downturn and unable to stimulate aggregate demand with their own resources.

In its original conception, then, the IMF was based on a recognition that markets often did not work well—that they could result in massive unemployment and might fail to make needed funds available to countries to help them restore their economies. The IMF was founded on the belief that there was a need for *collective action at the global level* for economic stability, just as the United Nations had been founded on the belief that there was a need for collective action at the global level for political stability. The IMF is a *public* institution, established with money provided by taxpayers around the world. This is important to remember because it does not report directly to either the citizens who finance it or those whose lives it affects. Rather, it reports to the ministries of finance and the central banks of the governments of the world. They assert their control through a complicated voting arrangement based largely on the economic power of the countries at the end of World War II. There have been some minor adjustments since, but the major developed countries run the show, with only one country, the United States, having effective veto. (In this sense, it is similar to the UN, where a historical anachronism determines who holds the veto—the victorious powers of World War II—but at least there the veto power is shared among five countries.)

Over the years since its inception, the IMF has changed markedly. Founded on the belief that markets often worked badly, it now champions market supremacy with ideological fervor. Founded on the belief that there is a need for international pressure on countries to have more expansionary economic policies—such as increasing expenditures, reducing taxes, or lowering interest rates to stimulate the economy— today the IMF typically provides funds only if countries engage in policies like cutting deficits, raising taxes, or raising interest rates that lead to a contraction of the economy. Keynes would be rolling over in his grave were he to see what has happened to his child.

The most dramatic change in these institutions occurred in the

1980s, the era when Ronald Reagan and Margaret Thatcher preached free-market ideology in the United States and the United Kingdom. The IMF and the World Bank became the new missionary institutions, through which these ideas were pushed on the reluctant poor countries that often badly needed their loans and grants. The ministries of finance in poor countries were willing to become converts, if necessary, to obtain the funds, though the vast majority of government officials, and, more to the point, people in these countries often remained skeptical. In the early 1980s, a purge occurred inside the World Bank, in its research department, which guided the Bank's thinking and direction. Hollis Chenery, one of America's most distinguished development economists, a professor at Harvard who had made fundamental contributions to research in the economics of development and other areas as well, had been Robert McNamara's confidant and adviser. McNamara had been appointed president of the World Bank in 1968. Touched by the poverty that he saw throughout the Third World, McNamara had redirected the Bank's effort at its elimination, and Chenery assembled a first-class group of economists from around the world to work with him. But with the changing of the guard came a new president in 1981, William Clausen, and a new chief economist, Ann Krueger, an international trade specialist, best known for her work on "rent seeking"—how special interests use tariffs and other protectionist measures to increase their incomes at the expense of others. While Chenery and his team had focused on how markets failed in developing countries and what governments could do to improve markets and reduce poverty, Krueger saw government as the problem. Free markets were the solution to the problems of developing countries. In the new ideological fervor, many of the first-rate economists that Chenery had assembled left.

Although the missions of the two institutions remained distinct, it was at this time that their activities became increasingly intertwined. In the 1980s, the Bank went beyond just lending for projects (like roads and dams) to providing broad-based support, in the form of *structural adjustment loans;* but it did this only when the IMF gave its approval—and with that approval came IMF-imposed conditions on the country. The IMF was supposed to focus on crises; but developing countries were always in need of help, so the IMF became a permanent part of life in most of the developing world.

The fall of the Berlin Wall provided a new arena for the IMF: managing the transition to a market economy in the former Soviet Union and the Communist bloc countries in Europe. More recently, as the crises have gotten bigger, and even the deep coffers of the IMF seemed insufficient, the World Bank was called in to provide tens of billions of dollars of emergency support, but strictly as a junior partner, with the guidelines of the programs dictated by the IMF. In principle, there was a division of labor. The IMF was supposed to limit itself to matters of *macroeconomics* in dealing with a country, to the government's budget deficit, its monetary policy, its inflation, its trade deficit, its borrowing from abroad; and the World Bank was supposed to be in charge of *structural issues*—what the country's government spent money on, the country's financial institutions, its labor markets, its trade policies. But the IMF took a rather imperialistic view of the matter: since almost any structural issue could affect the overall performance of the economy, and hence the government's budget or the trade deficit, it viewed almost everything as falling within its domain. It often got impatient with the World Bank, where even in the years when free-market ideology reigned supreme there were frequent controversies about what policies would best suit the conditions of the country. The IMF had the answers (basically, the same ones for every country), didn't see the need for all this discussion, and, while the World Bank debated what should be done, saw itself as stepping into the vacuum to provide the answers.

The two institutions could have provided countries with alternative perspectives on some of the challenges of development and transition, and in doing so they might have strengthened democratic processes. But they were both driven by the collective will of the G-7 (the governments of the seven most important advanced industrial countries),*

---

* These are the United States, Japan, Germany, Canada, Italy, France, and the UK. Today, the G-7 typically meets together with Russia (the G-8). The seven countries are no longer the seven largest economies in the world. Membership in the G-7, like permanent membership in the UN Security Council, is partly a matter of historical accident.

and especially their finance ministers and treasury secretaries, and too often, the last thing they wanted was a lively democratic debate about alternative strategies.

A half century after its founding, it is clear that the IMF has failed in its mission. It has not done what it was supposed to do—provide funds for countries facing an economic downturn, to enable the country to restore itself to close to full employment. In spite of the fact that our understanding of economic processes has increased enormously during the last fifty years, crises around the world have been more frequent and (with the exception of the Great Depression) deeper. By some reckonings, close to a hundred countries have faced crises.[3] Every major emerging market that liberalized its capital market has had at least one crisis. But this is not just an unfortunate streak of bad luck. Many of the policies that the IMF pushed, in particular, premature capital market liberalization, have contributed to global instability. And once a country was in crisis, IMF funds and programs not only failed to stabilize the situation but in many cases actually made matters worse, especially for the poor. The IMF failed in its original mission of promoting global stability; it has also been no more successful in the new missions that it has undertaken, such as guiding the transition of countries from communism to a market economy.

The Bretton Woods agreement had called for a third international economic organization—a World Trade Organization to govern international trade relations, a job similar to the IMF's governing of international financial relations. Beggar-thy-neighbor trade policies, in which countries raised tariffs to maintain their own economies but at the expense of their neighbors, were largely blamed for the spread of the depression and its depth. An international organization was required not just to prevent a recurrence but to encourage the free flow of goods and services. Although the General Agreement on Tariffs and Trade (GATT) did succeed in lowering tariffs enormously, it was difficult to reach the final accord; it was not until 1995, a half century after the end of the war and two-thirds of a century after the Great Depression, that the World Trade Organization came into being. But the WTO is markedly different from the other two organizations. It does not set rules itself; rather, it provides a forum in which trade negotiations go on and it ensures that its agreements are lived up to.

The ideas and intentions behind the creation of the international economic institutions were good ones, yet they gradually evolved over the years to become something very different. The Keynesian orientation of the IMF, which emphasized market failures and the role for government in job creation, was replaced by the free-market mantra of the 1980s, part of a new "Washington Consensus"—a consensus between the IMF, the World Bank, and the U.S. Treasury about the "right" policies for developing countries—that signaled a radically different approach to economic development and stabilization.

Many of the ideas incorporated in the consensus were developed in response to the problems in Latin America, where governments had let budgets get out of control while loose monetary policies had led to rampant inflation. A burst of growth in some of that region's countries in the decades immediately after World War II had not been sustained, allegedly because of excessive state intervention in the economy. The ideas that were developed to cope with problems arguably specific to Latin American countries, and which I will outline later in the book, were subsequently deemed to be applicable to countries around the world. In some cases, there was simply no evidence that they even worked for Latin America. In others, while they may have been effective in Latin America, the circumstances in other countries—poor developing countries in Africa or the economies in transition—were so different as to make them inappropriate.

However, most of the advanced industrial countries—including the United States and Japan—had built up their economies by wisely and selectively protecting some of their industries until they were strong enough to compete with foreign companies. While blanket protectionism has often not worked for countries that have tried it, neither has rapid trade liberalization. Forcing a developing country to open itself up to imported products that would compete with those produced by certain of its industries, industries that were dangerously vulnerable to competition from much stronger counterpart industries in other countries, can have disastrous consequences—socially and economically. Jobs have systematically been destroyed—poor farmers in developing countries simply couldn't compete with the highly subsidized goods from Europe and America—before the countries' industrial and agricultural sectors were able to grow strong and create new jobs. Even worse, the IMF's insistence on developing countries maintaining tight monetary policies has led to interest rates that would make job creation impossible even in the best of circumstances. And because trade liberalization occurred before safety nets were put into place, those who lost their jobs were forced into poverty. Liberalization has thus, too often, not been followed by the promised growth, but by increased misery. And even those who have not lost their jobs have been hit by a heightened sense of insecurity.

Capital controls are another example: European countries banned the free flow of capital until the 1970s. Some might say it's not fair to insist that developing countries with a barely functioning bank system risk opening their markets. But putting aside such notions of fairness, it's bad economics; the influx of hot money into and out of the country that so frequently follows after capital market liberalization leaves havoc in its wake. Small developing countries are like small boats. Rapid capital market liberalization, in the manner pushed by the IMF, amounted to setting them off on a voyage on a rough sea, before the holes in their hulls have been repaired, before the captain has received training, before life vests have been put on board. Even in the best of circumstances, there was a high likelihood that they would be overturned when they were hit broadside by a big wave.

Even if the IMF had subscribed to "mistaken" economic theories, it might not have mattered if its domain of activity had been limited to Europe, the United States, and other advanced industrialized countries that can fend for themselves. But the end of colonialism and communism has given the international financial institutions the opportunity to expand greatly their original mandates. Today* these institutions have become dominant players in the world economy. Not only countries seeking their help but also those seeking their "seal of approval" so that they can better access international capital markets must follow their economic prescriptions, prescriptions which reflect their free-market ideologies and theories.

The result for many people has been poverty and for many countries social and political chaos. The IMF has made mistakes in all the areas it has been involved in: development, crisis management, and in countries making the transition from communism to capitalism. Structural adjustment programs did not bring sustained growth even

---

* Throughout Part II, "today" and "currently" refer to *GAID*'s publishing date (2002).

to those, like Bolivia, that adhered to its strictures; in many countries, excessive austerity stifled growth; successful economic programs require extreme care in *sequencing*—the order in which reforms occur—and pacing. If, for instance, markets are opened up for competition too rapidly, before strong financial institutions are established, then jobs will be destroyed faster than new jobs are created. In many countries, mistakes in sequencing and pacing led to rising unemployment and increased poverty.[4] In the 1997 Asian crisis, IMF policies exacerbated the downturns in Indonesia and Thailand. Free market reforms in Latin America have had one or two successes—Chile is repeatedly cited—but much of the rest of the continent has still to make up for the lost decade of growth following the so-called successful IMF bailouts of the early 1980s, and many today have persistently high rates of unemployment—in Argentina, for instance, at double-digit levels since 1995—even as inflation has been brought down. The collapse in Argentina in 2001 is one of the most recent of a series of failures over the past few years. Given the high unemployment rate for almost seven years, the wonder is not that the citizens eventually rioted, but that they suffered quietly so much for so long. Even those countries that have experienced some limited growth have seen the benefits accrue to the well-off, and especially the *very* well-off—the top 10 percent—while poverty has remained high, and in some cases the income of those at the bottom has even fallen.

Underlying the problems of the IMF and the other international economic institutions is the problem of governance: who decides what they do. The institutions are dominated not just by the wealthiest industrial countries but by commercial and financial interests in those countries, and the policies of the institutions naturally reflect this. The choice of heads for these institutions symbolizes the institutions' problem, and too often has contributed to their dysfunction. While almost all of the activities of the IMF and the World Bank today are in the developing world (certainly, all of their lending), they are led by representatives from the industrialized nations. (By custom or tacit agreement the head of the IMF is always a European, that of the World Bank an American.) They are chosen behind closed doors, and it has never even been viewed as a prerequisite that the head should have any experience in the developing world. The institutions are not representative of the nations they serve.

The problems also arise from who *speaks* for each country. At the IMF, it is the finance ministers and the central bank governors. At the WTO, it is the trade ministers. Each of these ministers is closely aligned with particular constituencies *within* their countries. The trade ministries reflect the concerns of the business community—both exporters who want to see new markets opened up for their products and producers of goods who fear competition from new imports. These constituencies, of course, want to maintain as many barriers to trade as they can and keep whatever subsidies they can persuade Congress (or their parliament) to give them. The fact that the trade barriers raise the prices consumers pay or that the subsidies impose burdens on taxpayers is of less concern than the profits of the producers—and environmental and labor issues are of even less concern, other than as obstacles that have to be overcome. The finance ministers and central bank governors typically are closely tied to the financial community; they come from financial firms, and after their period of government service, that is where they return. Robert Rubin, the treasury secretary during much of the period described in this book, came from the largest investment bank, Goldman Sachs, and returned to the firm, Citigroup, that controlled the largest commercial bank, Citibank. The number-two person at the IMF during this period, Stan Fischer, went straight from the IMF to Citigroup. These individuals naturally see the world through the eyes of the financial community. The decisions of any institution naturally reflect the perspectives and interests of those who make the decisions; not surprisingly, as we shall see repeatedly in the following chapters, the policies of the international economic institutions are all too often closely aligned with the commercial and financial interests of those in the advanced industrial countries.

For the peasants in developing countries who toil to pay off their countries' IMF debts or the businessmen who suffer from higher value-added taxes upon the insistence of the IMF, the current system run by the IMF is one of taxation without representation. Disillusion with the international system of globalization under the aegis of the IMF grows as the poor in Indonesia, Morocco, or Papua New Guinea have fuel and food subsidies cut, as those in Thailand see AIDS increase as a result of IMF-forced cutbacks in health expenditures, and as families in many developing countries, having to pay for their children's education under so-called cost recovery programs, make the painful choice not to send their daughters to school.

Left with no alternatives, no way to express their concern, to press for change, people riot. The streets, of course, are not the place where issues are discussed, policies formulated, or compromises forged. But the protests have made government officials around the world think about alternatives to these Washington Consensus policies as the one and true way for growth and development. It has become increasingly clear not to just ordinary citizens but to policy makers as well, and not just those in the developing countries but those in the developed countries as well, that globalization as it has been practiced has not lived up to what its advocates promised it would accomplish—or to what it can and should do. In some cases it has not even resulted in growth, but when it has, it has not brought benefits to all; the net effect of the policies set by the Washington Consensus has all too often been to benefit the few at the expense of the many, the well-off at the expense of the poor. In many cases commercial interests and values have superseded concern for the environment, democracy, human rights, and social justice.

Globalization itself is neither good nor bad. It has the *power* to do enormous good, and for the countries of East Asia, who have embraced globalization *under their own terms*, at their own pace, it has been an enormous benefit, in spite of the setback of the 1997 crisis. But in much of the world it has not brought comparable benefits.

The experience of the United States during the nineteenth century makes a good parallel for today's globalization—and the contrast helps illustrate the successes of the past and today's failures. At that earlier time, when transportation and communication costs fell and previously local markets expanded, new national economies formed, and with these new national economies came national companies, doing business throughout the country. But the markets were not left to develop willy-nilly on their own; government played a vital role in shaping the evolution of the economy. The U.S. government obtained wide economic latitude when the courts broadly interpreted the constitutional provision that allows the federal government to regulate interstate commerce. The federal government began to regulate the financial system, set minimum wages and working conditions, and eventually provided unemployment and welfare systems to deal with the problems posed by a market system. The federal government also promoted some industries (the first telegraph line, for example, was laid by the federal government between Baltimore and Washington in 1842) and encouraged others, like agriculture, not just helping set up universities to do research but providing extension services to train farmers in the new technologies. The federal government played a central role not only in promoting American growth. Even if it did not engage in the kinds of active redistribution policies, at least it had programs whose benefits were widely shared—not just those that extended education and improved agricultural productivity, but also land grants that provided a minimum opportunity for all Americans.

Today, with the continuing decline in transportation and communication costs, and the reduction of man-made barriers to the flow of goods, services, and capital (though there remain serious barriers to the free flow of labor), we have a process of "globalization" analogous to the earlier processes in which national economies were formed. Unfortunately, we have no world government, accountable to the people of every country, to oversee the globalization process in a fashion comparable to the way national governments guided the nationalization process. Instead, we have a system that might be called *global governance without global government*, one in which a few institutions—the World Bank, the IMF, the WTO—and a few players—the finance, commerce, and trade ministries, closely linked to certain financial and commercial interests—dominate the scene, but in which many of those affected by their decisions are left almost voiceless. It's time to change some of the rules governing the international economic order, to think once again about how decisions get made at the international level—and in whose interests—and to place less emphasis on ideology and to look more at what works. It is crucial that the successful development we have seen in East Asia be achieved elsewhere. There is an enormous cost to continuing global instability. Globalization can be reshaped, and when it is, when it is properly, fairly run, with all countries having a voice in policies affecting them, there is a possibility that it will help create a new global economy in which growth is not only more sustainable and less volatile but the fruits of this growth are more equitably shared.

CHAPTER 6

BROKEN PROMISES

O N   MY   FIRST   day, February 13, 1997, as chief economist and senior vice president of the World Bank, as I walked into its gigantic, modern, gleaming main building on 19th Street in Washington, DC, the institution's motto was the first thing that caught my eye: *Our dream is a world without poverty*. In the center of the thirteen-story atrium there is a statue of a young boy leading an old blind man, a memorial to the eradication of river blindness (*onchocerciasis*). Before the World Bank, the World Health Organization, and others pooled their efforts, thousands were blinded annually in Africa from this preventable disease. Across the street stands another gleaming monument to public wealth, the headquarters of the International Monetary Fund. The marble atrium inside, graced with abundant flora, serves to remind visiting finance ministers from countries around the world that the IMF represents the centers of wealth and power.

These two institutions, often confused in the public mind, present marked contrasts that underline the differences in their cultures, styles, and missions: one is devoted to eradicating poverty, one to maintaining global stability. While both have teams of economists flying into developing countries for three-week missions, the World Bank has worked hard to make sure that a substantial fraction of its staff live permanently in the country they are trying to assist; the IMF generally has only a single "resident representative," whose powers are limited. IMF programs are typically dictated from Washington, and shaped by the short missions during which its staff members pore over numbers in the finance ministries and central banks and make themselves comfortable in five-star hotels in the capitals. There is more than symbolism in this difference: one cannot come to learn about, and love, a nation unless one gets out to the countryside. One should not see unemployment as just a statistic, an economic "body count," the unintended casualties in the fight against inflation or to ensure that Western banks get repaid. The unemployed are people, with families, whose lives are affected—sometimes devastated—by the economic policies that outsiders recommend, and, in the case of the IMF, effectively impose. Modern high-tech warfare is designed to remove physical contact: dropping bombs from 50,000 feet ensures that one does not "feel" what one does. Modern economic management is similar: from one's luxury hotel, one can callously impose policies about which one would think twice if one knew the people whose lives one was destroying.

Statistics bear out what those who travel outside the capital see in the villages of Africa, Nepal, Mindanao, or Ethiopia; the gap between the poor and the rich has been growing, and even the number in absolutely poverty—living on less than a dollar a day—has increased. Even where river blindness has been eliminated, poverty endures—this despite all the good intentions and promises made by the developed nations to the developing nations, most of which were once the colonial possessions of the developed nations.

Mind-sets are not changed overnight, and this is as true in the developed as in the developing countries. Giving developing countries their freedom (generally after little preparation for autonomy) often did not change the view of their former colonial masters, who continued to feel that they knew best. The colonial mentality—the "white man's burden" and the presumption that they knew what was best for the developing countries—persisted. America, which came to dominate the global economic scene, had much less of a colonial heritage, yet America's credentials too had been tarred, not so much by its "Manifest Destiny" expansionism as by the Cold War, in which principles of democracy were compromised or ignored, in the all-encompassing struggle against communism.

THE NIGHT BEFORE I started at the Bank, I held my last press conference as chairman of the President's Council of Economic Advisers. With the domestic economy so well under control, I felt that the greatest challenges for an economist now lay in the growing problem of world poverty. What could we do about the 1.2 billion people around the world living on less than a dollar a day, or the 2.8 billion people living on less than $2 a day—more than 45 percent of the world's population? What could I do to bring to reality the dream of a world without poverty? How could I embark on the more modest dream of a world with less poverty? I saw my task as threefold: thinking through what strategies might be most effective in promoting growth and reducing poverty; working with governments in the developing countries to put these strategies in place; and doing everything I could within the developed countries to advance the interests and concerns of the developing world, whether it was pushing for opening up their markets or providing more effective assistance. I knew the tasks were difficult, but I never dreamed that one of the major obstacles the developing countries faced was man-made, totally unnecessary, and lay right across the street—at my "sister" institution, the IMF. I had expected that not everyone in the international financial institutions or in the governments that supported them was committed to the goal of eliminating poverty; but I thought there would be an open debate about strategies—strategies which in so many areas seem to be failing, and especially failing the poor. In this, I was to be disappointed.

Ethiopia and the Struggle between Power Politics and Poverty

After four years in Washington, I had become used to the strange world of bureaucracies and politicians. But it was not until I traveled to Ethiopia, one of the poorest countries in the world, in March 1997, barely a month into the World Bank job, that I became fully immersed in the astonishing world of IMF politics and arithmetic. Ethiopia's per capita income was $110 a year and the country had suffered from successive droughts and famines that had killed 2 million people. I went to meet Prime Minister Meles Zenawi, a man who had led a seventeen-year guerrilla war against the bloody Marxist regime of Mengistu Haile Mariam. Meles's forces won in 1991 and then the government began the hard work of rebuilding the country. A doctor by training, Meles had formally studied economics because he knew that to bring his country out of centuries of poverty would require nothing less than economic transformation, and he demonstrated a knowledge of economics—and indeed a creativity—that would have put him at the head of any of my university classes. He showed a deeper understanding of economic principles—and certainly a greater knowledge of the circumstances in his country—than many of the international economic bureaucrats that I had to deal with in the succeeding three years.

Meles combined these intellectual attributes with personal integrity: no one doubted his honesty and there were few accusations of corruption within his government. His political opponents came mostly from the long-dominant groups around the capital who had lost political power with his accession, and they raised questions about his commitment to democratic principles. However, he was not an old-fashioned autocrat. Both he and the government were generally committed to a process of decentralization, bringing government closer to the people and ensuring that the center did not lose touch with the separate regions. The new constitution even gave each region the right to vote democratically to secede, ensuring that the political elites in the capital city, whoever they might be, could not risk ignoring the concerns of ordinary citizens in every part of the country, or that one part of the country could not impose its views on the rest. The government actually lived up to its commitment, when Eritrea declared its independence in 1993. (Subsequent events—such as the government's occupation of the university in Addis Ababa in the spring of 2000, with the imprisonment of some students and professors—show the precariousness, in Ethiopia as elsewhere, of basic democratic rights.)

When I arrived in 1997, Meles was engaged in a heated dispute with the IMF, and the Fund had suspended its lending program. Ethiopia's macroeconomic "results"—upon which the Fund was supposed to focus—could not have been better. There was no inflation; in fact, prices were falling. Output had been growing steadily since he had succeeded in ousting Mengistu.[1] Meles showed that, with the right policies in place, even a poor African country could experience sustained economic growth. After years of war and rebuilding, international assistance was beginning to return to the country. But Meles was having problems with the IMF. What was at stake was not just $127 million of IMF money provided through its so-called Enhanced Structural Adjustment Facility (ESAF) program (a lending program at highly subsidized rates to help very poor countries), but World Bank monies as well.

The IMF has a distinct role in international assistance. It is supposed to review each recipient's macroeconomic situation and make sure that the country is living within its means. If it is not, there is inevitably trouble down the road. In the short run, a country can live beyond its means by borrowing, but eventually a day of reckoning comes, and there is a crisis. The IMF is particularly concerned about inflation. Countries whose governments spend more than they take in in taxes and foreign aid often will face inflation, especially if they finance their deficits by printing money. Of course, there are other dimensions to good macroeconomic policy besides inflation. The term *macro* refers to the *aggregate* behavior, the overall levels of growth, unemployment, and inflation, and a country can have low inflation but no growth and high unemployment. To most economists, such a country would rate as having a disastrous macroeconomic framework. To most economists, inflation is not so much an end in itself, but a means to an end: it is because *excessively* high inflation often leads to low growth, and low growth leads to high unemployment, that inflation is so frowned upon. But the IMF often seems to confuse means with ends, thereby losing sight of what is ultimately of concern. A country like Argentina can get an "A" grade, even if it has double-digit unemployment for years, so long as its budget seems in balance and its inflation seems in control!

If a country does not come up to certain minimum standards, the IMF suspends assistance; and typically, when it does, so do other donors. Understandably, the World Bank and the IMF don't lend to countries unless they have a good macroframework in place. If countries have huge deficits and soaring inflation, there is a risk that money will not be well spent. Governments that fail to manage their overall economy typically do a poor job managing foreign aid. But if the macroeconomic indicators—inflation and growth—are solid, as they were in Ethiopia, surely the underlying macroeconomic framework must be good. Not only did Ethiopia have a sound macroeconomic framework but the World Bank had direct evidence of the competence of the government and its commitment to the poor. Ethiopia had formulated a rural development strategy, focusing its attention on the poor, and especially the 85 percent of the population living in the rural sector. It had dramatically cut back on military expenditures—remarkable for a government which had come to power through military means—because it knew that funds spent on weapons were funds that could not be spent on fighting poverty. Surely, this was precisely the kind of government to which the international community should have been giving assistance. But the IMF had suspended its program with Ethiopia, in spite of the good macroeconomic performance, saying it was worried about Ethiopia's budgetary position.

The Ethiopian government had two revenue sources, taxes and foreign assistance. A government's budget is in balance so long as its revenue sources equal its expenditures. Ethiopia, like many developing countries, derived much of its revenues from foreign assistance. The IMF worried that if this aid dried up, Ethiopia would be in trouble. Hence it argued that Ethiopia's budgetary position could only be judged solid if expenditures were limited to the taxes it collected.

The obvious problem with the IMF's logic is that it implies no poor country can ever spend money on anything it gets aid for. If Sweden, say, gives money to Ethiopia to build schools, this logic dictates that Ethiopia should instead put the money into its reserves. (All countries have, or should have, reserve accounts that hold funds for the proverbial rainy day. Gold is the traditional reserve, but today it has been replaced by hard currency and its interest-bearing relatives. The most common way to hold reserves is in U.S. Treasury bills.) But this is not why international donors give aid. In Ethiopia, the donors, who were working independently and not beholden to the IMF, wanted to see new schools and health clinics built, and so did Ethiopia. Meles put the matter more forcefully: He told me that he had not fought so hard for seventeen years to be instructed by some international bureaucrat that he could not build schools and clinics for his people once he had succeeded in convincing donors to pay for them.

The IMF view was not rooted in a long-held concern about project sustainability. Sometimes countries had used aid dollars to construct schools or clinics. When the aid money ran out, there was no money to maintain these facilities. The donors had recognized this problem and built it into their assistance programs in Ethiopia and elsewhere. But what the IMF alleged in the case of Ethiopia went beyond that concern. The Fund contended that international assistance was too unstable to be relied upon. To me, the IMF's position made no sense, and not just because of its absurd implications. I knew that assistance was often far more stable than tax revenues, which can vary markedly with economic conditions. When I got back to Washington, I asked my staff to check the statistics, and they confirmed that international assistance was more stable than tax revenues. Using the IMF reasoning about stable sources of revenue, Ethiopia, and other developing countries, should have counted foreign aid but not included tax revenues in their budgets. And if neither taxes nor foreign assistance were to be included in the revenue side of budgets, *every* country would be considered to be in bad shape.

But the IMF's reasoning was even more flawed. There are a number of appropriate responses to instability of revenues, such as setting aside additional reserves and maintaining flexibility of expenditures. If revenues, from any source, decline, and there are not reserves to draw upon, then the government has to be prepared to cut back expenditures. But for the kinds of assistance that constitute so much of what a poor country like Ethiopia receives, there is built-in flexibility; if the country does not receive money to build an additional school, it simply does not build the school. Ethiopia's government officials understood what was at issue, they understood the concern about what might happen if *either* tax revenues or foreign assistance should fall, and they had designed policies to deal with these contingencies. What they couldn't understand—and I couldn't understand—is why the IMF couldn't see the logic of their position. And much was at stake: schools and health clinics for some of the poorest people in the world.

In addition to the disagreement over how to treat foreign aid, I also became immediately entangled in another IMF-Ethiopia dispute over an early loan repayment. Ethiopia had repaid an American bank loan early, using some of its reserves. The transaction made perfect *economic* sense. In spite of the quality of the collateral (an airplane), Ethiopia was paying a far higher interest rate on its loan than it was receiving on its reserves. I, too, would have advised them to repay, particularly since in the event that funds would later be required, the government could presumably readily obtain funds using the plane as collateral. The United States and the IMF objected to the early repayment. They objected not to the logic of the strategy, but to the fact that Ethiopia had undertaken this course without IMF approval. But why should a sovereign country ask permission of the IMF for every action which it undertakes? One might have understood if Ethiopia's action threatened its ability to repay what was owed the IMF; but quite the contrary, because it was a sensible financial decision, it enhanced the country's ability to repay what was due.[2]

For years, the mantra at the 19th Street headquarters of the IMF in Washington had been accountability and judgment by results. The results of Ethiopia's largely self-determined policies should have demonstrated convincingly that it was a capable master of its own destiny. But the IMF felt countries receiving money from it had an obligation to report everything that might be germane; not to do so was grounds for suspension of the program, regardless of the reasonableness of the action. To Ethiopia, such intrusiveness smacked of a new form of colonialism; to the IMF, it was just standard operating procedure.

There were other sticking points in IMF-Ethiopia relations, concerning Ethiopian financial market liberalization. Good capital markets are the hallmark of capitalism, but nowhere is the disparity between developed and less developed countries greater than in their capital markets. Ethiopia's entire banking system (measured, for instance, by the size of its assets) is somewhat smaller than that of Bethesda, Maryland, a suburb on the outskirts of Washington with a population of 55,277. The IMF wanted Ethiopia not only to open up its financial markets to Western competition but also to divide its largest bank into several pieces. In a world in which U.S. megafinancial institutions like Citibank and Travelers, or Manufacturers Hanover and Chemical, say they have to merge to compete effectively, a bank the size of North East Bethesda National Bank really has no way to compete against a global giant like Citibank. When global financial institutions enter a country, they can squelch the domestic competition. And as they attract depositors away from the local banks in a country like Ethiopia, they may be far more attentive and generous when it comes to making loans to large multinational corporations than they will to providing credit to small businesses and farmers.

The IMF wanted to do more than just open up the banking system to foreign competition. It wanted to "strengthen" the financial system by creating an auction market for Ethiopia's government Treasury bills—a reform, as desirable as it might be in many countries, which was completely out of tune with that country's state of development. It also wanted Ethiopia to "liberalize" its financial market, that is, allow interest rates to be freely determined by market forces—something the United States and Western Europe did not do until after 1970, when their markets, and the requisite regulatory apparatus, were far more developed. The IMF was confusing ends with means. One of the prime objectives of a good banking system is to provide credit at good terms to those who will repay. In a largely rural country like Ethiopia, it is especially important for farmers to be able to obtain credit at reasonable terms to buy seed and fertilizer. The task of providing such credit is not easy; even in the United States, at critical stages of its development when agriculture was more important, the government took a crucial role in providing needed credit. The Ethiopian banking system was at least seemingly quite efficient, the difference between borrowing and lending rates being far lower than those in other developing countries that had followed the IMF's advice. Still, the Fund was unhappy, simply because it believed interest rates should be freely determined by international market forces, whether those markets were or were not competitive. To the Fund, a liberalized financial system was an end in itself. Its naive faith in markets made it confident that a liberalized financial system would lower interest rates paid on loans and thereby make more funds available. The IMF was so certain about the correctness of its dogmatic position that it had little interest in looking at actual experiences.

Ethiopia resisted the IMF's demand that it "open" its banking system, for good reason. It had seen what happened when one of its East African neighbors gave in to IMF demands. The IMF had insisted on financial market liberalization, believing that competition among banks would lead to lower interest rates. The results were disastrous: the move was followed by the very rapid growth of local and indigenous commercial banks, at a time when the banking legislation and bank supervision were inadequate, with the predictable results—fourteen banking failures in Kenya in 1993 and 1994 alone. In the end, interest rates increased, not decreased. Understandably, the government of Ethiopia was wary.

Committed to improving the living standards of its citizens in the rural sector, it feared that liberalization would have a devastating effect on its economy. Those farmers who had previously managed to obtain credit would find themselves unable to buy seed or fertilizer because they would be unable to get cheap credit or would be forced to pay higher interest rates which they could ill afford. This is a country wracked by droughts which result in massive starvation. Its leaders did not want to make matters worse. The Ethiopians worried that the IMF's advice would cause farmers' incomes to fall, exacerbating an already dismal situation.

Faced with Ethiopian reluctance to accede to its demands, the IMF suggested the government was not serious about reform and, as I have said, suspended its program. Happily, other economists in the World Bank and I managed to persuade the Bank management that lending more money to Ethiopia made good sense: it was a country desperately in need, with a first-rate economic framework and a government committed to improving the plight of its poor. World Bank lending tripled, even though it took months before the IMF finally relented on its position. In order to turn the situation around I had, with the invaluable help and support of colleagues, mounted a determined campaign of "intellectual lobbying." In Washington, my colleagues and I held conferences to encourage people at both the IMF and the World Bank to look again at issues of financial sector liberalization in very underdeveloped nations, and the consequences of unnecessarily imposed budgetary austerity in foreign aid–dependent poor countries, as in Ethiopia. I attempted to reach senior managers at the Fund, both directly and through colleagues at the World Bank, and those at the Bank working in Ethiopia made similar efforts to persuade their counterparts at the Fund. I used what influence I could through my connections with the Clinton administration, including talking to America's representative on the Fund. In short, I did everything I could to get the IMF program reinstated.

Assistance was restored, and I would like to think that my efforts helped Ethiopia. I learned, however, that immense time and effort are required to effect change, even from the inside, in an international bureaucracy. Such organizations are opaque rather than transparent, and not only does far too little information radiate from inside to the outside world, perhaps even less information from outside is able to penetrate the organization. The opaqueness also means that it is hard for information from the bottom of the organization to percolate to the top.

The tussle over lending to Ethiopia taught me a lot about how the IMF works. There was clear evidence the IMF was wrong about financial market liberalization and Ethiopia's macroeconomic position, but the IMF had to have its way. It seemingly would not listen to others, no matter how well informed, no matter how disinterested. Matters of substance became subsidiary to matters of process. Whether it made sense for Ethiopia to repay the loan was less important than the fact that it failed to consult the IMF. Financial market liberalization—how best this should be done in a country at Ethiopia's stage of development—was a matter of substance and experts could have been asked for their opinion. The fact that outside experts were not called in to help arbitrate what was clearly a contentious issue is consonant with the style of the IMF, in which the Fund casts itself as the monopoly supplier of "sound" advice. Even matters like the repayment of the loan—though properly not something on which the IMF should have taken a position at all, so long as Ethiopia's action enhanced rather than subtracted from its ability to repay what was owed—could have been referred to outsiders, to see whether the action was "reasonable." But doing so would have been anathema to the IMF. Because so much of its decision making was done behind closed doors—there was virtually no public discussion of the issues just raised—the IMF left itself open to suspicions that power politics, special interests, or other hidden reasons not related to the IMF's mandate and stated objectives were influencing its institutional policies and conduct.

It is hard even for a moderate-sized institution like the IMF to know a great deal about every economy in the world. Some of the best IMF economists were assigned to work on the United States, but when I served as chairman of the Council of Economic Advisers, I often felt that the IMF's limited understanding of the U.S. economy had led it to make misguided policy recommendations for America. The IMF economists felt, for instance, that inflation would start rising in the United States as soon as unemployment fell below 6 percent. At the Council, our models said they were wrong, but they were not terribly interested in our input. We were right, and the IMF was wrong: unemployment in the United States fell to below 4 percent and still inflation did not increase. Based on their faulty analysis of the U.S. economy, the IMF economists came up with a misguided policy prescription: raise interest rates. Fortunately, the Fed paid no attention to the IMF recommendation. Other countries could not ignore it so easily.

But to the IMF the lack of detailed knowledge is of less moment, because it tends to take a "one-size-fits-all" approach. The problems of this approach become particularly acute when facing the challenges of the developing and transition economies. The institution does not really claim expertise in development—its original mandate is supporting global economic stability, as I have said, not reducing poverty in developing countries—yet it does not hesitate to weigh in, and weigh in heavily, on development issues. Development issues are complicated; in many ways developing countries present far greater difficulties than more developed countries. This is because in developing nations, markets are often absent, and when present, often work imperfectly. Information problems abound, and cultural mores may significantly affect economic behavior.

Unfortunately, too often the training of the macroeconomists who predominate the IMF does not prepare them well for the problems that they have to confront in developing countries. In some of the universities from which the IMF hires regularly, the core curricula involve models in which there is never any unemployment. After all, in the standard competitive model—the model that underlies the IMF's market fundamentalism—demand always equals supply. If the demand for labor equals supply, there is never any *involuntary* unemployment. Someone who is not working has evidently chosen not to work. In this interpretation, unemployment in the Great Depression, when one out of four people was out of work, would be the result of a sudden increase in the desire for more leisure. It might be of some interest to psychologists why there was this sudden change in the desire for leisure, or why those who were supposed to be enjoying this leisure seemed so unhappy, but according to the standard model these questions go beyond the scope of economics. While these models might provide some amusement within academia, they seemed particularly ill suited to understanding the problems of a country like South Africa, which has been plagued with unemployment rates in excess of 25 percent since apartheid was dismantled.

The IMF economists could not, of course, ignore the existence of unemployment. Because under market fundamentalism—in which, *by assumption*, markets work perfectly and demand must equal supply for labor as for every other good or factor—there cannot be unemployment, the problem cannot lie with markets. It must lie elsewhere—with greedy unions and politicians interfering with the workings of free markets, by demanding—and getting—excessively high wages. There is an obvious policy implication—if there is unemployment, wages should be reduced.

But even if the training of the typical IMF macroeconomist had been better suited to the problems of developing countries, it's unlikely that an IMF mission, on a three-week trip to Addis Ababa, Ethiopia's capital, or the capital of any other developing country, could really develop policies appropriate for that country. Such policies are far more likely to be crafted by highly educated, first-rate economists already in the country, deeply knowledgeable about it and working daily on solving that country's problems. Outsiders can play a role, in sharing the experiences of other countries, and in offering alternative interpretations of the economic forces at play. But the IMF did not want to take on the mere role of an adviser, competing with others who might be offering their ideas. It wanted a more central role in shaping policy. And it could do this because its position was based on an ideology—market fundamentalism—that required little, if any, consideration of a country's particular circumstances and immediate problems. IMF economists could ignore the short-term effects their policies might have on the country, content in the belief that *in the long run* the country would be better off; any adverse short-run impacts would be merely pain that was necessary as part of the process. Soaring interest rates might, today, lead to starvation, but market efficiency requires free markets, and eventually, efficiency leads to growth, and growth benefits all. Suffering and pain became part of the process of redemption, evidence that a country was on the right track. To me, sometimes pain *is* necessary, but it is not a virtue in its own right. Well-designed policies can often avoid much of the pain; and some forms of pain—the misery caused by abrupt cuts in food subsidies, for example, which leads to rioting, urban violence, and the dissolution of the social fabric—are counterproductive.

The IMF has done a good job of persuading many that its ideo-
logically driven policies were necessary if countries are to succeed in
the long run. Economists always focus on the importance of scarcity and
the IMF often says it is simply the messenger of scarcity: countries cannot persistently live beyond their means. One doesn't, of course, need
a sophisticated financial institution staffed by Ph.D. economists to tell
a country to limit expenditures to revenues. But IMF reform programs
go well beyond simply ensuring that countries live within their means.

THERE ARE ALTERNATIVES to IMF-style programs, other programs
that may involve a reasonable level of sacrifice, which are not based on
market fundamentalism, programs that have had positive outcomes.
A good example is Botswana, 2,300 miles south of Ethiopia, a small
country of 1.5 million, which has managed a stable democracy since
independence.

At the time Botswana became fully independent in 1966 it was a
desperately poor country, like Ethiopia and most of the other countries
in Africa, with a per capita annual income of $100. It too was largely
agricultural, lacked water, and had a rudimentary infrastructure. But
Botswana is one of the success stories of development. Although the
country is now suffering from the ravages of AIDS, it averaged a growth
rate of more than 7.5 percent from 1961 to 1997.

Botswana was helped by having diamonds, but countries like the
Democratic Republic of the Congo, Nigeria, and Sierra Leone were
also rich in resources. In those countries, the wealth from this abundance fueled corruption and spawned privileged elites that engaged in
internecine struggles for control of each country's wealth. Botswana's
success rested on its ability to maintain a political consensus, based on a
broader sense of national unity. That political consensus, necessary to
any workable social contract between government and the governed,
had been carefully forged by the government, in collaboration with
outside advisers, from a variety of public institutions and private foundations, including the Ford Foundation. The advisers helped Botswana
map out a program for the country's future. Unlike the IMF, which
largely deals with the finance ministry and central banks, the advisers
openly and candidly explained their policies as they worked with the
government to obtain popular support for the programs and policies.

They discussed the program with senior Botswana officials, including cabinet ministers and members of Parliament, with open seminars as well as one-to-one meetings.

Part of the reason for this success was that the senior people in Botswana's government took great care in selecting their advisers. When the IMF offered to supply the Bank of Botswana with a deputy governor, the Bank of Botswana did not automatically accept him. The bank's governor flew to Washington to interview him. He turned out to do a splendid job. Of course, no success is without blemishes. On another occasion, the Bank of Botswana allowed the IMF to pick somebody to be director of research, and that turned out, at least in the view of some, to be far less successful.

The differences in how the IMF and the advisers from the Ford Foundation and other agencies approach developing countries has a multiplicity of consequences. While the IMF is vilified almost everywhere in the developing world, the warm relationship that was created between Botswana and its advisers was symbolized by the awarding of that country's highest medal to Steve Lewis, who at the time he advised Botswana was a professor of development economics at Williams.

The vital consensus that underlay Botswana's success was threatened two decades ago when Botswana had an economic crisis. One major sector, cattle raising, was threatened by drought, and problems in the diamond industry had put a strain on the country's budget and its foreign exchange position. Botswana was suffering exactly the kind of liquidity crisis the IMF had originally been created to deal with—a crisis that could be eased by financing a deficit to forestall recession and hardship. However, while that may have been Keynes's intent when he pushed for the establishment of the IMF, the institution does not now conceive of itself as a deficit financier, committed to maintaining economies at full employment. Rather, it has taken on the pre-Keynesian position of fiscal austerity in the face of a downturn, doling out funds only if the borrowing country conforms to the IMF's views about appropriate economic policy, which almost always entail contractionary policies leading to recessions or worse. Botswana, recognizing the volatility of its two main sectors, cattle and diamonds, had prudently set aside reserve funds for just such a crisis. As it saw its reserves dwindling, it knew that it would have to take further measures. Botswana tightened its belt, pulled together, and got through the crisis. But because of the broad understanding of economic policies that had been developed over the years and the consensus-based approach to policy making, the austerity did not cause the kinds of cleavages in society that have occurred so frequently elsewhere under IMF programs. Presumably, if the IMF had done what it should have been doing—providing funds quickly to countries with good economic policies in times of crisis, without searching around for conditionalities to impose—the country would have been able to navigate its way through the crisis with even less pain. (The IMF mission that came in 1981, quite amusingly, found it very difficult to impose new conditions, because Botswana had already done so many of the things that they would have insisted upon.) Since then, Botswana has not turned to the IMF for help.

The assistance of outside advisers—independent of the international financial institutions—had played a role in Botswana's success even earlier. Botswana would not have fared as well as it did if its original contract with the South African diamond cartel had been maintained. Shortly after independence, the cartel paid Botswana $20 million for a diamond concession in 1969, which reportedly returned $60 million in profits a year. In other words, the payback period was four months! A brilliant and dedicated lawyer seconded to the Botswana government from the World Bank argued forcefully for a renegotiation of the contract at a higher price, much to the consternation of the mining interests. De Beers (the South African diamond cartel) tried to tell people that Botswana was being greedy. They used what political muscle they could, through the World Bank, to stop him. In the end, they managed to extract a letter from the World Bank making it clear that the lawyer did not speak for the Bank. Botswana's response: That is precisely why we are listening to him. In the end, the discovery of the second large diamond mine gave Botswana the opportunity to renegotiate the whole relationship. The new agreement has so far served Botswana's interests well, and enabled Botswana and De Beers to maintain good relations.

Ethiopia and Botswana are emblematic of the challenges facing the more successful countries of Africa today: countries with leaders dedicated to the well-being of their people, fragile and in some cases imperfect democracies, attempting to create new lives for their peoples from the wreckage of a colonial heritage that left them without institutions or human resources. The two countries are also emblematic of the contrasts that mark the developing world: contrasts between success and failure, between rich and poor, between hopes and reality, between what is and what might have been.

I BECAME AWARE of this contrast when I first went to Kenya, in the late 1960s. Here was a rich and fertile country, with some of the most valuable land still owned by old colonial settlers. When I arrived, the colonial civil servants were also still there; now they were called advisers.

As I watched developments in East Africa over the ensuing years, and returned for several visits after becoming chief economist of the World Bank, the contrast between the aspirations in the 1960s and the subsequent developments were striking. When I first went, the spirit of *uhuru*, the Swahili word for freedom, and *ujama*, the word for self-help, were in the air. When I returned, the government offices were staffed by well-spoken and well-trained Kenyans; but the economy had been sinking for years. Some of the problems—the seemingly rampant corruption—were of Kenya's own making. But the high interest rates which had resulted from its following IMF advice, as well as other problems, could rightly be blamed at least in part on outsiders.

Uganda had begun the transition in perhaps better shape than any of the others, a relatively rich coffee-growing country, but it lacked trained native administrators and leaders. The British had allowed only two Africans to rise to the level of a master sergeant in their own army. One of them, unfortunately, was a Ugandan named Idi Amin, who ultimately became General Amin in Uganda's army and overthrew Prime Minister Milton Obote in 1971. (Amin enjoyed a certain measure of British confidence thanks to his service in the King's African Rifles in World War II and in Britain's struggle to suppress the Mau-Mau revolt in Kenya.) Amin turned the country into a slaughterhouse; as many as 300,000 people were killed because they were considered opponents of the "President for Life"—as Amin proclaimed himself in 1976. The reign of terror by an arguably psychopathic dictator ended only in 1979 when he was toppled by Ugandan exiles and forces from neighboring Tanzania. Today, the country is on the way to recovery, led by a charismatic leader, Yoweri Museveni, who has instituted major reforms with remarkable success, reducing illiteracy and AIDS. And he is as interesting in talking about political philosophy as he is in talking about development strategies.

BUT THE IMF is not particularly interested in hearing the thoughts of its "client countries" on such topics as development strategy or fiscal austerity, let alone politcal philosophy. All too often, the Fund's approach to developing countries has had the feel of a colonial ruler. A picture can be worth a thousand words, and a single picture snapped in 1998, shown throughout the world, has engraved itself in the minds of millions, particularly those in the former colonies. The IMF's managing director, Michel Camdessus (the head of the IMF is referred to as its "Managing Director"), a short, neatly dressed former French Treasury bureaucrat, who once claimed to be a Socialist, is standing with a stern face and crossed arms over the seated and humiliated president of Indonesia. The hapless president was being forced, in effect, to turn over economic sovereignty of his country to the IMF in return for the aid his country needed. In the end, ironically, much of the money went not to help Indonesia but to bail out the "colonial power's" private sector creditors. (Officially, the "ceremony" was the signing of a letter of agreement, an agreement effectively dictated by the IMF, though it often still keeps up the pretense that the letter of intent comes from the country's government!)

Defenders of Camdessus claim the photograph was unfair, that he did not realize that it was being taken and that it was viewed out of context. But that is the point—in day-to-day interactions, away from cameras and reporters, this is precisely the stance that the IMF bureaucrats take, from the leader of the organization on down. To those in the developing countries, the picture raised a very disturbing question: Had things really changed since the "official" ending of colonialism a half century ago? When I saw the picture, images of other signings of "agreements" came to mind. I wondered how similar this scene was to those marking the "opening up of Japan" with Admiral Perry's gunboat diplomacy or the end of the Opium Wars or the surrender of maharajas in India.

The stance of the IMF, like the stance of its leader, was clear: it was the font of wisdom, the purveyor of an orthodoxy too subtle to be grasped by those in the developing world. The message conveyed was all too often clear: in the best of cases there was a member of an elite—a minister of finance or the head of a central bank—with whom the Fund might have a meaningful dialogue. Outside of this circle, there was little point in even trying to talk.

A quarter of a century ago, those in the developing countries might rightly have given some deference to the "experts" from the IMF. But just as there has been a shift in the military balance of power, there has been an even more dramatic shift in the intellectual balance of power. The developing world now has its own economists—many of them trained at the world's best academic institutions. These economists have the significant advantage of lifelong familiarity with local politics, conditions, and trends. The IMF is like so many bureaucracies; it has repeatedly sought to extend what it does, beyond the bounds of the objectives originally assigned to it. As the IMF's mission creep gradually brought it outside its core area of competency in macroeconomics, into structural issues, such as privatization, labor markets, pension reforms, and so forth, and into broader areas of development strategies, the intellectual balance of power became even more tilted.

The IMF, of course, claims that it never dictates but always negotiates the terms of any loan agreement with the borrowing country. But these are one-sided negotiations in which all the power is in the hands of the IMF, largely because many countries seeking IMF help are in desperate need of funds. Although I had seen this so clearly in Ethiopia and the other developing countries with which I was involved, it was brought home again to me during my visit to South Korea in December 1997, as the East Asia crisis was unfolding. South Korea's economists knew that the policies being pushed on their country by the IMF would be disastrous. While, in retrospect, even the IMF agreed that it imposed excessive fiscal stringency, in prospect, few economists (outside the IMF) thought the policy made sense.[3] Yet Korea's economic officials remained silent. I wondered why they had kept this silence, but did not get an answer from officials inside the government until a subsequent visit two years later, when the Korean economy had recovered. The answer was what, given past experience, I had suspected all along. Korean officials reluctantly explained that they had been scared to disagree openly. The IMF could not only cut off its own funds, but could use its bully pulpit to discourage investments from private market funds by telling private sector financial institutions of the doubts the IMF had about Korea's economy. So Korea had no choice. Even implied criticism by Korea of the IMF program could have a disastrous effect: to the IMF, it would suggest that the government didn't fully understand "IMF economics," that it had reservations, making it less likely that it would actually carry out the program. (The IMF has a special phrase for describing such situations: the country has gone "off track." There is one "right" way, and any deviation is a sign of an impending derailment.) A public announcement by the IMF that negotiations had broken off, or even been postponed, would send a highly negative signal to the markets. This signal would at best lead to higher interest rates and at worst a total cutoff from private funds. Even more serious for some of the poorest countries, which have in any case little access to private funds, is that other donors (the World Bank, the European Union, and many other countries) make access to their funds contingent on IMF approval. Recent initiatives for debt relief have effectively given the IMF even more power, because unless the IMF approves the country's economic policy, there will be no debt relief. This gives the IMF enormous leverage, as the IMF well knows.

The imbalance of power between the IMF and the "client" countries inevitably creates tension between the two, but the IMF's own behavior in negotiations exacerbates an already difficult situation. In dictating the terms of the agreements, the IMF effectively stifles any discussions within a client government—let alone more broadly within the country—about alternative economic policies. In times of crises, the IMF would defend its stance by saying there simply wasn't time. But its behavior was little different in or out of crisis. The IMF's view was simple: questions, particularly when raised vociferously and openly, would be viewed as a challenge to the inviolate orthodoxy. If accepted, they might even undermine its authority and credibility. Government leaders knew this and took the cue: they might argue in private, but not in public. The chance of modifying the Fund's views was tiny, while the chance of annoying Fund leaders and provoking them to take a tougher position on other issues was far greater. And if they were angry or annoyed, the IMF could postpone its loans—a scary prospect for a country facing a crisis. But the fact that the government officials *seemed* to go along with the IMF's recommendation did not mean that they really agreed. And the IMF knew it.

Even a casual reading of the terms of the typical agreements between the IMF and the developing countries showed the lack of trust between the Fund and its recipients. The IMF staff monitored progress, not just on the relevant indicators for sound macromanagement—inflation, growth, and unemployment—but on intermediate variables, such as the money supply, often only loosely connected to the variables of ultimate concern. Countries were put on strict targets—what would be accomplished in thirty days, in sixty days, in ninety days. In some cases the agreements stipulated what laws the country's Parliament would have to pass to meet IMF requirements or "targets"—and by when.

These requirements are referred to as "conditions," and "conditionality" is a hotly debated topic in the development world.[4] Every loan document specifies basic conditions, of course. At a minimum, a loan agreement says the loan goes out on the condition that it will be repaid, usually with a schedule attached. Many loans impose conditions designed to increase the likelihood that they will be repaid. "Conditionality" refers to more forceful conditions, ones that often turn the loan into a policy tool. If the IMF wanted a nation to liberalize its financial markets, for instance, it might pay out the loan in installments, tying subsequent installments to verifiable steps toward liberalization. I personally believe that conditionality, at least in the manner and extent to which it has been used by the IMF, is a bad idea; there is little evidence that it leads to improved economic policy, but it does have adverse political effects because countries resent having conditions imposed on them. Some defend conditionality by saying that any banker imposes conditions on borrowers, to make it more likely that the loan will be repaid. But the conditionality imposed by the IMF and the World Bank was very different. In some cases, it even *reduced* the likelihood of repayment.

For instance, conditions that might weaken the economy in the short run, whatever their merits in the long, run the risk of exacerbating the downturn and thus making it more difficult for the country to repay the short-term IMF loans. Eliminating trade barriers, monopolies, and tax distortions may enhance long-run growth, but the disturbances to the economy, as it strives to adjust, may only deepen its downturn.

While the conditionalities could not be justified in terms of the Fund's fiduciary responsibility, they might be justified in terms of what it might have perceived as its moral responsibility, its obligation to do everything it could to strengthen the economy of the countries that had turned to it for help. But the danger was that even when well intentioned, the myriad of conditions—in some cases over a hundred, each with its own rigid timetable—detracted from the country's ability to address the central pressing problems.

The conditions went beyond economics into areas that properly belong in the realm of politics. In the case of Korea, for instance, the loans included a change in the charter of the Central Bank, to make it more independent of the political process, though there was scant evidence that countries with more independent central banks grow faster[5] or have fewer or shallower fluctuations. There is a widespread feeling that Europe's independent Central Bank exacerbated Europe's economic slowdown in 2001, as, like a child, it responded peevishly to the natural political concerns over the growing unemployment. Just to show that it was independent, it refused to allow interest rates to fall, and there was nothing anyone could do about it. The problems partly arose because the European Central Bank has a mandate to focus on inflation, a policy which the IMF has advocated around the world but one that can stifle growth or exacerbate an economic downturn. In the midst of Korea's crisis, the Korean Central Bank was told not only to be more independent but to focus exclusively on inflation, although Korea had not had a problem with inflation, and there was no reason to believe that mismanaged monetary policy had anything to do with the crisis. The IMF simply used the opportunity that the crisis gave it to push its political agenda. When, in Seoul, I asked the IMF team why they were doing this, I found the answer shocking (though by then it should not have come as a surprise): We always insist that countries have an independent central bank focusing on inflation. This was an issue on which I felt strongly. When I had been the president's chief economic adviser, we beat back an attempt by Senator Connie Mack of Florida to change the charter of the U.S. Federal Reserve Bank to focus exclusively on inflation. The Fed, America's central bank, has a mandate to focus not just on inflation but also on employment and growth. The president opposed the change, and we knew that, if anything, the American people thought the Fed already focused *too much* on inflation. The president made it clear that this was an issue he would fight, and as soon as this was made clear, the proponents backed off. Yet here was the

IMF—partially under the influence of the U.S. Treasury—imposing a political condition on Korea that most Americans would have found unacceptable for themselves.

Sometimes, the conditions seemed little more than a simple exercise of power: in its 1997 lending agreement to Korea, the IMF insisted on moving up the date of opening Korea's markets to certain Japanese goods although this could not possibly help Korea address the problems of the crisis. To some, these actions represented "seizing the window of opportunity," using the crisis to leverage in changes that the IMF and World Bank had long been pushing; but to others, these were simply acts of pure political might, extracting a concession, of limited value, simply as a demonstration of who was running the show.

While conditionality did engender resentment, it did not succeed in engendering development. Studies at the World Bank and elsewhere showed not just that conditionality did not *ensure* that money was well spent and that countries would grow faster but that there was little evidence it worked at all. Good policies cannot be bought.

THERE ARE SEVERAL reasons for the failure of conditionality. The simplest has to do with the economists' basic notion of fungibility, which simply refers to the fact that money going in for one purpose frees up other money for another use; the net impact may have nothing to do with the intended purpose. Even if conditions are imposed which ensure that this particular loan is used well, the loan frees up resources elsewhere, which may or may not be used well. A country may have two road projects, one to make it easier for the president to get to his summer villa, the other to enable a large group of farmers to bring their goods to a neighboring port. The country may have funds for only one of the two projects. The lender may insist as part of its conditionality that its money go for the project that increases the income of the rural poor; but in providing that money, it enables the government to fund the other.

There were other reasons why conditionality did not enhance economic growth. In some cases, they were the wrong conditions: financial market liberalization in Kenya and fiscal austerity in East Asia had adverse effects on the countries. In other cases, the way conditionality was imposed made the conditions politically unsustainable; when a new government came into power, they would be abandoned. Such conditions were seen as the intrusion by the new colonial power on the country's own sovereignty. The policies could not withstand the vicissitudes of the political process.

There was a certain irony in the stance of the IMF. It tried to pretend that it was above politics, yet it was clear that its lending program was, in part, driven by politics. The IMF made an issue of corruption in Kenya and halted its relatively small lending program largely because of the corruption it witnessed there. Yet it maintained a flow of money, billions of dollars, to Russia and Indonesia. To some, it seemed that while the Fund was overlooking grand larceny, it was taking a strong stand on petty theft. It should not have been kinder to Kenya—the theft was indeed large relative to the economy; it should have been tougher on Russia. The issue is not just a matter of fairness or consistency; the world is an unfair place, and no one really expected the IMF to treat a nuclear power the same way that it treated a poor African country of little strategic importance. The point was far simpler: the lending decisions were political—and political judgments often entered into IMF advice. The IMF pushed privatization in part because it believed governments could not, in managing enterprises, insulate themselves from political pressures. The very notion that one could separate economics from politics, or a broader understanding of society, illustrated a narrowness of perspective. If policies imposed by lenders induce riots, as has happened in country after country, then economic conditions worsen, as capital flees and businesses worry about investing more of their money. Such policies are not a recipe either for successful development or for economic stability.

The complaints against the IMF imposition of conditions extended beyond what conditions and how they were imposed, but were directed at how they were arrived at as well. The standard IMF procedure before visiting a client country is to write a draft report first. The visit is only intended to fine-tune the report and its recommendations, and to catch any glaring mistakes. In practice, the draft report is often what is known as boilerplate, with whole paragraphs being borrowed from the report of one country and inserted into another. Word processors make this easier. A perhaps apocryphal story has it that on one occasion a word processor failed to do a "search and replace," and the name of the country from which a report had been borrowed almost in its entirety was left in a document that was circulated. It is hard to know whether this was a one-off occurrence, done under time pressure, but the alleged foulup confirmed in the minds of many the image of "one-size-fits-all" reports. Even countries not borrowing money from the IMF can be affected by its views. It is not just through conditionality that the Fund imposes its perspectives throughout the world. The IMF has an annual consultation with every country in the world. The consultations, referred to as "Article 4" consultations after the article in its charter that authorized them, are supposed to ensure that each country is adhering to the articles of agreement under which the IMF was established (fundamentally ensuring exchange rate convertibility for trade purposes). Mission creep has affected this report as it has other aspects of IMF activity: the real Article 4 consultations are but a minor part of the entire surveillance process. The report is really the IMF's grading of the nation's economy.

While small countries often had to listen to the Article 4 evaluations, the United States and other countries with developed economies could basically ignore them. For instance, the IMF suffered from inflation paranoia, even when the United States was facing the lowest inflation rates in decades. Its prescription was therefore predictable: increase interest rates to slow down the economy. The IMF simply had no understanding of the changes that were then occurring, and had been occurring over the preceding decade in the U.S. economy that allowed it to enjoy faster growth, lower unemployment, and low inflation all at the same time. Had the IMF's advice been followed, the United States would not have experienced the boom in the American economy over the 1990s—a boom that brought unprecedented prosperity and enabled the country to turn around its massive fiscal deficit into a sizable surplus. The lower unemployment also had profound social consequences—issues to which the IMF paid little attention anywhere. Millions of workers who had been excluded from the labor force were brought in, reducing poverty and welfare roles at an unprecedented pace. This in turn brought down the crime rate. All Americans benefited. The low unemployment rate, in turn, encouraged individuals to take risks, to accept jobs without job security; and that willingness to take risks has proven an essential ingredient in America's success in the so-called New Economy.

The United States ignored the IMF's advice. Neither the Clinton administration nor the Federal Reserve paid much attention to it. The United States could do so with impunity because it was not dependent on the IMF or other donors for assistance, and we knew that the market would pay almost as little attention to it as we did. The market would not punish us for ignoring its advice or reward us for following it. But poor countries around the world are not so lucky. They ignore the Fund's advice only at their peril.

There are at least two reasons why the IMF should consult widely *within* a country as it makes its assessments and designs its programs. Those within the country are likely to know more about the economy than the IMF staffers—as I saw so clearly even in the case of the United States. And for the programs to be implemented in an effective and sustainable manner, there must be a commitment of the country behind the program, based on a broad consensus. Such a consensus can only be arrived at through discussion—the kind of open discussion that, in the past, the IMF shunned. To be fair to the IMF, in the midst of a crisis there is often little time for an open debate, the kind of broad consultation required to build a consensus. But the IMF has been in the African countries for years. If it is a crisis, it is a permanent ongoing crisis. There is time for consultations and consensus building—and in a few cases, such as Ghana, the World Bank (while my predecessor, Michael Bruno, was chief economist) succeeded in doing that, and these have been among the more successful cases of macroeconomic stabilization.

At the World Bank, during the time I was there, there was an increasing conviction that participation mattered, that policies and programs could not be imposed on countries but to be successful had to be "owned" by them, that consensus building was essential, that policies and development strategies had to be adapted to the situation in the country, that there should be a shift from "conditionality" to "selectivity," rewarding countries that had proven track records for using funds well with more funds, trusting them to continue to make good use of their funds, and providing them with strong incentives. This was reflected in the new Bank rhetoric, articulated forcefully by the Bank's president, James D. Wolfensohn: "The country should be put in the driver's seat." Even so, many critics say this process has not gone far enough and that the Bank still expects to remain in control. They worry that the country may be in the driver's seat of a dual-control car, in which the controls are really in the hands of the instructor. Changes in attitudes and operating procedures in the Bank will inevitably be slow, proceeding at different paces in its programs in different countries. But there remains a large gap between where the Bank is on these matters and where the IMF is, both in attitudes and procedures.

As much as it might like, the IMF, in its public rhetoric at least, could not be completely oblivious to the widespread demands for greater participation by the poor countries in the formulation of development strategies and for greater attention to be paid to poverty. As a result, the IMF and the World Bank have agreed to conduct "participatory" poverty assessments in which client countries join the two institutions in measuring the size of the problem as a first step. This was potentially a dramatic change in philosophy—but its full import seemed to escape the IMF. On one occasion, recognizing that the Bank was supposed to be taking the lead on poverty projects, just before the initial and, theoretically, consultative IMF mission to a certain client country prepared to depart, the IMF sent an imperious message to the Bank to have a draft of the client country's "participatory" poverty assessment sent to IMF headquarters "asap." Some of us joked that the IMF was confused. It thought the big philosophical change was that in joint Bank-IMF missions, the Bank could actually participate by having a say in what was written. The idea that citizens in a borrowing country might also participate was simply too much! Stories of this kind would be amusing were they not so deeply worrying.

Even if, however, the participatory poverty assessments are not perfectly implemented, they are a step in the right direction. Even if there remains a gap between the rhetoric and the reality, the recognition that those in the developing country ought to have a major voice in their programs is important. But if the gap persists for too long or remains too great, there will be a sense of disillusionment. Already, in some quarters, doubts are being raised, and increasingly loudly. While the participatory poverty assessments have engendered far more public discussion, more participation, than had previously been the case, in many countries expectations of participation and openness have not been fully realized, and there is growing discontent.

In the United States and other successful democracies citizens regard transparency, openness, knowing what government is doing, as an essential part of government accountability. Citizens regard these as *rights,* not favors conferred by the government. The Freedom of Information Act of 1966 has become an important part of American democracy. By contrast, in the IMF style of operation, citizens (an annoyance because they all too often might be reluctant to go along with the agreements, let alone share in the perceptions of what is good economic policy) were not only barred from discussions of agreements; they were not even told what the agreements were. Indeed, the prevailing culture of secrecy was so strong that the IMF kept much of the negotiations and some of the agreements secret from World Bank members even in joint missions! The IMF staff provided information strictly on a "need to know" basis. The "need to know" list was limited to the head of the IMF mission, a few people at IMF headquarters in Washington, and a few people in the client country's government. My colleagues at the Bank frequently complained that even those participating in a mission had to go to the government of the country who "leaked" what was going on. On a few occasions, I met with executive directors (the title for representatives that nations post to the IMF and the World Bank) who had apparently been kept in the dark.

One recent episode shows how far the consequences of lack of transparency can go. The notion that developing countries might have little voice in the international economic institutions is widely recognized. There may be a debate about whether this is just a historical anachronism or a manifestation of *realpolitik.* But we should expect that the U.S. government—including the U.S. Congress—should have some say, at least in how its executive director, the one who represents the United States at the IMF and the World Bank, votes. In 2001, Congress passed and the president signed a law requiring the United States to oppose proposals for the international financial institutions to charge fees for elementary school (a practice that goes under the seeming innocuous name of "cost recovery"). Yet the U.S. executive director simply ignored the law, and the secrecy of the institutions made it difficult for Congress—or anyone else—to see what was going on. Only because of a leak was the matter discovered, generating outrage even among congressmen and women accustomed to bureaucratic maneuvering.

Today, in spite of the repeated discussions of openness and transparency, the IMF still does not formally recognize the citizen's basic "right to know": there is no Freedom of Information Act to which an American, or a citizen of any other country, can appeal to find out what this international *public* institution is doing.

I should be clear: all of these criticisms of how the IMF operates do not mean the IMF's money and time is always wasted. Sometimes money has gone to governments with good policies in place—but not necessarily because the IMF recommended these policies. Then, the money did make a difference for the good. Sometimes, conditionality shifted the debate inside the country in ways that led to better policies. The rigid timetables that the IMF imposed grew partly from a multitude of experiences in which governments promised to make certain reforms, but once they had the money, the reforms were not forthcoming; sometimes, the rigid timetables helped force the pace of change. But all too often, the conditionality did not ensure either that the money was well used or that meaningful, deep, and long-lasting policy changes occurred. Sometimes, conditionality was even counterproductive, either because the policies were not well suited to the country or because the way they were imposed engendered hostility to the reform process. Sometimes, the IMF program left the country just as impoverished but with more debt and an even richer ruling elite.

The international institutions have escaped the kind of direct accountability that we expect of public institutions in modern democracies. The time has come to "grade" the international economic institution's performance and to look at some of those programs—and how well, or poorly, they did in promoting growth and reducing poverty.

CHAPTER 7

FREEDOM TO CHOOSE?

FISCAL AUSTERITY, PRIVATIZATION, and market liberalization were the three pillars of Washington Consensus advice throughout the 1980s and 1990s. The Washington Consensus policies were designed to respond to the very real problems in Latin America, and made considerable sense. In the 1980s, the governments of those countries had often run huge deficits. Losses in inefficient government enterprises contributed to those deficits. Insulated from competition by protectionist measures, inefficient private firms forced customers to pay high prices. Loose monetary policy led to inflation running out of control. Countries cannot persistently run large deficits; and sustained growth is not possible with hyperinflation. Some level of fiscal discipline is required. Most countries would be better off with governments focusing on providing essential public services rather than running enterprises that would arguably perform better in the private sector, and so privatization often makes sense. When trade liberalization—the lowering of tariffs and elimination of other protectionist measures—is done in the right way and at the right pace, so that new jobs are created as inefficient jobs are destroyed, there can be significant efficiency gains.

The problem was that many of these policies became ends in themselves, rather than means to more equitable and sustainable growth. In doing so, these policies were pushed too far, too fast, and to the exclusion of other policies that were needed.

The results have been far from those intended. Fiscal austerity pushed too far, under the wrong circumstances, can induce recessions, and high interest rates may impede fledgling business enterprises. The IMF vigorously pursued privatization and liberalization, at a pace and in a manner that often imposed very real costs on countries ill-equipped to incur them.

Privatization

In many developing—and developed—countries, governments all too often spend too much energy doing things they shouldn't do. This distracts them from what they should be doing. The problem is not so much that the government is too big, but that it is not doing the right thing. Governments, by and large, have little business running steel mills, and typically make a mess of it. (Although the most efficient steel mills in the world are those established and run by the Korean and Taiwanese governments, they are an exception.) In general, competing private enterprises can perform such functions more efficiently. This is the argument for privatization—converting state-run industries and firms into private ones. However, there are some important preconditions that have to be satisfied before privatization can contribute to an economy's growth. And the way privatization is accomplished makes a great deal of difference.

Unfortunately, the IMF and the World Bank have approached the issues from a narrow ideological perspective—privatization was to be pursued rapidly. Scorecards were kept for the countries making the transition from communism to the market: those who privatized faster were given the high marks. As a result, privatization often did not bring the benefits that were promised. The problems that arose from these failures have created antipathy to the very idea of privatization.

In 1998 I visited some poor villages in Morocco to see the impact that projects undertaken by the World Bank and nongovernmental organizations (NGOs) were having on the lives of the people there. I saw, for instance, how community-based irrigation projects were increasing farm productivity enormously. One project, however, had failed. An

NGO had painstakingly instructed local villagers on raising chickens, an enterprise that the village women could perform as they continued more traditional activities. Originally, the women obtained their seven-day-old chicks from a government enterprise. But when I visited the village, this new enterprise had collapsed. I discussed with villagers and government officials what had gone wrong. The answer was simple: The government had been told by the IMF that it should not be in the business of distributing chicks, so it ceased selling them. It was simply *assumed* that the private sector would immediately fill the gap. Indeed, a new private supplier arrived to provide the villagers with newborn chicks. The death rate of chicks in the first two weeks is high, however, and the private firm was unwilling to provide a guarantee. The villagers simply could not bear the risk of buying chicks that might die in large numbers. Thus, a nascent industry, poised to make a difference in the lives of these poor peasants, was shut down.

The assumption underlying this failure is one that I saw made repeatedly; the IMF simply assumed that markets arise quickly to meet every need, when in fact, many government activities arise because markets have *failed* to provide essential services. Examples abound. Outside the United States, this point often seems obvious. When many European countries created their social security systems and unemployment and disability insurance systems, there were no well-functioning private annuity markets, no private firms that would sell insurance against these risks that played such an important role in individuals' lives. Even when the United States created its social security system, much later, in the depths of the Great Depression as part of the New Deal, private markets for annuities did not work well—and even today one cannot get annuities that insure one against inflation. Again, in the United States, one of the reasons for the creation of the Federal National Mortgage Association (Fannie Mae) was that the private market did not provide mortgages at reasonable terms to low- and middle-income families. In developing countries, these problems are even worse; eliminating the government enterprise may leave a huge gap—and even if eventually the private sector enters, there can be enormous suffering in the meanwhile.

In Côte d'Ivoire, the telephone company was privatized, as is so often the case, *before* either an adequate regulatory or competition framework was put into place. The government was persuaded by the French firm that purchased the state's assets into giving it a monopoly, not only on the existing telephone services but on new cellular services as well. The private firm raised prices so high that, for instance, university students reportedly could not afford Internet connections, essential to prevent the already huge gap in digital access between rich and poor from widening even further.

The IMF argues that it is far more important to privatize quickly; one can deal with the issues of competition and regulation later. But the danger here is that once a vested interest has been created, it has an incentive, and the money, to maintain its monopoly position, squelching regulation and competition, and distorting the political process along the way. There is a natural reason why the IMF has been less concerned about competition and regulation than it might have been. Privatizing an unregulated monopoly can yield more revenue to the government, and the IMF focuses far more on macroeconomic issues, such as the size of the government's deficit, than on structural issues, such as the efficiency and competitiveness of the industry. Whether the privatized monopolies were more efficient in production than government, they were often more efficient in exploiting their monopoly position; consumers suffered as a result.

Privatization has also come not just at the expense of consumers but at the expense of workers as well. The impact on employment has perhaps been both the major argument for and against privatization, with advocates arguing that only through privatization can unproductive workers be shed, and critics arguing that job cuts occur with no sensitivity to the social costs. There is, in fact, considerable truth in both positions. Privatization often turns state enterprises from losses to profits by trimming the payroll. Economists, however, are supposed to focus on overall efficiency. There are social costs associated with unemployment, *which private firms simply do not take into account.* Given minimal job protections, employers can dismiss workers, with little or no costs, including, at best, minimal severance pay. Privatization has been so widely criticized because, unlike so-called greenfield investments—investments in new firms as opposed to private investors taking over existing firms—privatization often destroys jobs rather than creating new ones.

In industrialized countries, the pain of layoffs is acknowledged and somewhat ameliorated by the safety net of unemployment insurance. In less developed countries, the unemployed workers typically do not become a public charge, since there are seldom unemployment insurance schemes. There can be a large social cost nonetheless—manifested, in its worst forms, by urban violence, increased crime, and social and political unrest. But even in the absence of these problems, there are huge costs of unemployment. They include widespread anxiety even among workers who have managed to keep their jobs, a broader sense of alienation, additional financial burdens on family members who manage to remain employed, and the withdrawal of children from school to help support the family. These kinds of social costs endure long past the immediate loss of a job. They are often especially apparent in the case when a firm is sold to foreigners. Domestic firms may at least be attuned to the social context* and be reluctant to fire workers if they know there are no alternative jobs available. Foreign owners, on the other hand, may feel a greater obligation to their shareholders to maximize stock market value by reducing costs, and less of an obligation to what they will refer to as an "overbloated labor force."

It is important to restructure state enterprises, and privatization is often an effective way to do so. But moving people from low-productivity jobs in state enterprises to unemployment does not increase a country's income, and it certainly does not increase the welfare of the workers. The moral is a simple one, and one to which I shall return repeatedly: Privatization needs to be part of a more comprehensive program, which entails creating jobs *in tandem with* the inevitable job destruction that privatization often entails. Macroeconomic policies, including low interest rates, that help create jobs, have to be put in place. Timing (and sequencing) is everything. These are not just issues of pragmatics, of "implementation": these are issues of principle.

Perhaps the most serious concern with privatization, as it has so often been practiced, is corruption. The rhetoric of market fundamentalism asserts that privatization will reduce what economists call the "rent-

---

* I saw this forcefully in my discussions in Korea. Private owners showed an enormous social conscience in letting their workers go; they felt that there was a social contract, which they were reluctant to abrogate, even if it meant that they themselves would lose money.

seeking" activity of government officials who either skim off the profits of government enterprises or award contracts and jobs to their friends. But in contrast to what it was supposed to do, privatization has made matters so much worse that in many countries today privatization is jokingly referred to as "briberization." If a government is corrupt, there is little evidence that privatization will solve the problem. After all, the same corrupt government that mismanaged the firm will also handle the privatization. In country after country, government officials have realized that privatization meant that they no longer needed to be limited to annual profit skimming. By selling a government enterprise at below market price, they could get a significant chunk of the asset value for themselves rather than leaving it for subsequent officeholders. In effect, they could steal today much of what would have been skimmed off by future politicians. Not surprisingly, the rigged privatization process was designed to maximize the amount government ministers could appropriate for themselves, not the amount that would accrue to the government's treasury, let alone the overall efficiency of the economy. As we will see, Russia provides a devastating case study of the harm of "privatization at all costs."

Privatization advocates naively persuaded themselves these costs could be overlooked because the textbooks seemed to say that once private property rights were clearly defined, the new owners would ensure that the assets would be efficiently managed. Thus the situation would improve in the long term even if it was ugly in the short term. They failed to realize that without the appropriate legal structures and market institutions, the new owners might have an incentive to strip assets rather than use them as a basis for expanding industry. As a result, in Russia, and many other countries, privatization failed to be as effective a force for growth as it might have been. Indeed, sometimes it was associated with decline and proved to be a powerful force for undermining confidence in democratic and market institutions.

Liberalization

Liberalization—the removal of government interference in financial markets, capital markets, and of barriers to trade—has many dimensions. Today, even the IMF agrees that it has pushed that agenda too far—

that liberalizing capital and financial markets contributed to the global financial crises of the 1990s and can wreak havoc on a small emerging country.

The one aspect of liberalization that does have widespread support—at least among the elites in the advanced industrial countries—is trade liberalization. But a closer look at how it has worked out in many developing countries serves to illustrate why it is so often so strongly opposed, as seen in the protests in Seattle, Prague, and Washington, DC.

Trade liberalization is supposed to enhance a country's income by forcing resources to move from less productive uses to more productive uses; as economists would say, utilizing comparative advantage. But moving resources from low-productivity uses to *zero* productivity does not enrich a country, and this is what happened all too often under IMF programs. It is easy to destroy jobs, and this is often the immediate impact of trade liberalization, as inefficient industries close down under pressure from international competition. IMF ideology holds that new, more productive jobs will be created as the old, inefficient jobs that have been created behind protectionist walls are eliminated. But that is simply not the case—and few economists have believed in instantaneous job creation, at least since the Great Depression. It takes capital and entrepreneurship to create new firms and jobs, and in developing countries there is often a shortage of the latter, due to lack of education, and of the former, due to lack of bank financing. The IMF in many countries has made matters worse, because its austerity programs often also entailed such high interest rates—sometimes exceeding 20 percent, sometimes exceeding 50 percent, sometimes even exceeding 100 percent—that job and enterprise creation would have been an impossibility even in a good economic environment such as the United States. The necessary capital for growth is simply too costly.

The most successful developing countries, those in East Asia, opened themselves to the outside world but did so slowly and in a sequenced way. These countries took advantage of globalization to expand their exports and grew faster as a result. But they dropped protective barriers carefully and systematically, phasing them out only when new jobs were created. They ensured that there was capital available for new job and enterprise creation; and they even took an entrepreneurial role in promoting new enterprises. China is just dismantling its trade barriers, twenty years after its march to the market began, a period in which it grew extremely rapidly.

Those in the United States and the advanced industrialized countries should have found it easy to grasp these concerns. In the last two U.S. presidential campaigns, the candidate Pat Buchanan has exploited American workers' worries about job loss from trade liberalization. Buchanan's themes resonated even in a country with close to full employment (by 1999, the unemployment rate had fallen to under 4 percent), coupled with a good unemployment insurance system and a variety of assistance to help workers move from one job to another. The fact that, even during the booming 1990s, American workers could be so worried about the threat of liberalized trade to their jobs should have led to a greater understanding of the plight of workers in poor developing countries, where they live on the verge of subsistence, often on $2 a day or less, with no safety net in the form of savings, much less unemployment insurance, and in an economy with 20 percent or more unemployment.

The fact that trade liberalization all too often fails to live up to its promise—but instead simply leads to more unemployment—is why it provokes strong opposition. But the *hypocrisy* of those pushing for trade liberalization—and the way they have pushed it—has no doubt reinforced hostility to trade liberalization. The Western countries pushed trade liberalization for the products that they exported, but at the same time continued to protect those sectors in which competition from developing countries might have threatened their economies. This was one of the bases of the opposition to the new round of trade negotiations that was supposed to be launched in Seattle; previous rounds of trade negotiations had protected the interests of the advanced industrial countries—or more accurately, special interests within those countries—without concomitant benefits for the lesser developed countries. Protestors pointed out, quite rightly, that the earlier rounds of trade negotiations had lowered trade barriers on industrial goods, from automobiles to machinery, exported by the advanced industrial countries. At the same time, negotiators for these countries maintained their nations' subsidies on agricultural goods and kept closed the markets for these goods and for textiles, where many developing countries have a comparative advantage.

In the most recent Uruguay Round of trade negotiations, the subject of trade in services was introduced. In the end, however, markets were opened mainly for the services exported by the advanced countries—financial services and information technology—but not for maritime and construction services, where the developing countries might have been able to gain a toehold. The United States bragged about the benefits it received. But the developing countries did not get a proportionate share of the gains. One World Bank calculation showed that Sub-Saharan Africa, the poorest region in the world, saw its income decline by more than 2 percent as a result of the trade agreement. There were other examples of inequities that increasingly became the subject of discourse in the developing world, though the issues seldom made it into print in the more developed nations. Bolivia not only brought down its trade barriers to the point that they were lower than those in the United States but also cooperated with the United States in virtually eradicating the growth of coca, the basis of cocaine, even though this crop provided a higher income to its already poor farmers than any alternative. The United States responded, however, by keeping its markets closed to the alternative agriculture products, like sugar, that Bolivia's farmers might have produced for export—had America's markets been open to them.

Developing countries get especially angry over this sort of double standard because of the long history of hypocrisy and inequities. In the nineteenth century the Western powers—many of which had grown through using protectionist policies—had pushed unfair trade treaties. The most outrageous, perhaps, followed the Opium Wars, when the United Kingdom and France ganged up against a weak China, and together with Russia and the United States forced it, in the Treaty of Tientsin in 1858, not just to make trade and territorial concessions, ensuring it would export the goods the West wanted at low prices, but to open its markets *to opium*, so that millions in China would become addicted. (One might call this an almost diabolical approach to a "balance of trade.") Today, the emerging markets are not forced open under the threat of the use of military might, but through economic power, through the threat of sanctions or the withholding of needed assistance in a time of crisis. While the World Trade Organization was the forum within which international trade agreements were negotiated, U.S. trade negotiators and the IMF have often insisted on going further, accelerating the pace of trade liberalization. The IMF insists on this faster pace of liberalization as a condition for assistance—and countries facing a crisis feel they have no choice but to accede to the Fund's demands.

Matters are perhaps worse still when the United States acts unilaterally rather than behind the cloak of the WTO. The U.S. Trade Representative or the Department of Commerce, often prodded by special interests within the United States, brings an accusation against a foreign country; there is then a review process—involving only the U.S. government—with a decision made by the United States, after which sanctions are brought against the offending country. The United States sets itself up as prosecutor, judge, and jury. There is a quasi-judicial process, but the cards are stacked: both the rules and the judges favor a finding of guilty. When this arsenal is brought against other industrial countries, Europe and Japan, they have the resources to defend themselves; when it comes to the developing countries, even large ones like India and China, it is an unfair match. The ill will that results is far out of proportion to any possible gain for the United States. The process itself does little to reinforce confidence in a just international trading system.

The rhetoric the United States uses to push its position adds to the image of a superpower willing to throw its weight around for its own special interests. Mickey Kantor, when he was the U.S. Trade Representative in the first Clinton administration, wanted to push China to open its markets faster. The 1994 Uruguay Round negotiations, in which he himself had played a major role, established the WTO and set ground rules for members. The agreement had quite rightly provided a longer adjustment period for developing countries. At the time, the World Bank, and every economist, treated China—with its per capita income of $450—not only as a developing country but also as a low-income developing country. But Kantor was a hard negotiator. He insisted that it was a developed country, and should therefore have a quick transition.

Kantor had some leverage because China needed U.S. approval in order to join the WTO. The United States–China agreement that eventually led to China's being admitted to the WTO in November 2001 illustrates two aspects of the contradictions of the U.S. position. While the United States dragged out the bargaining with its unreasonable insistence that China was really a developed country, China began the adjustment process itself. In effect, unwittingly, the United States gave China the extra time it had wanted. But the agreement itself illustrates the double standards and inequity at play here. Ironically, while the United States insisted that China adjust quickly, as if it were a developed country—and because China had used the prolonged bargaining time well, it was able to accede to those demands—the United States also demanded, in effect, that America be treated as if *it* were a less developed country, that it be given not just the ten years of adjustment for lowering its barrier against textile imports that had been part of the 1994 negotiations, but an additional four years.

What is particularly disturbing is how special interests can undermine both U.S. credibility and broader national interests. This was seen most forcefully in April 1999, when Premier Zhu Rongji came to the United States partly to finish off negotiations for China's admission to the World Trade Organization, a move that was essential for the world trading regime—how could one of the largest trading countries be excluded?—but also for the market reforms in China itself. Over the opposition of the U.S. Trade Representative and the State Department, the U.S. Treasury insisted on a provision for faster liberalization of China's financial markets. China was quite rightly worried; it was precisely such liberalization that had led to the financial crises in neighboring countries in East Asia, at such costs. China had been spared because of its wise policies.

This American demand for liberalization of financial markets in China would not help secure global economic stability. It was made to serve the narrow interests of the financial community in the United States, which Treasury vigorously represents. Wall Street correctly believed that China represented a potential vast market for its financial services, and it was important that Wall Street get in, establish a strong toehold, before others. How shortsighted this was! It was clear that China would eventually be opened up. Hurrying the process up by a year or two can surely make little difference, except that Wall Street worries that its competitive advantage may disappear over time, as financial institutions in Europe and elsewhere catch up to the short-term advantages of their Wall Street competitors. But the potential cost was enormous. In the immediate aftermath of the Asian financial crisis, it was impossible for China to accede to Treasury's demands. For China, maintaining stability is essential; it could not risk policies that had proved so destabilizing elsewhere. Zhu Rongji was forced to return to China without a signed agreement. There had long been a struggle inside China between those pushing for and against reform. Those opposing reform argued that the West was seeking to weaken China, and would never sign a fair agreement. A successful end to the negotiations would have helped to secure the positions of the reformers in the Chinese government and added strength to the reform movement. As it turned out, Zhu Rongji and the reform movement for which he stood were discredited, and the reformists' power and influence were curtailed. Fortunately, the damage was only temporary, but still, the U.S. Treasury had shown how much it was willing to risk to pursue its special agenda.

EVEN THOUGH AN unfair trade agenda was pushed, at least there was a considerable body of theory and evidence that trade liberalization would, if implemented properly, be a good thing. The case for financial market liberalization was far more problematic. Many countries do have financial regulations that serve little purpose other than to increase the profits of some special interests, and these should be stripped away. But all countries regulate their financial markets, and excessive zeal in deregulation has brought on massive problems in capital markets even in developed countries around the world. To cite one example, the infamous savings-and-loan debacle in the United States, while it was a key factor in precipitating the 1991 recession and cost American taxpayers upward of $200 billion, was one of the least expensive (as a percentage of GDP) bailouts that deregulation has brought on, just as the U.S. recession was one of the mildest compared to ones in other economies that suffered similar crises.

While the more advanced industrialized countries, with their sophisticated institutions, were learning the hard lessons of financial deregulation, the IMF was carrying this Reagan-Thatcher message to the developing countries, countries which were particularly ill-equipped to manage what has proven, under the best of circumstances, to be a difficult task fraught with risks. Whereas the more advanced industrial countries did not attempt capital market liberalization until late in their development—European nations waited until the 1970s to get rid of their capital market controls—the developing nations have been encouraged to do so quickly.

The consequences—economic recession—of banking crises brought on by capital market deregulation, while painful for developed countries, were much more serious for developing countries. The poor countries have no safety net to soften the impact of recession. In addition, the limited competition in financial markets meant that liberalization did not always bring the promised benefits of lower interest rates. Instead, farmers sometimes found that they had to pay higher interest rates, making it more difficult for them to buy the seed and fertilizer necessary to eke out their bare subsistence living.

And as bad as premature and badly managed trade liberalization was for developing countries, in many ways capital market liberalization was even worse. Capital market liberalization entails stripping away the regulations intended to control the flow of hot money in and out of the country—short-term loans and contracts that are usually no more than bets on exchange rate movements. This speculative money cannot be used to build factories or create jobs—companies don't make long-term investments using money that can be pulled out on a moment's notice—and indeed, the risk that such hot money brings with it makes long-term investments in a developing country even less attractive. The adverse effects on growth are even greater. To manage the risks associated with these volatile capital flows, countries are routinely advised to set aside in their reserves an amount equal to their short-term foreign-denominated loans. To see what this implies, assume that a firm in a small developing country accepts a short-term $100 million loan from an American bank, paying 18 percent interest. Prudential policy on the part of the country would require that it would add $100 million to reserves. Typically reserves are held in U.S. Treasury bills, which in 2002 paid around 4 percent. In effect, the country was simultaneously borrowing from the United States at 18 percent and lending to the United States at 2 percent. The country as a whole has no more resources available for investing. American banks may make a tidy profit and the United States as a whole gains $16 million a year in interest. But it is hard to see how this allows the developing country to grow faster. Put this way, it clearly makes no sense. There is a further problem: a mismatch of incentives. With capital market liberalization, it is firms in a country's private sector that get to decide whether to borrow short-term funds from the American banks, but it is the government that must accommodate itself, adding to its reserves if it wishes to maintain its prudential standing.

The IMF, in arguing for capital market liberalization, relied on simplistic reasoning: Free markets are more efficient, greater efficiency allowed for faster growth. It ignored arguments such as the one just given, and put forward some further specious contentions, for instance, that without liberalization, countries would not be able to attract foreign capital, and especially direct investment. The Fund's economists have never laid claim to being great theorists; its claim to expertise lay in its global experience and its mastery of the data. Yet strikingly, not even the data supported the Fund's conclusions. China, which received the largest amount of foreign investment, did not follow any of the Western prescriptions (other than macrostability)—prudently forestalling full capital market liberalization. Broader statistical studies confirmed the finding that using the IMF's own definitions of liberalization, it did not entail faster growth or higher investment.

While China demonstrated that capital market liberalization was not needed to attract funds, the fact of the matter was that, given the high savings rates in East Asia (30–40 percent of GDP, in contrast to 18 percent in the United States and 17–30 percent in Europe), the region hardly needed additional funds; it already faced a daunting challenge in investing the flow of savings well.

The advocates of liberalization put forth another argument, one that looks particularly laughable in light of the global financial crisis that began in 1997, that liberalization would enhance stability by diversifying the sources of funding. The notion was that in times of downturn, countries could call upon foreigners to make up for a shortfall in domestic funds. The IMF economists were supposed to be practical people, well versed in the ways of the world. Surely, they must have known that bankers prefer to lend to those who do not need their funds; surely they must have seen how it is when countries face difficulties, that foreign lenders pull their money out—exacerbating the economic downturn.

While we shall take a closer look at why liberalization—especially when undertaken prematurely, before strong financial institutions are in place—increased instability, one fact remains clear: instability is not only bad for economic growth, but the costs of the instability are disproportionately borne by the poor.

The Role of Foreign Investment

Foreign investment is not one of the three main pillars of the Washington Consensus, but it is a key part of the new globalization. According to the Washington Consensus, growth occurs through liberalization, "freeing up" markets. Privatization, liberalization, and macrostability are supposed to create a climate to attract investment, including from abroad. This investment creates growth. Foreign business brings with it technical expertise and access to foreign markets, creating new employment possibilities. Foreign companies also have access to sources of finance, especially important in those developing countries where local financial institutions are weak. Foreign direct investment has played an important role in many—but not all—of the most successful development stories in countries such as Singapore and Malaysia and even China.

Having said this, there are some real downsides. When foreign businesses come in they often destroy local competitors, quashing the ambitions of the small businessmen who had hoped to develop homegrown industry. There are many examples of this. Soft drinks manufacturers around the world have been overwhelmed by the entrance of Coca-Cola and Pepsi into their home markets. Local ice cream manufacturers find they are unable to compete with Unilever's ice cream products.

One way to think about it is to recall the controversy in the United States over the large chains of drugstores and convenience stores. When Walmart comes into a community, there are often strong protests from local firms, who fear (rightly) that they will be displaced. Local shopkeepers worry they won't be able to compete with Walmart, with its enormous buying power. People living in small towns worry about what will happen to the character of the community if all local stores are destroyed. These same concerns are a thousand times stronger in developing countries. Although such concerns are legitimate, one has to maintain a perspective: the reason that Walmart is successful is that it provides goods to consumers at lower prices. The more efficient delivery of goods and services to poor individuals within developing countries is all the more important, given how close to subsistence so many live.

But critics raise several points. In the absence of strong (or effectively enforced) competition laws, after the international firm drives out the local competition it uses its monopoly power to raise prices. The benefits of low prices were short-lived.

Part of what is at stake is a matter of pacing; local businesses claim that, if they are given time, they can adapt and respond to the competition, that they can produce goods efficiently, that preserving local businesses is important for the strengthening of the local community, both economically and socially. The problem, of course, is that all too often policies first described as a temporary protection from foreign competition become permanent.

Many of the multinationals have done less than they might to improve the working conditions in the developing countries. Only gradually have they come to recognize the lessons that they learned all too slowly at home. Providing better working conditions may actually enhance worker productivity, and lower overall costs—or at least not raise costs very much.

Banking is another area where foreign companies often overrun local ones. The large American banks can provide greater security for depositors than do small local banks (unless the local government provides deposit insurance). The U.S. government has been pushing for opening up of financial markets in developing nations. The advantages are clear: the increased competition can lead to improved services. The greater financial strength of the foreign banks can enhance financial stability. Still, the threat foreign banks pose to the local banking sector is very real. Indeed, there was an extended debate in the United States on the same issue. National banking was resisted (until the Clinton administration, under Wall Street influence, reversed the traditional position of the Democratic Party) for fear that funds would flow to the major money centers, like New York, starving the outlying areas of needed funds. Argentina shows the dangers. There, before the collapse in 2001, the domestic banking industry had become dominated by foreign-owned banks, and while the banks easily provide funds to multinationals, and even large domestic firms, small and medium-size firms complained of a lack of access to capital. International banks' expertise—and information base—lies in lending to their traditional clients. Eventually, they may expand into these other niches, or new financial institutions may arise to address these gaps. And the lack of growth—to which the lack of finance contributed—was pivotal in that country's collapse. Within

Argentina, the problem was widely recognized; the government took some limited steps to fill the credit gap. But government lending could not make up for the market's failure.

Argentina's experience illustrates some basic lessons. The IMF and the World Bank have been stressing the importance of bank stability. It is easy to create sound banks, banks that do not lose money because of bad loans—simply require them to invest in U.S. Treasury bills. The challenge is not just to create sound banks but also to create sound banks that provide credit for growth. Argentina has shown how the failure to do that may itself lead to macroinstability. Because of a lack of growth it has had mounting fiscal deficits, and as the IMF forced cutbacks in expenditures and increases in taxes, a vicious downward spiral of economic decline and social unrest was set in motion.

Bolivia provides yet another example where foreign banks have contributed to macroeconomic instability. In 2001, a foreign bank that loomed large in the Bolivian economy suddenly decided, given the increased global risks, to pull back on lending. The sudden change in the credit supply helped plunge the economy into an even deeper economic downturn than falling commodity prices and the global economic slowdown were already bringing about.

There are additional concerns with respect to the intrusion of foreign banks. Domestic banks are more sensitive to what used to be called "window guidance"—subtle forms of influence by the central bank, for example, to expand credit when the economy needs stimulus and contract it when there are signs of overheating. Foreign banks are far less likely to be responsive to such signals. Similarly, domestic banks are far more likely to be responsive to pressure to address basic holes in the credit system—unserved and underserved groups, such as minorities and disadvantaged regions. In the United States, with one of the most developed credit markets, these gaps were felt to be so important that the Community Reinvestment Act (CRA) was passed in 1977, which imposed requirements on banks to lend to these underserved groups and areas. The CRA has been an important, if controversial, way of achieving critical social goals.

Finance, however, is not the only area in which foreign direct investment has been a mixed blessing. In some cases, new investors persuaded (often with bribes) governments to grant them special privileges, such as tariff protection. In many cases, the U.S., French, or governments of other advanced industrial countries weighed in—reinforcing the view within developing countries that it was perfectly appropriate for governments to meddle in and presumably receive payments from the private sector. In some cases, the role of government seemed relatively innocuous (although not necessarily uncorrupt). When U.S. Secretary of Commerce Ron Brown traveled abroad, he was accompanied by U.S. business people trying to make contacts with and gain entry into these emerging markets. Presumably, the chances of getting a seat on the plane were enhanced if one made significant campaign contributions.

In other cases, one government was called in to countervail the weight of another. In Côte d'Ivoire while the French government supported the French Telecom's attempt to exclude competition from an independent (American) cell phone company, the U.S. government pushed the claims of the American firm. But in many cases, governments went well beyond the realm of what was reasonable. In Argentina, the French government reportedly weighed in pushing for a rewriting of the terms of concessions for a water utility (Aguas Argentinas), after the French parent company (Suez Lyonnaise) that had signed the agreements found them less profitable than it had thought.

Perhaps of greatest concern has been the role of governments, including the American government, in pushing nations to live up to agreements that were vastly unfair to the developing countries, and often signed by corrupt governments in those countries. In Indonesia, at the 1994 meeting of leaders of APEC (Asia-Pacific Economic Cooperation) held at Jakarta, President Clinton encouraged American firms to come into Indonesia. Many did so, and often at highly favorable terms (with suggestions of corruption "greasing" the wheels—to the disadvantage of the people of Indonesia). The World Bank similarly encouraged private power deals there and in other countries, such as Pakistan. These contracts entailed provisions where the government was committed to purchasing large quantities of electricity at very high prices (the so-called take or pay clauses). The private sector got the profits; the government bore the risk. That was bad enough. But when the corrupt governments were overthrown (Mohammed Suharto in Indonesia in 1998, Nawaz Sharif in Pakistan in 1999), the U.S. government put pressure on the governments to fulfill the contract, rather than default or at least renegotiate the terms of the contract. There is, in fact, a long history of "unfair" contracts, which Western governments have used their muscle to enforce.[1]

There is more to the list of legitimate complaints against foreign direct investment. Such investment often flourishes only because of special privileges extracted from the government. While standard economics focuses on the *distortions* of incentives that result from such privileges, there is a far more insidious aspect: often those privileges are the result of corruption, the bribery of government officials. The foreign direct investment comes only at the price of undermining democratic processes. This is particularly true for investments in mining, oil, and other natural resources, where foreigners have a real incentive to obtain the concessions at low prices.

Moreover, such investments have other adverse effects—and often do not promote growth. The income that mining concessions brings can be invaluable but development is a transformation of society. An investment in a mine—say in a remote region of a country—does little to assist the development transformation, beyond the resources that it generates. It can help create a dual economy, an economy in which there are pockets of wealth. But a dual economy is not a developed economy. Indeed, the inflow of resources can sometimes actually impede development, through a mechanism that is called the "Dutch Disease." The inflow of capital leads to an appreciation of the currency, making imports cheap and exports expensive. The name comes from the Netherlands experience following the discovery of gas in the North Sea. Natural gas sales drove the Dutch currency up, seriously hurting the country's other export industries. It presented a challenging but solvable problem for that country; but for developing countries, the problem may be especially difficult.

Worse still, the availability of resources can alter incentives: as we saw in chapter 6, rather than devoting energy to creating wealth, in many countries that are well-endowed with resources, efforts are directed at appropriating the income (which economists refer to as "rents") associated with the natural resources.

The international financial institutions tended to ignore the problems I have outlined. Instead, the IMF's prescription for job creation—when it focused on that issue—was simple: Eliminate government intervention (in the form of oppressive regulation), reduce taxes, get inflation as low as possible, and invite foreign entrepreneurs in. In a sense, even here policy reflected the colonial mentality described in the previous chapter: of course, the developing countries would have to rely on foreigners for entrepreneurship. Never mind the remarkable successes of Korea and Japan, in which foreign investment played no role. In many cases, as in Singapore, China, and Malaysia, which kept the abuses of foreign investment in check, foreign direct investment played a critical role, not so much for the capital (which, given the high savings rate, was not really needed) or even for the entrepreneurship, but for the access to markets and new technology that it brought along.

Sequencing and Pacing

Perhaps of all the IMF's blunders, it is the mistakes in sequencing and pacing, and the failure to be sensitive to the broader social context, that have received the most attention—forcing liberalization before safety nets were put in place, before there was an adequate regulatory framework, before the countries could withstand the adverse consequences of the sudden changes in market sentiment that are part and parcel of modern capitalism; forcing policies that led to job destruction before the essentials for job creation were in place; forcing privatization before there were adequate competition and regulatory frameworks. Many of the sequencing mistakes reflected fundamental misunderstandings of both economic and political processes, misunderstandings that were particularly associated with those who believed in market fundamentalism. They argued, for instance, that once private property rights were established, all else would follow naturally—including the institutions and the kinds of legal structures that make market economies work.

Behind the free-market ideology there is a model, often attributed to Adam Smith, which argues that market forces—the profit motive—drive the economy to efficient outcomes *as if by an invisible hand.* One of the great achievements of modern economics is to show the sense in which, and the conditions under which, Smith's conclusion is correct. It turns out that these conditions are highly restrictive.[2] Indeed, more recent advances in economic theory—ironically occurring precisely during the period of the most relentless pursuit of the Washington Consensus policies—have shown that whenever information is imperfect and markets incomplete, which is to say always, *and especially in developing countries*, then the invisible hand works most imperfectly. Significantly, there are desirable government interventions which, in principle, can improve upon the efficiency of the market. These restrictions on the conditions under which markets result in efficiency are important—many of the key activities of government can be understood as responses to the resulting market failures. If information were perfect, we now know, there would be little role for financial markets—and little role for financial market regulation. If competition were automatically perfect, there would be no role for antitrust authorities.

The Washington Consensus policies, however, were based on a simplistic model of the market economy, the competitive equilibrium model, in which Adam Smith's invisible hand works, and works perfectly. Because in this model there is no need for government—that is, free, unfettered, "liberal" markets work perfectly—the Washington Consensus policies are sometimes referred to as "neo-liberal," based on "market fundamentalism," a resuscitation of the laissez-faire policies that were popular in some circles in the nineteenth century. In the aftermath of the Great Depression and the recognition of other failings of the market system, from massive inequality to unlivable cities marred by pollution and decay, these free-market policies have been widely rejected in the more advanced industrial countries, though within these countries there remains an active debate about the appropriate balance between government and markets.

EVEN IF SMITH'S invisible hand theory were relevant for advanced industrialized countries, the required conditions are not satisfied in developing countries. The market system requires clearly established property rights and the courts to enforce them; but often these are absent in developing countries. The market system requires competition and perfect information. But competition is limited and information is far from perfect—and well-functioning competitive markets can't be established overnight. The theory says that an efficient market economy requires that *all* of the assumptions be satisfied. In some cases, reforms in one area, without accompanying reforms in others, may actually make matters worse. This is the issue of sequencing. Ideology ignores these matters; it says simply move as quickly to a market economy as you can. But economic theory and history show how disastrous it can be to ignore sequencing.

The mistakes in trade, capital market liberalization, and privatization described earlier represent sequencing errors on a grand scale. The smaller-scale sequencing mistakes are even less noticed in the Western press. They constitute the day-to-day tragedies of IMF policies that affect the already desperately poor in the developing world. For example, many countries have marketing boards that purchase agricultural produce from the farmers and market it domestically and internationally. They often are a source of inefficiency and corruption, with farmers getting only a fraction of the ultimate price. Even though it makes little sense for the government to be engaged in this business, if the government suddenly gets out of it, it does not mean a vibrant competitive private sector will emerge automatically.

Several West African countries got out of the marketing board business under pressure from the IMF and World Bank. In some cases, it seemed to work; but in others, when the marketing board disappeared, a system of local monopolies developed. Limited capital restricted entry into this market. Few peasants could afford to buy a truck to carry their produce to market. They couldn't borrow the requisite funds either, given the lack of well-functioning banks. In some cases, people were able to get trucks to transport their goods, and the market did function initially; but then this lucrative business became the provenance of the local mafia. In either situation, the net benefits that the IMF and the World Bank promised did not materialize. Government revenue was lowered, the peasants were little if any better off than before, and a few local businessmen (mafiosi and politicians) were much better off.

Many marketing boards also engage in a policy of uniform pricing—paying farmers the same price no matter where they are located. While seemingly "fair," economists object to this policy because it effectively requires those farmers near markets to subsidize those far away. With market competition, farmers farther away from the place where the goods are actually sold receive lower prices; in effect, they bear the costs of transporting their goods to the market. The IMF forced one African country to abandon its uniform pricing before an adequate road system was in place. The price received by those in more isolated places was suddenly lowered markedly, as they had to bear the costs of transportation. As a result, incomes in some of the poorest rural regions in the country plummeted, and widespread hardship ensued. The IMF pricing scheme may have had some slight benefits in terms of increased efficiency, but we have to weigh these benefits against the social costs. Proper sequencing and pacing might have enabled one to gradually achieve the efficiency gains without these costs.

There is a more fundamental criticism of the IMF/Washington Consensus approach: It does not acknowledge that development requires a transformation of society. Uganda grasped this in its radical elimination of all school fees, something that budget accountants focusing solely on revenues and costs simply could not understand. Part of the mantra of development economics today is a stress on universal primary education, including educating girls. Countless studies have shown that countries, like those in East Asia, which have invested in primary education, including education of girls, have done better. But in some very poor countries, such as those in Africa, it has been very difficult to achieve high enrollment rates, especially for girls. The reason is simple: poor families have barely enough to survive; they see little direct benefit from educating their daughters, and the education systems have been oriented to enhancing opportunities mainly through jobs in the urban sector considered more suitable for boys. Most countries, facing severe budgetary constraints, have followed the Washington Consensus advice that fees should be charged. Their reasoning: statistical studies showed that small fees had little impact on school enrollment. But Uganda's President Museveni thought otherwise. He knew that he had to create a culture in which the expectation was that everyone went to school. And he knew he couldn't do that so long as there were any fees charged. So he ignored the advice of the outside experts and simply abolished all school fees. Enrollments soared. As each family saw others sending all of their children to school, it too decided to send its girls to school. What the simplistic statistical studies ignored is the power of *systemic* change.

If IMF strategies had simply failed to accomplish the full potential of development, that would have been bad enough. But the failures in many places have set back the development agenda, by unnecessarily corroding the very fabric of society. It is inevitable that the process of development and rapid change puts enormous stresses on society. Traditional authorities are challenged, traditional relationships are reassessed. That is why successful development pays careful attention to social stability—a major lesson not only of the story of Botswana in the previous chapter but also of Indonesia in the next, where the IMF insisted on abolishing subsidies for food and kerosene (the fuel used for cooking by the poor) just as IMF policies had exacerbated the country's recession, with incomes and wages falling and unemployment soaring. The riots that ensued tore the country's social fabric, exacerbating the ongoing depression. Abolishing the subsidies was not only bad social policy; it was bad economic policy.

These were not the first IMF-inspired riots, and had the IMF advice been followed more broadly, there surely would have been more. In 1995, I was in Jordan for a meeting with the crown prince and other senior government officials, when the IMF argued for cutting food subsidies to improve the government's budget. They had almost succeeded in getting agreement when King Hussein intervened and put a stop to it. He enjoyed his post, was doing a marvelous job, and wanted to keep it. In the highly volatile Middle East, food-inspired riots could well have overturned the government, and with that the fragile peace in the region. Weighed against the meager possible improvement in the budget situation, these events would have been far more harmful to the goal of prosperity. The IMF's narrow economic view made it impossible for it to consider these issues in their broader context.

Such riots are, however, like the tip of an iceberg: they bring to everyone's attention the simple fact that the social and political context cannot be ignored. But there were other problems. While in the 1980s Latin America needed to have its budgets brought into better balance and inflation brought under control, excessive austerity led to high unemployment, without an adequate safety net, which in turn contributed to high levels of urban violence, an environment hardly conducive to investment. Civil strife in Africa has been a major factor setting back its development agenda. Studies at the World Bank show that such strife is systematically related to adverse economic factors, including unemployment that can be produced by excessive austerity. Moderate inflation may not be ideal for creating an environment for investment, but violence and civil strife are even worse.

We recognize today that there is a "social contract" that binds citizens together, and with their government. When government policies abrogate that social contract, citizens may not honor their "contracts" with each other, or with the government. Maintaining that social contract is particularly important, and difficult, in the midst of the social upheavals that so frequently accompany the development transformation. In the green eye–shaded calculations of the IMF macroeconomics there is, too often, no room for these concerns.

Trickle-Down Economics

Part of the social contract entails "fairness," that the poor share in the gains of society as it grows, and that the rich share in the pains of society in times of crisis. The Washington Consensus policies paid little attention to issues of distribution or "fairness." If pressed, many of its proponents would argue that the best way to help the poor is to make the economy grow. They believe in trickle-down economics. *Eventually*, it is asserted, the benefits of that growth *trickle down* even to the poor. Trickle-down economics was never much more than just a belief, an article of faith. Pauperism seemed to grow in nineteenth-century England even though the country as a whole prospered. Growth in America in the 1980s provided the most recent dramatic example: while the economy grew, those at the bottom saw their real incomes decline. The Clinton administration had argued strongly against trickle-down economics; it believed that there had to be active programs to help the poor. And when I left the White House to go to the World Bank, I brought with me the same skepticism of trickle-down economics; if this had not worked in the United States, why would it work in developing countries? While it is true that sustained reductions in poverty cannot be attained without robust economic growth, the converse is not true: growth need not benefit all. It is not true that "a rising tide lifts all boats." Sometimes, a quickly rising tide, especially when accompanied by a storm, dashes weaker boats against the shore, smashing them to smithereens.

In spite of the obvious problems confronting trickle-down economics, it has a good intellectual pedigree. One Nobel Prize winner, Arthur Lewis, argued that inequality was good for development and economic growth, since the rich save more than the poor, and the key to growth was capital accumulation. Another Nobel Prize winner, Simon Kuznets, argued that while in the initial stages of development inequality increased, later on the trend was reversed.[3]

THE HISTORY OF the past fifty years has, however, not supported these theories and hypotheses. As we will see in the next chapter, East Asian countries—South Korea, China, Taiwan, Japan—showed that high savings did not require high inequality, that one could achieve rapid growth without a substantial increase in inequality. Because the governments did not believe that growth would automatically benefit the poor, and because they believed that greater *equality* would actually enhance growth, governments in the region took active steps to ensure that the rising tide of growth did lift most boats, that wage inequalities were kept in bounds, that some educational opportunity was extended to all. Their policies led to social and political stability, which in turn contributed to an economic environment in which businesses flourished. Tapping new reservoirs of talent provided the energy and human skills that contributed to the dynamism of the region.

Elsewhere, where governments adopted the Washington Consensus policies, the poor have benefited less from growth. In Latin America, growth has not been accompanied by a reduction in inequality, or even a reduction in poverty. In some cases poverty has actually increased, as evidenced by the urban slums that dot the landscape. The IMF talks with pride about the progress Latin America has made in market reforms over the past decade (though somewhat more quietly after the collapse of the star student Argentina in 2001, and the recession and stagnation that have afflicted many of the "reform" countries during the past five years), but has said less about the numbers in poverty.

Clearly, growth alone does not always improve the lives of all a country's people. Not surprisingly, the phrase "trickle-down" has disappeared from the policy debate. But, in a slightly mutated form, the idea is still alive. I call the new variant *trickle-down-plus*. It holds that growth is necessary and *almost* sufficient for reducing poverty—implying that the best strategy is simply to focus on growth, while mentioning issues like female education and health. But proponents of trickle-down-plus failed to implement policies that would effectively address either broader concerns of poverty or even specific issues such as the education of women. In practice, the advocates of trickle-down-plus continued with much the same policies as before, with much the same adverse effects. The overly stringent "adjustment policies" in country after country forced cutbacks in education and health: in Thailand, as a result, not only did female prostitution increase but expenditures on AIDS were cut way back; and what had been one of the world's most successful programs in fighting AIDS had a major setback.

The irony was that one of the major proponents of trickle-down-plus was the U.S. Treasury under the Clinton administration. Within the administration, in domestic politics, there was a wide spectrum of views, from New Democrats, who wanted to see a more limited role for government, to Old Democrats, who looked for more government intervention. But the central view, reflected in the annual Economic Report of the President (prepared by the Council of Economic Advisers), argued strongly against trickle-down economics—or even trickle-down-plus. Here was the U.S. Treasury pushing policies on other countries that, had they been advocated for the United States, would have been strongly contested *within the administration*, and almost surely defeated. The reason for this seeming inconsistency was simple: The IMF and the World Bank were part of Treasury's turf, an arena in which, with few exceptions, they were allowed to push their perspectives, just as other departments, within their domains, could push theirs.

PRIORITIES AND STRATEGIES

It is important not only to look at what the IMF puts on its agenda, but what it leaves off. Stabilization is on the agenda; job creation is off. Taxation, and its adverse effects, are on the agenda; land reform is off. There is money to bail out banks but not to pay for improved education and health services, let alone to bail out workers who are thrown out of their jobs as a result of the IMF's macroeconomic mismanagement.

Many of the items that were not on the Washington Consensus might bring both higher growth and greater equality. Land reform itself illustrates the choices at stake in many countries. In many developing countries, a few rich people own most of the land. The vast majority of the people work as tenant farmers, keeping only half, or less, of what they produce. This is termed *sharecropping*. The sharecropping system weakens incentives—where they share equally with the landowners, the effects are the same as a 50 percent tax on poor farmers. The IMF rails against high tax rates that are imposed against the rich, pointing out how they destroy incentives, but nary a word is spoken about these hidden taxes. Land reform, done properly, peacefully, and legally, ensuring that workers get not only land but access to credit, and the extension services that teach them about new seeds and planting techniques, could provide an enormous boost to output. But land reform represents a fundamental change in the structure of society, one that those in the elite that populates the finance ministries, those with whom the international financial institutions interact, do not necessarily like. If these institutions were really concerned about growth and poverty alleviation, they would have paid considerable attention to the issue: land reform preceded several of the most successful instances of development, such as those in Korea and Taiwan.

Another neglected item was financial sector regulation. Focusing on the Latin American crisis of the early 1980s, the IMF maintained that crises were caused by imprudent fiscal policies and loose monetary policies. But crises around the world had revealed a third source of instability, inadequate financial sector regulation. Yet the IMF pushed for reducing regulations—until the East Asia crisis forced it to change course. If land reform and financial sector regulation were underemphasized by the IMF and the Washington Consensus, in many places inflation was overemphasized. Of course, in regions like Latin America where inflation had been rampant, it deserved attention. But an *excessive* focus on inflation by the IMF led to high interest rates and high exchange rates, creating unemployment but not growth. Financial markets may have been pleased with the low inflation numbers, but workers—and those concerned with poverty—were not happy with the low growth and the high unemployment numbers.

Fortunately, poverty reduction has become an increasingly important development priority. We saw earlier that the trickle-down-plus strategies have not worked. Still, it is true that, on average, countries that have grown faster have done a better job of reducing poverty, as China and East Asia amply demonstrate. It is also true that poverty eradication requires resources, resources that can only be obtained with growth. Thus the existence of a correlation between growth and poverty reduction should come as no surprise. But this correlation does not prove that trickle-down strategies (or trickle-down-plus) constitute the best way to attack poverty. On the contrary, the statistics show that some countries have grown without reducing poverty, and some countries have been much more successful in reducing poverty, at any given growth rate, than others. The issue is not whether one is in favor of or against growth. In some ways, the growth/poverty debate seemed pointless. After all, almost everyone believes in growth.

The question has to do with the impact of *particular policies*. Some policies promote growth but have little effect on poverty; some promote growth but actually increase poverty; and some promote growth and reduce poverty at the same time. The last are called pro-poor growth strategies. Sometimes there are policies which are "win-win," policies like land reform or better access to education for the poor which hold out the promise of enhanced growth and greater equality. But many times there are trade-offs. Sometimes trade liberalization might enhance growth, but at the same time, at least in the short run, there will be increased poverty—especially if it is done rapidly—as some workers are thrown out of a job. And sometimes, there are lose-lose policies, policies for which there is little if any gain in growth but a significant increase in inequality. For many countries, capital market liberalization represents an example. The growth-poverty debate is about development strategies—strategies that look for policies that reduce poverty as they promote growth, that shun policies that increase poverty with little if any gain in growth, and that, in assessing situations where there are trade-offs, put a heavy weight on the impact on the poor.

Understanding the choices requires understanding the causes and nature of poverty. It is not that the poor are lazy; they often work harder, with longer hours, than those who are far better off. Many are caught in a series of vicious spirals: lack of food leads to ill health, which limits their earning ability, leading to still poorer health. Barely surviving, they cannot send their children to school, and without an education, their children are condemned to a life of poverty. Poverty is passed along from one generation to another. Poor farmers cannot afford to pay the money for the fertilizers and high-yielding seeds that would increase their productivity.

This is but one of many vicious cycles facing the poor. Partha Dasgupta of Cambridge University has emphasized another. In poor countries, like Nepal, the impoverished have no source of energy other than the neighboring forests; but as they strip the forests for the bare necessities of heating and cooking, the soil erodes, and as the environment degrades, they are condemned to a life of ever-increasing poverty.

Along with poverty come feelings of powerlessness. For its 2000 *World Development Report*, the World Bank interviewed thousands of poor in an exercise that was called *The Voices of the Poor*. Several themes— hardly unexpected—emerge. The poor feel that they are voiceless, and that they do not have control over their own destiny. They are buffeted by forces beyond their control.

And the poor feel insecure. Not only is their income uncertain— changes in economic circumstances beyond their control can lead to lower real wages and a loss of jobs, dramatically illustrated by the East Asia crisis—but they face health risks and continual threats of violence, sometimes from other poor people trying against all odds to meet the needs of their family, sometimes from police and others in positions of authority. While those in developed countries fret about the inadequacies of health insurance, those in developing countries must get by without any form of insurance—no unemployment insurance, no health insurance, no retirement insurance. The only safety net is provided by family and community, which is why it is so important, in the process of development, to do what one can to preserve these bonds.

To ameliorate the insecurity—whether the capriciousness of an exploitative boss or the capriciousness of a market increasingly buffeted by international storms—workers have fought for greater job security. But as hard as workers have fought for "decent jobs," the IMF has fought for what it euphemistically called "labor market flexibility," which sounds like little more than making the labor market work better but as applied has been simply a code name for lower wages, and less job protection.

Not all the downsides of the Washington Consensus policies for the poor could have been foreseen, but by now they are clear. We have seen how trade liberalization *accompanied by high interest rates* is an almost certain recipe for job destruction and unemployment creation—at the expense of the poor. Financial market liberalization *unaccompanied by an appropriate regulatory structure* is an almost certain recipe for economic instability—and may well lead to higher, not lower interest rates, making it harder for poor farmers to buy the seeds and fertilizer that can raise them above subsistence. Privatization, *unaccompanied by competition policies and oversight to ensure that monopoly powers are not abused*, can lead to higher, not lower, prices for consumers. Fiscal austerity, *pursued blindly*, in the wrong circumstances, can lead to high unemployment and a shredding of the social contract.

If the IMF underestimated the risks to the poor of its development strategies, it also underestimated the long-term social and political costs of policies that devastated the middle class, enriching a few at the top, and overestimated the benefits of its market fundamentalist policies. The middle classes have traditionally been the group that has pushed for the rule of law, that has pushed for universal public education, that has pushed for the creation of a social safety net. These are essential elements of a healthy economy and the erosion of the middle class has led to a concomitant erosion of support for these important reforms.

At the same time that it underestimated the costs of its programs, the IMF overestimated the benefits. Take the problem of unemployment. To the IMF and others who believe that when markets function normally demand must equal supply, unemployment is a symptom of an interference in the free workings of the market. Wages are too high (for instance, because of union power). The obvious remedy to unemployment was to lower wages; lower wages will increase the demand for labor, bringing more people onto employment rolls. While modern economic theory (in particular, theories based on asymmetric information and incomplete contracts) has explained why even with highly competitive markets, including labor markets, unemployment can persist—so the argument that says that unemployment must be due to unions or government minimum wages is simply wrong—there is another criticism of the strategy of lowering wages. Lower wages *might* lead some firms to hire a few more workers; but the number of newly hired workers may be relatively few, and the misery caused by the lower wages on all the other workers might be very grave. Employers and owners of capital might be quite happy, as they see their profits soar. These will endorse the IMF/market fundamentalist model with its policy prescriptions with enthusiasm! Asking people in developing countries to pay for schools is another example of this narrow worldview. Those who said charges should be imposed argued that there would be little effect on enrollment and that the government needed the revenue badly. The irony here was that the simplistic models miscalculated the impact on enrollment of eliminating school fees; by failing to take into account the *systemic* effects of policy, not only did they fail to take into account the broader impacts on society, they even failed in the more narrow attempts to estimate accurately the consequences for school enrollment.

If the IMF had an overly optimistic view of the markets, it had an overly pessimistic view of government; if government was not the root of all evil, it certainly was more part of the problem than the solution. But the lack of concern about the poor was not just a matter of views of markets and government, views that said that markets would take care of everything and government would only make matters worse; it was also a matter of values—how concerned we should be about the poor and who should bear what risks.

THE RESULTS OF the policies enforced by Washington Consensus have not been encouraging: for most countries embracing its tenets development has been slow, and where growth has occurred, the benefits have not been shared equally; crises have been mismanaged; the transition from communism to a market economy (as we shall see) has been a disappointment. Inside the developing world, the questions run deep. Those who followed the prescriptions, endured the austerity, are asking: When do we see the fruits? In much of Latin America, after a short burst of growth in the early 1990s, stagnation and recession have set in. The growth was not sustained—some might say not sustainable. Indeed, at this juncture, the growth record of the so-called post-reform era looks no better, and in some countries much worse, than in the pre-reform import substitution period (when countries used protectionist policies to help domestic industries compete against imports) of the 1950s and 1960s. The average annual growth rate in the region in the 1990s, at 2.9 percent after the reforms, was just more than half that in the 1960s at 5.4 percent. In retrospect, the growth strategies of the 1950s and 1960s were not sustained (critics would say they were unsustainable); but the slight upsurge in growth in the early 1990s also did not last (these also, critics would say, were unsustainable). Indeed, critics of the Washington Consensus point out that the burst of growth in the early 1990s was little more than a catch-up, not even making up for the lost decade of the 1980s, the decade after the last major crisis, during which growth stagnated. Throughout the region people are asking, has reform failed, or has globalization failed? The distinction is perhaps artificial—globalization was at the center of the reforms. Even in the countries that have managed some growth, such as Mexico, the benefits have accrued largely to the upper 30 percent, and have been even more concentrated in the top 10 percent. Those at the bottom have gained little; many are even worse off.

The Washington Consensus reforms have exposed countries to greater risk, and the risks have been borne disproportionately by those least able to cope with them. Just as in many countries the pacing and sequencing of reforms has resulted in job destruction outmatching job creation, so too has the exposure to risk outmatched the ability to create institutions for coping with risk, including effective safety nets.

There were, of course, important messages in the Washington Consensus, including lessons about fiscal and monetary prudence, lessons which were well understood by the countries that succeeded; but most did not have to learn them from the IMF.

Sometimes the IMF and the World Bank have unfairly taken the blame for the messages they deliver—no one likes to be told that they have to live within their means. But the criticism of the international economic institutions goes deeper: while there was much that was good on their development agenda, even reforms that are desirable in the long run have to be implemented carefully. It's now widely accepted that pacing and sequencing cannot be ignored. But even more important, there is more to development than these lessons suggest. There *are* alternative strategies—strategies that differ not only in emphases but even in policies; strategies, for instance, which include land reform but do not include capital market liberalization, which provide for competition policies before privatization, which ensure that job creation accompanies trade liberalization.

These alternatives made use of markets, but recognized that there was an important role for government as well. They recognized the importance of reform, but that reforms needed to be paced and sequenced. They saw change not just as a matter of economics, but as part of a broader evolution of society. They recognized that for long-term success, there had to be broad support of the reforms, and if there was to be broad support, the benefits had to be broadly distributed.

We have already called attention to some of these successes: the limited successes in Africa, for instance, in Uganda, Ethiopia, and Botswana; and the broader successes in East Asia, including China. In chapter 9, we shall take a closer look at some of the successes in transition, such as Poland. The successes show that development and transition are possible; the successes in development are well beyond that which almost anyone imagined a half century ago. The fact that so many of the success cases followed strategies that were markedly different from those of the Washington Consensus is telling.

Each time and each country is different. Would other countries have met the same success if they had followed East Asia's strategy? Would the strategies which worked a quarter of a century ago work in today's global economy? Economists can disagree about the answers to these questions. But countries need to consider the alternatives and, through democratic political processes, make these choices for themselves. It should be—and it should have been—the task of the international economic institutions to provide the countries the wherewithal to make these *informed* choices on their own, with an understanding of the consequences and risks of each. The essence of freedom is the right to make a choice—and to accept the responsibility that comes with it.

CHAPTER 8

THE EAST ASIA CRISIS

How IMF Policies Brought the World
to the Verge of a Global Meltdown

WHEN THE THAI baht collapsed on July 2, 1997, no one knew that this was the beginning of the greatest economic crisis since the Great Depression—one that would spread from Asia to Russia and Latin America and threaten the entire world. For ten years the baht had traded at around 25 to the dollar; then overnight it fell by about 25 percent. Currency speculation spread and hit Malaysia, Korea, the Philippines, and Indonesia, and by the end of the year what had started as an exchange rate disaster threatened to take down many of the region's banks, stock markets, and even entire economies. The crisis is over now, but countries such as Indonesia will feel its effects for years. Unfortunately, the IMF policies imposed during this tumultuous time worsened the situation. Since the IMF was founded precisely to avert and deal with crises of this kind, the fact that it failed in so many ways led to a major rethinking of its role, with many people in the United States and abroad calling for an overhaul of many of the Fund's policies and the institution itself. Indeed, in retrospect, it became clear that the IMF policies not only exacerbated the downturns but were partially responsible for the onset: excessively rapid financial and capital market liberalization was probably the single most important cause of the crisis, though mistaken policies on the part of the countries themselves played a role as well. Today the IMF acknowledges many, but not all, of its mistakes—its officials realize how dangerous, for instance, excessively rapid capital market liberalization can be—but its change in views comes too late to help the countries afflicted.

The crisis took most observers by surprise. Not long before the crisis, even the IMF had forecast strong growth. Over the preceding three decades East Asia had not only grown faster and done better at reducing poverty than any other region of the world, developed or less developed, but it had also been more stable. It had been spared the ups and downs that mark all market economies. So impressive was its performance that it was widely described as the "East Asia Miracle." Indeed, reportedly, so confident had the IMF been about the region that it assigned a loyal staff member as director for the region, as an easy preretirement posting.

When the crisis broke out, I was surprised at how strongly the IMF and the U.S. Treasury seemed to criticize the countries—according to the IMF, the Asian nations' institutions were rotten, their governments corrupt, and wholesale reform was needed. These outspoken critics were hardly experts on the region, but what they said contradicted so much of what I knew about it. I had been traveling to and studying the area for three decades. I had been asked by the World Bank, by Lawrence Summers himself when he was its vice president for research, to participate in a major study of the East Asia Miracle, to head the team looking at the financial markets. Almost two decades before, as the Chinese began their transition to a market economy, I had been called upon by them to discuss their development strategy. In the White House, I continued my close involvement, heading, for instance, the team that wrote the annual economic report for APEC (the Asia-Pacific Economic Cooperation, the group of countries around the Pacific rim, whose annual meetings of heads of states had come increasingly into prominence as the economic importance of the region grew). I participated actively in the National Security Council in the debates about China—and indeed, when tensions over the administration's "containment" policy got too heated, I was the cabinet member sent to meet with China's premier, Zhu Rongji, to calm the waters. I was one of the few foreigners ever invited to join the country's top leaders at their yearly August retreat for policy discussions.

How, I wondered, if these countries' institutions were so rotten, had they done so well for so long? The difference in perspectives, between what I knew about the region and what the IMF and the Treasury alleged, made little sense, until I recalled the debate that had raged over the East Asia Miracle itself. The IMF and the World Bank had almost consciously avoided studying the region, though presumably, because of its success, it would have seemed natural for them to turn to it for lessons for others. It was only under pressure from the Japanese that the World Bank had undertaken the study of economic growth in East Asia (the final report was titled *The East Asian Miracle*) and then only after the Japanese had offered to pay for it. The reason was obvious: The countries had been successful not only in spite of the fact that they had not followed most of the dictates of the Washington Consensus, but *because* they had not. Though the experts' findings were toned down in the final published report, the World Bank's Asian Miracle study laid out the important roles that the government had played. These were far from the minimalist roles beloved of the Washington Consensus.

There were those, not just in the international financial institutions but in academia, who asked, was there really a miracle? "All" that East Asia had done was to save heavily and invest well! But this view of the "miracle" misses the point. No other set of countries around the world had managed to save at such rates *and* invest the funds well. Government policies played an important role in enabling the East Asian nations to accomplish both things simultaneously.[1]

When the crisis broke out, it was almost as if many of the region's critics were glad: their perspective had been vindicated. In a curious disjunction, while they were loath to credit the region's governments with any of the successes of the previous quarter century, they were quick to blame the governments for the failings.

Whether one calls it a miracle or not is beside the point: the increases in incomes and the reductions in poverty in East Asia over the last three decades have been unprecedented. No one visiting these countries can fail to marvel at the developmental transformation, the changes not only in the economy but also in society, reflected in every statistic imaginable. Thirty years ago, thousands of backbreaking rickshaws were pulled for a pittance; today, they are only a tourist attraction, a photo opportunity for the camera-snapping tourists. The combination of high savings rates, government investment in education, and state-directed industrial policy all served to make the region an economic powerhouse.

Growth rates were phenomenal for decades and the standard of living rose enormously for tens of millions of people. The benefits of growth were shared widely. There were problems in the way the Asian economies developed, but overall, the governments had devised a strategy that worked, a strategy which had but one item in common with the Washington Consensus policies—the importance of macrostability. As in the Washington Consensus, trade was important, but the emphasis was on promoting exports, not removing impediments to imports. Trade was eventually liberalized, but only gradually, as new jobs were created in the export industries. While the Washington Consensus policies emphasized rapid financial and capital market liberalization, the East Asian countries liberalized only gradually—some of the most successful, like China, still have a long way to go. While the Washington Consensus policies emphasized privatization, government at the national and local levels helped create efficient enterprises that played a key role in the success of several of the countries. In the Washington Consensus view, industrial policies, in which governments try to shape the future direction of the economy, are a mistake. But the East Asian governments took that as one of their central responsibilities. In particular, they believed that if they were to close the income gap between themselves and the more developed countries, they had to close the knowledge and technology gap, so they designed education and investment policies to do that. While the Washington Consensus policies paid little attention to inequality, the East Asian countries focused on reducing poverty and limiting inequality, believing that such policies were important for maintaining social cohesion, and that social cohesion was necessary to provide a climate favorable to investment and growth. Most broadly, while the Washington Consensus policies emphasized a minimalist role for government, in East Asia, governments helped shape and direct markets.

When the crisis began, those in the West did not realize its severity. Asked about aid for Thailand, President Bill Clinton dismissed the collapse of the baht as "a few glitches in the road" to economic prosperity.[2] The confidence and imperturbability of Clinton was shared by the financial leaders of the world, as they met in September 1997 in Hong Kong for the annual meeting of the IMF and World Bank. IMF officials there were so sure of their advice that they even asked for a change in its charter to allow it to put *more* pressure on developing countries to liberalize their capital markets. Meanwhile, the leaders of the Asian countries, and especially the finance ministers I met with, were terrified. They viewed the hot money that came with liberalized capital markets as the source of their problems. They knew that major trouble was ahead: a crisis would wreak havoc on their economies and their societies, and they feared that IMF policies would prevent them from taking the actions that they thought might stave off the crisis, at the same time that the policies they would insist upon should a crisis occur would worsen the impacts on their economy. They felt, however, powerless to resist. They even knew what could and should be done to prevent a crisis and minimize the damage—but knew that the IMF would condemn them if they undertook those actions and they feared the resulting withdrawal of international capital. In the end, only Malaysia was brave enough to risk the wrath of the IMF; and though Prime Minister Mahathir's policies—trying to keep interest rates low, trying to put brakes on the rapid flow of speculative money out of the country—were attacked from all quarters, Malaysia's downturn was shorter and shallower than that of any of the other countries.[3]

At the Hong Kong meeting, I suggested to the ministers of the Southeast Asian countries with whom I met that there were some concerted actions which they could take together; if they all imposed capital controls—controls intended to prevent the damage as the speculative money rushed out of their countries—in a coordinated way, they might be able to withstand the pressures that would undoubtedly be brought down upon them by the international financial community, and they could help insulate their economies from the turmoil. They talked about getting together later in the year to map out a plan. But hardly had their bags been unpacked from the trip to Hong Kong than the crisis spread, first to Indonesia, and then, in early December, to South Korea. Meanwhile, other countries around the world had been attacked by currency speculators—from Brazil to Hong Kong—and withstood the attack, but at high cost.

There are two familiar patterns to these crises. The first is illustrated by South Korea, a country with an impressive track record. As it emerged from the wreckage of the Korean War, South Korea formulated a growth strategy which increased per capita income eightfold in thirty years, reduced poverty dramatically, achieved universal literacy, and went far in closing the gap in technology between itself and the more advanced countries. At the end of the Korean War, it was poorer than India; by the beginning of the 1990s, it had joined the Organisation for Economic Co-operation and Development (OECD), the club of the advanced industrialized countries. Korea had become one of the world's largest producers of computer chips, and its large conglomerates, Samsung, Daewoo, and Hyundai, produced goods known throughout the world. But whereas in the early days of its transformation it had tightly controlled its financial markets, under pressure from the United States it had reluctantly allowed its firms to borrow abroad. But by borrowing abroad, the firms exposed themselves to the vagaries of the international market: in late 1997, rumors flashed through Wall Street that Korea was in trouble. It would not be able to roll over the loans from Western banks that were coming due, and it did not have the reserves to pay them off. Such rumors can be self-fulfilling prophecies. I heard these rumors at the World Bank well before they made the newspapers—and I knew what they meant. Quickly, the banks which such a short time earlier were so eager to lend money to Korean firms decided not to roll over their loans. When they all decided not to roll over their loans, their prophecy came true: Korea *was* in trouble.

The second was illustrated by Thailand. There, a speculative attack (combined with high short-term indebtedness) was to blame. Speculators, believing that a currency will devalue, try to move out of the currency and into dollars; with free convertibility—that is, the ability to change local currency for dollars or any other currency—this can easily be done. But as traders sell the currency, its value is weakened—confirming their prophecy. Alternatively, and more commonly, the government tries to support the currency. It sells dollars from its reserves (money the country holds, often in dollars, against a rainy day), buying up the local currency, to sustain its value. But eventually, the government runs out of hard currency. There are no more dollars to sell. The currency plummets. The speculators are satisfied. They have bet right. They can move back into the currency—and make a nice profit. The magnitude of the returns can be enormous. Assume a speculator goes to a Thai bank, borrows 24 billion baht, which, at the original exchange rate, can be converted into $1 billion. A week later the exchange rate falls; instead of there being 24 baht to the dollar, there are now 40 baht to the dollar. He takes $600 million, converting it back to baht, getting 24 billion baht to repay the loan. The remaining $400 million is his profit—a tidy return for one week's work, and the investment of little of his own money. Confident that the exchange rate would not appreciate (that is, go from 24 baht to the dollar to, say, 20 to the dollar), there was hardly any risk; at worst, if the exchange rate remained unchanged, he would lose one week's interest. As perceptions that a devaluation is imminent grow, the chance to make money becomes irresistible and speculators from around the world pile in to take advantage of the situation.

If the crises had a familiar pattern, so too did the IMF's responses: it provided huge amounts of money (the total bailout packages, including support from G-7 countries, was $95 billion)[4] so that the countries could sustain the exchange rate. It thought that if the market believed that there was enough money in the coffers, there would be no point in attacking the currency, and thus "confidence" would be restored. The money served another function: it enabled the countries to provide dollars to the firms that had borrowed from Western bankers to repay the loans. It was thus, in part, a bailout to the international banks as much as it was a bailout to the country; the lenders did not have to face the full consequences of having made bad loans. And in country after country in which the IMF money was used to sustain the exchange rate temporarily at an unsustainable level, there was another consequence: rich people inside the country took advantage of the opportunity to convert their money into dollars at the favorable exchange rate and whisk it abroad. As we shall note in the next chapter, the most egregious example occurred in Russia, after the IMF lent it money in July 1998. But this phenomenon, which is sometimes given the more neutral sounding name of "capital flight," also played a key role in the previous important crisis, in Mexico during 1994–95.

The IMF combined the money with conditions, in a package which was supposed to rectify the problems that caused the crisis. It is these other ingredients, as much as the money, that are supposed to persuade markets to roll over their loans, and to persuade speculators to look elsewhere for easy targets. The ingredients typically include higher interest rates—in the case of East Asia, much, much higher interest rates—plus cutbacks in government spending and increases in taxes. They also include "structural reforms," that is, changes in the structure of the economy which, it is believed, lies behind the country's problems. In the case of East Asia, not only were conditions imposed that mandated hikes in interest rates and cutbacks in spending; additional conditions required countries to make political as well as economic changes, major reforms, such as increased openness and transparency and improved financial market regulation, as well as minor reforms, like the abolition of the clove monopoly in Indonesia.

The IMF would claim that imposing these conditions was the responsible thing to do. It was providing billions of dollars; it had a responsibility to make sure not just that it was repaid but that the countries "did the right thing" to restore their economic health. If structural problems had *caused* the macroeconomic crisis, those problems had to be addressed. The breadth of the conditions meant that the countries accepting Fund aid had to give up a large part of their economic sovereignty. Some of the objection to the IMF programs was based on this, and the resulting undermining of democracy; and some were based on the fact that the conditions did not (and arguably were not designed to) restore the economies' health. But, as we noted in chapter 6, some of the conditions had nothing to do with the problem at hand.

The programs—with all of their conditions and with all of their money—failed. They were supposed to arrest the fall in the exchange rates; but these continued to fall, with hardly a flicker of recognition by the markets that the IMF had "come to the rescue." In each case, embarrassed by the failure of its supposed medicine to work, the IMF charged the country with failing to take the necessary reforms seriously. In each case, it announced to the world that there were fundamental problems that had to be addressed before a true recovery could take place. Doing so was like crying fire in a crowded theater: investors, more convinced by the diagnosis of the problems than by the prescriptions, fled.[5] Rather than restoring confidence that would lead to an inflow of capital into the country, IMF criticism exacerbated the stampede of capital out. Because of this, and the other reasons to which I turn shortly, the perception throughout much of the developing world, one I share, is that the IMF itself had become a part of the countries' problem rather than part of the solution. Indeed, in several of the crisis countries, ordinary people as well as many government officials and business people continue to refer to the economic and social storm that hit their nations simply as "the IMF"—the way one would say "the plague" or "the Great Depression." History is dated by "before" and "after" the IMF, just as countries that are devastated by an earthquake or some other natural disaster date events by "before" or "after" the earthquake.

As the crisis progressed, unemployment soared, GDP plummeted, banks closed. The unemployment rate was up fourfold in Korea, threefold in Thailand, tenfold in Indonesia. In Indonesia, almost 15 percent of males working in 1997 had lost their jobs by August 1998, and the economic devastation was even worse in the urban areas of the main island, Java. In South Korea, urban poverty almost tripled, with almost a quarter of the population falling into poverty; in Indonesia, poverty doubled. In some countries, like Thailand, people thrown out of jobs in the cities could return to their rural homes. However, this put increasing pressure on those in the rural sector. In 1998, GDP in Indonesia fell by 13.1 percent, in Korea by 6.7 percent, and in Thailand by 10.8 percent. Three years after the crisis, Indonesia's GDP was still 7.5 percent below that before the crisis, Thailand's 2.3 percent lower.

In some cases, fortunately, outcomes were less bleak than was widely anticipated. Communities in Thailand worked together to ensure that their children's education was not interrupted, with people voluntarily contributing to help keep their neighbors' kids in school. They also made sure that everyone had enough food, and because of this the incidence of malnutrition did not increase. In Indonesia, a World Bank program seemed to succeed in arresting the anticipated adverse effects on education. It was poor urban workers—hardly well off by any standards—who were made most destitute by the crisis. The usurious interest rates which threw small businesses into bankruptcy contributed to the erosion of the middle class, and will have the longest lasting effects on the social, political, and economic life of the region.

Deteriorating conditions in one country helped bring down its neighbors. The slowdown in the region had global repercussions: global economic growth slowed, and with the slowing of global growth, commodity prices fell. From Russia to Nigeria, the many emerging countries that depended on natural resources were in deep, deep trouble. As investors who had risked their money in these countries saw their wealth plummeting, and as *their* bankers called in their loans, they had to cut back their investments in other emerging markets. Brazil, dependent neither on oil nor on trade with the countries in deep trouble, with economic features far different from these countries, was brought into the unfolding global financial crisis by the generalized fear of foreign investors and the retrenchment in their lending. Eventually, almost every emerging market, even Argentina, which the IMF had long held up as the poster child of reform, largely for its success in bringing down inflation, was affected.

HOW IMF/U.S. TREASURY POLICIES LED TO THE CRISIS

The disturbances capped a half decade of an American-led global triumph of market economics following the end of the Cold War. This period saw international attention focus on newly emerging markets, from East Asia to Latin America, and from Russia to India. Investors saw these countries as a paradise of high returns and seemingly low risk. In the short space of seven years, private capital flows from the developed to the less developed countries increased sevenfold while public flows (foreign aid) stayed steady.[6]

International bankers and politicians were confident that this was the dawn of a new era. The IMF and the U.S. Treasury believed, or at least argued, that full capital account liberalization would help the region grow even faster. The countries in East Asia had no need for additional capital, given their high savings rate, but still capital account liberalization was pushed on these countries in the late 1980s and early 1990s. I believe that capital account liberalization was *the single most important factor leading to the crisis*. I have come to this conclusion not just by carefully looking at what happened in the region, but by looking at what happened in the almost one hundred other economic crises of the last quarter century. Because economic crises have become more frequent (and deeper), there is now a wealth of data through which one can analyze the factors contributing to crises.[7] It has also become increasingly clear that all too often capital account liberalization represents risk without a reward. Even when countries have strong banks, a mature stock market, and other institutions that many of the Asian countries did not have, it can impose enormous risks.

Probably no country could have withstood the sudden change in investor sentiment, a sentiment that reversed this huge inflow to a huge outflow as investors, both foreign and domestic, put their funds elsewhere. Inevitably, such large reversals would precipitate a crisis, a recession, or worse. In the case of Thailand, this reversal amounted to 7.9 percent of GDP in 1997, 12.3 percent of GDP in 1998, and 7 percent of GDP in the first half of 1999. It would be equivalent to a reversal in capital flows for the United States of an average $765 billion per year between 1997 and 1999. While developing countries' ability to withstand the reversal was weak, so too was their ability to cope with the consequences of a major downturn. Their remarkable economic performance—no major economic recession in three decades—meant that the East Asian countries had not developed unemployment insurance schemes. But even had they turned their mind to the task, it would not have been easy: in the United States, unemployment insurance for those who are self-employed in agriculture is far from adequate, and this is precisely the sector that dominates in the developing world.

The complaint against the IMF, however, runs deeper: it is not just that the Fund pushed the liberalization policies which led to the crisis, but that they pushed these policies even though there was little evidence that such policies promoted growth, and there was ample evidence that they imposed huge risks on developing countries.

Here was a true irony—if such a gentle word can be used. In October 1997, at the very beginning of the crisis, the Fund was advocating the expansion of precisely those polices which underlay the increasing frequency of crises. As an academic, I was shocked that the IMF and the U.S. Treasury would push this agenda with such force, in the face of a virtual absence of theory and evidence suggesting that it was in the economic interests of either the developing countries or global economic stability—and in the presence of evidence to the contrary. Surely, one might have argued, there must be *some* basis for their position, beyond serving the naked self-interest of financial markets, which saw capital market liberalization as just another form of market access—more markets in which to make more money. Recognizing that East Asia had little need for additional capital, the advocates of capital market liberalization came up with an argument that even at the time I thought was unconvincing, but in retrospect looks particularly strange—that it would enhance the countries' economic stability! This was to be achieved by allowing greater diversification of sources of funding.[8] It is hard to believe that these advocates had not seen the data that showed that capital flows were pro-cyclical. That is to say that capital flows out of a country in a recession, precisely when the country needs it most, and flows in during a boom, exacerbating inflationary pressures. Sure enough, just at the time the countries needed outside funds, the bankers asked for their money back.

Capital market liberalization made the developing countries subject to both the rational and the irrational whims of the investor community, to their irrational exuberance and pessimism. Keynes was well aware of the often seemingly irrational changes in sentiments. In *The General Theory of Employment, Interest and Money* (1935), he referred to these huge and often inexplicable swings in moods as "animal spirits." Nowhere were these spirits more evident than in East Asia. Slightly before the crisis, Thai bonds paid only 0.85 percent higher interest than the safest bonds in the world, that is, they were regarded as extremely safe. A short while later, the risk premium on Thai bonds had soared.

There was a second, hardly more credible argument that the advocates of capital market liberalization put forward—again without evidence. They contended that capital market controls impeded economic efficiency and that, as a result, countries would grow better without these controls. Thailand provides a case in point for why this argument was so flawed. Before liberalization, Thailand had severe limitations on the extent to which banks could lend for speculative real estate. It had imposed these limits because it was a poor country that wanted to grow, and it believed that investing the country's scarce capital in manufacturing would both create jobs and enhance growth. It also knew that throughout the world, speculative real estate lending is a major source of economic instability. This type of lending gives rise to bubbles (the soaring of prices as investors clamor to reap the gain from the seeming boom in the sector); these bubbles always burst; and when they do, the economy crashes. The pattern is familiar, and was the same in Bangkok as it was in Houston: as real estate prices rise, banks feel they can lend more on the basis of the collateral; as investors see prices going up, they want to get in on the game before it's too late—and the bankers give them the money to do it. Real estate developers see quick profits by putting up new buildings, until excess capacity results. The developers can't rent their space, they default on their loans, and the bubble bursts.

The IMF, however, contended that the kinds of restraints that Thailand had imposed to prevent a crisis interfered with the efficient market allocation of resources. If the market says, build office buildings, commercial construction *must be* the highest return activity. If the market says, as it *effectively* did after liberalization, build empty office buildings, then so be it; again, according to IMF logic, the market *must* know best. While Thailand was desperate for more public investment to strengthen its infrastructure and relatively weak secondary and university education systems, billions were squandered on commercial real estate. These buildings remain empty today, testimony to the risks posed by excessive market exuberance and the pervasive market failures that can arise in the presence of inadequate government regulation of financial institutions.[9]

The IMF, of course, was not alone in pushing for liberalization. The U.S. Treasury, which, as the IMF's largest shareholder and the only one with veto power has a large role in determining IMF policies, pushed liberalization too.

I was in President Clinton's Council of Economic Advisers in 1993 when South Korea's trade relations with the United States came up for discussion. The negotiations included a host of minor issues—such as opening up South Korea's markets to American sausages—and the important issue of financial and capital market liberalization. For three decades, Korea enjoyed remarkable economic growth without significant international investment. Growth had come based on the nation's own savings and on its own firms managed by its own people. It did not need Western funds and had demonstrated an alternative route for the importation of modern technology and market access. While its neighbors, Singapore and Malaysia, had invited in multinational companies, South Korea had created its own enterprises. Through good products and aggressive marketing, South Korean companies had sold their goods around the world. South Korea recognized that continued growth and integration in the global markets would require some liberalization, or deregulation, in the way its financial and capital markets were run. South Korea was also aware of the dangers of poor deregulation: it had seen what happened in the United States, where deregulation had culminated in the 1980s savings-and-loan debacle. In response, South Korea had carefully charted out a path of liberalization. This path was too slow for Wall Street, which saw profitable opportunities and did not want to wait. While Wall Streeters defended the principles of free markets and a limited role for government, they were not above asking help from government to push their agenda for them. And as we shall see, the Treasury Department responded with force.

At the Council of Economic Advisers we weren't convinced that South Korean liberalization was an issue of U.S. *national* interest, though obviously it would help the *special* interests of Wall Street. Also we were worried about the effect it would have on global stability. We wrote a memorandum, or "think piece," to lay out the issues, stimulate a debate, and help focus attention on the matter. We prepared a set of criteria for evaluating which market-opening measures are most vital to U.S. national interests. We argued for a system of *prioritization*. Many forms of "market access" are of little benefit to the United States. While some specific groups might benefit a great deal, the country as a whole would gain little. Without prioritization, there was a risk of what happened during the previous Bush administration: one of the supposedly great achievements in opening up Japan's market was that Toys "R" Us could sell Chinese toys to Japanese children—good for Japanese children and Chinese workers, but of little benefit to America. Though it is hard to believe that such a mild-mannered proposal could be greeted with objections, it was. Lawrence Summers, at the time undersecretary of the Treasury, adamantly opposed the exercise, saying such prioritization was unnecessary. It was the responsibility of the National Economic Council (NEC) to coordinate economic policy, to balance the economic analysis of the Council of Economic Advisers with the political pressures that were reflected in the various agencies, and decide what issues to take to the president for final decision.

The NEC, then headed by Robert Rubin, decided the issue was of insufficient importance to be brought to the president for consideration. The real reason for the opposition was only too transparent. Forcing Korea to liberalize faster would not create many jobs in America, nor would it likely lead to significant increases in American GDP. Any system of prioritization would therefore not put these measures high on the agenda.[10] But worse, it was not even clear that the United States would, as a whole, even benefit, and it was clear that Korea might in fact be worse off. The U.S. Treasury, which argued to the contrary both that it was important for the United States and that it would not lead to instability, prevailed. In the final analysis, such matters are the Department of the Treasury's province, and it would be unusual for the position of the Treasury to be overridden. The fact that the debate was conducted behind closed doors meant that other voices could not be heard; perhaps if they had, if there had been more transparency in American decision making, it is possible that the outcome might have been different. Instead, Treasury won, and the United States, Korea, and the global economy lost. Treasury would probably claim that the liberalization itself was not at fault; the problem was that liberalization was done in the wrong way. But that was precisely one of the points that the Council of Economic Advisers raised: It was very likely that a quick liberalization would be done poorly.

THE FIRST ROUND OF MISTAKES

There is little doubt that IMF and Treasury policies contributed to an environment that enhanced the likelihood of a crisis by encouraging, in some cases insisting on, an unwarrantedly rapid pace toward financial and capital market liberalization. However, the IMF and Treasury made their most profound mistakes in their initial response to the crisis. Of the many failures outlined below, today there is widespread agreement on all but the criticism of IMF monetary policy.

At the onset, the IMF seemed to have misdiagnosed the problem. It had handled crises in Latin America, caused by profligate government spending and loose monetary policies that led to huge deficits and high inflation; and while it may not have handled those crises well—the region experienced a decade of stagnation after the so-called successful IMF programs, and even the creditors had eventually to absorb large losses—it at least had a game plan that had a certain coherency. East Asia was vastly different from Latin America; governments had surpluses and the economy enjoyed low inflation, but corporations were deeply indebted.

The diagnosis made a difference for two reasons. First, in the highly inflationary environment of Latin America, what was needed was a decrease in the excess demand. Given the impending recession in East Asia, the problem was not excess demand but insufficient demand. Dampening demand could only make matters worse.

Second, if firms have a low level of indebtedness, high interest rates, while painful, can still be absorbed. With high levels of indebtedness, imposing high interest rates, even for short periods of time, is like signing a death warrant for many of the firms—and for the economy.

In fact, while the Asian economies did have some weaknesses that needed to be addressed, they were no worse than those in many other countries, and surely nowhere near as bad as the IMF suggested. Indeed, the rapid recovery of Korea and Malaysia showed that, in large measure, the downturns were not unlike the dozens of recessions that have plagued market economies in the advanced industrial countries in the two hundred years of capitalism. The countries of East Asia not only had an impressive record of growth, as we have already noted, but they had had fewer downturns over the previous three decades than any of the advanced industrial countries. Two of the countries had had only one year of negative growth; two had had no recession in thirty years. In these and other dimensions, there was more to praise in East Asia than to condemn; and if East Asia was vulnerable, it was a newly acquired vulnerability—largely the result of the capital and financial market liberalization for which the IMF was itself partly culpable.

Hooverite Contractionary Policies: An Anomaly in the Modern World

For more than seventy years there has been a standard recipe for a country facing a severe economic downturn. The government must stimulate aggregate demand, either by monetary or fiscal policy—cut taxes, increase expenditures, or loosen monetary policy. When I was chairman of the Council of Economic Advisers, my main objective was to maintain the economy at full employment and maximize long-term growth. At the World Bank, I approached the problems of the countries in East Asia with the same perspective, evaluating policies to see which would be most effective in both the short and long term. The crisis economies of East Asia were clearly threatened with a major downturn and needed stimulation. The IMF pushed exactly the opposite course, with consequences precisely of the kind that one would have predicted.

At the time of the onset of the crisis, East Asia was in rough macrobalance—with low inflationary pressures and government budgets in balance or surplus. This had two obvious implications. First, the collapse of the exchange rate and the stock markets, the breaking of the real estate bubbles, accompanied by falling investment and consumption, would send it into a recession. Second, the economic collapse would result in collapsing tax revenues, and leave a budget gap. Not since Herbert Hoover have responsible economists argued that one should focus on the actual deficit rather than the structural deficit, that is, the deficit that would have been there had the economy been operating at full employment. Yet this is precisely what the IMF advocated.

Today, the IMF admits that the fiscal policy it recommended was excessively austere.[11] The policies made the recession far worse than it needed to be. During the crisis, however, in the *Financial Times* the IMF's first deputy managing director Stanley Fischer defended the IMF's policies, writing, in effect, that *all* the IMF was asking of the countries was to have a balanced budget![12] Not for sixty years have respectable economists believed that an economy going into a recession should have a balanced budget.

I felt intensely about this issue of balanced budgets. While I was at the Council of Economic Advisers, one of our major battles was over the balanced budget amendment to the Constitution. This amendment would have required the federal government to limit its expenditures to its revenues. We, *and Treasury,* were against it because we believed that it was bad economic policy. In the event of a recession, it would be all the more difficult to use fiscal policy to help the economy recover. As the economy goes into a recession, tax revenues decrease, and the amendment would have required the government to cut back expenditures (or increase taxes), which would have depressed the economy further.

Passing the amendment would have been tantamount to the government walking away from one of its central responsibilities, maintaining the economy at full employment. Despite the fact that expansionary fiscal policy was one of the few ways out of recession, and despite the administration's opposition to the balanced budget amendment, the U.S. Treasury and the IMF advocated the equivalent of a balanced budget amendment for Thailand, Korea, and other East Asian countries.

Beggar-Thyself Policies

Of all the mistakes the IMF committed as the East Asia crisis spread from one country to another in 1997 and 1998, one of the hardest to fathom was the Fund's failure to recognize the important interactions among the policies pursued in the different countries. Contractionary policies in one country not only depressed that country's economy but had adverse effects on its neighbors. By continuing to advocate contractionary policies the IMF exacerbated the *contagion*, the spread of the downturn from one country to the next. As each country weakened, it reduced its imports from its neighbors, thereby pulling its neighbors down.

The beggar-thy-neighbor policies of the 1930s are generally thought to have played an important role in the spread of the Great Depression. Each country hit by a downturn tried to bolster its own economy by cutting back on imports and thus shifting consumer demand to its own products. A country would cut back on imports by imposing tariffs and by making competitive devaluations of its currency, which made its own goods cheaper and other countries' more expensive. However, as each country cut back on imports, it succeeded in "exporting" the economic downturn to its neighbors. Hence the term *beggar-thy-neighbor*.

The IMF devised a strategy that had an effect which was even worse than the beggar-thy-neighbor policies that had devastated countries around the world during the depression of the 1930s. Countries were told that when facing a downturn they must cut back on their trade deficit, and even build a trade surplus. This might be logical if the central objective of a country's macroeconomic policy were to repay foreign creditors. By building up a war chest of foreign currency, a country will be better able to pay its bills—never mind the cost to those inside the country or elsewhere. Today, unlike the 1930s, enormous pressure is put on a country not to increase tariffs or other trade barriers in order to decrease imports, even if it faces a recession. The IMF also inveighed strongly against further devaluation. Indeed, the whole point of the bailouts was to *prevent* a further decrease in the exchange rate. This itself might seem peculiar, given the IMF's otherwise seeming faith in markets: why not let market mechanisms determine exchange rates, just as they determine other prices? But intellectual consistency has never been the hallmark of the IMF, and its single-minded worries about inflation being set off by devaluation have always prevailed. With tariffs and devaluations ruled out, there were but two ways to build a trade surplus. One was to increase exports; but this is not easy, and cannot be done quickly, particularly when the economies of your major trading partners are weak and your own financial markets are in disarray, so exporters cannot obtain finance to expand. The other was to reduce imports—by cutting incomes, that is, inducing a major recession. Unfortunately for the countries, and the world, this was the only option left. And this is what happened in East Asia in the late 1990s: contractionary fiscal and monetary policies combined with misguided financial policies led to massive economic downturns, cutting incomes, which reduced imports and led to huge trade surpluses, giving the countries the resources to pay back foreign creditors.

If one's objective was to increase the size of reserves, the policy was a success. But at what expense to the people in the country, and their neighbors! Hence the name of these policies—"beggar-thyself." The consequence for any country's trading partners was exactly the same as if beggar-thy-neighbor policies had actually been pursued. Each country's imports were cut back, which is the same as other countries' exports being cut. From the neighbors' perspectives, they couldn't care less *why* exports were cut; what they saw was the consequence, a reduction of sales abroad. Thus the downturn was exported around the region. Only this time, there was not even the saving grace that as the downturn was exported, the domestic economy was strengthened. As the downturn spread around the world, slower growth in the region led to a collapse in commodity prices, like oil, and the collapse in those prices wrought havoc in oil-producing countries like Russia.

Of all the failures of the IMF, this is perhaps the saddest, because it represented the greatest betrayal of its entire raison d'être. It did worry about contagion—contagion from one capital market to another transmitted through the fears of investors—though as we saw in the last section, the policies it had pushed had made the countries far more vulnerable to the volatility of investor sentiment. A collapse in the exchange rate in Thailand might make investors in Brazil worry about markets there. The buzzword was *confidence*. A lack of confidence in one country could spread to a lack of confidence in emerging markets. But more generally, the IMF's performance as market psychologist left something to be desired. Creating deep recessions with massive bankruptcies and/or pointing out deep-seated problems in the best performing region of the emerging markets are policies hardly designed to restore confidence. But even had it done better in restoring confidence, questions should have been raised: in focusing on protecting investors, it had forgotten about those in the countries it was supposed to be helping; in focusing on financial variables, like exchange rates, it had almost forgotten about the real side of the economy. It had lost sight of its original mission.

Strangling an Economy with High Interest Rates

Today, the IMF agrees that the *fiscal* policies (those relating to the levels of government deficits) it pushed were excessively contractionary, but it does not own up to the mistakes of monetary policy. When the Fund entered East Asia, it forced countries to raise interest rates to what, in conventional terms, would be considered astronomical levels. I remember meetings where President Clinton was frustrated that the Federal Reserve Bank, headed by Alan Greenspan, an appointee from past administrations, was about to raise interest rates one-quarter or one-half percentage point. He worried that it would destroy "his" recovery. He felt he had been elected on a platform of "It's the economy, stupid," and "Jobs, Jobs, Jobs" and he didn't want the Fed to hurt his plans. He knew that the Fed was concerned with inflation, but thought those fears were excessive—a sentiment which I shared, and which the subsequent events bore out. The president worried about the adverse effect interest rate increases would have on unemployment, and the economic recovery just getting underway. And this in the country with one of the best business environments in the world. Yet in East Asia, IMF bureaucrats, who were even less politically accountable, forced interest rate increases not ten but fifty times greater—interest rate increases of more than 25 percentage points. If Clinton worried about the adverse effects of a half-point increase on an economy experiencing a nascent recovery, he would have been apoplectic about the effect of those huge increases in interest rates on an economy plunging into a recession. Korea first raised its interest rates to 25 percent, but was told that to be serious it must allow interest rates to go still higher. Indonesia raised its interest rates in a preemptive move before the crisis, but was told that that was not good enough. Nominal interest rates soared.

The reasoning behind these policies was simple, if not simplistic. If a country raised interest rates, it would make it more attractive for capital to flow into that country. Capital flows into the country would help support the exchange rate and thus stabilize the currency. End of argument.

At first glance, this appears logical. However, consider the case of South Korea as an example. Recall that in South Korea the crisis was started by foreign banks refusing to roll over their short-term loans. They refused because they worried about South Korean firms' ability to repay. Bankruptcy—default—was at the center of the discussion. But in the IMF model—as in the models of most of the macroeconomics textbooks written two decades ago—bankruptcy plays no role. To discuss monetary policy and finance without bankruptcy is like *Hamlet* without the Prince of Denmark. At the heart of the analysis of the macroeconomy *should* have been an analysis of what an increase in interest rates would do to the chances of default and to the amount that creditors can recover in the event of default. Many of the firms in East Asia were highly indebted, and had huge debt equity ratios. Indeed, the excessive leverage had repeatedly been cited as one of South Korea's weaknesses, *even by the IMF.* Highly leveraged companies are particularly sensitive to interest rate increases, especially to the extremely high levels urged by the IMF. At very high interest rate levels, a highly leveraged company goes bankrupt quickly. Even if it does not go bankrupt, its equity (net worth) is quickly depleted as it is forced to pay huge amounts to creditors.

The Fund recognized that the underlying problems in East Asia were weak financial institutions and overleveraged firms; yet it pushed high interest rate policies that actually exacerbated those problems. The consequences were precisely as predicted: The high interest rates increased the number of firms in distress, and thereby increased the number of banks facing nonperforming loans.[13] This weakened the banks further. The increased distress in the corporate and financial sectors exacerbated the downturn that the contractionary policies were inducing through the reduction in aggregate demand. The IMF had engineered a simultaneous contraction in aggregate demand *and* supply.

In defending its policies, the IMF said they would help restore market confidence in the affected countries. But clearly countries in deep recession did not inspire confidence. Consider a Jakarta businessman who has put almost all of his wealth into East Asia. As the regional economy plummets—as contractionary policies take hold and amplify the downturn—he suddenly realizes that his portfolio is hardly sufficiently diversified, and shifts investment to the booming U.S. stock market. Local investors, just like international investors, were not interested in pouring money into an economy going into a tailspin. Higher interest rates did not attract more capital into the country. On the contrary, the higher rates made the recession worse and actually drove capital *out* of the country.

The IMF came up with another defense, of no more validity. They argued that if interest rates were not greatly increased, the exchange rate would collapse, and this would be devastating to the economy, as those who had dollar-denominated debts would not be able to pay them. But the fact was that, for reasons that should have been apparent, raising interest rates did not stabilize the currency; the countries were thus forced to lose on both accounts. Moreover, the IMF never bothered to look at the details of what was going on inside the countries. In Thailand, for instance, it was the already bankrupt real estate firms and those that lent to them who had the most foreign-denominated debt. Further devaluations might have harmed the foreign creditors but would not have made these firms any more dead. In effect, the IMF made the small businesses and other innocent bystanders pay for those who had engaged in excessive dollar borrowing—and to no avail.

When I pleaded with the IMF for a change in policies, and pointed out the disaster that would ensue if the current course were to be continued, there was a curt reply: If I were proven correct, the Fund would change its policies. I was appalled by this wait-and-see attitude. All economists know there are long lags in policy. The benefits of changing course will not be felt for six to eighteen months, while enormous damage could be done in the meantime.

That damage was done in East Asia. Because many firms were highly leveraged, many were forced into bankruptcy. In Indonesia, an estimated 75 percent of all businesses were put into distress, while in Thailand close to 50 percent of bank loans became nonperforming. Unfortunately, it is far easier to destroy a firm than to create a new one. Lowering interest rates would not un-bankrupt a firm that had been forced into bankruptcy: its net worth would still have been wiped out. The IMF's mistakes were costly, and slow to reverse.

Naive geopolitical reasoning, vestiges of Kissinger-style *realpolitik* compounded the consequences of these mistakes. In 1997, Japan offered $100 billion to help create an Asian Monetary Fund, in order to finance the required stimulative actions. But Treasury did everything it could to squelch the idea. The IMF joined in. The reason for the IMF's position was clear: While the IMF was a strong advocate of competition in markets, it did not want competition in its own domain, and the Asian Monetary Fund would provide that. The U.S. Treasury's motivations were similar. As the only shareholder of the IMF with veto power, the United States had considerable say in IMF policies. It was widely known that Japan disagreed strongly with the IMF's actions—I had repeated meetings with senior Japanese officials in which they expressed misgivings about IMF policies that were almost identical to my own.[14] With Japan, and possibly China, as the likely major contributors to the Asian Monetary Fund, their voices would predominate, providing a real challenge to American "leadership"—and control.

The importance of control—including control over the media—was brought home forcefully in the early days of the crisis. When World Bank Vice President for East Asia Jean Michel Severino pointed out in a widely discussed speech that several countries in the region were going into a deep recession, or even depression, there was a strong response from Treasury. It was made clear that it was simply unacceptable to use the R (for recession) or D (for depression) words, even though by then it was clear that Indonesia's GDP was likely to fall between 10 to 15 percent, a magnitude that clearly warranted the use of those harsh terms.

Eventually, Summers, Fischer, Treasury, and the IMF could not ignore the depression. Japan once again made a generous offer to help under the Miyazawa Initiative, named after Japan's finance minister. This time the offer was scaled down to $30 billion, and was accepted. But even then the United States argued that the money should be spent not to stimulate the economy through fiscal expansion, but for corpo-rate and financial restructuring—effectively, to help bail out American and other foreign banks and other creditors. The squashing of the Asian Monetary Fund is still resented in Asia and many officials have spoken to me angrily about the incident. Three years after the crisis, the countries of East Asia finally got together to begin, quietly, the creation of a more modest version of the Asian Monetary Fund, under the innocuous name of the Chang Mai Initiative, named after the city in northern Thailand where it was launched.

THE SECOND ROUND OF MISTAKES: BUMBLING RESTRUCTURING

As the crisis worsened, the need for "restructuring" became the new mantra. Banks that had bad loans on their books should be shut down, companies that owed money should be closed or taken over by their creditors. The IMF focused on this rather than simply performing the role it was supposed to fill: providing liquidity to finance needed expen-ditures. Alas, even this focus on restructuring failed, and much of what the IMF did helped push the sinking economies down further.

Financial Systems

The East Asia crisis was, first and foremost, a crisis of the financial sys-tem, and this needed to be dealt with. The financial system can be com-pared to the brain of the economy. It allocates scarce capital among competing uses by trying to direct it to where it is most effective, in other words, where it yields the highest returns. The financial system also monitors the funds to ensure that they are used in the way prom-ised. If the financial system breaks down, firms cannot get the working capital they need to continue existing levels of production, let alone finance expansion through new investment. A crisis can give rise to a vicious circle wherein banks cut back on their finance, leading firms to cut back on their production, which in turn leads to lower output and lower incomes. As output and incomes plummet, profits fall, and some firms are even forced into bankruptcy. When firms declare bankruptcy, banks' balance sheets become worse, and the banks cut back lending even further, exacerbating the economic downturn.

If enough firms fail to repay their loans, banks may even collapse. A collapse of even a single large bank can have disastrous consequences. Financial institutions determine creditworthiness. This information is highly specific, cannot easily be transmitted, and is embedded in the records and institutional memory of the bank (or other financial institution). When a bank goes out of business, much of the creditworthiness information it has on its borrowers is destroyed, and that information is expensive to recreate. Even in more advanced countries, a typical small or medium-sized enterprise may obtain credit from at most two or three banks. When a bank goes out of business in good times, many of its customers will have difficulty finding an alternative supplier of credit overnight. In developing countries, where sources of finance are even more limited, if the bank that a business relies upon fails, finding a new source of funds—especially during an economic downturn—may be nearly impossible.

Fears of this vicious circle have induced governments throughout the world to strengthen their financial systems through prudent regulation. Repeatedly, free marketeers have bridled against these regulations. When their voices have been heeded the consequences have been disastrous, whether in Chile in 1982–83, in which Chilean gross domestic product fell by 13.7 percent and one in five workers was unemployed, or the United States in the Reagan era, where, as we noted earlier, deregulation led to the savings-and-loan debacle, costing American taxpayers more than $200 billion.

A recognition of the importance of maintaining credit flows has similarly guided policy makers in trying to deal with the problems of financial restructuring. Fears about the adverse effects of this "destruction of informational capital" partially explain why the United States, during the S&L debacle, closed down very few banks outright. Most of the weak banks were taken over by or merged into other banks, and customers hardly knew of the switch. In this way, the information capital was preserved. Even so, the S&L crisis was an important contributing factor to the 1991 recession.

Inducing a Bank Run

Although financial system weaknesses were far more pervasive in East Asia than in the United States, and the IMF's rhetoric continually focused on these weaknesses as underlying the East Asia crisis, the IMF failed to understand how financial markets work and their impact on the rest of the economy. Its crude macromodels never embraced a broad picture of financial markets at the aggregate level, but were even more deficient at the microlevel—that is, at the level of the firm. The Fund did not adequately take into account the corporate and financial distress to which its so-called stabilization policies, including the high interest rates, contributed so strongly.

As they approached the problem of restructuring, IMF teams in East Asia focused on shutting down weak banks; it was as if they had a Darwinian model of competition in mind, so the weak banks *must* not survive. There was some basis for their position. Elsewhere, allowing weak banks to continue to operate *without tight supervision* resulted in their making highly risky loans. They gambled by making high-risk, high-return loans—if they were lucky, the loans would be repaid, and the higher interest rates would bring them back to solvency. If they were unlucky, they would go out of business—with the government picking up the pieces—but that is what would happen to them in any case if they did not embark on the risky loan strategy. But too often, such risky loans indeed turn out to be bad loans, and when the day of reckoning comes, the government faces an even bigger bailout than if the bank had been shut down earlier. This was one of the lessons that had emerged so clearly from the U.S. savings-and-loan debacle: the refusal of the Reagan administration to deal with the problem for years meant that when the crisis could no longer be ignored, the cost to the taxpayer was far larger. But the IMF overlooked another critical lesson: the importance of keeping credit flowing.

Its strategy for financial restructuring involved triage—separating out the really sick banks, which should be closed immediately, from the healthy banks. A third group were those that were sick but reparable. Banks are required to have a certain ratio of capital to their outstanding loans and other assets; this ratio is termed the *capital adequacy ratio*. Not surprisingly, when many loans are nonperforming, many banks fail to meet their capital adequacy ratio. The IMF insisted that banks either shut down or *quickly* meet this capital adequacy ratio. But this insistence on banks quickly meeting capital adequacy standards exacerbated the downturn. The Fund made the kind of mistake that we warn students about in the first course in economics, called "the fallacy of composition." When only one bank has a problem, then insisting on its meeting its capital adequacy standards makes sense. But when many, or most, banks are in trouble, that policy can be disastrous. There are two ways of increasing the ratio of capital to loans: increasing capital or reducing loans. In the midst of a downturn, especially of the magnitude of that in East Asia, it is hard to raise new capital. The alternative is to reduce outstanding loans. But as each bank calls in its loans, more and more firms are put into distress. Without adequate working capital, they are forced to cut back on their production, cutting into the demand for products from other firms. The downward spiral is exacerbated. And with more firms in distress, the capital adequacy ratio of banks can even be worsened. The attempt to improve the financial position of the banks backfired.

With a large number of banks shut down, and with those managing to survive facing an increasingly large number of loans in distress, and unwilling to take on new customers, more and businesses found themselves without access to credit. Without credit, the one glimmer of hope for a recovery would be squashed. The depreciation of the currency meant that exports should have boomed, as the goods from the region became cheaper, by 30 percent or more. But while export volumes increased, they did not increase nearly as much as expected, and for a simple reason: to expand exports, firms needed to have working capital to produce more. As banks shut down and cut back on their lending, firms could not even get the working capital required to maintain production, let alone to expand.

Nowhere was the IMF's lack of understanding of financial markets so evident as in its policies toward closing banks in Indonesia. There, some sixteen private banks were closed down, and notice was given that other banks might be subsequently shut down as well; but depositors, except for those with very small accounts, would be left to fend for themselves. Not surprisingly, this engendered a run on the remaining private banks, and deposits were quickly shifted to state banks, which were thought to have an implicit government guarantee. The effects on the Indonesia banking system, and economy, were disastrous, compounding the mistakes in fiscal and monetary policy already discussed, and almost sealing that country's fate: a depression had become inevitable.

In contrast, South Korea ignored outside advice, and recapitalized its two largest banks rather than closing them down. This is part of why Korea recovered relatively quickly.

Corporate Restructuring

While attention focused on financial restructuring, it was clear that the problems in the financial sector could not be resolved unless the problems in the corporate sector were effectively addressed. With 75 percent of the firms in Indonesia in distress, and half of the loans in Thailand nonperforming, the corporate sector was entering a stage of paralysis. Firms that are facing bankruptcy are in a state of limbo: it is not clear who really owns them, the current owners or the creditors. Issues of ownership are not fully resolved until the firm emerges from bankruptcy. But without clear owners, there is always a temptation for current management and the old owners to strip assets, and such asset stripping did occur. In the United States and other countries, when companies go into bankruptcy, trustees are appointed by the courts to prevent this. But in Asia there were neither the legal frameworks nor the personnel to implement trusteeships. It was thus imperative that bankruptcies and corporate distress be resolved quickly, before stripping could occur. Unfortunately, IMF's misguided economics, having contributed to the mess through the high interest rates which forced so many firms into distress, conspired with ideology and special interests to dampen the pace of restructuring.

The IMF's strategy for corporate restructuring—restructuring the firms that were effectively in bankruptcy—was no more successful than its strategy for restructuring banks. It confused *financial* restructuring—entailing straightening out who really owns the firm, the discharge of debt or its conversion to equity—with *real* restructuring, the nuts-and-bolts decisions: what the firm should produce, how it should produce its output, and how it should be organized. In the presence of the massive economic downturn, there were real macrobenefits from rapid financial restructuring. Individual participants in the bargaining surrounding bankruptcy workouts would fail to take into account these systemic benefits. It might pay them to drag their feet—and bankruptcy negotiations are often protracted, taking more than a year or two. When only a few firms in an economy are bankrupt, this delay has little social cost; when many firms are in distress, the social cost can be enormous, as the macroeconomic downturn is prolonged. It is thus imperative that the government do whatever it can to facilitate a quick resolution.

I took the view that the government should play an active role in pushing this financial restructuring, ensuring that there were real owners. My view was that once ownership issues were resolved, the new owners should set about the task of deciding the issues of real restructuring. The IMF took the opposite view, saying that the government should *not* take an active role in financial restructuring, but push for real restructuring, selling assets, for instance, to reduce South Korea's *seeming* excess capacity in chips and bringing in outside (typically foreign) management. I saw no reason to believe that international bureaucrats, trained in macromanagement, had any special insight into corporate restructuring in general, or the chip industry in particular. While restructuring is, in any case, a slow process, the governments of Korea and Malaysia took an active role, and succeeded within a remarkably short period of time, two years, in completing the financial restructuring of a remarkably large fraction of the firms in distress. By contrast, restructuring in Thailand, which followed the IMF strategy, languished.

THE MOST GRIEVOUS MISTAKES:
RISKING SOCIAL AND POLITICAL TURMOIL

The social and political consequences of mishandling the Asian crisis may never be measured fully. When the IMF's managing director Michel Camdessus, and G-22 finance ministers and central bank governors (the finance ministers and central bank governors from the major industrial countries, plus the major Asian economies, including Australia) met in Kuala Lumpur, Malaysia, in early December 1997, I warned of the danger of social and political unrest, especially in countries where there has been a history of ethnic division (as in Indonesia, where there had been

massive ethnic rioting some thirty years earlier), if the excessively contractionary monetary and fiscal policies that were being imposed continued. Camdessus calmly responded that they needed to follow Mexico's
example; they had to take the painful measures if they were to recover.
Unfortunately, my forecasts turned out to be all too right. Just over
five months after I warned of the impending disaster, riots broke out.
While the IMF had provided some $23 billion to be used to support the
exchange rate and bail out creditors, the far, far smaller sums required to
help the poor were not forthcoming. In American parlance, there were
billions and billions for corporate welfare, but not the more modest millions for welfare for ordinary citizens. Food and fuel subsidies for the
poor in Indonesia were drastically cut back, and riots exploded the next
day. As had happened thirty years earlier, the Indonesian businessmen
and their families became the victims.

It was not just that IMF policy might be regarded by softheaded liber-
als as inhumane. Even if one cared little for those who faced starvation,
or the children whose growth would be stunted by malnutrition, it was
simply bad economics. Riots do not restore business confidence. They
drive capital out of a country; they do not attract capital into a country.
And riots are predictable—like any social phenomenon, not with cer-
tainty, but with a high probability. It was clear Indonesia was ripe for
such social upheaval. The IMF itself should have known this; around the
world, the IMF has inspired riots when its policies cut off food subsidies.

After the riots in Indonesia, the IMF reversed its position; food subsidies were restored. But again, the IMF showed that it had not learned the
basic lesson of "irreversibility." Just as a firm that was bankrupted by the
high interest rates does not become "un-bankrupted" when the interest
rates were lowered, a society that is rendered asunder by riots induced
by cutting out food subsides just as it is plunging into depression is not
brought together when the food subsidies are restored. Indeed, in some
quarters, the bitterness is all the greater: if the food subsidies could have
been afforded, why were they taken away in the first place?

I had the opportunity to talk to Malaysia's prime minister after the
riots in Indonesia. His country had also experienced ethnic riots in the
past. Malaysia had done a lot to prevent their recurrence, including putting in a program to promote employment for ethnic Malays. Mahathir
knew that all the gains in building a multiracial society could be lost,

had he let the IMF dictate its policies to him and his country and then riots had broken out. For him, preventing a severe recession was not just a matter of economics, it was a matter of the survival of the nation.

RECOVERY: VINDICATION OF THE IMF POLICIES?

By the beginning of the new millennium, the crisis was over. Many Asian countries were growing again, their recovery slightly stalled by the global slowdown that began in 2000. The countries that managed to avoid a recession in 1998, Taiwan and Singapore, fell into one in 2001; Korea is doing far better. With a worldwide downturn affecting the United States and Germany as well, no one talked about weak institutions and poor governments as the cause of recessions; now, they seemed to have remembered that such fluctuations have always been part of market economies.

But although some at the IMF believe their interventions were successful, it's widely agreed that serious mistakes were made. Indeed, the nature of the recovery shows this. Almost every economic downturn comes to an end. But the Asian crisis was more severe than it should have been, recovery took longer than it needed to, and prospects for future growth are not what they should be.

On Wall Street, a crisis is over as soon as financial variables begin to turn around. So long as exchange rates are weakening or stock prices falling, it is not clear where the bottom lies. But once the bottom has been reached, the losses are at least capped and the worst is known. However, to truly measure recovery, stabilization of exchange rates or interest rates is not enough. People do not live off exchange rates or interest rates. Workers care about jobs and wages. Although the unemployment rate and real wages may have bottomed out, that is not enough for the worker who remains unemployed or who has seen his income fall by a quarter. There is no true recovery until workers return to their jobs and wages are restored to pre-crisis levels. Even as the new millennium began, incomes in the countries of East Asia affected by the crisis are still 20 percent below what they would have been had their growth continued at the pace of the previous decade. In Indonesia, output in 2001 was still 5.3 percent lower than in 1997, and even Thailand, the IMF's best pupil, had not attained its pre-crisis level, let alone made up for the lost growth. This is not the first instance of the IMF declaring victory prematurely: Mexico's crisis in 1995 was declared over as soon as the banks and international lenders started to get repaid; but five years after the crisis, workers were just getting back to where they were beforehand. The very fact that the IMF focuses on financial variables, not on measure of real wages, unemployment, GDP, or broader measures of welfare, is itself telling.

The question of how best to manage a recovery is difficult, and the answer clearly depends on the cause of the problem. For many downturns, the best prescription is the standard Keynesian one: expansionary fiscal and monetary policy. The problems in East Asia were more complicated, because *part* of the problem was weaknesses in finance—weak banks and firms with excess leverage. But a deepening recession makes these problems worse. Pain is not a virtue in its own right; pain by itself does not help the economy; and the pain caused by IMF policies, deepening recession, made recovery more difficult. Sometimes, as in Latin America, in Argentina, Brazil, and a host of other countries during the 1970s, crises are caused by profligate governments spending beyond their means, and in those cases, the government will need to cut back expenditures or increase taxes—decisions which are painful, at least in the political sense. But because East Asia had neither loose monetary policies nor profligate public sectors—inflation was low and stable, and budgets prior to the crisis were in surplus—those were not the right measures for dealing with East Asia's crisis.

The problem with the IMF's mistakes is that they are likely to be long-lasting. The IMF often talked as if what the economy needed was a good purgative. Take the pain; the deeper the pain, the stronger the subsequent growth. In the IMF theory, then, a country concerned about its *long-run* prospects—say twenty years from now—should swallow hard and accept a deep downturn. People today would suffer, but their children at least would be better off. Unfortunately, the evidence does not support the IMF's theory. An economy which has a deep recession may grow faster as it recovers, but it never makes up for the lost time. The deeper today's recession, the lower the likely income even twenty years from now. It is not, as the IMF claims, that they are likely to be better off. The effects of a recession are long-lasting. There is an important implication: The deeper the recession today, not only is output lower today, but the lower output is likely to be for years to come. In a way, this is good news, since it means that the best medicine for today's health of the economy and the best medicine for tomorrow's coincide. It implies that economic policy should be directed at minimizing the depth and duration of any economic downturn. Unfortunately, this was neither the intention nor the impact of the IMF prescriptions.

Malaysia and China

By contrasting what happened in Malaysia and in China, two nations that chose not to have IMF programs, with the rest of East Asia, which did, the negative effects of the IMF policies will show clearly. Malaysia was severely criticized during the crisis by the international financial community. Though Prime Minister Mahathir's rhetoric and human rights policies often leave much to be desired, many of his economic policies were a success.

Malaysia was reluctant to join the IMF program, partly because officials there did not want to be dictated to by outsiders but also because they had little confidence in the IMF. Early on in the 1997 crisis, IMF chief Michael Camdessus announced that Malaysia's banks were in a weak position. An IMF/World Bank team was quickly dispatched to look at the country's banking system. While there was a high level of nonperforming loans (15 percent), Malaysia's Central Bank had imposed strong regulations which had resulted in banks making adequate provisions for these losses. Moreover, Malaysia' strong regulatory stance had prevented banks from exposure to foreign exchange volatility (the danger of borrowing in dollars and lending in ringgit), and had even limited the foreign indebtedness of the companies to which these banks lent (precautionary prescriptions which were, at the time, not part of the IMF standard package).

The standard way to assess the strength of a banking system is to subject it, in simulation exercises, to stress tests and evaluate its response under different economic circumstances. The Malaysian banking system fared quite well. Few banking systems could survive a long recession, or a depression, and Malaysia's was no exception; but Malaysia's banking system was remarkably strong. During one of my many visits to Malaysia, I saw the discomfort of the IMF staffers writing the report: how to formulate it without contradicting the managing director's assertions and yet remain consistent with the evidence.

Within Malaysia itself, the issue of the appropriate response to the crisis was hotly debated. Finance Minister Anwar Ibrahim proposed "an IMF program without the IMF," that is, raising interest rates and cutting back on expenditures. Mahathir remained skeptical. Eventually, he dumped his finance minister and economic policies were reversed.

As the regional crisis grew into a global crisis, and international capital markets went into a seizure, Mahathir acted again. In September 1998, Malaysia pegged the ringgit at 3.80 to the dollar, cut interest rates, and decreed that all offshore ringgit be repatriated by the end of the month. The government also imposed tight limits on transfers of capital abroad by residents in Malaysia and froze the repatriation of foreign portfolio capital for twelve months. These measures were announced as short term, and were carefully designed to make it clear that the country was not hostile to long-term foreign investment. Those who had invested money in Malaysia and had profits were allowed to take them out. On September 7, 1998, in a now-famous column in *Fortune* magazine, the noted economist Paul Krugman urged Mahathir to impose capital controls. But he was in the minority. Malaysia's Central Bank governor Ahmad Mohamed Don and his deputy, Fong Weng Phak, both resigned, reportedly because they disagreed with the imposition of the controls. Some economists—those from Wall Street joined by the IMF—predicted disaster when the controls were imposed, saying foreign investors would be scared off for years to come. They expected foreign investment to plummet, the stock market to fall, and a black market in the ringgit, with its accompanying distortions, to form. And, they warned, while the controls would lead to a drying up of capital *inflows*, they would be ineffective in stopping capital *outflows*. Capital flight would occur anyway. Pundits predicted that the economy would suffer, growth would be halted, the controls would never be lifted, and that Malaysia was postponing addressing the underlying problems. Even Treasury Secretary Robert Rubin, usually of such quiet demeanor, joined in the communal tongue-lashing.

In fact, the outcome was far different. My team at the World Bank worked with Malaysia to convert the capital controls into an exit tax. Since rapid capital flows into or out of a country cause large disturbances, they generate what economists call "large externalities"—effects on other, ordinary people not involved in these capital flows. Such flows lead to massive disturbances to the overall economy. Government has the right, even the obligation, to take measures to address such disturbances. In general, economists believe that market-based interventions such as taxes are more effective and have fewer adverse side effects than direct controls, so we at the World Bank encouraged Malaysia to drop direct controls and impose an exit tax. Moreover, the tax could be gradually lowered, so that there would be no large disturbance when the interventions were finally removed.

Things worked just as planned. Malaysia removed the tax just as it had promised, one year after the imposition of controls. In fact, Malaysia had once before imposed temporary capital controls, and had removed them as soon as things stabilized. This historical experience was ignored by those who attacked the country so roundly. In the one-year interim, Malaysia had restructured its banks and corporations, proving the critics, who had said that it was only with the discipline that comes from free capital markets that governments ever do anything serious, wrong once again. Indeed, it had made far more progress in that direction than Thailand, which followed the IMF prescriptions. In retrospect, it was clear that Malaysia's capital controls allowed it to recover more quickly, with a shallower downturn,[15] and with a far smaller legacy of national debt burdening future growth. The controls allowed it to have lower interest rates than it could otherwise have had; the lower interest rates meant that fewer firms were put into bankruptcy, and so the magnitude of publicly funded corporate and financial bailout was smaller. The lower interest rates meant too that recovery could occur with less reliance on fiscal policy, and consequently less government borrowing. Today, Malaysia stands in a far better position than those countries that took IMF advice. There was little evidence that the capital controls discouraged foreign investors. Foreign investment actually increased.[16] Because investors are concerned about economic stability, and because Malaysia had done a far better job in maintaining that stability than many of its neighbors, it was able to attract investment.

CHINA WAS THE other country that followed an independent course. It is no accident that the two large developing countries spared the ravages of the global economic crisis—India and China—both had capital controls. While developing world countries with liberalized capital markets actually saw their incomes decline, India grew at a rate in excess of 5 percent and China at close to 8 percent. This is all the more remarkable given the overall slowdown in world growth, and in trade in particular, during that period. China achieved this by following the prescriptions of economic orthodoxy. These were not the Hooverite IMF prescriptions, but the standard prescriptions that economists have been teaching for more than half a century: When faced with an economic downturn, respond with expansionary macroeconomic policy. China seized the opportunity to combine its short-run needs with long-run growth objectives. The rapid growth over the preceding decade, anticipated to continue into the next century, created enormous demands on infrastructure. There were large opportunities for public investments with high returns, including projects underway that were sped up, and projects that were already designed but had been put on the shelf for lack of funds. The standard medicines worked, and China averted a growth slowdown.

While making economic policy decisions, China was aware of the link between macrostability and its microeconomy. It knew that it needed to continue restructuring its corporate and financial sector. However, it also recognized that an economic slowdown would make it all the more difficult to proceed with a reform agenda. An economic slowdown would throw more firms into distress and make more loans nonperforming, thereby weakening the banking system. An economic slowdown would also increase unemployment, and rising unemployment would make the social costs of restructuring the state enterprises much higher. And China recognized the links between economics and political and social stability. It had in its recent history all too often experienced the consequences of instability, and wanted none of that. In all respects, China fully appreciated the *systemic* consequences of macroeconomic policies, consequences that the IMF policies habitually overlooked.

This is not to say that China is out of the woods. The restructuring of its banking and state-owned enterprises still represents a challenge for it in the years ahead. But these are challenges that can be far better addressed in the context of a strong macroeconomy.

Though the differences in individual circumstances make the reasons either for the occurrence of a crisis or for quick recovery hard to ascertain, I think it is no accident that the only major East Asian country, China, to avert the crisis took a course directly opposite that advocated by the IMF, and that the country with the shortest downturn, Malaysia, also explicitly rejected an IMF strategy.

Korea, Thailand, and Indonesia

Korea and Thailand provide further contrasts. After a short period of policy vacillation from July through October 1997, Thailand followed IMF prescriptions almost perfectly. Yet more than three years after the beginning of the crisis, it was still in recession, with a GDP approximately 2.3 percent below the pre-crisis level. Little corporate restructuring had taken place, and close to 40 percent of the loans were still nonperforming.

In contrast, Korea did not close down banks according to the standard IMF prescription, and the Korean government, like Malaysia's, took a more active role in restructuring corporations. Moreover, Korea kept its exchange rate low, rather than letting it rebound. This was ostensibly to enable it to reestablish its reserves, but by buying dollars for its reserves it depressed the value of the won. Korea kept the exchange rate low in order to sustain exports and limit imports. Moreover, Korea did not follow the IMF's advice concerning *physical* restructuring. The IMF acted as if it knew more about the global chip industry than these firms who had made it their business, and argued that Korea should quickly get rid of the excess capacity. Korea, smartly, ignored this advice. As the demand for chips recovered, the economy recovered. Had the IMF's advice been followed, the recovery would have been far more muted.

In evaluating the recoveries, most analysts put Indonesia aside, simply because the economy has been dominated by political events and social turmoil. However, the political and social turmoil are themselves attributable in no small measure to IMF policies, as we have seen. No one will know whether there could have been a more graceful transition from Suharto, but few would argue that it could have been more tumultuous.

Effects on the Future

Despite the many hardships, the East Asia crisis has had salutary effects. East Asian countries will undoubtedly develop better financial regulatory systems, and better financial institutions overall. Though its firms had already demonstrated a remarkable ability to compete in the global marketplace, Korea is likely to emerge with a more competitive economy. Some of the worst aspects of corruption, the so-called crony capitalism, will have been checked.

However, the manner in which the crisis was addressed—particularly the use of high interest rates—is likely to have a significantly adverse effect on the region's intermediate, and possibly long-term, economic growth. There is a certain irony in the central reason for this. Weak, underregulated financial institutions are bad because they lead to bad resource allocations. While East Asia's banks were far from perfect, over the preceding three decades their achievements in allocating the enormous flows of capital were, in fact, quite impressive—this was what sustained their rapid growth. Although the intention of those pushing for "reforms" in East Asia was to improve the ability of the financial system to allocate resources, in fact, the IMF's policies are likely to have impaired the *overall* efficiency of the market.

Around the world, very little new investment is financed by raising new equity (selling shares of stock in a company). Indeed, the only countries with widely diversified share ownership are the United States, the United Kingdom, and Japan, all of which have strong legal systems and strong shareholder protections. It takes time to develop these legal institutions, and few countries have succeeded in doing so. In the meantime, firms around the world must rely on debt. But debt is inherently risky. IMF strategies, such as capital market liberalization and raising interest rates to exorbitant levels when a crisis occurs, make borrowing even riskier. To respond rationally, firms will engage in lower levels of borrowing and force themselves to rely more heavily on retained earnings. Thus growth in the future will be constrained, and capital will not flow as freely as it otherwise would to the most productive uses. In this way, IMF policies lead to less efficient resource allocation, particularly capital allocation, which is the scarcest resource in developing countries. The IMF does not take this impairment into account because its models do not reflect the realities of how capital markets actually work, including the impact of the imperfections of information on capital markets.

EXPLAINING THE MISTAKES

While the IMF now agrees it made serious mistakes in its fiscal policy advice, in how it pushed bank restructuring in Indonesia, in perhaps pushing capital market liberalization prematurely, and in underestimating the importance of the interregional impacts, by which the downfall of one country contributed to that of its neighbors, it has not admitted to the mistakes in its monetary policy, nor has it even sought to explain why its models failed so miserably in predicting the course of events. It has not sought to develop an alternative intellectual frame—implying that in the next crisis, it may well make the same mistakes. (In January 2002, the IMF chalked up one more failure to its credit—Argentina. Part of the reason is its insistence once again on contractionary fiscal policy.)

Part of the explanation of the *magnitude* of the failures has to do with hubris: no one likes to admit a mistake, especially a mistake of this magnitude or with these consequences. Neither Fischer nor Summers, neither Rubin nor Camdessus, neither the IMF nor the U.S. Treasury wanted to think that their policies were misguided. They stuck to their positions, in spite of what I viewed as overwhelming evidence of their failure. (When the IMF finally decided to support lower interest rates and reversed its support for fiscal contraction in East Asia, it said it was because the time was right. I would suggest that it reversed courses partly due to public pressure.)

But in Asia other theories abound, including a conspiracy theory that I do not share which views the policies either as a deliberate attempt to weaken East Asia—the region of the world that had shown the greatest growth over the previous forty years—or at least to enhance the incomes of those on Wall Street and the other money centers. One can understand how this line of thinking developed: The IMF first told countries in Asia to open up their markets to hot short-term capital. The countries did it and money flooded in, but just as suddenly flowed out. The IMF then said interest rates should be raised and there should be a fiscal contraction, and a deep recession was induced. As asset prices plummeted, the IMF urged affected countries to sell their assets even at bargain basement prices. It said the companies needed solid foreign management (conveniently ignoring that these companies had a most enviable record of growth over the preceding decades, hard to reconcile with bad management) and that this would only happen if the companies were sold to foreigners—not just managed by them. The sales were handled by the same foreign financial institutions that had pulled out their capital, precipitating the crisis. These banks then got large commissions from their work selling the troubled companies or splitting them up, just as they had got large commissions when they had originally guided the money into the countries in the first place. As the events unfolded, cynicism grew even greater: some of these American and other financial companies didn't do much restructuring; they just held the assets until the economy recovered, making profits from buying at the fire sale prices and selling at more normal prices.

I believe that there is a simpler set of explanations—the IMF was not participating in a conspiracy, but it was reflecting the interests and ideology of the Western financial community. Modes of operation which were secretive insulated the institution and its policies from the kind of intensive scrutiny that might have forced it to use models and adopt policies that were appropriate to the situation in East Asia. The failures in East Asia bear much in common with those in development and in transition, and in chapters 12 and 13 we will take a closer look at the common causes.

AN ALTERNATIVE STRATEGY

In response to the complaints I continue to raise about the IMF-Treasury strategy, my critics have rightly asked what I would have done. This chapter has already hinted at the basic strategy: Maintain the economy at as close to full employment as possible. Attaining that objective, in turn, entails an expansionary (or at least not contractionary) monetary and fiscal policy, the exact mix of which would depend on the country in question. I agreed with the IMF on the importance of financial restructuring—addressing the problems of weak banks—but I would have approached it totally differently, with a primary objective of maintaining the flow of finance, and a standstill on existing debt repayment: a debt restructuring, such as that which eventually worked for Korea. Maintaining the flow of finance, in turn, would require greater efforts at restructuring existing institutions. And a key part of corporate restructuring would entail the implementation of a special bankruptcy provision aimed at the quick resolution of distress resulting from the macroeconomic disturbances that were well beyond the normal. The U.S. bankruptcy code has provisions which allow for relatively quick reorganization of a firm (rather than liquidation), called *Chapter 11*. Bankruptcy induced by macroeconomic disturbances, as in East Asia, call for an even faster resolution—in what I refer to as a *super-Chapter 11*.

With or without such a provision, strong intervention of government was required. But the intervention of the government would have aimed at financial restructuring—establishing clear ownership of firms, enabling them to reenter credit markets. That would have enabled them to take full advantage of the opportunities for export that resulted from their lower exchange rate. It would have eliminated the incentive for asset stripping; it would have provided them with strong incentives to engage in any real restructuring that was required—and the new owners and managers would have been in a far better position to guide this restructuring than international or domestic bureaucrats, who, as the expression goes, had never met a payroll. Such financial restructuring did not require huge bailouts. The disillusionment with the large bailout strategy is now almost universal. I cannot be sure that my ideas would have worked, but there is little doubt in my mind that the chance of success with this strategy was far greater than with the IMF's plan, which failed in ways that were perfectly predictable, at huge costs.

The IMF did not learn quickly from its failures in East Asia. With slight variants, it repeatedly tried the large bailout strategy. With the failures in Russia, Brazil, and Argentina, it has become clear that an alternative strategy is required, and there is today increasing support for at least some of the key elements of the approach I have just described. Today, five years after the onset of the crisis, the IMF and the G-7 are all talking about giving greater emphasis to bankruptcy and standstills (short-term freezes on payments), and even the temporary use of capital controls. We will return to these reforms later, in chapter 13.

The Asian crisis has brought many changes that will stand the countries in good stead in the future. Corporate governance and accounting standards have improved—in some cases putting these countries toward the top of the emerging markets. The new constitution in Thailand promises a stronger democracy (including a provision embracing the citizens' "right to know," not even included in the U.S. Constitution), promising a level of transparency certainly beyond that of the international financial institutions. Many of these changes put in place conditions for even more robust growth in the future.

But offsetting these gains are some real losses. The way the IMF approached the crisis has left in most of the countries a legacy of private and public debt. It has not only frightened firms off the excessively high debt that characterized Korea, but even off more cautious debt levels: the exorbitant interest rates forcing thousands of firms into bankruptcy showed how even moderate levels of debt could be highly risky. As a result, firms will have to rely more on self-finance. In effect, capital markets will work less efficiently—a casualty too of the IMF's ideological approach to improving market efficiency. And most important, growth of living standards will be slowed.

The IMF policies in East Asia had exactly the consequences that have brought globalization under attack. The failures of the international institutions in poor developing countries were long-standing; but these failures did not grab the headlines. The East Asia crisis made vivid to those in the more developed world some of the dissatisfaction that those in the developing world had long felt. What took place in Russia through most of the 1990s provides some even more arresting examples why there is such discontent with international institutions, and why they need to change.

CHAPTER 9

WHO LOST RUSSIA?

W
ITH THE FALL of the Berlin Wall in late 1989, one of the most important economic transitions of all time began. It was the second bold economic and social experiment of the century.[1] The first was Russia's transition to communism seven decades earlier. Over the years, the failures of this first experiment became apparent. As a consequence of the 1917 Revolution and the Soviet hegemony over a large part of Europe after World War II, some 8 percent of the world's population that lived under the Soviet Communist system forfeited both political freedom and economic prosperity. The second transition in Russia as well as in Eastern and Southeastern Europe is far from over, but this much is clear: in Russia it has fallen far short of what the advocates of the market economy had promised, or hoped for. For the majority of those living in the former Soviet Union, economic life under capitalism has been even worse than the old Communist leaders had said it would be. Prospects for the future are bleak. The middle class has been devastated, a system of crony and mafia capitalism has been created, and the one achievement, the creation of a democracy with meaningful freedoms, including a free press, appears fragile at best, particularly as formerly independent TV stations are shut down one by one. While those in Russia must bear much of the blame for what has happened, the Western advisers, espe-

cially from the United States and the IMF, who marched in so quickly to preach the gospel of the market economy, must also take some blame. At the very least, they provided support to those who led Russia and many of the other economies down the paths they followed, arguing for a new religion—market fundamentalism—as a substitute for the old one—Marxism—which had proved so deficient.

Russia is an ever-unfolding drama. Few anticipated the sudden dissolution of the Soviet Union and few anticipated the sudden resignation of Boris Yeltsin. Some see the oligarchy, the worst excesses of the Yeltsin years, as already curbed; others simply see that some of the oligarchs have fallen from grace. Some see the increases in output that have occurred in the years since its 1998 crisis as the beginning of a renaissance, one which will lead to the recreation of a middle class; others see it as taking years just to repair the damage of the past decade. Incomes today are markedly lower than they were a decade ago, and poverty is much higher. The pessimists see the country as a nuclear power wavering with political and social instability. The optimists (!) see a semiauthoritarian leadership establishing stability, but at the price of the loss of some democratic freedoms.

Russia experienced a burst of growth after 1998, based on high oil prices and the benefits of the devaluation which the IMF so long opposed. But as oil prices have come down, and the benefits of the devaluation have been reaped, growth too has slowed. Since then, as Russia deindustrialized, it became increasingly dependent on oil. When the oil prices boomed, as in the years before the global financial crisis, Russia boomed; when the oil prices fell, Russia went into recession.

It is not surprising that the debate over who lost Russia has had such resonance. At one level, the question is clearly misplaced. In the United States it evokes memories of the debate a half century ago about who lost China, when the Communists took over that country. But China was not America's to lose in 1949, nor was Russia America's to lose a half century later. In neither case did America and the Western European countries have control over the political and social evolution. At the same time, it is clear that something has clearly gone wrong, not only in Russia but also in most of the more than twenty countries that emerged from the Soviet empire.

The IMF and other Western leaders claim that matters would have been far worse were it not for their help and advice. We had then, and we have now, no crystal ball to tell us what would happen if alternative policies were pursued. We have no way of running a controlled experiment, going back in time to try an alternative strategy. We have no way of being *certain* of what might have been.

But we do know that certain political and economic judgment calls were made, and we know that the outcomes have been disastrous. In some cases, the link between the policies and the consequences is easy to see: The IMF worried that a devaluation of the ruble would set off a round of inflation. Its insistence on Russia maintaining an overvalued currency and its supporting that with billions of dollars of loans ultimately crushed the economy. (When the ruble was finally devalued in 1998, inflation did not soar as the IMF had feared, and the economy experienced its first significant growth.) In other cases, the links are more complicated. But the experiences of the few countries that followed different policies in managing their transitions help guide us through the maze. It is essential that the world make an informed judgment about the IMF policies in Russia, what drove them and why they were so misguided. Those, myself included, who have had an opportunity to see firsthand how decisions were made and what their consequences were have a special responsibility to provide their interpretations of relevant events.

There is a second reason for a reappraisal. Now, more than ten years after the fall of the Berlin Wall, it is clear that the transition to a market economy will be a long struggle, and many, if not most, of the issues that seemed settled only a few years ago will need to be revisited. Only if we understand the mistakes of the past can we hope to design policies that are likely to be effective in the future.

The leaders of the 1917 Revolution recognized that what was at stake was more than a change in economics; it was a change in society in all of its dimensions. So, too, the transition from communism to a market economy was more than just an economic experiment: it was a transformation of societies and of social and political structures. Part of the reason for the dismal results of the economic transition was the failure to recognize the centrality of these other components.

The first Revolution recognized how difficult the task of transformation was, and the revolutionaries believed that it could not be accomplished by democratic means; it had to be led by the "dictatorship of the proletariat." Some of the leaders of the second revolution in the 1990s at first thought that, freed from the shackles of communism, the Russian people would quickly appreciate the benefits of the market. But some of the Russian market reformers (as well as their Western supporters and advisers) had very little faith or interest in democracy, fearing that if the Russian people were allowed to choose, they would not choose the "correct" (that is *their*) economic model. In Eastern Europe and the former Soviet Union, when the promised benefits of market reform failed to materialize in country after country, democratic elections rejected the extremes of market reform, and put social democratic parties or even "reformed" Communist parties, many with former Communists at the helm, into power. It is not surprising that many of the market reformers showed a remarkable affinity to the old ways of doing business: in Russia, President Yeltsin, with enormously greater powers than his counterparts in any Western democracy, was encouraged to circumvent the democratically elected Duma (parliament) and to enact market reforms by decree.[2] It is as if the market Bolsheviks, native true believers, as well as the Western experts and evangelists of the new economic religion who flew into the post-Socialist countries, attempted to use a benign version of Lenin's methods to steer the post-communism, "democratic" transition.

THE CHALLENGES AND OPPORTUNITIES OF TRANSITION

As the transition began in the early 1990s, it presented both great challenges and opportunities. Seldom before had a country deliberately set out to go from a situation where government controlled virtually every aspect of the economy to one where decisions occurred through markets. The People's Republic of China had begun its transition in the late 1970s, and was still far from a full-fledged market economy. One of the most successful transitions had been Taiwan, 100 miles off the shore of mainland China. It had been a Japanese colony since the end of the nineteenth century. With China's 1949 revolution, it became the refuge for the old Nationalist leadership, and from their base in Taiwan, they claimed sovereignty over the entire mainland, keeping the name—"the Republic of China." They had nationalized and redistributed the land, established and then partially privatized an array of major industries, and more broadly created a vibrant market economy. After 1945 many countries, including the United States, moved from wartime mobilization to a peacetime economy. At the time, many economists and other experts feared a major recession would follow wartime demobilization, which entailed not only a change in how decisions were made (ending versions of command economies in which wartime governments made the major decisions about production and returning to private sector management of production) but also an enormous reallocation of production of goods, for example, from tanks to cars. But by 1947, the second full postwar year, production in the United States was 9.6 percent higher than 1944, the last full war year. By the end of the war, 37 percent of GDP (1945) was devoted to defense. With peace, this number was brought down rapidly to 7.4 percent (1947).

There was one important difference between the transition from war to peace, and from communism to a market economy, as I will detail later: Before World War II, the United States had the basic market institutions in place, even though during the war many of these were suspended and superseded by a "command and control" approach. In contrast, Russia needed both resource redeployment *and* the wholesale creation of market institutions.

But Taiwan and China faced similar problems to the economies in transition. Both faced the challenge of a major transformation of their societies, including the establishment of the institutions that underlay a market economy. Both have had truly impressive successes. Rather than prolonged transition recession, they had close to double-digit growth. The radical economic reformers who sought to advise Russia and many of the other countries on transition paid scant attention to these experiences, and the lessons that could be learned. It was not because they believed that Russian history (or the history of the other countries making the transition) made these lessons inapplicable. They studiously ignored the advice of Russian scholars, whether they were experts in its history, economics, or society, for a simple reason: they believed that the *market revolution* which was about to occur made all of the knowledge available from these other disciplines irrelevant. What the market fundamentalists preached was textbook economics—an oversimplified version of market economics which paid scant attention to the dynamics of change.

Consider the problems facing Russia (or the other countries) in 1989. There were institutions in Russia that had names *similar* to those in the West, but they did not perform the same functions. There were banks in Russia, and the banks did garner savings; but they did not make decisions about who got loans, nor did they have the responsibility for monitoring and making sure that the loans were repaid. Rather, they simply provided the "funds," as dictated by the government's central planning agency. There were firms, enterprises producing goods in Russia, but the enterprises did not make decisions: they produced what they were told to produce, with inputs (raw material, labor, machines) that were allocated to them. The major scope for entrepreneurship lay in getting around problems posed by the government: the government would give enterprises quotas on output, without necessarily providing the inputs needed, but in some cases providing more than necessary. Entrepreneurial managers engaged in trades to enable themselves to fulfill their quotas, in the meanwhile getting a few more perks for themselves than they could have enjoyed on their official salaries. These activities—which had always been necessary to make the Soviet system merely function—led to the corruption that would only increase as Russia moved to a market economy.[3] Circumventing what laws were in force, if not breaking them outright, became part of the way of life, a precursor to the breakdown of the "rule of law" which was to mark the transition.

As in a market economy, under the Soviet system there were prices, but the prices were set by government fiat, not by the market. Some prices, such as those for basic necessities, were kept artificially low—enabling even those at the bottom of the income distribution to avoid poverty. Prices for energy and natural resources also were kept artificially low—which Russia could only afford because of its huge reservoirs of these resources.

Old-fashioned economics textbooks often talk about market economics as if it had three essential ingredients: prices, private property, and profits. Together with competition, these provide incentives, coordinate economic decision making, ensuring that firms produce what individuals want at the lowest possible cost. But there has also long been a recognition of the importance of *institutions*. Most important are legal and regulatory frameworks, to ensure that contracts are enforced, that there is an orderly way of resolving commercial disputes, that when borrowers cannot repay what is owed, there are orderly bankruptcy procedures, that competition is maintained, and that banks that take depositors are in a position to give the money back to depositors when they ask. This framework of laws and agencies helps ensure that securities markets operate in a fair manner, that managers do not take advantage of shareholders nor majority shareholders of minority shareholders. In the nations with mature market economies, the legal and regulatory frameworks had been built up over a century and a half, in response to problems encountered in unfettered market capitalism. Bank regulation came into place after massive bank failures; securities regulation after major episodes in which unwary shareholders were cheated. Countries seeking to create a market economy did not have to relive these disasters: they could learn from the experiences of others. But while the market reformers may have mentioned this institutional infrastructure, they gave it short shrift. They tried to take a shortcut to capitalism, creating a market economy without the underlying institutions, and institutions without the underlying institutional infrastructure. Before you set up a stock market, you have to make sure there are real regulations in place. New firms need to be able to raise new capital, and this requires banks that are real banks, not the kinds of banks that characterized the old regime, or banks that simply lend money to government. A real and effective banking system requires strong banking regulations. New firms need to be able to acquire land, and this requires a land market and land registration.

Similarly, in Soviet-era agriculture, farmers used to be given the seeds and fertilizer they needed. They did not have to worry about getting these and other inputs (such as tractors) or marketing their output. Under a market economy, markets for inputs and outputs had to be created, and this required new firms or enterprises. Social institutions are also important. Under the old system in the Soviet Union, there was no unemployment, and hence no need for unemployment insurance. Workers typically worked for the same state enterprise for their entire lives, and the firm provided housing and retirement benefits. In post-

1989 Russia, however, if there were to be a labor market, individuals would have to be able to move from firm to firm. But if they could not obtain housing, such mobility would be almost impossible. Hence, a housing market was necessary. A minimal level of social sensitivity means that employers will be reluctant to fire workers if there is nothing for them to fall back on. Hence, there could not be much "restructuring" without a social safety net. Unfortunately, neither a housing market nor a real safety net existed in the Russia of 1989.

The challenges facing the economies of the former Soviet Union and the other Communist bloc nations in transition were daunting: they had to move from one price system—the distorted price system that prevailed under communism—to a market price system; they had to create markets and the institutional infrastructure that underlies them; and they had to privatize all the property which previously had belonged to the state. They had to create a new kind of entrepreneurship—not just the kind that was good at circumventing government rules and laws—and new enterprises to help redeploy the resources that had previously been so inefficiently used.

No matter how one looked at it, these economies faced hard choices, and there were fierce debates about which choices to make. The most contentious centered on the speed of reform: some experts worried that if they did not privatize quickly, creating a large group of people with a vested interest in capitalism, there would be a reversion to communism. But others worried that if they moved too quickly, the reforms would be a disaster—economic failures compounded by political corruption—opening up the way to a backlash, either from the extreme left or right. The former school was called "shock therapy," the latter "gradualist."

The views of the shock therapists—strongly advocated by the U.S. Treasury and the IMF—prevailed in most of the countries. The gradualists, however, believed that the transition to a market economy would be better managed by moving at a reasonable speed, in good order ("sequencing"). One didn't need to have *perfect* institutions; but, to take one example, privatizing a monopoly before an effective competition or regulatory authority was in place might simply replace a government monopoly with a private monopoly, even more ruthless in exploiting the consumer. Ten years later, the wisdom of the gradualist approach is at last being recognized: the tortoises have overtaken the hares. The gradualist critics of shock therapy not only accurately predicted its failures but also outlined the reasons why it would not work. Their only failure was to underestimate the magnitude of the disaster.

If the challenges posed by transition were great, so were the opportunities. Russia was a rich country. While three-quarters of a century of communism may have left its populace devoid of an understanding of market economics, it had left them with a high level of education, especially in technical areas so important for the New Economy. After all, Russia was the first country to send a man into space.

The economic theory explaining the failure of communism was clear: Centralized planning was doomed to failure, simply because no government agency could glean and process all the relevant information required to make an economy function well. Without private property and the profit motive, incentives—especially managerial and entrepreneurial incentives—were lacking. The restricted trade regime, combined with huge subsidies and arbitrarily set prices, meant the system was rife with distortions.

It followed that replacing centralized planning with a decentralized market system, replacing public ownership with private property, and eliminating or at least reducing the distortions by liberalizing trade, would cause a burst of economic output. The cutback in military expenditures—which had absorbed a huge share of GDP when the USSR was still in existence, five times larger than in the post–Cold War era—provided even more room for increases in standards of living. Instead, however, the standard of living in Russia, and many of the other East European transition countries, fell.

THE "REFORM" STORY

The first mistakes occurred almost immediately as the transition began. In the enthusiasm to get on with a market economy, most prices were freed overnight in 1992, setting in motion an inflation that wiped out savings, and moved the problem of macrostability to the top of the agenda. Everybody recognized that with hyperinflation (inflation at double-digit rates *per month*), it would be difficult to have a successful transition. Thus, the first round of shock therapy—instantaneous price liberalization—necessitated the second round: bringing inflation down. This entailed tightening monetary policy—raising interest rates.

While most of the prices were completely freed, some of the most important prices were kept low—those for natural resources. With the newly declared "market economy," this created an open invitation: If you can buy, say, oil and resell it in the West, you could make millions or even billions of dollars. So people did. Instead of making money by creating new enterprises, they got rich from a new form of the old entrepreneurship—exploiting mistaken government policies. And it was this "rent-seeking" behavior that would provide the basis of the claim by reformers that the problem was not that the reforms had been too quick, but that they had been too slow. If only *all* prices had been freed immediately! There is considerable validity in this argument, but as a defense of the radical reforms it is disingenuous. Political processes never give the technocrat free rein, and for good reason: as we have seen, technocrats often miss out on important economic, social, and political dimensions. Reform, even in well-functioning political and economic systems, is always "messy." Even if it made sense to push for instantaneous liberalization, the more relevant question is, how should one have proceeded with liberalization if one could not succeed in getting important sectors, like energy prices, liberalized quickly?

Liberalization and stabilization were two of the pillars of the radical reform strategy. Rapid privatization was the third. But the first two pillars put obstacles in the way of the third. The initial high inflation had wiped out the savings of most Russians so there were not enough people in the country who had the money to buy the enterprises being privatized. Even if they could afford to buy the enterprises, it would be difficult to revitalize them, given the high interest rates and lack of financial institutions to provide capital.

Privatization was supposed to be the first step in the process of restructuring the economy. Not only did ownership have to change but so did management; and production had to be reoriented, from producing what firms were told to produce to producing what consumers wanted. This restructuring would, of course, require new investment, and in many cases job cuts. Job cuts help overall efficiency, of course, only if they result in workers moving from low-productivity jobs to high-productivity employment. Unfortunately, too little of this positive restructuring occurred, partly because the strategy put almost insurmountable obstacles in the way.

The radical reform strategy did not work: gross domestic product in Russia fell, year after year. What had been envisioned as a short transition recession turned into one of a decade or more. The bottom seemed never in sight. The devastation—the loss in GDP—was greater than Russia had suffered in World War II. In the period 1940–46 the Soviet Union industrial production fell 24 percent. In the period 1990–98, Russian industrial production fell 42.9 percent—almost equal to the fall in GDP (45 percent). Those familiar with the history of the earlier transition in the Russian Revolution, *into* communism, could draw some comparisons between that socioeconomic trauma and the post-1989 transition: farm livestock decreased by half, investment in manufacturing came almost to a stop. Russia was able to attract some foreign investment in natural resources; Africa had shown long ago that if you price natural resources low enough, it is easy to attract foreign investment in them.

The stabilization/liberalization/privatization program was, of course, not a growth program. It was intended to set the preconditions for growth. Instead, it set the preconditions for decline. Not only was investment halted, but capital was used up—savings vaporized by inflation, the proceeds of privatization or foreign loans largely misappropriated. Privatization, accompanied by the opening of the capital markets, led not to wealth creation but to asset stripping. It was perfectly logical. An oligarch who has just been able to use political influence to garner assets worth billions, after paying only a pittance, would naturally want to get his money out of the country. Keeping money in Russia meant investing it in a country in deep depression, and risking not only low returns but having the assets seized by the next government, which would inevitably complain, quite rightly, about the "illegitimacy" of the privatization process. Anyone smart enough to be a winner in the privatization sweepstakes would be smart enough to put their money in the booming U.S. stock market, or into the safe haven of secretive offshore bank accounts. It was not even a close call; and not surprisingly, billions poured out of the country.

The IMF kept promising that recovery was around the corner. By 1997, it had reason for this optimism. With output having already fallen

40 percent since 1990, how much further down could it go? Besides, the country was doing much of what the Fund had stressed. It had liberalized, if not completely; it had stabilized, if not completely (inflation rates were brought down dramatically); and it had privatized. But of course it is easy to privatize quickly, if one does not pay any attention to *how* one privatizes: essentially give away valuable state property to one's friends. Indeed, it can be highly profitable for governments to do so—whether the kickbacks come back in the form of cash payments or in campaign contributions (or both).

But the glimpses of recovery seen in 1997 were not to last long. Indeed, the mistakes the IMF made in a distant part of the world were pivotal. In 1998, the fallout from the East Asia crisis hit. The crisis had led to a general skittishness about investing in emerging markets, and investors demanded higher returns to compensate them for lending capital to these countries. Mirroring the weaknesses in GDP and investment were weaknesses in public finance: the Russian government had been borrowing heavily. Though it had difficulty making budget ends meet, the government, pressured by the United States, the World Bank, and the IMF to privatize rapidly, had turned over its state assets for a pittance, and done so before it had put in place an effective tax system. The government created a powerful class of oligarchs and businessmen who paid but a fraction of what they owed in taxes, much less what they would have paid in virtually any other country.

Thus, at the time of the East Asia crisis, Russia was in a peculiar position. It had an abundance of natural resources, but its government was poor. The government was virtually giving away its valuable state assets, yet it was unable to provide pensions for the elderly or welfare payments for the poor. The government was borrowing billions from the IMF, becoming increasingly indebted, while the oligarchs, who had received such largesse from the government, were taking billions out of the country. The IMF had encouraged the government to open up its capital accounts, allowing a free flow of capital. The policy was supposed to make the country more attractive for foreign investors; but it was virtually a one-way door that facilitated a rush of money out of the country.

The 1998 Crisis

The country was deeply in debt, and the higher interest rates that the East Asia crisis had provoked created an enormous additional strain. This rickety tower collapsed when oil prices fell. Due to recessions and depressions in Southeast Asia, which IMF policies had exacerbated, oil demand not only failed to expand as expected but actually contracted. The resulting imbalance between demand and supply of oil turned into a dramatic fall in crude oil prices (down over 40 percent in the first six months of 1998 compared to the average prices in 1997). Oil is both a major export commodity and a source of government tax revenue for Russia, and the drop in prices had a predictably devastating effect. At the World Bank, we became aware of the problem early in 1998, when prices looked ready to fall even below Russia's cost of extraction plus transportation. Given the exchange rate at the time, Russia's oil industry could cease being profitable. A devaluation would then be inevitable.

It was clear that the ruble was overvalued. Russia was flooded with imports, and domestic producers were having a hard time competing. The switch to a market economy and away from the military was supposed to allow a redeployment of resources to produce more consumer goods, or more machines to produce consumer goods. But investment had halted, and the country was not producing consumer goods. The overvalued exchange rate—combined with the other macroeconomic policies foisted on the country by the IMF—had crushed the economy, and while the official unemployment rate remained subdued, there was massive disguised unemployment. The managers of many firms were reluctant to fire workers, given the absence of an adequate safety net. Though unemployment was disguised, it was no less traumatic: while the workers only pretended to work, the firms only pretended to pay. Wage payments fell into massive arrears, and when workers were paid, it was often with bartered goods rather than rubles.

If for these people, and for the country as a whole, the overvalued exchange rate was a disaster, for the new class of businessmen the overvalued exchange rate was a boon. They needed fewer rubles to buy their Mercedes, their Chanel handbags, and imported Italian gourmet foods. For the oligarchs trying to get their money out of the country, too, the overvalued exchange rate was a boon—it meant that they could get more dollars for their rubles, as they squirreled away their profits in foreign bank accounts.

Despite this suffering on the part of the majority of Russians, the reformers and their advisers in the IMF feared a devaluation, believing that it would set off another round of hyperinflation. They strongly resisted any change in the exchange rate and were willing to pour billions of dollars into the country to avoid it. By May, and certainly by June of 1998, it was clear Russia would need outside assistance to maintain its exchange rate. Confidence in the currency had eroded. In the belief that a devaluation was inevitable, domestic interest rates soared and more money left the country as people converted their rubles into dollars. Because of this fear of holding rubles, and the lack of confidence in the government's ability to repay its debt, by June 1998 the government had to pay almost 60 percent interest rates on its ruble loans (GKOs, the Russian equivalent of U.S. Treasury bills). That figure soared to 150 percent in a matter of weeks. Even when the government promised to pay back in dollars, it faced high interest rates (yields on dollar-denominated debt issued by the Russian government rose from slightly over 10 percent to almost 50 percent, 45 percentage points higher than the interest rate the U.S. government had to pay on its Treasury bills at the time); the market thought there was a high probability of default, and the market was right. Even that rate was lower than it might otherwise have been because many investors believed that Russia was too big and too important to fail. As the New York investment banks pushed loans to Russia, they whispered about how big the IMF bailout would have to be.

The crisis mounted in the way that these crises so frequently do. Speculators could see how much in the way of reserves was left, and as reserves dwindled, betting on a devaluation became increasingly a one-way bet. They risked almost nothing betting on the ruble's crash. As expected, the IMF came to the rescue with a multi-billion-dollar package in July 1998.[4]

In the weeks preceding the crisis, the IMF pushed policies that made the crisis, when it occurred, even worse. The Fund pushed Russia into borrowing more in foreign currency and less in rubles. The argument was simple: The ruble interest rate was much higher than the dollar interest rate. By borrowing in dollars, the government could save money. But there was a fundamental flaw in this reasoning. Basic economic theory argues that the difference in the interest rate between dollar bonds and ruble bonds should reflect the expectation of a devaluation. Markets equilibrate so that the risk-adjusted cost of borrowing (or the return to lending) is the same. I have much less confidence in markets than does the IMF, so I have much less faith that in fact the risk-adjusted cost of borrowing is the same, regardless of currency. But I also have much less confidence than the Fund that the Fund's bureaucrats can predict exchange rate movements better than the market. In the case of Russia, the IMF bureaucrats believed that they were smarter than the market—they were willing to bet Russia's money that the market was wrong. This was a misjudgment that the Fund was to repeat, in varied forms, time and time again. Not only was the judgment flawed; it exposed the country to enormous risk: if the ruble did devalue, Russia would find it far more difficult to repay the dollar-denominated loans.[5] The IMF chose to ignore this risk. By inducing greater foreign borrowing, by making Russia's position once it devalued so much less tenable, the IMF was partly culpable for the eventual suspension of payments by Russia on its debts.

The Rescue

Hoping to restore confidence in Russia's economy, the IMF approved an $11.2 billion loan on July 20, 1997, as part of a $22.6 billion package from international lenders. Russia received $4.8 billion immediately, and this money was spent in a failed attempt to bolster the value of the ruble. The World Bank was asked to provide a $6 billion loan.

This was hotly debated inside the World Bank. There were many of us who had been questioning lending to Russia all along. We questioned whether the benefits to possible future growth were large enough to justify loans that would leave a legacy of debt. Many thought that the IMF was making it easier for the government to put off meaningful reforms, such as collecting taxes from the oil companies. The evidence of corruption in Russia was clear. The Bank's own study of corruption had identified that region as among the most corrupt in the world. The West knew that much of those billions would be diverted from their intended purposes to the families and associates of corrupt officials and their oligarch friends. While the Bank and the IMF had seemingly taken a strong stance against lending to corrupt governments, it appeared that there were two standards. Small nonstrategic countries like Kenya were denied loans because of corruption while countries such as Russia where the corruption was on a far larger scale were continually lent money.

Apart from these moral issues, there were straightforward economic issues. The IMF's bailout money was supposed to be used to support the exchange rate. However, if a country's currency is overvalued and this causes the country's economy to suffer, maintaining the exchange rate makes little sense. If the exchange rate support works, the country suffers. But in the more likely case that the support does not work, the money is wasted, and the country is deeper in debt. Our calculations showed that Russia's exchange rate was overvalued, so providing money to maintain that exchange rate was simply bad economic policy. Moreover, calculations at the World Bank before the loan was made, based on estimates of government revenues and expenditures over time, strongly suggested that the July 1998 loan would not work. Unless a miracle brought interest rates down drastically, by the time autumn rolled around, Russia would be back in crisis.

There was another route by which I reached the conclusion that a further loan to Russia would be a great mistake. Russia was a naturally resource-rich country. If it got its act together, it didn't need money from the outside; and if it didn't get its act together, it wasn't clear that any money from the outside would make much difference. Under either scenario, the case against giving money seemed compelling.

In spite of strong opposition from its own staff, the Bank was under enormous political pressure from the Clinton administration to lend money to Russia. The Bank managed a compromise, publicly announcing a very large loan, but providing the loan in tranches—installments. A decision was taken to make $300 million available immediately, with the rest available only later, as we saw how Russia's reforms progressed. Most of us thought that the program would fail long before the additional money had to be forthcoming. Our predictions proved correct. Remarkably, the IMF seemed able to overlook the corruption, and the attendant risks with what would happen with the money. It actually thought that maintaining the exchange rate at an overvalued level was a good thing, and that the money would enable it to do this for more than a couple months. It provided billions to the country.

The Rescue Fails

Three weeks after the loan was made, Russia announced a unilateral suspension of payments and a devaluation of the ruble.[6] The ruble crashed. By January 1999, the ruble had declined in real effective terms by more than 75 percent from its July 1998 level.[7] The August 17 announcement precipitated a global financial crisis. Interest rates to emerging markets soared higher than they had been at the peak of the East Asia crisis. Even developing countries that had been pursuing sound economic policies found it impossible to raise funds. Brazil's recession deepened, and eventually it too faced a currency crisis. Argentina and other Latin American countries only gradually recovering from previous crises were again pushed nearer the brink. Ecuador and Colombia went over the brink and into crisis. Even the United States did not remain untouched. The New York Federal Reserve Bank engineered a private bailout of one of the nation's largest hedge funds, Long Term Capital Management, since the Fed feared its failure could precipitate a global financial crisis.

The surprise about the collapse was not the collapse itself, but the fact that it really did take some of the IMF officials—including some of the most senior ones—by surprise. They had genuinely believed that their program would work.

Our own forecasts proved only partially correct: we thought that the money might sustain the exchange rate for three months; it lasted three weeks. We felt that it would take days or even weeks for the oligarchs to bleed the money out of the country; it took merely hours and days. The Russian government even "allowed" the exchange rate to appreciate. As we have seen, this meant the oligarchs would need to spend fewer rubles to purchase their dollars. A smiling Viktor Gerashchenko, the chairman of the Central Bank of Russia, told the president of the World Bank and me that it was simply "market forces at work." When the IMF was confronted with the facts—the billions of dollars that it had given (loaned) Russia were showing up in Cypriot and Swiss bank accounts just days after the loan was made—it claimed that these weren't *their* dollars. The argument demonstrated either a remarkable lack of understanding of economics or a level of disingenuousness that rivaled Gerashchenko's, or both. When money is sent to a country, it is not sent in the form of marked dollar bills. Thus, one cannot say it is "my" money that went anywhere. The IMF had lent Russia the dollars—funds that allowed Russia, in turn, to give its oligarchs the dollars to take out of the country. Some of us quipped that the IMF would have made life easier all around if it had simply sent the money directly into the Swiss and Cyprus bank accounts.

It was, of course, not just the oligarchs who benefited from the rescue. The Wall Street and other Western investment bankers, who had been among those pressing the hardest for a rescue package, knew it would not last: they too took the short respite provided by the rescue to rescue as much as they could, to flee the country with whatever they could salvage.

By lending Russia money for a doomed cause, IMF policies led Russia into deeper debt, with nothing to show for it. The cost of the mistake was not borne by the IMF officials who gave the loan, or America who had pushed for it, or the Western bankers and the oligarchs who benefited from the loan, but by the Russian taxpayer.

There was one positive aspect of the crisis: The devaluation spurred Russia's import-competing sectors—goods actually produced in Russia finally took a growing share of the home market. This "unintended consequence" ultimately led to the long-awaited growth in Russia's real (as opposed to black) economy. There was a certain irony in this failure: macroeconomics was supposed to be the IMF's strength, and yet even here it had failed. These macroeconomic failures compounded the other failures, and contributed mightily to the enormity of the decline.

THE FAILED TRANSITIONS

Seldom has the gap between expectations and reality been greater than in the case of the transition from communism to the market. The combination of privatization, liberalization, and decentralization was supposed to lead quickly, after perhaps a short transition recession, to a vast increase in production. It was expected that the benefits from transition would be greater in the long run than in the short run, as old, inefficient machines were replaced, and a new generation of entrepreneurs was created. Full integration into the global economy, with all the benefits that that would bring, would also come quickly, if not immediately.

These expectations for economic growth were not realized, not only in Russia but in *most* of the economies in transition. Only a few of the former Communist countries—such as Poland, Hungary, Slovenia, and Slovakia—have a GDP equal to that of a decade ago. For the rest, the magnitudes of the declines in incomes are so large that they are hard to fathom. According to World Bank data, Russia in 2000 had a GDP that was less than two-thirds of what it was in 1989. Moldova's decline is the most dramatic, with output in 2000 less than a third of what it was a decade before. Ukraine's 2000 GDP was just a third of what it was ten years earlier.

Underlying the data were true symptoms of Russia's malady. Russia had quickly been transformed from an industrial giant—a country that had managed with Sputnik to put the first satellite into orbit—into a natural resource exporter; resources, and especially oil and gas, accounted for over half of all exports. While the Western reform advisers were writing books with titles like *The Coming Boom in Russia* or *How Russia Became a Market Economy,* the data itself was making it hard to take seriously the rosy pictures they were painting, and more dispassionate observers were writing books like *The Sale of the Century: Russia's Wild Ride from Communism to Capitalism.*[8]

The magnitude of GDP decline in Russia (not to mention other former Communist countries) is the subject of controversy, and some argue that because of the growing and critical informal sector—from street vendors to plumbers, painters, and other service providers, whose economic activities are typically hard to capture in national income statistics—the numbers represent an overestimate of the size of the decline. However, others argue that because so many of the transactions in Russia entail barter (over 50 percent of industrial sales),[9] and because the "market" prices are typically higher than these "barter" prices, the statistics actually underestimate the decline.

Taking all this into account, there is still a consensus that most individuals have experienced a marked deterioration in their basic standard of living, reflected in a host of social indicators. While in the rest of the world life spans were increasing markedly, in Russia they were over three years shorter, and in Ukraine almost three years shorter. Survey data of household consumption—what people eat, how much they spend on clothing, and what type of housing they live in—corroborates a marked decline in standards of living, on par with those suggested by the fall in GDP statistics. Given that the government was spending less on defense, standards of living should have increased even more than GDP. To put it another way, assume that somehow previous expenditures on consumption could have been preserved, and a third of the expenditures on military could have been shifted into new production of consumption goods, and that there had been no restructuring to increase efficiency or to take advantage of the new trade opportunities. Consumption—living standards—would then have increased by 4 percent, a small amount but far better than the actual decline.

Increased Poverty and Inequality

These statistics do not tell the whole story of the transition in Russia. They ignore one of the most important successes: How do you value the benefits of the new democracy, as imperfect as it might be? But they also ignore one of the most important failures: The increase in poverty and inequality.

While the size of the national economic pie was shrinking, it was being divided up more and more inequitably so the average Russian was getting a smaller and smaller slice. In 1989, only 2 percent of those living in Russia were in poverty. By late 1998, that number had soared to 23.8 percent, using the $2 a day standard. More than 40 percent of the country had less than $4 a day, according to a survey conducted by the World Bank. The statistics for children revealed an even deeper problem, with more than 50 percent living in families in poverty. Other post-Communist countries have seen comparable, if not worse, increases in poverty.[10]

Shortly after I arrived at the World Bank, I began taking a closer look at what was going on, and at the strategies that were being pursued. When I raised my concerns about these matters, an economist at the Bank who had played a key role in the privatizations responded heatedly. He cited the traffic jams of cars, many of them Mercedes, leaving Moscow on a summer weekend, and the stores filled with imported luxury goods. This was a far different picture from the empty and colorless retail establishments under the former regime. I did not disagree that a substantial number of people had been made wealthy enough to cause a traffic jam, or to create a demand for Gucci shoes and other imported luxury items sufficient for certain stores to prosper. At many European resorts, the wealthy Russian has replaced the wealthy Arab of two decades ago. In some, street signs are even given in Russian along with the native language. But a traffic jam of Mercedes in a country with a per capita income of $4,730 (as it was in 1997) is a sign of a sickness, not health. It is a clear sign of a society that concentrates its wealth among the few, rather than distributing it among the many.

While the transition has greatly increased the number of those in poverty, and led a few at the top to prosper, the middle class in Russia has perhaps been the hardest hit. The inflation first wiped out their meager savings, as we have seen. With wages not keeping up with inflation, their real incomes fell. Cutbacks in expenditures on education and health further eroded their standards of living. Those who could, emigrated. (Some countries, like Bulgaria, lost 10 percent or more of their population, and an even larger fraction of their educated workforce.) The bright students in Russia and other countries of the former Soviet Union that I've met work hard, with one ambition in mind: to migrate to the West. These losses are important not just for what they imply today for those living in Russia, but for what they portend for the future: historically, the middle class has been central to creating a society based on the rule of law and democratic values.

The magnitude of the increase in inequality, like the magnitude and duration of the economic decline, came as a surprise. Experts did expect some increase in inequality, or at least measured inequality. Under the old regime, incomes were kept similar by suppressing wage differences. The Communist system, while it did not make for an easy life, avoided the extremes of poverty, and kept living standards relatively equal, by providing a high common denominator for education, housing, health care and child care services. With a switch to a market economy, those who worked hard and produced well would reap the rewards for their efforts, so some increase in inequality was inevitable. However, it was expected that Russia would be spared the inequality arising from inherited wealth. Without this legacy of inherited inequality, there was the promise of a more egalitarian market economy. How differently matters have turned out! Russia today has a level of inequality comparable with the worst in the world, those Latin American societies which were based on a semifeudal heritage.[11]

Russia has gotten the worst of all possible worlds—an enormous decline in output and an enormous increase in inequality. And the prognosis for the future is bleak: extremes of inequality impede growth, particularly when they lead to social and political instability.

HOW MISGUIDED POLICIES LED TO THE FAILURES OF TRANSITION

We have already seen some of the ways that the Washington consensus policies contributed to the failures: privatization done the wrong way had not led to increased efficiency or growth but to asset stripping and decline. We have seen how the problems were compounded by interactions between reforms, as well as their pace and sequencing: capital market liberalization and privatization made it easier to take money out of the country; privatization before a legal infrastructure was in place enhanced the ability and incentive for asset stripping rather than reinvesting in the country's future. A full description of what went on, and a full analysis of the ways in which IMF programs contributed to the decline of the country, is a book in itself. Here, I want to sketch three examples. In each case, defenders of the IMF will say that things would have been worse, but for their programs. In some cases—such as the absence of competition policies—the IMF will insist that such policies were part of the program, but, alas, Russia did not implement them. Such a defense is ingenuous: with dozens of conditions, *everything* was in the IMF program. Russia knew, however, that when it came to the inevitable charade in which the IMF would threaten to cut off aid, Russia would bargain hard, an agreement (not often fulfilled) would be reached, and the money spigot opened up again. What was important were the monetary targets, the budget deficits, and the pace of privatization—the number of firms that had been turned over to the private sector, never mind how. Almost everything else was secondary; much—like competition policy—was virtually window-dressing, a defense against critics who said they were leaving out important ingredients to a successful transition strategy. As I repeatedly pushed for stronger competition policies, those inside Russia who agreed with me, who were trying to establish a true market economy, who were trying to create an effective competition authority, repeatedly thanked me.

Deciding what to emphasize, establishing priorities, is not easy. Textbook economics often provides insufficient guidance. Economic theory says that for markets to work well, there must be both competition and private property. If reform was easy, one would wave a magic wand and have both. The IMF chose to emphasize privatization, giving short shrift to competition. The choice was perhaps not surprising: corporate and financial interests often oppose competition policies, for these policies restrict their ability to make profits. The consequences of the IMF's mistake here were far more serious than just high prices: privatized firms sought to establish monopolies and cartels, to enhance their profits, undisciplined by effective antitrust policies. And as so often happens, the profits of monopoly prove especially alluring to those who are willing to resort to mafialike techniques either to obtain market dominance or to enforce collusion.

Inflation

Earlier we saw how the rapid liberalization at the beginning had led to the burst of inflation. The sad part of Russia's story was that each mistake was followed by another, which compounded the consequences.

Having set off the rapid inflation through abrupt price liberalization in 1992, it was necessary for the IMF and the Yeltsin regime to contain it. But balance has never been the strong suit of the IMF, and its excessive zeal led to excessively high interest rates. There is little evidence that lowering inflation below a moderate level increases growth. The most successful countries, like Poland, ignored the IMF's pressure and maintained inflation at around 20 percent through the critical years of adjustment. IMF's star pupils, like the Czech Republic, which pushed inflation down to 2 percent, saw their economy stagnate. There are some good reasons to believe that excessive zeal in fighting inflation can dampen real economic growth. The high interest rate clearly stifled new investment. Many of the new, privatized firms, even those who might have begun without an eye to looting them, saw that they could not expand and turned to asset stripping. The IMF-driven high interest rates led to an overvaluation of the exchange rate, making imports cheap and exports difficult. No wonder then that any visitor to Moscow after 1992 could see the stores filled with imported clothing and other goods, but would be hard-pressed to find much with a "Made in Russia" label. And this was true even five years after the transition began.

The tight monetary policies also contributed to the use of barter. With a shortage of money, workers were paid in kind—with whatever it was that the factory produced or had available, from toilet paper to shoes. While the flea markets that were established everywhere throughout the country as workers tried to get cash to buy the bare necessities of life gave a semblance of entrepreneurial activity, they masked huge inefficiencies. High rates of inflation are costly to an economy because they interfere with the workings of the price system. But barter is every bit as destructive to the effective workings of the price system, and the excesses of monetary stringency simply substituted one set of inefficiencies for a possibly even worse set.

Privatization

The IMF told Russia to privatize as fast as possible; how privatization was done was viewed as secondary. Much of the failure of which I wrote earlier—both the decline in incomes and the increase in inequality—can be directly linked to this mistake. In a World Bank review of the ten-year history of transition economies, it became apparent that privatization, in the absence of the institutional infrastructure (like corporate governance), had no positive effect on growth.[12] The Washington Consensus had again just gotten it wrong. It is easy to see the links between the way privatization was done and the failures.

For instance, in Russia and other countries, the lack of laws ensuring good corporate governance meant that those who could get control of a corporation had an incentive to steal assets from the minority shareholders; and managers had similar incentives vis-à-vis shareholders. Why expend energy in creating wealth when it was so much easier to steal it? Other aspects of the privatization process, as we have seen, enhanced the incentives as well as opportunities for corporate theft. Privatization in Russia turned over large national enterprises, typically to their old managers. Those insiders knew how uncertain and difficult was the road ahead. Even if they were predisposed to do so, they dared not wait for the creation of capital markets and the hosts of other changes that would be required for them to reap the full value of any investments and restructuring. They focused on what they could get out of the firm in the next few years, and all too often, this was maximized by stripping assets.

Privatization was also supposed to eliminate the role of the state in the economy; but those who assumed that had a far too naive view of the role of the state in the modern economy. It exercises its influence in a myriad of ways at a myriad of levels. Privatization did reduce the power of the central government, but that devolution left the local and regional governments with far wider discretion. A city or an *oblast* (regional government) could use a host of regulatory and tax measures to extort "rents" from firms that operated in their jurisdiction. In advanced industrial countries there is a rule of law which keeps local and state governments from abusing their potential powers; not so in Russia. In advanced industrial countries, competition among communities makes each try to make itself more attractive to investors. But in a world in which high interest rates and an overall depression make such investments unlikely in any case, local governments spent little time creating attractive "environments for investment" and focused instead on seeing how much they could extract from existing enterprises—just as the owners and managers of newly privatized firms themselves did. And when these privatized firms operated across many jurisdictions, authorities in one district reasoned that they had better take what they could grab before others took their own bites out of assets. And this only reinforced the incentive of managers to grab whatever they could as quickly as possible. After all, the firms would be left destitute in any case. It was a race to the bottom. There were incentives for asset stripping at every level.

Just as the radical "shock therapy" reformers claim that the problem with liberalization was not that it was too fast, but that it was not fast enough, so too with privatization. While the Czech Republic, for example, was praised by the IMF even as it faltered, it became clear that the country's rhetoric had outpaced its performance: it had left the banks in state hands. If a government privatizes corporations, but leaves banks in the state's hands, or without effective regulation, that government does not create the hard budget constraints that lead to efficiency, but rather an alternative, less transparent way of subsidizing firms—and an open invitation to corruption. Critics of Czech privatization claim the problem was not that privatization was too rapid, but that it was too slow. But no country has succeeded in privatizing everything, overnight, well, and it is likely that were a government to try to do instantaneous privatization, there would be a mess. The task is too difficult, the incentives for malfeasance too high. The failures of the rapid privatization strategies were predictable—and predicted.

Not only did privatization, as it was imposed in Russia (as well as in far too many of its former Soviet bloc dependencies), not contribute to the economic success of the country; it undermined confidence in government, in democracy, and in reform. The result of giving away its rich natural resources before it had in place a system to collect natural resource taxes was that a few friends and associates of Yeltsin became billionaires, but the country was unable to pay pensioners their $15-a-month pension.

The most egregious example of bad privatization was the loans-for-share program. In 1995, the government, instead of turning to the Central Bank for needed funds, turned to private banks. Many of these private banks belonged to friends of the government who had been given bank charters. In an environment with underregulated banks, the charters were effectively a license to print money, to make loans either to themselves or their friends or to the government. As a condition of the loan, the government put up shares of its own enterprises as collateral. Then—surprise!—the government defaulted on its loans; the private banks took over the companies in what might be viewed as a sham sale (though the government did go through a charade of having "auctions"); and a few oligarchs became instant billionaires. These privatizations had no political legitimacy. And, as noted previously, the fact that they had no legitimacy made it even more imperative that the oligarchs take their funds quickly out of the country—before a new government that might try to reverse the privatizations or undermine their position came to power.

Those who benefited from the largesse of the state, or more accurately from Yeltsin's largesse, worked hard to ensure Yeltsin's reelection. Ironically, while there was always a presumption that part of Yeltsin's giveaway went to finance his campaign, some critics think that the oligarchs were far too smart to use their money to pay for the election campaign; there was plenty of government slush funds that could be used. The oligarchs provided Yeltsin with something that was far more valuable—modern campaign management techniques and positive treatment by the TV networks they controlled.

The loans-for-share scheme constituted the final stage of the enrichment of the oligarchs, the small band of people (some of whom owed their origins, reportedly at least, partly to mafialike connections) who came to dominate not just the economic but the political life of the country. At one point, they claimed to control 50 percent of the country's wealth! Defenders of the oligarchs liken them to America's robber barons, the Harrimans and Rockefellers. But there is a big difference between the activities of such figures in nineteenth-century capitalism, even those carving out railway and mining baronies in America's Wild West, and the Russian oligarchy's exploitation of Russia, what has been called the Wild East. America's robber barons created wealth, even as they accumulated fortunes. They left a country much richer, even if they got a big slice of the larger pie. Russia's oligarchs stole assets, stripped them, leaving their country much poorer. The enterprises were left on the verge of bankruptcy, while the oligarch's bank accounts were enriched.

The Social Context

The officials who applied Washington Consensus policies failed to appreciate the social context of the transition economies. This was especially problematic, given what had happened during the years of communism.

Market economies entail a host of economic relationships—exchanges. Many of these exchanges involve matters of trust. An individual lends another money, trusting that he will be repaid. Backing up this trust is a legal system. If individuals do not live up to their contractual obligations, they can be forced to do so. If an individual steals property from another, he can be brought to court. But in countries with mature market economies and adequate institutional infrastructures, individuals and corporations resort only occasionally to litigation.

Economists often refer to the glue that holds society together as "social capital." Random violence and Mafia capitalism are often cited as reflections of the erosion of social capital, but in some of the countries of the former Soviet Union that I visited, one could see everywhere, in more subtle ways, direct manifestations of the erosion of social capital. It is not just a question of the misbehavior of a few managers; it is an almost anarchic theft by all from all. For instance, the landscape in Kazakhstan is dotted with greenhouses—missing their glass. Of course, without the glass, they fail to function. In the early days of the transition, there was so little confidence in the future that each individual took what he could: each believed that others would take the glass out of the greenhouse—in which case the greenhouse (and their livelihood) would be destroyed. But if the greenhouse was, in any case, fated to be destroyed, it made sense for each to take what he could—even if the value of the glass was small.

The way in which transition proceeded in Russia served to erode this social capital. One got wealthy not by working hard or by investing, but by using political connections to get state property on the cheap in privatizations. The social contract, which bound citizens together with their government, was broken, as pensioners saw the government giving away valuable state assets, but claiming that it had no money to pay their pensions.

The IMF's focus on macroeconomics—and in particular on inflation—led it to shunt aside issues of poverty, inequality, and social capital. When confronted about this myopia of focus, it would say, "Inflation is especially hard on the poor." But its policy framework was not designed to minimize the impact on the poor. And by ignoring the impacts of its policies on the poor and on social capital, the IMF actually impeded *macroeconomic* success. The erosion of social capital created an environment that was not conducive to investment. The Russian government's (and the IMF's) lack of attention to a minimal safety net slowed down the process of restructuring, as even hardheaded plant managers often found it difficult to fire workers, knowing there was little standing between their fired workers and extreme hardship, if not starvation.

Shock Therapy

The great debate over reform strategy in Russia centered on the pace of reform. Who was right, in the end—the "shock therapists" or the "gradualists"? Economic theory, which focuses on equilibrium and idealized models, has less to say about dynamics, the order, timing, and pacing of reforms, than one would like—though IMF economists often tried to convince client countries otherwise. The debaters resorted to metaphors to convince others of the merits of their side. The rapid reformers said, "You can't cross a chasm in two leaps," while the gradualists argued that it took nine months to make a baby, and talked about crossing the river by feeling the stones. In some cases, what separated the two views was more a difference in perspective than reality. I was present at a seminar in Hungary where one participant said, "We must have rapid reform! It must be accomplished in five years." Another said, "We should have gradual reform. It will take us five years." Much of the debate was more about the manner of reform than the speed.

We have already encountered two of the essential critiques of the gradualists: "Haste makes waste"—it is hard to design good reforms well; and sequencing matters. There are, for instance, important prerequisites for a successful mass privatization, and creating these prerequisites takes time.[13] Russia's peculiar pattern of reforms demonstrates that incentives do matter, but that Russia's kind of ersatz capitalism did not provide the incentives for wealth creation and economic growth but rather for asset stripping. Instead of a smoothly working market economy, the quick transition led to a disorderly Wild East.

The Bolshevik Approach to Market Reform

Had the radical reformers looked beyond their narrow focus on economics, they would have found that history shows that most of the experiments in radical reform were beset by problems. This is true from the French Revolution in 1789, to the Paris Commune of 1871, to the

Bolshevik Revolution in Russia in 1917, and to China's Cultural Revolution of the 1960s and 1970s. It is easy to understand the forces giving rise to each of these revolutions, but each produced its own Robespierre, its own political leaders who were either corrupted by the revolution or took it to extremes. By contrast, the successful American "Revolution" was not a true revolution in society; it was a *revolutionary* change in political structures, but it represented an *evolutionary* change in the structure of society. The radical reformers in Russia were trying simultaneously for a revolution in the economic regime and in the structure of society. The saddest commentary is that, in the end, they failed in both: a market economy in which many old party apparatchiks had simply been vested with enhanced powers to run and profit from the enterprises they formerly managed, in which former KGB officials still held the levers of power. There was one new dimension: a few new oligarchs, able and willing to exert immense political and economic power.

In effect, the radical reformers employed Bolshevik strategies—though they were reading from different texts. The Bolsheviks tried to impose communism on a reluctant country in the years following 1917. They argued that the way to build socialism was for an elite cadre to "lead" (often a euphemism for "force") the masses onto the correct path, which was not necessarily the path the masses wanted or thought best. In the "new" post-Communist revolution in Russia, an elite, spearheaded by international bureaucrats, similarly attempted to force rapid change on a reluctant population.

Those who advocated the Bolshevik approach not only seemed to ignore the history of such radical reforms but also postulated that political processes would work in ways for which history provided no evidence. For instance, economists such as Andrei Shleifer, who recognized the importance of the institutional infrastructure for a market economy, believed that privatization, no matter how implemented, would lead to a political demand for the institutions that govern private property.

Shleifer's argument can be thought of as an (unwarranted) extension of Coase's theorem. The economist Ronald H. Coase, who was awarded a Nobel Prize for his work, argued that in order to achieve efficiency, well-defined property rights are essential. Even if one distributed assets to someone who did not know how to manage them well, in a society with well-defined property rights that person would have an incentive to sell to someone who could manage the assets efficiently. That is why, advocates of rapid privatization argued, one didn't really need to pay close attention to how privatization was accomplished. It is now recognized that the conditions under which Coase's conjecture is valid are highly restrictive[14]—and certainly weren't satisfied in Russia as it embarked on its transition.

Shleifer and company, however, took Coase's ideas further than Coase himself would have done. They believed that political processes were governed in the same way as economic processes. If a group with vested interests in property could be created, it would demand the establishment of an institutional infrastructure necessary to make a market economy work, and its demands would be reflected in the political process. Unfortunately, the long history of political reforms suggests that the distribution of income does matter. It has been the middle class that has demanded the reforms that are often referred to as "the rule of law." The very wealthy usually do far better for themselves behind closed doors, bargaining special favors and privileges. Certainly it has not been demands from the Rockefellers and the Bill Gates of the world that have led to strong competition policies. Today, in Russia, we do not see demands for strong competition policy forthcoming from the oligarchs, the new monopolists. Demands for the rule of law have come from these oligarchs, who obtained their wealth through behind-the-scenes special deals within the Kremlin, only as they have seen their special influence on Russia's rulers wane.

Demands for an open media, free from concentration in the hands of a few, came from the oligarchs, who sought to control the media in order to maintain their power—but only when the government sought to use its power to deprive them of theirs. In most democratic and developed countries such concentrations of economic power would not long be tolerated by a middle class forced to pay monopoly prices. Americans have long been concerned with the dangers of concentration of media power, and concentrations of power in the United States on a scale comparable to that in Russia today would be unacceptable. Yet U.S. and IMF officials paid little attention to the dangers posed by the concentration of media power; rather, they focused on the rapidity of privatization, a sign that the privatization process was proceeding apace. And they took comfort, indeed even pride, in the fact that the concentrated private media was being used, and used effectively, to keep their friends Boris Yeltsin and the so-called reformers in power.

One of the reasons that it is important to have an active and critical media is to ensure that the decisions that get made reflect not just the interests of a few but the general interest of society. It was essential for the continuation of the Communist system that there not be public scrutiny. One of the problems with the failure to create an effective, independent, and competitive media in Russia was that the policies—such as the loans-for-share scheme—were not subjected to the public critique that they deserved. Even in the West, however, the critical decisions about Russian policy, both at the international economic institutions and in the U.S. Treasury, went on largely behind closed doors. Neither the taxpayers in the West, to whom these institutions were supposed to be accountable, nor the Russian people, who paid the ultimate price, knew much about what was going on at the time. Only now are we wrestling with the question of "Who lost Russia?"—and why. The answers, as we are beginning to see, are not edifying.

CHAPTER 10

UNFAIR FAIR TRADE
LAWS AND OTHER
MISCHIEF

THE IMF IS a political institution. The 1998 bailout was dictated by a concern to maintain Boris Yeltsin in power, though on the basis of all the *principles* which should have guided lending, it made little sense. The quiet acquiescence, if not outright support, to the corrupt loans-for-share privatization was partially based on the fact that the corruption too was for good purpose—to get Yeltsin reelected.[1] IMF policies in these areas were inextricably linked to the political judgments of the Clinton administration's Treasury.

Within the administration as a whole, there were, in fact, misgivings about Treasury's strategy. After the defeat of the reformers in December 1993, Strobe Talbott, at the time in charge of Russia policy (later to become deputy secretary of state), expressed the widespread apprehensive view of the shock therapy strategy: Had there been too much shock and too little therapy? We at the Council of Economic Advisers felt strongly that the United States was giving bad advice to Russia and using taxpayers' money to induce them to accept it. But Treasury claimed Russian economic policy as its own turf; turned aside any attempts to have an open dialogue, either within government or outside; and stood stubbornly by its commitment to shock therapy and rapid privatization.

Political judgments as much as economics lay behind the stances of the people at the Treasury. They worried about the imminent danger of backsliding into communism. The gradualists worried that the real danger was the failure of shock therapy: increasing poverty and falling incomes would undermine support for market reforms. Again, the gradualists proved right. The Moldova elections in February 2000, in which the old Communists got 70 percent of the seats in the Duma, were perhaps the most extreme case, but disillusionment with radical reform and shock therapy is now common among the economies in transition.[2] Seeing the transition as the last round in the battle between good and evil, between markets and communism, led to one further problem: the IMF and U.S. Treasury treated most of the ex-Communists with disdain and distrust, except for a few chosen ones who became their allies. There were, of course, some die-hard Communists, but some, perhaps many of those who had served in the Communist governments, were far from true believers. Instead, they were pragmatists who wanted to get ahead in the system. If the system required that they join the Communist Party, that did not seem an overly excessive price to pay. Many were as happy as anyone else to see the end of the Communist domination and the restoration of democratic processes. If these people carried over anything from their Communist days, it was a belief that the state bore a responsibility for taking care of those in need, and a belief in a more egalitarian society.

In fact, many of these ex-Communists became what, in European terms, are called Social Democrats of various persuasions. In American political terms they might range anywhere from the old New Deal Democrats to the more recent New Democrats, though most would have been closer to the former than the latter. It was ironic that the Democratic Clinton administration, seemingly embracing views highly consonant with these Social Democrats, would so often ally itself in the economies in transition with reformers who leaned to the right, the disciples of Milton Friedman and of radical market reforms, who paid too little attention to the social and distributional consequences of policy.

In Russia, there was no one but ex-Communists to be dealt with. Yeltsin himself was an ex-Communist—a candidate member of the Politburo. In Russia, the Communists were never really ousted from power. Almost all of Russia's reformers were well-connected ex-Communists. At one time, it seemed the fault line would lie between those who were closely connected to the KGB and Gosplan—the centers of political and economic control under the old regime—and everyone else. The "good guys" were the apparatchiks who had run businesses, like Viktor Chernomyrdin, the head of Gazprom, who succeeded Gaidar as prime minister, practical men with whom we could deal. While some of these "practical men" were ready to steal as much of the state's wealth for themselves and their friends as they could get away with, they were clearly no left-wing ideologues. While (mistaken or not) judgments about who would likely lead Russia into the promised land of free markets may have guided decisions about whom the United States (and the IMF) should ally itself with in the early days of the transition, by 2000 a hard pragmatism had set in. If there had been idealism in the beginning, the failings of Yeltsin and many of those around him had led to cynicism. Putin was embraced with seeming warmth by the Bush administration as someone we could work with, his KGB credentials of little moment. It had taken a long time for us to finally stop judging people by whether they were or were not Communists during the old regime—or even by what they did under the old regime. If mistaken ideology may have blinded us in dealing with emerging leaders and parties in the countries in transition, as well as the design of economic policies, mistaken political judgments played no less a role. Many of those with whom we allied ourselves were less interested in creating the kind of market economy that has worked so well in the West than in enriching themselves.

As time went on, and the problems with the reform strategy and the Yeltsin government became clearer, the reactions of people in both the IMF and the U.S. Treasury proved not unlike those of officials earlier inside the U.S. government as the failures of the Vietnam War became clearer: to ignore the facts, to deny the reality, to suppress the discussion, to throw more and more good money after bad. Russia was about to "turn a corner"; growth was about to occur; the next loan would enable Russia finally to get going; Russia had now shown that it would live up to the conditions of the loan agreements; and so on and so forth. As the prospects of success looked increasingly bleak, as the end to the crisis looked increasingly around still another corner, the rhetoric changed: the emphasis switched from confidence in Yeltsin to fearing the threat of the alternative.

The sense of anxiety was palpable. I received a call one day from the office of a very senior adviser to the Russian government. He wanted to organize a brainstorming session in Russia on what the country might do to get itself going. The best that the IMF had been able to provide in years of advice was stabilization; it had nothing to offer in the way of growth. And it was clear that stabilization—at least as presented by the IMF—did not lead to growth. When the IMF and the U.S. Treasury got wind of this, they leaped into action. Treasury (reportedly at the most senior level) called the president of the Bank and I was ordered not to go. But, while Treasury would like to think of the World Bank as its own property, other countries can, when carefully orchestrated, outflank even the U.S. Treasury secretary. And so it happened here: with the appropriate calls and letters from Russia, I proceeded to Russia to do what the Russians had asked—to open a discussion unfettered by either IMF ideology or U.S. Treasury's special interests.

My visit was fascinating. The breadth of the discussions was impressive. There were a number of bright people struggling to craft a strategy for economic growth. They knew the numbers—but to them the decline in Russia was not just a matter of statistics. Many people I talked to recognized the importance of what had been left out of, or given insufficient attention in, the IMF programs. They knew that growth requires more than stabilization, privatization, and liberalization. They worried that the pressure from the IMF for rapid privatization, which they were still feeling, would lead to still more problems. Some recognized the importance of creating strong competition policies, and bemoaned the lack of support that they were receiving. But what struck me most was the incongruity between the spirit in Washington and in Moscow. In Moscow, there was (at the time) a healthy policy debate. Many were concerned, for instance, that the high exchange rate was suppressing growth—and they were right. Others worried that a devaluation would set off inflation—and they too were right. These are complicated matters, and in democracies, they need to be debated and discussed. Russia was trying to do that, trying to open up the discussion to different voices. It was Washington—or more accurately, the IMF and the U. S. Treasury—that was afraid of democracy, that wanted to suppress debate. I could not but note, and feel sad about, the irony.

As the evidence of the failures mounted, and as it became increasingly clear that the United States had been backing a weak horse, the U.S.

administration tried even harder to clamp down on criticisms and public discussion. Treasury tried to eliminate discussions from within the Bank with the press, to be sure that only their interpretations of what was going on would be heard. Yet it was remarkable how, even as evidence on possible corruption unfolded in U.S. newspapers, the Treasury Department hardly wavered in its strategy.

For many, the loans-for-share privatization scheme discussed in chapter 9 (in which a few oligarchs got control of a vast portion of the country's rich natural resources) became the critical point at which the United States should have spoken out. Within Russia, the United States was not unjustly perceived as having allied itself with corruption. In what would have been perceived as a public display of support, Deputy Treasury Secretary Lawrence Summers invited to his house Anatoly Chubais, who had been in charge of privatization, who organized the loans-for-share scam, and who not surprisingly has become one of the least popular public officials in all Russia. The U.S. Treasury and the IMF entered into the political life of Russia. By siding so firmly for so long with those at the helm when the huge inequality was created through this corrupt privatization process, the United States, the IMF, and the international community have indelibly associated themselves with policies that, at best, promoted the interests of the wealthy at the expense of the average Russian.

When U.S. and European newspapers finally exposed the corruption publicly, Treasury's condemnation had a hollow and disingenuous ring. The reality is that the Duma's inspector general brought these charges to Washington long before the news stories broke. Within the World Bank, I was urged not to meet with him, lest we give credence to his charges. If the extent of corruption was not known, it was because ears and eyes were covered.

WHAT SHOULD HAVE BEEN DONE

The West's long-term interests would have been far better served had we stayed out of close involvement with particular leaders, and provided broad-based support to democratic processes. This could have been done by supporting young and emerging leaders in Moscow and in the provinces who were against corruption and who were trying to create a true democracy.

I wish there had been an open debate about America's Russian strategy at the beginning of the Clinton administration, a debate more reflective of the discussion going on in the outside world. I believe that if Clinton had been confronted with the arguments, he would have adopted a more balanced approach. He would have been more sensitive to the concerns of the poor, and more aware of the importance of political processes than the people at Treasury. But as is so often the case, the president was never given a chance to hear the full range of issues and views. Treasury viewed the issue as too important to let the president have an important role in making the decisions. Perhaps because of the lack of interest from the American people, Clinton himself did not feel that this issue was important enough for him to demand an accounting in greater detail.

U.S. INTERESTS AND RUSSIAN REFORM

There are many in Russia (and elsewhere) who believe the failed policies were not just accidental: the failures were deliberate, intended to eviscerate Russia, to remove it as a threat for the indefinite future. This rather conspiratorial view credits those at the IMF and the U.S. Treasury with both greater malevolence and greater wisdom than I think they had. I believe that they actually thought the policies they were advocating would succeed. They believed that a strong Russian economy and a stable Russian reform-oriented government were in the interests of both the United States and global peace.

But the policies were not totally altruistic. U.S. economic interests—or more accurately, U.S. financial and commercial market interests—were reflected in the policies. For instance, the July 1998 bailout was just as much a bailout of Western banks that stood to lose billions of dollars (and eventually did lose billions) as it was a bailout of Russia. But it was not just Wall Street's direct interests that influenced policy; it was the ideology that prevailed in the financial community. For instance, Wall Street regards inflation as the worst thing in the world: it erodes the real value of what is owed to creditors, which leads to increases in interest rates, which in turn lead to declines in bond prices. To financiers, unemployment is far less of a concern. For Wall Street, nothing could be more sacrosanct than private property; no wonder then the emphasis on privatization. Their commitment to competition is far less passionate— after all, it was the U.S. secretary of the Treasury, Paul O'Neill, who in his previous position as head of Alcoa engineered the global alumi- num cartel and worked to suppress competition in the global aluminum market. And notions of social capital and political participation may not even appear on their radar screen; they feel far more comfortable with an independent central bank than one whose actions are more directly under the control of political processes. (In the case of Russia, there was a certain irony in this stance; in the aftermath of the 1998 crisis, it was Russia's independent central banker that threatened to push a more infla- tionary policy than the IMF—and some members of the government— wanted, and it was the independence of the Central Bank that partly accounted for its ability to ignore charges of corruption.)

Broader special economic interests in the United States affected poli- cies in ways that conflicted with broader national interests and made the country look more than a little hypocritical. The United States supports free trade, but all too often, when a poor country does manage to find a commodity it can export to the United States, domestic American pro- tectionist interests are galvanized. This mix of labor and business inter- ests uses the many trade laws—officially referred to as "fair trade laws," but known outside the United States as "unfair fair trade laws"—to con- struct barbed-wire barriers to imports. These laws allow a company that believes a foreign rival is selling a product below cost to request that the government impose special tariffs to protect it. Selling products below cost is called dumping, and the duties are called dumping duties. Often, however, the U.S. government determines costs on the basis of little evidence, and in ways which make little sense. To most economists, the dumping duties are simply naked protectionism. Why, they ask, would a rational firm sell goods below cost?

The Aluminum Case

During my term in government, perhaps the most grievous instance of U.S. special interests interfering in trade—and the reform process—

occurred in early 1994, just after the price of aluminum plummeted. In response to the fall in price, U.S. aluminum producers accused Russia of dumping aluminum. Any economic analysis of the situation showed clearly that Russia was not dumping. Russia was simply selling aluminum at the international price, which was lowered both because of a global slowdown in demand occasioned by slower global growth and because of the cutback in Russian aluminum use for military planes. Moreover, new soda can designs used substantially less aluminum than before, and this also led to a decline in the demand. As I saw the price of aluminum plummet, I knew the industry would soon be appealing to the government for some form of relief, either new subsidies or new protection from foreign competition. But even I was surprised at the proposal made by the head of Alcoa, Paul O'Neill: a global aluminum cartel. Cartels work by restricting output, thereby raising prices. O'Neill's interest was no surprise to me; what did surprise me was the idea that the U.S. government would not only condone a cartel but actually play a pivotal role in setting one up. He also raised the specter of using the antidumping laws if the cartel was not created. These laws allow the United States to impose special duties on goods that are sold at below a "fair market value," and particularly when they are sold below the cost of production. The issue, of course, was not whether Russia was or was not dumping. Russia was selling its aluminum at international prices. Given the excess capacity in its industry and the low price of Russian electricity, much if not all of what it was selling on international markets was being sold above its costs of production. However, the way the dumping laws are typically implemented, countries can be charged with dumping even when they were—from an economic point of view—not dumping. The U.S. estimates costs of production using a peculiar methodology, which, if applied to American firms, would probably conclude that most American firms were dumping as well; but worse, the Department of Commerce, which acts simultaneously as judge, jury, and prosecutor, estimates costs based on what it calls BIA, best information available, which is typically that provided by the American firms trying to keep out the foreign competition. In the case of Russia and the other former Communist countries, it often estimates costs by looking at costs in a comparable country. In one case, Poland was charged with dumping golf carts:

the supposedly "comparable" country was Canada. In the case of aluminum, had dumping charges been brought, there was a reasonable chance that sufficiently high duties would be imposed so that Russia would not be able to sell its aluminum in the United States. It might be able to sell its aluminum elsewhere (unless other countries followed the U.S. lead), in which case international aluminum prices would have continued to have been depressed. For Alcoa, a global cartel was thus preferable: it offered a better chance of getting the high prices that Alcoa wanted.

I opposed the cartel. What makes market economies work is competition. Cartels are illegal inside the United States, and they should be illegal globally. The Council of Economic Advisers had become a strong ally of the Antitrust Division of the U.S. Justice Department in pushing for strong enforcement of competition laws. For the United States now to help create a global cartel was a violation of every principle. Here, however, more was at stake. Russia was struggling to create a market economy. The cartel would hurt Russia, by restricting its sales of one of the few goods that it could market internationally. And creating the cartel would be teaching Russia the wrong lesson about how market economies work.

On a quick trip to Russia, I talked to Gaidar, then the first deputy prime minister in charge of economics; he and I both knew that Russia was not dumping—in the sense in which that word would be used by economists—but we both knew how the U.S. laws work. Were dumping charges brought, there was a good chance that dumping duties would be levied. Nonetheless, he knew how bad a cartel would be for Russia, both economically and in terms of the impact on the reforms he was trying to put into place. He agreed that we should resist as strongly as we could. He was willing to face the risk of the imposition of dumping duties.

I worked hard to convince those in the National Economic Council that it would be a mistake to support O'Neill's idea, and I made great progress. But in a heated subcabinet meeting, a decision was made to support the creation of an international cartel. People in the Council of Economic Advisers and the Department of Justice were livid. Ann Bingaman, the assistant attorney general for antitrust, put the cabinet on notice that there might have been a violation of the antitrust laws in the presence of the subcabinet. Reformers within the Russian government were adamantly opposed to the establishment of the cartel and had communicated their feelings directly to me. They knew that the quantitative restrictions that the cartel would impose would give more power back to the old-line ministries. With a cartel, each country would be given certain quotas, amounts of aluminum they could produce or export. The ministries would control who got the quotas. This was the kind of system with which they were familiar, the kind of system that they loved. I worried that the excess profits generated by the trade restrictions would give rise to a further source of corruption. We did not fully grasp that in the new Mafiaized Russia, it would also give rise to a bloodbath in the struggle over who got the quotas.

While I had managed to convince almost everyone of the dangers of the cartel solution, two voices dominated. The State Department, with its close connections to the old-line state ministries, supported the establishment of a cartel. The State Department prized order above all else, and cartels do provide order. The old-line ministries, of course, were never convinced that this movement to prices and markets made sense in the first place, and the experience with aluminum simply served to confirm their views. Rubin, at that time head of the National Economic Council, played a decisive role, siding with State. At least for a while, the cartel did work. Prices were raised. The profits of Alcoa and other producers were enhanced. The American consumers—and consumers throughout the world—lost, and indeed, the basic principles of economics, which teach the value of competitive markets, show that the losses to consumers outweigh the gains to producers. But in the case at point, more was at issue: we were trying to teach Russia about market economics. They learned a lesson, but it was the wrong lesson, a lesson that was to cost them dearly over the succeeding years: the way to do well in market economics was to go to the government! We did not intend to teach crony-capitalism 101, and they probably did not need to take crony-capitalism 101 from us; they probably could have learned all that was required on their own. But we unwittingly provided them with a bad example.[3]

National Security for Sale

The aluminum case was not the first, nor would it be the last instance, where special interests dominated over the national and global goal of a successful transition. At the end of the Bush administration and the beginning of the Clinton administration, a historical "swords to plow-shares" agreement was made between Russia and the United States. A U.S. government enterprise called the United States Enrichment Corporation (USEC) would buy Russian uranium from deactivated nuclear warheads and bring it to the United States. The uranium would be de-enriched so that it could no longer be used for nuclear weapons, and would then be used in nuclear power plants. The sale would provide Russia with needed cash, which it could use to better keep its nuclear material under control.

Unbelievable as it may seem, the fair trade laws were again invoked, to impede this transfer. The American uranium producers argued that Russia was dumping uranium on U.S. markets. Just as in the case of aluminum, there was no economic validity to this charge. However, the U.S. unfair fair trade laws are not written on the basis of economic principles. They exist solely to protect American industries adversely affected by imports.

When the U.S. government's import of uranium for purposes of disarmament was challenged by American uranium producers under the fair trade laws, it became clear that a change in these laws was needed. The Department of Commerce and the U.S. Trade Representative were—with high-level coaxing—finally persuaded to propose changes in the laws to Congress. Congress turned the proposals down. It has remained unclear to me whether Commerce and the U.S. Trade Representative sabotaged efforts at getting a change in the laws by presenting the proposal to Congress in a way that made the outcome inevitable, or whether they fought against a Congress which has always taken a strong protectionist stand.

Equally striking was what happened next, in the mid-1990s. Much to the embarrassment of the Reagan and Bush administrations, the United States was far behind in the sweepstakes on privatization in the 1980s. Margaret Thatcher had privatized billions, while the United States had privatized only a $2 million helium plant in Texas. The difference, of course, was that Thatcher had far more and far larger nationalized industries that she could privatize. At last privatization advocates in the United States thought of something that few others would, or could, privatize: USEC, which not only enriches uranium for nuclear reactors but also for atomic bombs. The privatization was beset by problems. USEC had been entrusted with bringing in the enriched uranium from Russia; as a private firm, this was a kind of monopoly power that would not have passed scrutiny of the antitrust authorities. Worse still, we at the Council of Economic Advisers had analyzed the incentives of a privatized USEC, and had shown convincingly that it had every incentive to keep the Russian uranium out of the United States. This was a real concern: there were major worries about nuclear proliferation—about nuclear material getting into the hands of a rogue state or a terrorist organization—and having a weakened Russia with enriched uranium to sell to anyone willing to pay was hardly a pretty picture. USEC adamantly denied that it would ever act counter to broader U.S. interests, and affirmed that it would always bring in Russian uranium as fast as the Russians were willing to sell; but the very week that it made these protestations, I got hold of a secret agreement between USEC and the Russian agency. The Russians had offered to triple their deliveries, and USEC had not only turned them down but paid a handsome amount in what could only be termed "hush money" to keep the offer (and USEC's refusal) secret. One might have thought that this itself would have been enough to stop the privatization, but not so: the U.S. Treasury was as adamant about privatization at home as it was in Russia.

Interestingly, this, America's only major privatization of the decade, has been beset with problems almost as bad as those that have befallen privatization elsewhere, so much so that bipartisan bills have been introduced into Congress to renationalize the enterprise. Our forecasts that the privatization would interfere with the importation of the enriched uranium from Russia proved all too prescient. Indeed, at one point, it looked as if all exports to the United States might be held up. In the end, USEC asked for huge subsidies to continue with the importation. The rosy economic picture painted by USEC (and the U.S. Treasury) proved false, and investors became angry as they saw share prices plummet. There was nervousness about a firm with bare financial viability in charge of our nation's production of enriched uranium. Within a couple of years of privatization, questions were being raised about whether Treasury could, with a straight face, give the financial certification required by the law for USEC to continue to operate.

LESSONS FOR RUSSIA

Russia had a crash course in market economics, and we were the teachers. And what a peculiar course it was. On the one hand, they were given large doses of free market, textbook economics. On the other hand, what they saw *in practice* from their teachers departed markedly from this ideal. They were told that trade liberalization was necessary for a successful market economy, yet when they tried to export aluminum and uranium (and other commodities as well) to the United States, they found the door shut. Evidently, America had succeeded without trade liberalization; or, as it is sometimes put, "trade is good, but imports are bad." They were told that competition is vital (though not much emphasis was put on this), yet the U.S. government was at the center of creating a global cartel in aluminum, and gave the monopoly rights to import enriched uranium to the U.S. monopoly producer. They were told to privatize rapidly and honestly, yet the one attempt at privatization by the United States took years and years, and in the end its integrity was questioned. The United States lectured everyone, especially in the aftermath of the East Asia crisis, about crony capitalism and its dangers. Yet issues of the use of influence appeared front and center not only in the instances described in this chapter but in the bailout of Long Term Capital Management described in the last.

If the West's preaching is not taken seriously everywhere, we should understand why. It is not just past injuries, such as the unfair trade treaties referred to in earlier chapters. It is what we are doing today. Others look not only at what we say, but also at what we do. It is not always a pretty picture.

CHAPTER 11

BETTER ROADS
TO THE MARKET

As the failures of the radical reform strategies in Russia and elsewhere have become increasingly evident, those who pushed them claim that they had no choices. But there were alternative strategies available. This was brought home forcefully at a meeting in Prague in September 2000, when former government officials from a number of the Eastern European countries—both those that were experiencing success and those whose performance was disappointing—reappraised their experiences. The government of the Czech Republic headed by Vaclav Klaus initially got high marks from the IMF because of its policy of rapid privatization; but its management of the overall transition process resulted in a GDP that, by the end of the 1990s, was lower than the country's 1989 level. Officials in his government said they had no choice in the policies adopted. But this contention was challenged by speakers from the Czech Republic and those from the other countries. There were alternatives; other countries made different choices—and there is a clear link between the different choices and the different outcomes.

Poland and China employed alternative strategies to those advocated by the Washington Consensus. Poland is the most successful of the Eastern European countries; China has experienced the fastest rate of growth of any major economy in the world over the past twenty years. Poland started with "shock therapy" to bring hyperinflation down to more moderate levels, and its initial and limited use of this measure has led many to think that this was one of the shock therapy transitions. But that is totally wrong. Poland quickly realized that shock therapy was appropriate for bringing down hyperinflation, but was inappropriate for societal change. It pursued a gradualist policy of privatization, while simultaneously building up the basic institutions of a market economy, such as banks that actually lend, and a legal system that could enforce contracts and process bankruptcies fairly. It recognized that without those institutions, a market economy cannot function. (In contrast to Poland, the Czech Republic privatized corporations before it privatized the banks. The state banks continued to lend to the privatized corporations; easy money flowed to those favored by the state, and privatized entities were not subjected to rigorous budgetary constraint, which allowed them to put off real restructuring.) Poland's former deputy premier and finance minister, Grzegorz W. Kolodko, has argued that the success of his nation was due to its explicit rejection of the doctrines of the Washington Consensus.[1] The country did not do what the IMF recommended—it did not engage in rapid privatization, and it did not put reducing inflation to lower and lower levels over all other macroeconomic concerns. But it did emphasize some things to which the IMF had paid insufficient attention—such as the importance of democratic support for the reforms, which entailed trying to keep unemployment low, providing benefits for those who were unemployed and adjusting pensions for inflation, and creating the institutional infrastructure required to make a market economy function.

The gradual process of privatization allowed restructuring to take place prior to privatization, and the large firms could be reorganized into smaller units. A new, vibrant small enterprise sector was thus created, headed by young managers willing to invest for their future.[2]

Similarly, China's success over the past decade stands in marked contrast to Russia's failure. While China grew at an average rate of over 10 percent in the 1990s, Russia declined at an average annual rate of 5.6 percent. By the end of the decade, real incomes (so-called purchasing power) in China were comparable to those in Russia. Whereas China's transition has entailed the largest reduction in poverty in history in such a short time span (from 358 million in 1990 to 208 million in 1997, using China's admittedly lower poverty standard of $1 a day), Russia's transition has entailed one of the largest increases in poverty in history in such a short span of time (outside of war and famine).

The contrast between China's strategy and that of Russia could not be clearer, and it began from the very first moves along the path to transition. China's reforms began in agriculture, with the movement from the commune (collective) system of production in agriculture to the "individual responsibility" system—effectively, *partial* privatization. It was not complete privatization: individuals could not buy and sell land freely; but the gains in output showed how much could be gained from even partial and limited reforms. This was an enormous achievement, involving hundreds of millions of workers, accomplished in a few years. But it was done in a way that engendered widespread support: a successful trial in one province, followed by trials in several others, equally successful. The evidence was so compelling that the central government did not have to *force* this change; it was willingly accepted. But the Chinese leadership recognized that they could not rest on their laurels, and the reforms had to extend to the entire economy.

At this juncture, they called upon several American advisers, including Kenneth Arrow and myself. Arrow had been awarded the Nobel Prize partly for his work on the foundations of a market economy; he had provided the mathematic underpinnings that explained why, *and when*, market economies work. He had also done path-breaking work on dynamics, on how economies changed. But unlike those transition gurus who marched into Russia armed with textbook economics, Arrow recognized the limitations of these textbook models. He and I each stressed the importance of competition, of creating the institutional infrastructure for a market economy. Privatization was secondary. The most challenging questions that were posed by the Chinese were questions of dynamics, and especially how to move from distorted prices to market prices. The Chinese came up with an ingenious solution: a two-tier price system in which what a firm produced under the old quotas (what it was required to produce under the old command-and-control system) is priced using old prices, but anything produced in excess of the old quota is priced using free-market prices. The system allowed full incentives *at the margin*—which, as economists are well aware, is where they matter—but avoided the huge redistributions that would have occurred if the new prices were instantaneously to prevail over the entire output. It allowed the market to "grope" for the undistorted prices, a process that is not always smooth, with minimal disturbance. Most important, the Chinese gradualist approach avoided the pitfall of rampant inflation that had marked the shock therapies of Russia and the other countries under IMF tutelage, and all the dire consequences that followed, including the wiping out of savings accounts. As soon as it had accomplished its purpose, the two-tier price system was abandoned.

In the meanwhile, China unleashed a process of *creative* destruction: of eliminating the old economy by creating a new one. Millions of new enterprises were created by the townships and villages, which had been freed from the responsibility of managing agriculture and could turn their attention elsewhere. At the same time, the Chinese government invited foreign firms into the country, to participate in joint ventures. And foreign firms came in droves—China became the largest recipient of foreign direct investment among the emerging markets, and number eight in the world, below only the United States, Belgium, the United Kingdom, Sweden, Germany, the Netherlands, and France.[3] By the end of the decade, its ranking was even higher. It set out, simultaneously, to create the "institutional infrastructure"—an effective securities and exchange commission, bank regulations, and safety nets. As safety nets were put into place and new jobs were created, it began the task of restructuring the old state-owned enterprises, downsizing them as well as the government bureaucracies. In a short span of a couple of years, it privatized much of the housing stock. The tasks are far from over, the future far from clear, but this much is undisputed: the vast majority of Chinese live far better today than they did twenty years ago.

The "transition" from the authoritarianism of the ruling Communist Party in China, however, is a more difficult problem. Economic growth and development do not automatically confer personal freedom and civil rights. The interplay between politics and economics is complex. Fifty years ago, there was a widespread view that there was a trade-off between growth and democracy. Russia, it was thought, might be able to grow faster than America, but it paid a high price. We now know that the Russians gave up their freedom but did not gain economically. There are cases of successful reforms done under dictatorship—Pinochet in Chile is one example. But the cases of dictatorships destroying their economies are even more common.

Stability is important for growth and anyone familiar with China's history realizes that the fear of instability runs deep in this nation of over 1 billion people. Ultimately, growth and prosperity, widely shared, are necessary, if not sufficient, for long-run stability. The democracies of the West have, in turn, shown that free markets (often disciplined by governments) succeed in bringing growth and prosperity in a climate of individual freedom. As valid as these precepts are for the past, they are likely to be even more so for the New Economies of the future.

In its quest for both stability and growth, China put creating competition, new enterprises and jobs, before privatization and restructuring existing enterprises. While China recognized the importance of macrostabilization, it never confused ends with means, and it never took fighting inflation to an extreme. It recognized that if it was to maintain social stability, it had to avoid massive unemployment. Job creation had to go in tandem with restructuring. Many of its policies can be interpreted in this light. While China liberalized, it did so gradually and in ways which ensured that resources that were displaced were redeployed to more efficient uses, not left in fruitless unemployment. Monetary policy and financial institutions facilitated the creation of new enterprises and jobs. Some money did go to support inefficient state enterprises, but China thought that it was more important, not only politically but also economically, to maintain social stability, which would be undermined by high unemployment. Although China did not rapidly privatize its state enterprises, as new enterprises were created the state ones dwindled in importance, so much so that twenty years after the transition began, they accounted for only 28.2 percent of industrial production. It recognized the dangers of full capital market liberalization, while it opened itself up to foreign direct investment.

The contrast between what happened in China and what has happened in countries like Russia, which bowed to IMF ideology, could not be starker. In case after case, it seemed that China, a newcomer to market economies, was more sensitive to the incentive effects of each of its policy decisions than the IMF was to its.

Township and village public enterprises were central in the early years of transition. IMF ideology said that because these were *public* enterprises, they could not have succeeded. But the IMF was wrong. The township and village enterprises solved the governance problem, a problem to which the IMF gave scant attention, but which underlay many of the failures elsewhere. The townships and villages channeled their precious funds into wealth creation, and there was strong competition for success. Those in the townships and villages could see what was happening to their funds; they knew whether jobs were being created and incomes increased. Although there may not have been democracy, there was accountability. New industries in China were sited in rural areas. This helped to reduce the social upheaval that inevitably accompanies industrialization. Thus China built the foundation of a New Economy on existing institutions, maintaining and enhancing its social capital, while in Russia it eroded.

The ultimate irony is that many of the countries that have taken a more gradualist policy have succeeded in making deeper reforms more rapidly. China's stock market is larger than Russia's. Much of Russia's agriculture today is managed little differently than it was a decade ago, while China managed the transition to the "individual responsibility system" in less than five years. The contrasts I have depicted between Russia on the one hand and China and Poland on the other could be repeated elsewhere in the economies in transition. The Czech Republic received accolades early on from the IMF and the World Bank for its rapid reforms; it later became apparent that it had created a capital market which did not raise money for new investment, but allowed a few smart money managers (more accurately, white-collar criminals—if they did what they did in the Czech Republic in the United States, they would be behind bars) to walk off with millions of dollars of others' money. As a result of these and other mistakes in its transition, *relative to where it was in 1989*, the republic has fallen behind—in spite of its huge advantages in location and the high level of education of its populace. In contrast, Hungary's privatization may have gotten off to a slow start, but its firms have been restructured, and are now becoming internationally competitive.

Poland and China show that there were alternative strategies. The political, social, and historical context of each country differs; one cannot be sure that what worked in these countries would have worked in Russia, and would have been politically feasible there. By the same token, some argue that comparing the successes is unfair, given the markedly different circumstances. Poland began with a stronger market tradition than Russia; it even had a private sector during the Communist era. But China began from a less advanced position. The presence of entrepreneurs in Poland prior to the transition might have enabled Poland to undertake a more rapid privatization strategy; yet Poland as well as China chose a more gradualist approach.

Poland is alleged to have had an advantage because it was more industrialized, China because it was less so. China, according to these critics, was still in the midst of industrialization and urbanization; Russia faced the more delicate task of reorienting an already industrialized but moribund economy. But one could argue just the converse: development is not easy, as the rarity of successes clearly demonstrates. If transition is difficult, and development is difficult, it is not obvious why doing both simultaneously should be easy. The difference between China's success and Russia's failure in reforming agriculture was, if anything, even greater than the two countries' success in reforming industry.

One attribute of the success cases is that they are "homegrown," designed by people within each country, sensitive to the needs and concerns of their country. There was no cookie-cutter approach in China or Poland or Hungary. These and all the other successful transitioning countries were pragmatic—they never let ideology and simple textbook models determine policy.

Science, even an imprecise science like economics, is concerned with predictions and analyzing *causal* links. The predictions of the gradualists were borne out—both in the countries that followed their strategies, and in the shock therapy countries that followed the alternative course. By contrast, the predictions of the shock therapists were not.

In my judgment, the successes in countries that did not follow IMF prescriptions were no accident. There was a clear link between the policies pursued and the outcomes, between the successes in China and Poland and what they did, and the failure in Russia, and what it did. The outcomes in Russia were, as we have noted, what the critics of shock therapy predicted—only worse. The outcomes in China were precisely the opposite of what the IMF would have predicted—but were totally consonant with what the gradualists had suggested, only better.

The excuse of the shock therapists that measures called for by their prescription were never fully implemented is not convincing. In economics, no prescription is followed precisely, and policies (and advice) must be predicated on the fact that fallible individuals working within complex political processes will implement them. If the IMF failed to recognize this, that itself is a serious indictment. What is worse is that many of the failures were foreseen by independent observers and experts—and ignored.

The criticism of the IMF is not just that its predictions were not borne out. After all, no one, not even the IMF, could be sure of the consequences of the far-ranging changes that were entailed by the transition from communism to a market economy. The criticism is that the Fund's vision was too narrow—it focused only on the economics—and that it employed a particularly limited economic model.

We now have far more evidence about the reform process than we did five years ago when the IMF and the World Bank rushed to the judgment that their strategies were working.[4] Just as matters look strikingly different today than they did in the mid-1990s, so too in another decade, we may, given outcomes of reforms now underway, have to revise our judgments. From the current vantage point, however, some things seem clear. The IMF said that those who engaged in shock therapy, while they might feel more pain in the short run, would be more successful in the long. Hungary, Slovenia, and Poland have shown that gradualist policies lead to less pain in the short run, greater social and political stability, and faster growth in the long. In the race between the tortoise and the hare, it appears that the tortoise has won again. The radical reformers, whether the star pupils like the Czech Republic or the slightly unruly ones like Russia, have lost.[5]

THE ROAD TO THE FUTURE

Those who are responsible for the mistakes of the past have had scant advice for where Russia should go in the future. They repeat the same mantras—the need to continue with stabilization, privatization, and liberalization. The problems caused by the past now have forced them to recognize the need for strong institutions, but they have little advice to offer on what that means or how it is to be achieved. At meeting after meeting on Russian policy, I was struck by the absence of a strategy either for attacking poverty or enhancing growth. Indeed, the World Bank discussed scaling back on its programs in the rural sector. This made sense for the Bank, given the problems that its previous programs in this area had caused, but it made no sense for Russia, given that this was where much of the country's poverty lay. The only "growth" strategy proposed was that the country had to adopt policies that would repatriate the capital that had fled the country. Those who held this position overlooked that this recommendation could mean making a permanent fixture of the oligarchs, and the kleptocracy and crony/Mafia capitalism that they represented. There was no other reason for them to bring their capital back, when they could earn good returns in the West. Moreover, the IMF and U.S. Treasury never addressed the fact that they were supporting a system that lacked political legitimacy, where many of those with wealth had obtained their money by stealth and political connections with a leader—Boris Yeltsin—who too had lost all credibility and legitimacy. Sadly, for the most part, Russia must treat what has happened as pillage of national assets, a theft for which the nation can never be recompensed. Russia's objective in the future must be to try to stop further pillage, to attract legitimate investors by creating a rule of law and, more broadly, an attractive business climate.

The 1998 crisis had one benefit, to which I referred earlier: the devaluation of the ruble spurred growth, not so much in exports, but in import substitutes; it showed that the IMF policies had indeed been stifling the economy, keeping it below its potential. The devaluation, combined with a stroke of luck—the enormous increase in oil prices in the late 1990s—fueled a recovery, from an admittedly low base. There are lasting benefits from this growth spurt; some of the enterprises that took advantage of the favorable circumstances seem on the road to seizing new opportunities and continued growth. There are other positive signs: some of those who took advantage of the system of ersatz capitalism to become very wealthy are working for a change in the rules, to make sure that what they did to others cannot be done to them. There are moves in some quarters for better corporate governance—some of the oligarchs, while they are not willing to risk all of their money in Russia, would like to entice others to risk more of theirs, and know that to do so they have to behave better than they have in the past. But there are other, less positive signs. Even in the heyday of very high oil prices, Russia was barely able to make its budget balance; it should have been putting money aside for the likelihood of a "rainy day" when oil prices come down. Russia's recovery remains uncertain. As we noted earlier, years after the beginning of the transition, Russia had still failed to become a "normal" market economy—let alone a real democracy. Its dependence on natural resources meant that its economy fluctuated with the vagaries of oil and gas prices. It had evolved into a sui generis form of state capitalism, with parts of the economy dominated by oligarchs who had little choice but to do Putin's bidding. A transition that was supposed to bring unprecedented prosperity resulted in Russian per capita income increasing from 15 percent of that of the United States in 1989 to 16 percent of that of the United States twenty-six years later!

Russia has learned many lessons. In the aftermath of communism, many of its people swung from the old religion of Marx to the new religion of free markets. The sheen has been taken off this new religion, and a new pragmatism has settled in.

There are some policies that might make a difference. In cataloging what has to be done, it is natural to begin by thinking about the mistakes of the past: the lack of attention to the underpinnings of a market economy—from financial institutions that lend to new enterprises, to laws that enforce contracts and promote competition, to an independent and honest judiciary.

Russia must go beyond its focus on macrostabilization and encourage economic growth. Throughout the 1990s, the IMF focused on making countries work on getting budgets in order and controlling the growth of the money supply. Although when conducted in *moderation*, this stabilization may be a prerequisite to growth, it is hardly a growth strategy. In fact, the stabilization strategy contracted aggregate demand. This decrease in aggregate demand interacted with misguided restructuring strategies, to contract aggregate supply. In 1998, there was an active debate about the role of demand and supply. The IMF argued that any increase in aggregate demand would be inflationary. If this were true, it would be a terrible admission of failure. In six years, Russia's productive capacity had been cut by more than 40 percent—far deeper than the reduction in defense, a far greater loss in capacity than occurs in any but the worst wars. I knew that the IMF policies had contributed greatly to the reduction in productive capacity, but I believed that lack of aggregate demand still remained a problem. As it turned out, the IMF again proved to be wrong: when the devaluation occurred, at last domestic producers could compete with foreign imports, and they were able to meet the new demands. Production increased. There had indeed been excess capacity, which IMF policies had left idle for years.

Growth will only succeed if Russia creates an investment-friendly environment. This entails actions at all levels of government. Good policies at the national level can be undone by bad policies at the local and regional level. Regulations at all levels can make it difficult to establish new businesses. Unavailability of land can be an impediment just as lack of availability of capital can be. Privatization does little good if local government officials squeeze firms so hard that they have no incentive to invest. This implies that issues of federalism have to be attacked head-on. A federalist structure that provides compatible incentives at all levels has to be put into place. This will be difficult. Policies aimed at curtailing abuses at lower levels of government can themselves be abused, to give excessive power to the center, and deprive local and regional authorities of the capacity to devise creative and entrepreneurial growth strategies. Although Russia has stagnated overall, there has been progress in a few localities—and there is concern that the Kremlin's recent attempts at reining in local authorities will in fact stifle these local initiatives.

But there is one factor essential to establishing a good business climate, something which will prove particularly difficult to achieve given what has happened over the past decade: political and social stability. The huge inequality, the enormous poverty, which has been created over the past decades provides fertile ground for a variety of movements, from nationalism to populism, some of which may not only be a threat to Russia's economic future but to global peace. It will be difficult—and likely take considerable time—to reverse the inequality that was created so quickly.

Finally, Russia must collect taxes. Collections should be least difficult in Russia's dominant natural resource businesses, since revenues and output in the natural resources sector are *in principle* easily monitored, so taxes should be easy to collect. Russia must put firms on notice that if taxes are not paid in, say, sixty days, their property will be seized. If taxes are not paid and the government does seize the property, it can reprivatize it in a way that has more legitimacy than the discredited loans-for-share privatization under Yeltsin. On the other hand, if the businesses do pay their taxes, Russia, the Russian government, will have the resources to attack some of the important outstanding problems.

And just as those who owe taxes must pay what they owe, those who owe money to banks—especially the banks that are now in the hands of the government as a result of defaults—must be made to pay those debts. Again, this may entail an effective renationalization of the enterprise, a renationalization to be followed by a more legitimate privatization than had occurred previously.

The success of this agenda is predicated on there being a relatively honest government interested in improving the common weal. We in the West should realize this: there is relatively little that we can do to bring that about. The hubris of those in the Clinton administration and the IMF, that they could "pick" those to support, push reform programs that worked, and usher in a new day for Russia, has been shown for what it was: the arrogant attempt by those who knew little of the country, using a narrow set of economic conceptions, to change the course of history, an attempt that was doomed to failure. We can help support the kinds of institutions that are the underpinnings of democracies—building up think tanks, creating space for public dialogue, supporting independent media, helping to educate a new generation that understands how democracies work. At the national, regional, and provincial level there are many young officials who would like to see their country take a different course, and broad-based support—intellectual as much as financial—could make a difference. If the devastation of its middle class represents the longest-term threat to Russia, then while we cannot fully reverse the damage that has been done, at least we can work to stop its further erosion.

George Soros has shown that the assistance provided by a single individual can make a difference; surely the concerted efforts of the West, if well directed, could do even more. As we forge broader democratic interactions, we should distance ourselves from those that are allied to the power structures of the past as well as the newly emerging power structures of the oligarchs—at least as far as *realpolitik* will allow. This above all else: We should do no harm. IMF loans to Russia were harmful. It is not only that these loans and the policy decisions behind them have left the country more indebted and impoverished, and maintained exchange rates at high levels that squelched the economy; they were also intended to maintain the existing groups in power, as corrupt as it was clear they were, so to the extent that they succeeded in this deliberate intervention in the political life of the country, they arguably set back a deeper reform agenda that went beyond creating a particular, narrow vision of a market economy to the creation of a vibrant democracy. My conclusion as I sat in the meetings debating the 1998 loan remains as true today as it was then: If Russia, an oil- and natural resource–rich country, is able to get its act together, it will not need these loans; and if it does not, the loans will be of little benefit. It is not money that Russia needs. It is something else, something the rest of the world can give; but it will require a very different kind of program.

DEMOCRATIC ACCOUNTABILITY
AND THE FAILURES

I have painted a bleak picture of Russia in transition: massive poverty, a few oligarchs, a devastated middle class, a declining population, and disillusionment with market processes. This indictment should be balanced with a recognition of the achievements. Russia now has a fragile democracy, far better than the totalitarian regime of the past. It suffers from a largely captive media—formerly, too much under the control of a few oligarchs, now too much under the control of the state—but a media that still presents a diversity of viewpoints far wider than under the state control system of the past. Young, well-educated, dynamic entrepreneurs, while they too often seek to migrate to the West rather than face the difficulties of doing business in Russia or the other former Soviet republics, represent the promise of a more vibrant private sector in the future.

In the end, Russia and its leaders must be held accountable for Russia's recent history and its fate. To a large extent, Russians, at least a small elite, created their country's predicament. Russians made the key decisions—like the loans-for-share privatization. Arguably, the Russians were far better at manipulating Western institutions than the Westerners were at understanding Russia. Senior government officials, like Anatoly Chubais, have openly admitted how they misled (or worse, lied to) the IMF.* They felt they had to, to get the money they needed.

But we in the West, and our leaders, have played a far from neutral and not insignificant role. The IMF let itself be misled, because it wanted to believe that its programs were working, because it wanted to continue lending, because it wanted to believe that it was reshaping Russia. And we surely did have some influence on the course of the country: we gave our imprimatur to those who were in power. That the West seemed willing to deal with them—big time with billions of dollars—gave them credibility; the fact that others might not be able to elicit such support clearly counted against them. Our tacit support for the loans-for-share program may have quieted criticisms; after all, the IMF was the expert on transition; it had urged privatization as rapidly as possible and the loans-for-share was, if nothing else, rapid. That it was corrupt was evidently not a source of concern. The support, the policies—and the billions of dollars of IMF money—may not just have enabled the corrupt government with its corrupt policies to remain in power; they may even have reduced pressure for more meaningful reforms.

We placed our bets on favored leaders and pushed particular strategies of transition. Some of those leaders have turned out to be incompetent, others to have been corrupt, and some both. Some of those policies have turned out to be wrong, others to have been corrupt, and some both. It makes no sense to say that the policies were right, and simply not implemented well. Economic policy must be predicated not on an ideal world but on the world as it is. Policies must be designed not for how they might be implemented in an ideal world but for how they will be implemented in the world in which we live. Judgment calls were made not to pursue more promising alternative strategies. Today, just as Russia begins to hold its leaders accountable for the consequences of their decisions, we too should hold our leaders accountable.

---

* When Chubais was asked if the Russian government has the right to lie to the IMF about the true fiscal situation, he literally said: "In such situations, the authorities have to do it. We ought to. The financial institutions understand, despite the fact that we conned them out of $20 billion, that we had no other way out." See R. C. Paddock, "Russia Lied to Get Loans, Says Aide to Yeltsin," *Los Angeles Times*, September 9, 1998.

CHAPTER 12

THE IMF'S
OTHER AGENDA

THE INTERNATIONAL MONETARY Fund's less-than-successful efforts in the 1980s and 1990s raise troubling questions about the way the Fund sees the process of globalization—how it sees its objectives and how it seeks to accomplish these objectives as part of its role and mission.

The Fund believes it is fulfilling the tasks assigned to it: promoting global stability, helping developing countries in transition achieve not only stability but also growth. Until recently it debated whether it should be concerned with poverty—that was the responsibility of the World Bank—but today it has even taken that on board as well, at least rhetorically. I believe, however, that it has failed in its mission, that the failures are not just accidental but the consequences of how it has understood its mission.

Many years ago former president of General Motors and secretary of defense Charles E. Wilson's famous remark to the effect that "What's good for General Motors is good for the country" became the symbol of a particular view of American capitalism. The IMF often seems to have a similar view—"what the financial community views as good for the global economy is good for the global economy and should be done." In some instances, this is true; in many, it is not. In some instances, what the financial community may think is in its interests is actually not, because the prevalent free-market ideology blurs clear thinking about how best to address an economy's ills.

Losing Intellectual Coherency:
From Keynes's IMF to Today's IMF

There was a certain coherency in Keynes's (the intellectual godfather of the IMF) conception of the Fund and its role. Keynes identified a market failure—a reason why markets could not be left to themselves—that might benefit from collective action. He was concerned that markets might generate persistent unemployment. He went further. He showed why there was a need for *global* collective action, because the actions of one country spilled over to others. One country's imports are another country's exports. Cutbacks in imports by one country, for whatever reason, hurt other countries' economies.

There was another market failure: he worried that in a severe downturn, monetary policy might be ineffective, but that some countries might not be able to borrow to finance the expenditure increases or compensate for tax cuts needed to stimulate the economy. Even if a country was seemingly creditworthy, it might not be able to get money. Keynes not only identified a set of market failures; he explained why an institution like the IMF could improve matters: by putting pressure on countries to maintain their economy at full employment, and by providing liquidity for those countries facing downturns that could not afford an expansionary increase in government expenditures, *global* aggregate demand could be sustained.

Today, however, market fundamentalists dominate the IMF; they believe that markets by and large work well and that governments by and large work badly. We have an obvious problem: a public institution created to address certain failures in the market but currently run by economists who have both a high level of confidence in markets and little confidence in public institutions. The inconsistencies at the IMF appear particularly troubling when viewed from the perspective of the advances in economic theory in the last three decades.

The economics profession has developed a systematic approach to *the market failure theory of governmental action*, which attempts to identify why markets might not work well and why collective action is necessary. At the international level, the theory identifies why individual governments might fail to serve global economic welfare, and how global collective action, concerted action by governments working together, often through international institutions, would improve things. Developing an intellectually coherent view of international policy for an international agency such as the IMF thus requires identifying important instances in which markets might fail to work, and analyzing how particular policies might avert or minimize the damage done by these failures. It should go further, showing how the particular interventions are the *best* way to attack the market failures, to address problems *before* they occur, and to remedy them when they do.

As we have noted, Keynes provided such an analysis, explaining why countries might not pursue sufficiently expansionary policies on their own—they would not take into account the benefits it would bring to other countries. That was why the Fund, in its original conception, was intended to put international pressure on countries to have more expansionary policies than they would choose of their own accord. Today, the Fund has reversed course, putting pressure on countries, particularly developing ones, to implement more contractionary policies than these countries would choose of their own accord. But while seemingly rejecting Keynes's views, today's IMF has, in my judgment, not articulated a coherent theory of market failure that would justify its own existence and provide a rationale for its particular interventions in the market. As a result, as we have seen, all too often the IMF forged policies which, in addition to exacerbating the very problems they sought to address, allowed these problems to play out over and over again.

A New Role for a New Exchange Rate Regime?

Some thirty years ago, the world switched to a system of flexible exchange rates. There was a coherent theory behind the switch: exchange rates, like other prices, should be determined by market forces. Attempts by government to intervene in the determination of this price are no more successful than attempts to intervene in the determination of any other price. Yet, as we have seen, the IMF has recently undertaken massive interventions. Billions of dollars were spent trying to sustain the exchange rates of Brazil and Russia at unsustainable levels. The IMF justifies these interventions on the grounds that *sometimes* markets exhibit excessive pessimism—they "overshoot"—and the calmer hand of the international bureaucrat can then help stabilize markets. It struck me as curious that an institution committed to the doctrine that markets work well, if not perfectly, should decide that this one market—the exchange rate market—requires such massive intervention. The IMF has never put forward a good explanation either for why this expensive intervention is desirable in this particular market—or for why it is undesirable in other markets.

I agree with the IMF that markets may exhibit excessive pessimism. But I also believe that markets may exhibit excessive optimism, and that it is not just in the exchange rate market that these problems occur. There is a wider set of imperfections in markets, and especially capital markets, requiring a wider set of interventions.

For instance, it was excessive exuberance that led to Thailand's real estate and stock market bubble, a bubble reinforced, if not created, by hot speculative money flowing into the country. The exuberance was followed by excessive pessimism when the flow abruptly reversed. In fact, this change in the direction of speculative capital was the root cause of the excessive volatility in exchange rates. If this is a phenomenon comparable to a *disease*, it makes sense to treat the disease rather than just its manifestation, exchange rate volatility. But IMF free-market ideology led the Fund to make it easier for speculative hot money to flow into and out of a country. In treating the symptoms directly, by pouring billions of dollars into the market, the IMF actually made the underlying disease worse. If speculators only made money off each other, it would be an unattractive game—a highly risky activity, which *on average* made a zero return, as the gains by some were matched by equal losses from others. What makes speculation profitable is the money coming from governments, supported by the IMF. When the IMF and the Brazilian government, for instance, spent some $50 billion maintaining the exchange rate at an overvalued level in late 1998, where did the money go? The money doesn't disappear into thin air. It goes into somebody's pocket—much of it into the pockets of the speculators. Some speculators may win, some may lose, but speculators as a whole make an amount equal to what the government loses. In a sense, it is the IMF that keeps the speculators in business.

Contagion

There is another, equally striking example of how the IMF's lack of a coherent and reasonably complete theory can lead to policies which exacerbate the very problems the IMF is supposed to solve. Consider what happens when the Fund attempts to quarantine "contagion." In essence, the Fund argues that it must intervene, and quickly, if it determines that an ongoing crisis in one country will spill over to others, that is, the crisis will spread like an infectious, contagious disease.

If contagion is a problem, it is important to understand the workings of the mechanism through which it occurs, just as epidemiologists, in trying hard to contain an infectious disease, work hard to understand its transmission mechanism. Keynes had a coherent theory; the downturn in one country leads that country to import less, and this hurts its neighbors. We saw in chapter 8 how the IMF, while talking about contagion, took actions in the Asian financial crisis that actually accelerated transmission of the disease, as it forced country after country to tighten their belts. The reductions in incomes led quickly to large reductions in imports, and in the closely integrated economies of the region, these led to the successive weakening of neighboring countries. As the region imploded, the declining demand for oil and other commodities led to the collapse of commodity prices, which wrought havoc in other countries, thousands of miles away, whose economies depended on the export of those commodities.

Meanwhile the IMF clung to fiscal austerity as the antidote, claiming that was essential to restore investor confidence. The East Asia crisis spread from there to Russia through the collapse of oil prices, not through any mysterious connection between "confidence" on the part of investors, foreign and domestic, in the East Asia Miracle economies and the Mafia capitalism of Russia. Because of the lack of a coherent and persuasive theory of contagion, the IMF had spread the disease rather than contained it.

When Is a Trade Deficit a Problem?

Problems of coherence plague not only the IMF's remedies but also its diagnoses. IMF economists worry a lot about balance of payments deficits; such deficits are, in their calculus, a sure sign of a problem in the offing. But in railing against such deficits, they often pay little attention to what the money is actually being used for. If a government has a fiscal surplus (as Thailand did in the years before the 1997 crisis), then the balance of payments deficit essentially arises from *private* investment exceeding private savings. If a firm in the private sector borrows a million dollars at 5 percent interest and invests it in something that yields a 20 percent return, then it's not a problem for it to have borrowed the million dollars. The investment will more than pay back the borrowing. Of course, even if the firm makes a mistake in judgment, and the returns are 3 percent, or even zero, there is no problem. The borrower then goes into bankruptcy, and the creditor loses part or all of his loan. This may be a problem for the creditor, but it is not a problem that the country's government—or the IMF—need worry about.

A *coherent approach* would have recognized this. It would have also recognized that if some country imports more than it exports (i.e., it has a trade deficit), another country must be exporting more than it imports (it has a trade surplus). It is an unbreakable law of international accounting that the sum of all deficits in the world must add up to the sum of all surpluses. This means that if China and Japan insist on having a trade surplus, then some countries must have deficits. One cannot just inveigh against the deficit countries; the surplus countries are equally at fault. If Japan and China maintain their surpluses, and Korea converts its deficit into a surplus, the problem of deficit *must* appear on somebody else's doorstep.

Still, large trade deficits can be a problem. They can be a problem because they imply a country has to borrow year after year. And if those who are providing the capital change their minds and stop making loans, the country can be in big trouble—a crisis. It is spending more to buy goods from abroad than it gets from selling its goods abroad. When others refuse to continue to finance the trade gap, the country will have to adjust quickly. In a few cases, the adjustment can be made easily: if a country is borrowing heavily to finance a binge of car buying (as was the case recently in Iceland), then if foreigners refuse to provide the financing for the cars, the binge stops, and the trade gap closes. But more typically the adjustment does not work so smoothly. And problems are even worse if the country has borrowed short term, so that creditors can demand back *now* what they have lent to finance previous years' deficits, whether they were used to finance consumption splurges or long-term investments.

Bankruptcy and Moral Hazard

When the adjustment does not occur smoothly, there is a crisis. Such crises occur, for instance, when a real estate bubble bursts, as it did in Thailand. Those who borrowed from abroad to finance their real estate ventures could not repay their loans. Bankruptcy became widespread. How the IMF handles bankruptcy represents still another arena where the Fund's approach is plagued with intellectual inconsistencies.

In standard market economics, if a lender makes a bad loan, he bears the consequence. The borrower may well go into bankruptcy, and countries have laws on how such bankruptcies should be worked out. This is the way market economies are supposed to work. Instead, repeatedly, the IMF programs provide funds for governments to bail out Western creditors. The creditors, anticipating an IMF bailout, have weakened incentives to ensure that the borrowers will be able to repay. This is the infamous moral hazard problem well known in the insurance industry and, now, in economics. Insurance reduces your incentive to take care, to be prudent. A bailout in the event of a crisis is like "free" insurance. If you are a lender, you take less care in screening your applicants—when you know you will be bailed out if the loans go sour. Similarly prudent firms facing foreign exchange volatility can insure against it. But if the IMF intervenes to stabilize the exchange rate—arguing that otherwise there would be defaults—then borrowers are being encouraged to incur excess risk—and not worry about it. These moral hazard problems were particularly relevant in the lead-up to the ruble crisis in Russia in 1998. In that instance, even as the Wall Street creditors were making loans to Russia, they were letting it be known how large a bailout they thought was needed and, given Russia's nuclear status, they believed Russia would get.

The IMF, focusing on the symptoms, tries to defend its interventions by saying that without them, the country will default, and as a result it will not be able to get credit in the future. A coherent approach would have recognized the fallacy in this argument. *If* capital markets work well—certainly, if they worked anywhere near as well as the IMF market fundamentalists seem to argue—then they are forward-looking; in assessing what interest rates to charge, they look at the risk *going forward*. A country that has discharged a heavy overhang of debt, even by defaulting, is in better shape to grow, and thus *more* able to repay any additional borrowing. That is part of the rationale for bankruptcy in the first place: the discharge or restructuring of debt allows firms—and countries—to move forward and grow. Eighteenth-century debtor prisons may have provided strong incentives for individuals not to go into bankruptcy, but they did not help debtors get reestablished. Not only were they inhumane, but they did not enhance overall economic efficiency.

History supports this theoretical analysis. In the most recent instance, Russia, which had a massive debt default in 1998 and was widely criticized for not even consulting creditors, was able to borrow from the market by 2001 and capital began to flow back to the country. Likewise, capital started flowing back to South Korea, even though the nation effectively forced a restructuring of its debt, giving foreign creditors a choice of rolling over loans or not being repaid.

Consider how the IMF, if it had developed a coherent model, might have approached one of the most difficult problems in East Asia: whether or not to raise interest rates in the midst of the crisis. Raising them, of course, would force thousands of firms into bankruptcy. The contention of the IMF was that failing to raise rates would lead to a collapse of the exchange rate, and the collapse of the exchange rate would lead to even more bankruptcy. Put aside, for the moment, the question of whether raising interest rates (with the resulting exacerbation of the recession) would lead to a stronger exchange rate (in real life it did not). Put aside, too, the empirical question of whether more firms would be hurt by raising interest rates or the fall in the exchange rate (at least in Thailand, the evidence strongly suggested that the damage from a further fall in the exchange rate would be smaller). The *problem* of economic disruption caused by exchange rate devaluations is *caused* by the firms that choose not to buy insurance against the collapse of the exchange rate. A coherent analysis of the problem would have begun by asking why the seeming market failure—why do firms not buy the insurance? And any analysis would have suggested that the IMF itself was a big part of the problem: IMF interventions to support the exchange rate, as noted above, make it less necessary for firms to buy insurance, exacerbating in the future the very problem the intervention was supposed to address.

From Bailout to Bail-In

As the IMF's failures became increasingly evident, it sought new strategies, but the lack of coherency ensured that its quest for viable alternatives had little chance of success. The extensive criticism of its bailout strategy induced it to try what some have called a "bail-in" strategy. The IMF wanted the private sector institutions to be "in" on any bailouts. It began to insist that before it lent money to a country in a bailout, there had to be extensive "participation" by the private sector lenders; they would have to take a "haircut," forgiving a substantial part of the debt that was owed. Not surprisingly, this new strategy was first tried not on major countries like Brazil and Russia, but on powerless countries like Ecuador and Romania, too weak to resist the IMF. The strategy quickly proved to be both problematic in conception and flawed in implementation, with highly negative consequences for the countries targeted for the experiment.

Romania was a particularly mystifying example. It was not threatening a default; it only wanted new money from the IMF to signal that it was creditworthy, which would help to lower the interest rates it paid. But new lenders will only lend if they get an interest rate commensurate with the risk they face. New lenders cannot be forced to take a "haircut." If the IMF had based its policies on a coherent theory of well-functioning capital markets, it would have realized this.

But there was a more serious problem, which goes to the IMF's core mission. The Fund was created to deal with the liquidity crises caused by the credit market's occasional irrationality, its refusal to lend to countries that were in fact creditworthy. Now the IMF was handing power over its lending policies to the same individuals and institutions that precipitated crises. Only if they were willing to lend could it be willing to lend. These lenders quickly saw the profound implications of the change, even if the IMF did not. If creditors refuse to lend the client country money, or to go along with a settlement, the borrowing country will not be able to get funds—not just from the IMF but from the World Bank and other institutions which made their lending contingent on IMF approval. The creditors suddenly had enormous leverage. A twenty-eight-year-old man in the Bucharest branch of an international private bank, by making a loan of a few million dollars, had the power to decide whether or not the IMF, the World Bank, and the EU would provide Romania with more than a billion dollars of money. In effect, the Fund had delegated its responsibility for assessing whether to lend to the country to this twenty-eight-year-old. Not surprisingly, the twenty-eight-year-old, and other thirty- and thirty-five-year-old bankers in the branches of the other international banks in Bucharest, quickly grasped their newly granted bargaining powers. Each time the Fund lowered the amount of money it demanded that the private banks put up, the private banks lowered the amount that they were willing to offer. At one point, Romania appeared to be only $36 million of private sector loans short to receive the billion-dollar aid package. The private banks assembling the money required by the IMF demanded not only top dollar (high interest rates) but, at least in one case, some discreet relaxation of Romania's regulatory rules. This "regulatory forbearance" would allow the creditor to do things he might otherwise not be able to do—to lend more, or to make riskier, higher interest rate loans—increasing his profits, but increasing the riskiness of the banking system, and undermining the very reason for regulation. Less competent or more corrupt governments might have been tempted, but Romania did not accept the offer, partly because it was not really that desperate for money in the first place.

The issue can be seen another way. The IMF's decision to make a loan is supposed to be based on how a country is addressing its fundamental macroeconomic problems. Under the "participatory" strategy, a country could have a perfectly satisfactory set of macropolicies, but if it could not raise the amount that the IMF said it had to raise from the private banks, it might not be able to receive funds from any of the sources. The IMF is supposed to have the expertise on these questions, not the twenty-eight-year-old bank officer in Bucharest.

Eventually, at least in the case of Romania, the failings of the strategy became evident even to the IMF, and it proceeded to provide funds to the country even though the private sector had not provided the amounts the IMF had "insisted" upon.

The Best Defense Is an Offense: Expanding the Role of the IMF as "Lender of Last Resort"

In the light of increasing perceptions of the Fund's failures and growing demands that its scope be cut back, in 1999 the IMF's first deputy manager, Stanley Fischer, proposed that the Fund expand its role to make it a lender of last resort. Given that the IMF had failed to use the powers it had well, the proposal to increase its power was quite bold. It was based on an appealing analogy: Inside countries, central banks act as a lender of last resort, lending money to banks which are "solvent but not liquid," that is, which have a positive net worth, but which cannot obtain funds from elsewhere. The IMF would perform the same role for countries. Had the IMF had a coherent view of the capital market, it would have quickly seen the flaw in the idea.[1] Under the perfect market theory, if a business is solvent, it should be able to borrow money from the market; any firm that is solvent *is* liquid. Just as IMF economists, who normally seem to have such faith in markets, believe that they can judge better than the market what the exchange rate should be, so too do they seem to think that they can judge better than the market whether the borrowing country is creditworthy.

I don't believe capital markets work perfectly. Ironically, while I think they work far less well than IMF economists typically suggest, I think that they are somewhat more "rational" than the IMF seems to believe when it intervenes. There are advantages to IMF lending; often the Fund lends when the capital markets simply refuse to do so. But at the same time, I recognize that the country pays dearly for the "cheap" money it gets from the IMF. If a national economy goes sour and default looms, the IMF is the preferred creditor. It gets paid back first—even if others, such as foreign creditors, do not. These get what's left over. They might get nothing. So a rational private sector financial institution is going to insist on a risk premium—a higher interest rate to cover the higher likelihood of not getting paid back. If more of a country's money goes to the IMF, there is less to go to private sector foreign lenders, and these lenders will insist on a commensurately higher interest rate. A coherent theory of the capital market would have made the IMF more aware of this—and made it more reluctant to lend the billions and billions it has provided in bailout packages. A more coherent theory of markets would have had the IMF, in times of crisis, looking harder for alternatives, like those we discussed in chapter 8.

THE IMF'S NEW AGENDA?

The fact that a lack of coherence has led to a multitude of problems is perhaps not surprising. The question is, why the lack of coherence? Why does it persist, on issue after issue, even after the problems are pointed out? Part of the explanation is that the problems that the IMF has to confront are difficult; the world is complex; the Fund's economists are practical men striving to make hard decisions quickly, rather than academics calmly striving for intellectual coherence and consistency. But I think that there is a more fundamental reason: The IMF is pursuing not just the objectives set out in its original mandate, of enhancing global stability and ensuring that there are funds for countries facing a threat of recession to pursue expansionary policies. It is also pursuing the interests of the financial community. This means the IMF has objectives that often conflict.

The tension is all the greater because this conflict can't be brought out into the open: if the new role of the IMF were publicly acknowledged, support for that institution might weaken, and those who have succeeded in changing the mandate almost surely knew this. Thus the new mandate had to be clothed in ways that *seemed* at least superficially consistent with the old. Simplistic free market ideology provided the curtain behind which the real business of the "new" mandate could be transacted. The change in mandate and objectives, while it may have been quiet, was hardly subtle: from serving global *economic* interests to serving the interests of global *finance*.

I should be clear: the IMF never *officially* changed its mandate, nor did it ever formally set out to put the interests of the financial community over the stability of the global economy or the welfare of poor countries. We cannot talk meaningfully about the motivations and intentions of any institution, only of those who constitute and govern it. Even then, we often cannot ascertain true motivations—there may be a gap between what they say are their intentions and their true motivations. As social scientists, we can, however, attempt to describe the behavior of an institution in terms of what it *appears* to be doing. Looking at the IMF *as if* it were pursuing the interests of the financial community provides a way of making sense of what might otherwise seem to be contradictory and intellectually incoherent behaviors.

Moreover, the IMF's behavior should come as no surprise: it approached the problems from the perspectives and ideology of the financial community, and these naturally were closely (though not perfectly) aligned with its interests. As we have noted before, many of its key personnel came from the financial community, and many of its key personnel, having served these interests well, left to well-paying jobs in the financial community. In modern democracies, there are concerns about such *revolving doors*, where those in government service move quickly from and to private sector jobs in firms that may benefit from government services or contracts, or that are affected by government regulations, for the obvious reason. Citizens worry, will government officials be tempted to treat potential future employers especially well, in the hopes that by doing so their future prospects will be enhanced, even if there is no explicit quid pro quo? Economists—and ordinary citizens—believe that incentives matter. If so, how could they not affect behavior, if ever so subtly, in these situations? Sensitive to these concerns, most democracies have imposed constraints on these revolving doors, even though in doing so, some talented individuals might be discouraged from public service. The IMF is so far removed from democratic accountability that these concerns did not seem to weigh at all; moving from the IMF to a bank that had benefited from an IMF bail-out was par for the course.

But one does not need to look for venality. The IMF (or at least many of its senior officials and staff members) believed that capital market liberalization would lead to faster growth for the developing countries, believed it so strongly that it gave little credence to any evidence that suggested otherwise. The IMF never wanted to harm the poor and believed that the policies it advocated would eventually benefit them; it believed in trickle-down economics and, again, did not want to look too closely at evidence that might suggest otherwise. It believed that the discipline of the capital markets would help poor countries grow, and therefore it believed that keeping in good stead with the capital markets was of first-order importance.

LOOKING AT THE IMF policies this way, its emphasis on getting foreign creditors repaid rather than helping domestic businesses remain open becomes more understandable. The IMF may not have become the bill collector of the G-7, but it clearly worked hard (though not always successfully) to make sure that the G-7 lenders got repaid. There was an alternative to its massive interventions, as we saw in chapter 8, an alternative that would have been better for the developing nations, and in the longer run, better for global stability. The IMF could have facilitated the workout process; it could have tried to engineer a standstill (the temporary interruption of payments) that would have given the countries—and their firms—time to recoup, to restart their stalled economies. It could have tried to create an accelerated bankruptcy process.[2] But bankruptcy and standstills were not (at the time) welcome options, for they meant that the creditors would not be repaid. Many of the loans were uncollateralized, so in the event of bankruptcy, little might be recovered.

The IMF worried that a default, by breaking the sanctity of contracts, would undermine capitalism. In this, they were wrong in several respects. Bankruptcy is an unwritten part of every credit contract; the law provides for what will happen if the debtor cannot pay the creditor. Because bankruptcy is an implicit part of the credit contract, bankruptcy does not violate the "sanctity" of the credit contract. But there is another, equally important, *unwritten* contract, that between citizens and their society and government, what is sometimes called "the social contract." This contract requires the provision of basic social and economic protections, including reasonable opportunities for employment. While misguidingly working to preserve what it saw as the sanctity of the credit contract, the IMF was willing to tear apart the even more important social contract. In the end, it was the IMF policies which undermined the market as well as the long-run stability of the economy and society.

IT IS UNDERSTANDABLE then why the IMF and the strategies it foists on countries around the world are greeted with such hostility. The billions of dollars which it provides are used to maintain exchange rates at unsustainable levels for a short period, during which the foreigners and the rich are able to get their money out of the country at more favorable terms (through the open capital markets that the IMF has pushed on the countries). For each ruble, for each rupiah, for each cruzeiro, those in the country get more dollars as long as the exchange rates are sustained. The billions too are often used to pay back foreign creditors, even when the debt was private. What had been private liabilities were in effect in many instances nationalized.

In the Asian financial crisis, this was great for the American and European creditors, who were glad to get back the money they had lent to Thai or Korean banks and businesses or at least more of it than they otherwise would have. But it was not so great for the workers and other taxpayers of Thailand and Korea, whose tax money is used to repay the IMF loans, whether or not they got much benefit from the money. But adding insult to injury, after the billions are spent to maintain the exchange rate at an unsustainable level and to bail out the foreign creditors, after their governments have knuckled under to the pressure of the IMF to cut back on expenditures, so that the countries face a recession in which millions of workers lose their jobs, there seems to be no money around when it comes to finding the far more modest sums to pay subsidies for food or fuel for the poor. No wonder that there is such anger against the IMF.

If one sees the IMF as an institution pursuing policies that are in the interests of creditors, other IMF policies also become more understandable. We noted earlier the focus on the trade deficit. After the crisis, the massive contractionary policies imposed on the East Asian countries led to quick reductions in imports and a massive rebuilding of reserves. From the perspective of an institution worried about the ability to repay creditors, this made sense: without reserves, the countries would not be able to repay the dollar loans that they and the firms in their country owed. But if one had focused more on the issue of global stability and the economic recovery of the countries and the region, one would have taken a more lax approach to the rebuilding of reserves, and at the same time instituted other policies to insulate the countries from the effects of the vagaries of international speculators. Thailand had run out of reserves because they had been used in 1997 to fight off speculators. Once it was decided that Thailand needed quickly to rebuild reserves, it was inevitable that it would have a deep recession. The IMF's beggar-thyself policies, which, as we saw in chapter 8, have replaced the beggar-thy-neighbor policies of the Great Depression, were even worse in spreading the global crisis. From the perspective of the creditors, the policies sometimes worked, and remarkably quickly: In Korea, reserves went from essentially zero to almost $97 billion by July 2001; in Thailand, from essentially negative to more than $31 billion by July 2001. For the creditors, of course, all of this was good news; they could now rest assured that Korea had the dollars to repay any loans, should the creditors demand it.

I would have taken a strategy that was sympathetic to the concerns of the debtors, less focused on the interests of the creditors. I would have said that it was more important to keep the economy going and to postpone building up reserves for a couple of years until the economy was back on track. I would have explored other ways of providing short-term stability—not only the standstills or bankruptcies to which I referred earlier, but short-term capital controls and "exit taxes" of the kind that Malaysia used. There are ways of protecting a country against the ravages of speculators, or even of short-term lenders or investors who have suddenly changed their sentiments. No policy comes without its risks or price; but these alternatives would almost surely have imposed lower costs and risks on those *inside* the crisis countries, even if they had imposed higher costs on the creditors.

Defenders of the IMF's policies point to the fact that the creditors did have to bear some of the costs. Many were not fully repaid. But this misses the point on two counts: The creditor-friendly policies attempted to *reduce* the losses from what they otherwise would have been. They did not engineer a full bailout, but a partial one; they did not stop the exchange rate from falling, but they worked to prevent it from falling further. Secondly, the IMF did not always succeed in doing what it set out to do. The IMF pushed contractionary policies in Indonesia too far, so that in the end, the interests of the creditors were not well served. More broadly, global financial stability was arguably not only in the interests of the global economy but also in the interests of the financial markets; yet many of the IMF's policies—from the capital market liberalization to the massive bailouts—almost surely contributed to global instability.

The fact that the IMF was concerned about and reflected the perspectives of the financial community also helps explain some of its defensive rhetoric. In the East Asia crisis, the IMF and the U.S. Treasury quickly sought to blame the problems on the borrowing countries, and in particular on their lack of transparency. Even then, it was clear that lack of transparency does not cause crises nor can transparency inoculate a country against crises. Prior to the East Asia crisis, the most recent financial crisis was the real estate crash in the late 1980s and early 1990s in Sweden, Norway, and Finland, some of the most transparent nations in the world. There were many countries that were far less transparent than Korea, Malaysia, and Indonesia—and they did not have a crisis. If transparency is the key to the economic riddle, then the countries of East Asia should have had *more* crises earlier, since the data showed that they were becoming more, not less, transparent. Despite its alleged failures on the transparency front, East Asia had not only shown remarkable growth but also remarkable stability. If the East Asian countries were as "highly vulnerable" as the IMF and the Treasury claimed, it was a new-found vulnerability based not on an increased lack of transparency but on another familiar factor: the premature capital and financial market liberalization that the IMF had pushed on these countries.

In retrospect, there was a "transparent" reason for this focus on transparency:[3] it was important for the financial community, the IMF, and the U.S. Treasury to shift blame. The policies that the Fund and Treasury had pushed in East Asia, Russia, and elsewhere were to blame: capital market liberalization had led to destabilizing speculation, financial market liberalization to bad lending practices. As their recovery programs failed to work as they said they would, they had further incentive to try to say the real problem lay not with their programs but elsewhere, with the afflicted countries.

Closer scrutiny, however, showed that the industrialized nations were at fault in many other ways; weak banking regulation in Japan, for instance, might have provided an incentive for banks to lend to Thailand at such attractive rates that the borrowers could not resist borrowing more than was prudent. Banking regulatory policies in the United States and other major industrialized countries also encouraged unwise lending—banks were allowed to treat short-term foreign lending as safer than long-term. This encouraged short-term lending, and the short-term loans were among the important sources of instability in East Asia.

The major investment firms also wanted to exculpate their advisers, who had encouraged their clients to put their money into these countries. Fully backed up by the governments in the United States and the other major industrialized nations, investment advisers from Frankfurt to London to Milan could claim that there was no way they could have been expected to know how bad things really were, given the lack of transparency in East Asian countries. These experts quietly slid over the fact that in a fully open and transparent market, one with perfect information, returns are low. Asia had been an attractive investment—it produced high returns—precisely because it was more risky. The advisers' belief that they had *better* information—and their clients' thirst for high returns—drove funds to the region. The key problems—South Korea's high indebtedness, Thailand's huge trade deficits and real estate boom that inevitably would bust, Suharto's corruption—were well known, and the risks these posed should have been disclosed to investors.

The international banks too found it convenient to shift blame. They wanted to blame the borrowers and bad lending practices of the Thai and South Korean banks, which, they alleged, were making bad loans with the connivance of the corrupt governments in their countries—and the IMF and the U.S. Treasury again joined them in the attack. From the start, one should have been suspicious of the IMF/Treasury arguments. Despite their attempt to get the major international lenders off the hook, the hard truth is that every loan has both a borrower and a lender. If the loan is inherently bad, the lender is as much at fault as the borrower. Moreover, banks in the Western developed countries were lending to the large Korean firms, knowing full well how leveraged many Korean firms were. The bad loans were a result of bad judgment, not of any pressure from the United States or other Western governments, and were made in spite of the Western banks' allegedly good risk management tools. No wonder, then, that these big banks wanted to shift the scrutiny away from themselves. The IMF had good reason for supporting them, for the Fund itself shared in the culpability. Repeated IMF bailouts elsewhere had contributed to lack of due diligence on the part of the lenders.

There was an even more profound issue at stake. The U.S. Treasury had during the early 1990s heralded the global triumph of capitalism. Together with the IMF, it had told countries that followed the "right policies"—the Washington Consensus policies—they would be assured of growth. The East Asia crisis cast doubt on this new worldview *unless it could be shown that the problem was not with capitalism, but with the Asian countries and their bad policies*. The IMF and the U.S. Treasury had to argue that the problem was not with the reforms—implementing liberalization of capital markets, above all, that sacred article of faith—but with the fact that the reforms had not been carried far enough. By focusing on the weaknesses of the crisis countries, they not only shifted blame away from their own failures—both the failures of policy and the failures in lending—but they attempted to use the experience to push their agenda still further.

CHAPTER 13

THE WAY AHEAD

G LOBALIZATION TODAY IS not working for many of the world's poor. It is not working for much of the environment. It is not working for the stability of the global economy. The transition from communism to a market economy has been so badly managed that, with the exception of China, Vietnam, and a few Eastern European countries, poverty has soared as incomes have plummeted.

To some, there is an easy answer: Abandon globalization. That is neither feasible nor desirable. As I noted in chapter 5, globalization has also brought huge benefits—East Asia's success was based on globalization, especially on the opportunities for trade, and increased access to markets and technology. Globalization has brought better health, as well as an active global civil society fighting for more democracy and greater social justice. The problem is not with globalization, but with how it has been managed. Part of the problem lies with the international economic institutions, with the IMF, World Bank, and WTO, which help set the rules of the game. They have done so in ways that, all too often, have served the interests of the more advanced industrialized countries—and particular interests within those countries—rather than those of the developing world. But it is not just that they have served those interests; too often, they have approached globalization from particular narrow mind-sets, shaped by a particular vision of the economy and society.

The demand for reform is palpable—from congressionally appointed commissions and foundation-supported groups of eminent economists writing reports on changes in the global financial architecture to the protests that mark almost every international meeting. In response, there has already been some change. The new round of trade negotiations that was agreed to in November 2001 at Doha, Qatar, has been characterized as the "development round," intended not just to open up markets further but to rectify some of the imbalances of the past, and the debate at Doha was far more open than in the past. The IMF and the World Bank have changed their rhetoric—there is much more talk about poverty, and at least at the World Bank, there is a sincere attempt to live up to its commitment to "put the country in the driver's seat" in its programs in many countries. But many of the critics of the international institutions are skeptical. They see the changes as simply the institutions facing the political reality that they *must* change their rhetoric if they are to survive. These critics doubt that there is real commitment. They were not reassured when, in 2000, the IMF appointed to its number two position someone who had been chief economist at the World Bank during the period when it took on market fundamentalist ideology. Some critics are so doubtful about these reforms that they continue to call for more drastic actions such as the abolition of the IMF, but I believe this is pointless. Were the Fund to be abolished, it would most likely be recreated in some other form. In times of international crises, government leaders like to feel there is someone in charge, that an international agency is doing something. Today, the IMF fills that role.

I believe that globalization can be reshaped to realize its potential for good and I believe that the international economic institutions can be reshaped in ways that will help ensure that this is accomplished. But to understand how these institutions should be reshaped, we need to understand better why they have failed, and failed so miserably.

Interests and Ideology

In the last chapter we saw how, by looking at the policies of the IMF *as if* the organization was pursuing the interests of the financial markets, rather than simply fulfilling its original mission of helping countries in crises and furthering global economic stability, one could make sense of what otherwise seemed to be a set of intellectually incoherent and inconsistent policies.

If financial interests have dominated thinking at the International Monetary Fund, commercial interests have had an equally dominant role at the World Trade Organization. Bilateral trade agreements have been even worse. Embedded in such agreements are often provisions, designed by large multinationals, which require governments to compensate foreign investors for a decrease in their future expected profits, if the government passes a regulation which adversely affects them—no matter how important the regulation is for protecting public health, safety, the environment, or even ensuring economic stability. Private corporations are allowed to sue governments, with the adjudication occurring in private arbitration panels in which the corporations get to pick one of the three judges. The intent is to have a chilling effect on regulations, especially concerning the environment, and it's worked.

While the institutions seem to pursue commercial and financial interests above all else, they do not see matters that way. They genuinely believe the agenda that they are pursuing is in the *general interest*. In spite of the evidence to the contrary, many trade and finance ministers, and even some political leaders, believe that everyone will eventually benefit from trade and capital market liberalization. Many believe this so strongly that they support forcing countries to accept these "reforms," through whatever means they can, even if there is little popular support for such measures.

The greatest challenge is not just in the institutions themselves but in mind-sets: Caring about the environment, making sure the poor have a say in decisions that affect them, promoting democracy and fair trade are necessary if the potential benefits of globalization are to be achieved. The problem is that the institutions have come to reflect the mind-sets of those to whom they are accountable. The typical central bank governor begins his day worrying about inflation statistics, not poverty statistics; the trade minister worries about export numbers, not pollution indices.

The world is a complicated place. Each group in society focuses on a part of the reality that affects it the most. Workers worry about jobs and wages, financiers about interest rates and being repaid. A high interest rate is good for a creditor—provided he or she gets paid back. But workers see high interest rates as inducing an economic slowdown; for them, this means unemployment. No wonder that they see the danger in high interest rates. For the financier who has lent his money out long-term, the real danger is inflation. Inflation may mean that the dollars he gets repaid will be worth less than the dollars he lent.

In public policy debates, few argue openly in terms of their own self-interest. Everything is couched in terms of *general interest*. Assessing how a particular policy is likely to affect the general interest requires a model, a view of how the entire system works. Adam Smith provided one such model, arguing in favor of markets; Karl Marx, aware of the adverse effects that capitalism seemed to be having on workers of his time, provided an alternative model. Despite its many well-documented flaws, Marx's model has had enormous influence, especially in developing countries where for the billions of poor capitalism seemed not to be delivering on its promises. But with the collapse of the Soviet empire, its weaknesses have become all too evident. And with that collapse, and the global economic dominance of the United States, the market model has prevailed.

But there is not just *one* market model. There are striking differences between the Japanese version of the market system and the German, Swedish, and American versions. There are several countries with per capita income comparable to that of the United States, but where inequality is lower, poverty is less, and health and other aspects of living standards higher (at least in the judgment of those living there). While the market is at the center of both the Swedish and American versions of capitalism, government takes on quite different roles. In Sweden, the government takes on far greater responsibilities promoting social welfare; it continues to provide far better public health, far better unemployment insurance, and far better retirement benefits than does the United States. Yet it has been every bit as successful, even in terms of the innovations associated with the "New Economy." For many Americans, but not all, the American model has worked well; for most Swedes, the American model is viewed as unacceptable—they believe their model has served them well. For Asians, a variety of Asian models has worked well, and this is true for Malaysia and Korea as well as China and Taiwan, even taking into account the global financial crisis.

Over the past fifty years, economic science has explained why, and the conditions under which, markets work well *and when they do not.* It has shown why markets may lead to the underproduction of some things—like basic research—and the overproduction of others—like pollution. The most dramatic market failures are the periodic slumps, the recessions and depressions, that have marred capitalism over the past two hundred years, that leave large numbers of workers unemployed and a large fraction of the capital stock underutilized. But while these are the most obvious examples of market failures, there are a myriad of more subtle failures, instances where markets failed to produce efficient outcomes.

Government can, and has, played an essential role not only in mitigating these market failures but also in ensuring *social justice.* Market processes may, by themselves, leave many people with too few resources to survive.

In countries that have been most successful, in the United States and in East Asia, government has performed these roles and performed them, for the most part, reasonably well. Governments provided a high-quality education to all and furnished much of the infrastructure—including the institutional infrastructure, such as the legal system, which is required for markets to work effectively. They regulated the financial sector, ensuring that capital markets worked more in the way that they were supposed to. They provided a safety net for the poor. And they promoted technology, from telecommunications to agriculture to jet engines and radar. While there is a vigorous debate in the United States and elsewhere about what the *precise* role of government should be, there is broad agreement that government has a role in making any society, any economy, function efficiently—and humanely.

There are important disagreements about economic and social policy in our democracies. Some of these disagreements are about values—how concerned should we be about our environment (how much environmental degradation should we tolerate, if it allows us to have a higher measured GDP); how concerned should we be about the poor (how much sacrifice in our total income should we be willing to make, it if allows some of the poor to move out of poverty, or to be slightly better off); or how concerned should we be about democracy (are we willing to compromise on basic rights, such as the rights to association, if we believe that as a result, the economy will grow faster). Some of these disagreements are about how the economy functions. The *analytic propositions* are clear: whenever there is imperfect information or markets (that is always), there are, in principle, interventions by the government—even a government that suffers from the same imperfections of information—which can increase the markets' efficiency. As we saw in chapter 7, the assumptions underlying market fundamentalism do not hold in developed economies, let alone in developing countries. But the advocates of market fundamentalism still argue that the inefficiencies of markets are relatively small and the inefficiencies of government are relatively large. They see government more as part of the problem than the solution; unemployment is blamed on government setting too-high wages, or allowing unions too much power.

Adam Smith was far more aware of the limitations of the market, including the threats posed by imperfections of competition, than those who claim to be his latterday followers. Smith too was more aware of the social and political context in which all economies must function. Social cohesion is important if an economy is to function: urban violence in Latin America and civil strife in Africa create environments that are hostile to investment and growth. But while social cohesion can affect economic performance, the converse is also true: excessively austere policies—whether they be contractionary monetary or fiscal policies in Argentina, or cutting off food subsidies to the poor in Indonesia—predictably give rise to turmoil. This is especially the case when it is believed that there are massive inequities—such as billions going to corporate and financial bailouts in Indonesia, leaving nothing left for those forced into unemployment.

In my own work—both in my writings and in my role as the president's economic adviser and chief economist of the World Bank—I have advocated a balanced view of the role of government, one which recognizes both the limitations and failures of markets *and* government, but which sees the two as working together, in partnership, with the precise nature of that partnership differing among countries, depending on their stages of both political and economic development.

But at whatever stage of political and economic development a country is, government makes a difference. Weak governments and too-intrusive governments have both hurt stability and growth. The Asia financial crisis was brought on by a lack of adequate regulation of the financial sector, Mafia capitalism in Russia by a failure to enforce the basics of law and order. Privatization without the necessary institutional infrastructure in the transition countries led to asset stripping rather than wealth creation. In other countries, privatized monopolies, without regulation, were more capable of exploiting consumers than the state monopolies. By contrast, privatization accompanied by regulation, corporate restructuring, and strong corporate governance[1] has led to higher growth.

My point here, however, is not to resolve these controversies, or to push for my particular conception of the role of government and markets, but to emphasize that there are real disagreements about these issues among even well-trained economists. Some critics of economics and economists jump to the conclusion that economists always disagree, and therefore try to dismiss *whatever* economists say. That is wrong. On some issues—like the necessity of countries living within their means, and the dangers of hyperinflation—there is widespread agreement.

The problem is that the IMF (and sometimes the other international economic organizations) presents as received doctrine propositions and policy recommendations for which there is not widespread agreement; indeed, in the case of capital market liberalization, there was scant evidence in support and a massive amount of evidence against. While there is agreement that no economy can succeed under hyperinflation, there is no consensus about the gains from lowering inflation to lower and lower levels; there is little evidence that pushing inflation to lower and lower levels yields gains commensurate with the costs, and some economists even think that there are *negative* benefits from pushing inflation too low.[2]

The discontent with globalization arises not just from economics seeming to be pushed over everything else, but because a particular view of economics—market fundamentalism—is pushed over all other views. Opposition to globalization in many parts of the world is not to globalization per se—to the new sources of funds for growth or to the new export markets—but to the particular set of doctrines, the Washington Consensus policies that the international financial institutions have imposed. And it is not just opposition to the policies themselves, but to the notion that there is a single set of policies that is right. This notion flies in the face both of economics, which emphasizes the importance of trade-offs, and of ordinary common sense. In our own democracies we have active debates on every aspect of economic policy; not just on macroeconomics, but on matters like the appropriate structure of bankruptcy laws or the privatization of Social Security. Much of the rest of the world feels as if it is being deprived of making its own choices, and even forced to make choices that countries like the United States have rejected.

But while the commitment to a particular ideology deprived countries of the choices that should have been theirs, it also contributed strongly to their failures. The economic structures in each of the regions of the world differ markedly; for instance, East Asian firms had high levels of debt, those in Latin America relatively little. Unions are strong in Latin America, relatively weak in much of Asia. Economic structures also change over time—a point emphasized by the New Economy discussions of recent years. The advances in economics of the past thirty years have focused on the role of financial institutions, on information, on changing patterns of global competition. I have noted how these changes altered views concerning the efficiency of the market economy. They also altered views concerning the appropriate responses to crises.

At the World Bank and the IMF, these new insights—and more important, their implications for economic policy—were often resisted, just as these institutions had resisted looking at the experiences of East Asia, which had *not* followed the Washington Consensus policies and had grown faster than any other region of the world. This failure to take on board the lessons of modern economic science left these institutions ill-prepared to deal with the East Asia crisis when it occurred, and less able to promote growth around the world.

The IMF felt it had little need to take these lessons on board because it knew the answers; if economic science did not provide them, ideology—the simple belief in free markets—did. Ideology provides a lens through which one sees the world, a set of beliefs that are held so firmly that one hardly needs empirical confirmation. Evidence that contradicts those beliefs is summarily dismissed. For the believers in free and unfettered markets, capital market liberalization was *obviously* desirable; one didn't need evidence that it promoted growth. Evidence that it caused instability would be dismissed as merely one of the adjustment costs, part of the pain that had to be accepted in the transition to a market economy.

The Need for International Public Institutions

We cannot go back on globalization; it is here to stay. The issue is how can we make it work. And if it is to work, there have to be global public institutions to help set the rules.

These international institutions should, of course, focus on issues where global collective action is desirable, or even necessary. Over the past three decades there has been an increased understanding of the circumstances under which collective action, at whatever level, is required. Earlier, I discussed how collective action is required when markets by themselves do not result in efficient outcomes. When there are externalities—when the actions of individuals have effects on others for which they neither pay nor are compensated—the market will typically result in the overproduction of some goods and the underproduction of others. Markets cannot be relied upon to produce goods that are essentially public in nature, like defense.[3] In some areas, markets fail to exist;[4] governments have provided student loans, for instance, because the market, on its own, failed to provide funding for investments in human capital. And for a variety of reasons, markets are often not self-regulating—there are booms and busts—so the government has an important role in promoting economic stability.

Over the past decade, there has been an increased understanding of the appropriate level—local, national, or global—at which collective action is desirable. Actions the benefits of which accrue largely locally (such as actions related to local pollution) should be conducted at the local level; while those that benefit the citizens of an entire country should be undertaken at the national level. Globalization has meant that there is increasing recognition of arenas where impacts are global. It is in these arenas where global collective action is required—and systems of global governance are essential. The recognition of these areas has been paralleled by the creation of global institutions to address such concerns. The United Nations can be thought of as focusing upon issues of global political security, while the international financial institutions, and in particular the IMF, are supposed to focus on global economic stability. Both can be thought of as dealing with externalities that can take on global dimensions. Local wars, unless contained and defused, can draw in others, until they become global conflagrations. An economic downturn in one country can lead to slowdowns elsewhere. In 1998 the great concern was that a crisis in emerging markets might lead to a global economic meltdown.

But these are not the only arenas in which global collective action is essential. There are global environmental issues, especially those that concern the oceans and atmosphere. Global warming caused by the industrial countries' use of fossil fuels, leading to concentrations of greenhouse gasses (CO_2), affects those living in preindustrial economies, whether in a South Sea island or in the heart of Africa. The hole in the ozone layer caused by the use of chlorofluorocarbons (CFCs) similarly affects everyone—not just those who made use of these chemicals. As the importance of these international environmental issues has grown, international conventions have been signed. Some have worked remarkably well, such as the one directed at the ozone problem (the Montreal Protocol of 1987); while others, such as those that address global warming, have yet to make a significant dent in the problem.

There are also global health issues like the spread of highly contagious diseases such as AIDS, which respect no boundaries. The World Health Organization has succeeded in eradicating a few diseases, notably river blindness and smallpox, but in many areas of global public health the challenges ahead are enormous. Knowledge itself is an important global public good: the fruits of research can be of benefit to anyone, anywhere, at essentially no additional cost.

International humanitarian assistance is a form of collective action that springs from a shared compassion for others. As efficient as markets may be, they do not ensure that individuals have enough food, clothes to wear, or shelter. The World Bank's main mission is to eradicate poverty, not so much by providing humanitarian assistance at the time of crisis as by enabling countries to grow, to stand on their own.

Although specialized institutions in most of these areas have evolved in response to specific needs, the problems they face are often interrelated. Poverty can lead to environmental degradation, and environmental degradation can contribute to poverty. People in poor countries like

Nepal with little in the way of heat and energy resources are reduced to deforestation, stripping the land of trees and brush to obtain fuel for heating and cooking, which leads to soil erosion, and thus to further impoverishment.

Globalization, by increasing the interdependence among the people of the world, has enhanced the need for global collective action and the importance of global public goods. That the global institutions which have been created in response have not worked perfectly is not a surprise: the problems are complex and collective action at any level is difficult. But in previous chapters we have documented complaints that go well beyond the charge that they have not worked perfectly. In some cases their failures have been grave; in other cases they have pursued an agenda that is unbalanced—with some benefiting from globalization much more than others, and some actually being hurt.

Governance

So far, we have traced the failures of globalization to the fact that in setting the rules of the game, commercial and financial interests and mind-sets have seemingly prevailed within the international economic institutions. A particular view of the role of government and markets has come to prevail—a view which is not universally accepted even within the developed countries, but which is being forced upon the developing countries and the economies in transition.

The question is, why has this come about? And the answer is not hard to find: It is the finance ministers and central bank governors who sit around the table at the IMF making decisions, the trade ministers at the WTO. Even when they stretch, to push policies that are in their countries' broader national interests (or occasionally, stretching further, to push policies that are in a broader global interest), they see the world through particular, inevitably more parochial, perspectives.

I have argued that there needs to be a change in mind-set. But the mind-set of an institution is inevitably linked to whom it is *directly* accountable. Voting rights matter, and who has a seat at the table—even with limited voting rights—matters. It determines whose voices get heard. The IMF is not just concerned with technical arrangements among bankers, such as how to make bank check-clearing systems more efficient. The IMF's actions affect the lives and livelihoods of billions throughout the developing world; yet they have little say in its actions. The workers who are thrown out of jobs as a result of the IMF programs have no seat at the table; while the bankers, who insist on getting repaid, are well represented through the finance ministers and central bank governors. The consequences for policy have been predictable: bailout packages which pay more attention to getting creditors repaid than to maintaining the economy at full employment. The consequences for the choice of the institution's management have equally been predictable: there has been more of a concern with finding a leader whose views are congruent with the dominant "shareholders" than with finding one that has expertise in the problems of the developing countries, the mainstay of the Fund's business today.

Governance at the WTO is more complicated. It is the voices of trade that are heard. No wonder, then, that little attention is often paid to concerns about the environment. Yet while the voting arrangements at the IMF ensure that the rich countries predominate, at the WTO each country has a single vote, and decisions are largely by consensus. But in practice, the United States, Europe, and Japan have dominated in the past. This may now be changing. At the last meeting at Doha, the developing countries insisted that if another round of trade negotiations was to be initiated, their concerns had to be heard—and they achieved some notable concessions. With China's joining the WTO, the developing countries have a powerful voice on their side—though the interests of China and those of many of the other developing countries do not fully coincide.

The most fundamental change that is required to make globalization work in the way that it should is a change in governance. This entails, at the IMF and the World Bank, a change in voting rights, and in all of the international economic institutions changes to ensure that it is not just the voices of trade ministers that are heard in the WTO or the voices of the finance ministries and treasuries that are heard at the IMF and World Bank.

Such changes are not going to be easy. The United States is unlikely to give up its effective veto at the IMF. The advanced industrial countries are not likely to give up their votes so that the developing countries can have more votes. They will even put up specious arguments: voting rights, as in any corporation, are assigned on the basis of capital contributions. China would long ago have been willing to increase its capital contribution, if that was required to give it more voting rights. U.S. Treasury Secretary Paul O'Neill has tried to give the impression that it is the American taxpayers, its plumbers and carpenters, who pay for the multi-billion-dollar bailouts—and because they pay the costs, they ought to have the vote. But that is wrong. The money comes ultimately from the workers and other taxpayers in the developing countries, for the IMF almost always gets repaid.

But although change is not easy, it is possible. The changes that the developing countries wrenched from the developed countries in November 2001 as the price for beginning another round of trade negotiations show that, at least in the WTO, there has been a change in bargaining power.

Still, I am not sanguine that fundamental reforms in the *formal* governance of the IMF and World Bank will come soon. Yet in the short run, there are changes in *practices* and *procedures* that can have significant effects. At the World Bank and the IMF there are twenty-four seats at the table. Each seat speaks for several countries. In the present configuration, Africa has very few seats simply because it has so few votes, and it has so few votes because, as we noted, votes are allocated on the basis of economic power. Even without changing the voting arrangements, one could have more African seats; their voice would be heard even if their votes were not counted.

Effective participation requires that the representatives of the developing countries be well informed. Because the countries are poor, they simply cannot afford the kinds of staff that the United States, for instance, can muster to support its positions at all the international economic institutions. If the developed countries were serious about paying more attention to the voices of the developing countries, they could help fund a think tank—independent from the international economic organizations—that would help them formulate strategies and positions.

Transparency

Short of a fundamental change in their governance, the most important way to ensure that the international economic institutions are more responsive to the poor, to the environment, to the broader political and social concerns that I have emphasized is to increase openness and transparency. We have come to take for granted the important role that an informed and free press has in reining in even our democratically elected governments: any mischief, any minor indiscretion, any favoritism, is subject to scrutiny, and public pressure works powerfully. Transparency is even more important in public institutions like the IMF, the World Bank, and the WTO, because their leaders are not elected directly. Though they are public, there is no *direct* accountability to the public. But while this should imply that these institutions be even more open, in fact, they are even less transparent.

The problem of lack of transparency affects each of the international institutions, though in slightly different ways. At the WTO, the negotiations that lead up to agreements are all done behind closed doors, making it difficult—until it is too late—to see the influence of corporate and other special interests. The deliberations of the WTO panels that rule on whether there has been a violation of the WTO agreements occur in secret. It is perhaps not surprising that the trade lawyers and ex–trade officials who often comprise such panels pay, for instance, little attention to the environment; but by bringing the deliberations more out into the open, public scrutiny would either make the panels more sensitive to public concerns or force a reform in the adjudication process.

The IMF comes by its penchant for secrecy naturally: central banks, though public institutions, have traditionally been secretive. Within the financial community, secrecy is viewed as natural—in contrast to academia, where openness is the accepted norm. Before September 11, 2001, the secretary of treasury even defended the secrecy of the offshore banking centers. The billions of dollars in the Cayman Islands and other such centers are not there because those islands provide better banking services than Wall Street, London, or Frankfurt; they are there because the secrecy allows them to engage in tax evasion, money laundering, and other nefarious activities. Only after September 11 was it recognized that among those other nefarious activities was the financing of terrorism.

But the IMF is not a private bank; it is a public institution.

The absence of open discourse means that models and policies are not subjected to timely criticism. Had the actions and policies of the IMF during the 1997 crisis been subject to conventional democratic processes, and there had been a full and open debate in the crisis countries about the proffered IMF policies, it is possible that they would never have been adopted, and that far saner policies would have emerged. That discourse might not only have exposed the faulty economic assumptions on which the policy prescriptions were based but also revealed that the interests of the creditors were being placed ahead of those of workers and small businesses. There were alternative courses of actions, where less of the risk was borne by these less powerful parties, and these alternative courses of actions might have been given the serious consideration that they deserved.

Earlier, in my days at the Council of Economic Advisers, I had seen and come to understand the strong forces that drove secrecy. Secrecy allows government officials the kind of discretion that they would not have if their actions were subject to public scrutiny. Secrecy not only makes their life easy but allows special interests full sway. Secrecy also serves to hide the mistakes, whether innocent or not, whether the result of a failure to think matters through or not. As it is sometimes put, "Sunshine is the strongest antiseptic."

Even when policies are not driven by special interests, secrecy engenders suspicions—whose interests are really being served?—and such suspicions, even when groundless, undermine the political sustainability of the policies. It is this secrecy, and the suspicions it gives rise to, that has helped sustain the protest movement. One of the demands of the protestors has been for greater openness and transparency.

These demands had a special resonance because the IMF itself emphasized the importance of transparency during the East Asia crisis. One of the clearly *unintended* consequences of the IMF's rhetorical emphasis on transparency was that eventually, when the transparency spotlight was turned around to shine on the IMF itself, it was found wanting.[5]

Secrecy also undermines democracy. There can be democratic accountability only if those to whom these public institutions are supposed to be accountable are well informed about what they are doing—including what choices they confronted and how those decisions were made. We saw in chapter 6 how modern democracies had come to recognize the citizens' basic *right to know*, implemented through laws such as America's Freedom of Information Act. We saw also, however, that while nominally espousing transparency and openness, the IMF and the World Bank have not yet embraced these ideas. They must.

REFORMING THE IMF AND THE
GLOBAL FINANCIAL SYSTEM

There are some common themes facing reform in all of the international economic institutions, but each institution has a set of problems of its own. I begin with the IMF, partly because it brings out more clearly some problems that are present to a lesser extent in other institutions.

I began the previous chapter by asking, How could an organization with such talented (and high paid) government bureaucrats make so many mistakes? I suggested that *part* of its problems arose from the dissonance between its supposed objective, the objective for which it was originally created, promoting global economic stability, and the newer objectives—such as capital market liberalization—which did more to serve the interests of the financial community than of global stability. This dissonance led to intellectual incoherency and inconsistencies that were more than just matters of academic interest. No wonder, then, that it was hard to derive coherent policies. Economic science was too often replaced by ideology, an ideology that gave clear directions, if not always guidance that worked, and an ideology that was broadly consonant with the interests of the financial community, even if, when it failed to work, those interests themselves were not well served.

One of the important distinctions between *ideology* and *science* is that science recognizes the limitations on what one knows. There is always uncertainty. By contrast, the IMF never likes to discuss the uncertainties associated with the policies that it recommends, but rather, likes to project an image of being infallible. This posture and mind-set makes it difficult for it to learn from past mistakes—how can it learn from those mistakes if it can't admit them? While many organizations would like outsiders to believe that they are indeed infallible, the problem with the IMF is that it often acts as if it *almost* believes in its infallibility.

The IMF has admitted to mistakes in the East Asia crisis, acknowledging that the contractionary fiscal policies exacerbated the downturn, and that the strategy for restructuring the financial system in Indonesia led to a bank run, which only made matters worse. But, not surprisingly, the Fund—and the U.S. Treasury, which was responsible for pushing many of the policies—has tried to limit the criticisms and their discussion. Both were furious when a World Bank report touched on these and other mistakes and got front-page coverage in the *New York Times*. Orders to muzzle the critics were issued. More tellingly, the IMF never pursued the issues further. It never asked why the mistakes had occurred, what was wrong with the models, or what could be done to prevent a recurrence in the next crisis—and there surely will be another crisis in the future. (In January 2002, Argentina was going through a crisis. Once again, the IMF bailout policies failed to work; the contractionary fiscal policies that it insisted upon pushed the economy into an ever deeper recession.) The IMF never asked why its models *systematically* underestimated the depth of recessions—or why its policies are *systematically* excessively contractionary.

The Fund tries to defend its stance of institutional infallibility, saying that if it showed it was wavering in its conviction that its policies were correct, it would lose credibility—and the success of its policies requires that markets give it credibility. Here again, there is real irony. Does the IMF, always praising the "perfection and rationality" of the market, really believe that it enhances its credibility by making overly confident forecasts? Predictions that repeatedly don't pan out make the Fund look rather less than infallible, especially if the markets are as rational as it claims. Today, the IMF has lost much of its credibility, not only in developing countries but also with its cherished constituency, the financial community. Had the IMF been more honest, more forthright, more modest, it would arguably be in a better standing today.

Sometimes, IMF officials give another reason for their failure to discuss alternative policies and the risks associated with each. They say that it would simply confuse the developing countries—a patronizing attitude that reflects a deep skepticism about democratic processes.

It would be nice if the IMF, having had these problems pointed out, would change its mind-set and its modes of behavior. But this is not likely to be the case. Indeed, the Fund has been remarkably slow in learning from its mistakes—partly, as we have seen, because of the strong role of ideology and its belief in institutional infallibility, partly because its hierarchical organizational structure is used to ensure its prevailing worldviews dominate throughout the institution. The IMF is not, in the jargon of modern business schools, a "learning organization," and like other organizations that find it difficult to learn and adapt, it finds itself in difficulties when the environment around it changes.

Earlier in this chapter, I argued that a fundamental change in mindset is likely to occur only with a change in governance, but that such changes are unlikely in the near term. Increased transparency would help; but even there, meaningful reforms were being resisted.

A broad consensus—outside the IMF—has developed that the IMF should limit itself to its core area, managing crises; that it should no longer be involved (outside crises) in development or the economies of transition. I strongly concur—partly because the other reforms that would enable it to promote democratic, equitable, and sustainable development and transition are simply not forthcoming.

There are other dimensions to narrowing the focus. The IMF currently is responsible for the collection of valuable economic statistics, and though by and large it does a good job, the data it reports are compromised by its operating responsibilities; to make its programs *seem* to work, to make the numbers "add up," economic forecasts have to be adjusted. Many users of these numbers do not realize that they are not like ordinary forecasts; in these instances, GDP forecasts are not based on a sophisticated statistical model, or even on the best estimates of those who know the economy well, but are merely the numbers that have been *negotiated* as part of an IMF program. Such conflicts of interest invariably arise when the operating agency is also responsible for statistics, and many governments have responded by creating an independent statistical agency.

Another activity of the Fund is surveillance, reviewing a country's economic performance, under the Article 4 consultations discussed in chapter 6. This is the mechanism through which the IMF pushes its particular perspectives on developing countries that are not dependent on its aid. Because an economic slowdown in one country can have adverse effects on others, it does make sense for countries to put pressure on each other to maintain their economic strength; there is a global public good. The problem is the report card itself. The IMF emphasizes inflation; but unemployment and growth are equally important. And its policy recommendations too reflect its particular perspectives on the balance of government and markets. My direct experience with these Article 4 consultations in the United States convinces me that this too is a task that should be taken over by others. Because the most direct impact of one country's slowdown is on its neighbors, and the neighbors are much more attuned to the circumstances in the country, regional surveillance is a viable alternative.

Forcing the IMF to return to its original mission—narrowing its focus—enables greater accountability. We can attempt to ascertain whether it has prevented crises from happening, creating a more stable global environment, and whether it has resolved them well. But clearly, narrowing focus does not solve the institution's problem: part of the complaint is that it has pushed policies, such as capital market liberalization, which have increased global instability, and that its big bailout policies, whether in East Asia, or Russia, or Latin America, have failed.

Reform Efforts

In the aftermath of the East Asia crisis, and the failures of the IMF policies, there was a general consensus that something was wrong with the international economic system, something needed to be done to make the global economy more stable. However, many of those at the U.S. Treasury and IMF felt that only minor changes were needed. To compensate for the lack of grandness in the changes, they conceived a grandiose title for the reform initiative, *reform of the global financial architecture*. The term was intended to suggest a major change in the rules of the game that would prevent another crisis.

Underneath the rhetoric, there were some real issues. But just as those in charge at the IMF did everything to shift the blame away from their mistakes and away from the systemic problems, they did everything they could to curtail the reforms, except to the extent that they result in *more* power and money to the IMF and *more obligations* (such as compliance with new standards set by the advanced industrial countries) on the emerging markets.

These doubts are reinforced by the way discussions of reform have proceeded. The "official" reform debate has been centered in the same institutions and dominated by the same governments that have effectively "run" globalization for over fifty years. Around the world today, there is a great deal of cynicism about the reform debate. Faced with the same people at the table who had been responsible for the system all along, the developing countries wondered if it was likely that real change would occur. As far as these "client countries" were concerned, it was a charade in which the politicians pretended to do something to redress the problems while financial interests worked to preserve as much of the status quo as they could. The cynics were partly right, but only partly so. The crisis brought to the fore the sense that something was wrong with the process of globalization, and this perception mobilized critics across a wide landscape of issues, from transparency to poverty to the environment to labor rights.

Inside the organizations themselves, among many influential members there is a sense of complacency. The institutions have altered their rhetoric. They talk about "transparency," about "poverty," about "participation." Even if there is a gap between the rhetoric and the reality, the rhetoric has an effect on the institutions' behavior, on transparency, on the concern for poverty. They have better Web sites and there is more openness. The participatory poverty assessments have generated more involvement and a greater awareness of the poverty impacts of programs. But these changes, as profound as they seem to those inside the institutions, appear superficial to outsiders. The IMF and World Bank still have disclosure standards far weaker than those of governments in democracies like the United States, or Sweden, or Canada. They attempt to hide critical reports; it is only their inability to prevent leaks that often forces the eventual disclosure. There is mounting unhappiness in developing countries with the new programs involving participatory poverty assessments, as those participating are told that important matters, such as the macroeconomic framework, are off limits.[6]

There are other instances where there has been more change in what is said than in what is done. Today, the dangers of short-term capital flows and premature capital and financial market liberalization are occasionally acknowledged even by senior officials at the IMF. This constitutes a major change in the official stance of the Fund—though it is still too soon to see whether, or how, the change in rhetoric will be reflected in policies implemented within countries.[7] So far, the evidence does not look promising, as one simple episode illustrates. Shortly after the new managing director Horst Köhler took office, he undertook a tour of some member countries. In a visit to Thailand at the end of May 2000, he noted what had by then become conventional wisdom outside the IMF, and was beginning to seep into the IMF itself: the dangers of capital market liberalization. Neighboring Indonesia quickly picked up on the opening, and by the time he visited there in June, its government had announced plans to explore interventions into the capital market. But quickly, the Indonesians—and Köhler—were set straight by the IMF staff. The bureaucracy won again: capital market liberalization might, in theory, be problematic; but capital market interventions (controls) evidently were not to be on the table for those seeking IMF assistance.

There were other gestures to reform, halfhearted or half-baked.[8] As criticism of the large bailouts in the 1990s mounted, there was a succession of failed reforms. First came the precautionary lending package—lending before a crisis actually had occurred—to Brazil, which forestalled that country's crisis but for a few months, and at great cost. Then there was the contingent credit line, another measure designed to have money ready when a crisis erupted.[9] That too didn't work, mainly because no one seemed interested in it on the proposed terms.[10] It was recognized that the bailouts may have contributed to moral hazard, to weak lending practices, and so a bail-in strategy whereby creditors would have to bear part of the costs was put into place, though not for major countries like Russia, but rather for the weak and powerless, like Ecuador, Ukraine, Romania, and Pakistan. As I explained in chapter 12, by and large the bail-in strategies were a failure. In some cases, such as Romania, they were abandoned, though not until after considerable damage to that country's economy; in other cases, like Ecuador, they were enforced, with even more devastating effects. The new U.S. Treasury secretary and the IMF's new managing director both expressed reservations about the overall effectiveness of the large bailout strategy, but then went ahead with more of the same—$11 billion and $21.6 billion lent to Turkey and Argentina in 2000 and 2001, respectively. The eventual failure of the Argentine bailout seems to have finally forced the *beginning* of a rethinking of strategy.

Even when there was widespread, but not universal, consensus on reforms, resistance arose from those in financial centers, sometimes supported by the U.S. Treasury. In the East Asia crisis, as attention was focused on transparency, it became clear that to know what was going on in emerging markets, one had to know what hedge funds and offshore banking centers were doing. Indeed, there was a worry that more transparency elsewhere would lead to more transactions going through these channels, and there would overall be less information about what was going on. Secretary Summers took the side of the hedge funds and the offshore banking centers, resisting calls for increased transparency, arguing that excessive transparency might reduce incentives for gathering information, the "price discovery" function in the technical jargon. Reforms in the offshore banking centers, established as tax and regulatory avoidance havens, only took on momentum after September 11. This should not come as a surprise; these facilities exist as a result of deliberate policies in the advanced industrial countries, pushed by financial markets and the wealthy.

Other, even seemingly minor reforms faced strong resistance, sometimes from the developing as well as developed countries. As it became clear that short-term indebtedness played a key role in the crisis, attention focused on bond provisions that allowed what seemed to be a long-term bond to be converted into a short-term indebtedness overnight.[11] And as demands for bail-in of creditors grew, so too did demands for provisions in bonds that would facilitate their "forced" participation in workouts, so-called collective action clauses. The bond markets have, so far successfully, resisted both reforms—even as these reforms have seemingly received some support from the IMF. The critics of these reforms argued that such provisions might make credit more costly to the borrowing country; but they miss the central point. Today, there are huge costs to borrowing, especially when things go badly, but only a fraction of those costs are borne by the borrower.

What Is Needed

The recognition of the problems has come a long way. But the reforms of the international financial system have only just begun. In my mind, among the key reforms required are the following:

1. Acceptance of the dangers of capital market liberalization, and that short-term capital flows ("hot money") impose huge externalities, costs borne by those not directly party to the transaction (the lenders and borrowers). Whenever there are such large externalities, interventions—including those done through the banking and tax systems[12]—are desirable. Rather than resisting these interventions,

the international financial institutions should be directing their efforts to making them work better.

2. Bankruptcy reforms and standstills. The appropriate way of addressing problems when private borrowers cannot repay creditors, whether domestic or foreign, is through bankruptcy, not through an IMF-financed bailout of creditors. What is required is bankruptcy reform that recognizes the special nature of bankruptcies that arise out of macroeconomic disturbances; what is needed is a super-Chapter 11, a bankruptcy provision that expedites restructuring and gives greater presumption for the continuation of existing management. Such a reform will have the further advantage of inducing more due diligence on the part of creditors, rather than encouraging the kind of reckless lending that has been so common in the past.[13] Trying to impose more creditor-friendly bankruptcy reforms, taking no note of the special features of macro-induced bankruptcies, is not the answer. Not only does this fail to address the problems of countries in crises; it is a medicine which likely will not take hold—as we have seen so graphically in East Asia, one cannot simply graft the laws of one country onto the customs and norms of another. The problems of defaults on *public* indebtedness (as in Argentina) are more complicated, but again there needs to be more reliance on bankruptcies and standstills, a point that the IMF too seems belatedly to have accepted. But the IMF cannot play the central role. The IMF is a major creditor, and it is dominated by the creditor countries. A bankruptcy system in which the creditor or his representative is also the bankruptcy judge will never be accepted as fair.

3. Less reliance on bailouts. With increased use of bankruptcies and standstills, there will be less need for the big bailouts, which failed so frequently, with the money either going to ensure that Western creditors got paid back more than they otherwise would, or that exchange rates were maintained at overvalued levels longer than they otherwise would have been (allowing the rich inside the country to get more of their money out at more favorable terms, but leaving the country more indebted). As we have seen, the bailouts have not just failed to work; they have contributed to the prob-

lem, by reducing incentives for care in lending, and for covering of exchange risks.

4. Improved banking regulation—both design and implementation—in the developed and the less developed countries alike. Weak bank regulation in developed countries can lead to bad lending practices, an export of instability. While there may be some debate whether the design of the risk-based capital adequacy standards adds to the stability of the financial systems in the developed countries, there is little doubt that it has contributed to global instability, by encouraging short-term lending. Financial sector deregulation and the excessive reliance on capital adequacy standards has been misguided and destabilizing; what is required is a broader, less ideological approach to regulation, adapted to the capacities and circumstances of each country. Thailand was right to have restricted speculative real estate lending in the 1980s. It was wrong to encourage the Thais to eliminate these restrictions. There are a number of other restrictions such as speed limits (restrictions on the rate of increase of banks' assets), which are likely to enhance stability. Yet the reforms cannot, at the same time, lose sight of the broader goals: a safe and sound banking system is important, but it must also be one that supplies capital to finance enterprise and job creation.[14]

5. Improved risk management. Today, countries around the world face enormous risk from the volatility of exchange rates. While the problem is clear, the solution is not. Experts—including those at the IMF—have vacillated in the kinds of exchange-rate systems that they have advocated. They encouraged Argentina to peg its currency to the dollar. After the East Asia crisis, they argued that countries should either have a freely floating exchange rate or a fixed peg. With the disaster in Argentina, this advice is likely to change again. No matter what reforms occur to the exchange rate mechanism, countries will still face enormous risks. Small countries like Thailand buying and selling goods to many countries face a difficult problem, as the exchange rates among the major currencies vary by 50 percent or more. Fixing their exchange rate to one currency will not resolve the problems; it can actually exacerbate fluctuations with respect to other currencies. But there are other dimensions to risk. The Latin American debt crisis in the 1980s[15]

was brought about by the huge increase in interest rates, a result of Federal Reserve Chairman Paul Volcker's tight money policy in the United States. Developing countries have to learn to manage these risks, probably by buying insurance against these fluctuations in the international capital markets. Unfortunately, today the countries can only buy insurance for short-run fluctuations. Surely the developed countries are much better able to handle these risks than the less developed countries, and they should help develop these insurance markets. It would therefore make sense for the developed countries and the international financial institutions to provide loans to the developing countries in forms that mitigate the risks, e.g., by having the creditors absorb the risks of large real interest fluctuations.

6. Improved safety nets. Part of the task of risk management is enhancing the capabilities of the vulnerable within the country to absorb risks. Most developing countries have weak safety nets, including a lack of unemployment insurance programs. Even in more developed countries, safety nets are weak and inadequate in the two sectors that predominate in developing countries, agriculture and small businesses, so international assistance will be essential if the developing countries are to make substantial strides in improving their safety nets.

7. Improved response to crises. We have seen the failure of the crisis responses in the 1997–98 crisis. The assistance given was badly designed and poorly implemented. The programs did not take sufficiently into account the lack of safety nets, that maintaining credit flows was of vital importance, and that collapse in trade between countries would spread the crisis. The policies were based not only on bad forecasts but on a failure to recognize that it is easier to destroy firms than to recreate them, that the damage caused by high interest rates will not be reversed when they are lowered. There needs to be a restoration of balance: the concerns of workers and small businesses have to be balanced with the concerns of creditors; the impacts of policies on domestic capital flight have to balance the seemingly excessive attention currently paid to outside investors. Responses to future financial crises will have to be placed within a social and political context. Apart from the devastation of

the riots that happen when crises are mismanaged, capital will not be attracted to countries facing social and political turmoil, and no government, except the most repressive, can control such turmoil, especially when policies are perceived to have been imposed from the outside.

Most important, there needs to be a return to basic economic principles; rather than focusing on ephemeral investor psychology, on the unpredictability of confidence, the IMF needs to return to its original mandate of providing funds to restore aggregate demand in countries facing an economic recession. Countries in the developing world repeatedly ask why, when the United States faces a downturn, does it argue for expansionary fiscal and monetary policy, and yet when they face a downturn, just the opposite is insisted upon. As the United States went into a recession in 2001, the debate was not whether there should be a stimulus package, but its design. By now, the lessons of Argentina and East Asia should be clear: confidence will never be restored to economies that remain mired in deep recessions. The conditions that the IMF imposes on countries in return for money need not only to be far more narrowly circumscribed but also to reflect this perspective.

There are other changes that would be desirable: forcing the IMF to disclose the expected "poverty" and unemployment impact of its programs would direct its attention to these dimensions. Countries should know the likely consequences of what it recommends. If the Fund systematically errs in its analyses—if, for instance, the increases in poverty are greater than it predicted—it should be held accountable. Questions can be asked: Is there something systematically wrong with its models? Or is it trying to deliberately mislead policy making?

REFORMING THE WORLD BANK AND DEVELOPMENT ASSISTANCE

Part of the reason that I remain hopeful about the possibility of reforming the international economic institutions is that I have seen change occur at the World Bank. It has not been easy, nor has it gone as far as I would have liked. But the changes have been significant.

By the time I arrived, the new president, James Wolfensohn, was well on his way to trying to make the Bank more responsive to the concerns of developing countries. Though the new direction was not always clear, the intellectual foundations not always firm, and support within the Bank far from universal, the Bank had begun seriously to address the fundamental criticisms levied at it. Reforms involved changes in philosophy in three areas: development; aid in general and the Bank's aid in particular; and relationships between the Bank and the developing countries.

In reassessing its course, the Bank examined how successful development has occurred.[16] Some of the lessons that emerged from this reassessment were ones that the World Bank had long recognized: the importance of living within one's budget constraints, the importance of education, including female education, and of macroeconomic stability. However, some new themes also emerged. Success came not just from promoting primary education but also from establishing a strong technological basis, which included support for advanced training. It is possible to promote equality and rapid growth *at the same time*; in fact, more egalitarian policies appear to help growth. Support for trade and openness is important,[17] but it was the jobs created by export expansion, not the job losses from increased imports, that gave rise to growth. When governments took actions to promote exports and new enterprises, liberalization worked; otherwise, it often failed. In East Asia, government played a pivotal role in successful development by helping create institutions that promote savings and the efficient allocation of investment. Successful countries also emphasized competition and enterprise creation over privatization and the restructuring of existing enterprises.

Overall, the successful countries have pursued a comprehensive approach to development. Thirty years ago, economists of the left and the right often seemed to agree that the improvement in the efficiency of resource allocation and the increase in the supply of capital were at the heart of development. They differed only as to whether those changes should be obtained through government-led planning or unfettered markets. In the end, neither worked. Development encompasses not just resources and capital but a transformation of society.[18] Clearly, the international financial institutions cannot be held responsible for this transformation, but they can play an important role. And at the very least, they should not become impediments to a successful transformation.

Assistance

But the way assistance is often given may do exactly that—create impediments to effective transitions. We saw in chapter 6 that *conditionality*—the imposition of a myriad of conditions, some often political in nature—as a precondition for assistance did not work; it did not lead to better policies, to faster growth, to better outcomes. Countries that think reforms have been imposed on them do not really feel invested in and committed to such reforms. Yet their participation is essential if real societal change is to happen. Even worse, the conditionality has undermined democratic processes. At last, there is a glimmering of recognition, even by the IMF, that conditionality has gone too far, that the dozens of conditions make it difficult for developing countries to focus on priorities. But while there has, accordingly, been an attempt to refine conditionality, within the World Bank the discussion of reform has been taken further. Some argue that conditionality should be replaced by *selectivity*, giving aid to countries with a proven track record, allowing them to choose for themselves their own development strategies, ending the micromanagement that has been such a feature of the past. The evidence is that aid given selectively can have significant impacts both in promoting growth and in reducing poverty.

Debt Forgiveness

The developing countries require not only that aid be given in a way that helps their development but also that there be more aid. Relatively small amounts of money could make enormous differences in promoting health and literacy. In real terms, adjusted for inflation, the amounts of development assistance have actually been declining, and even more so either as a percentage of developed country income or on a per capita basis for those in the developing countries. There needs to be a basis for funding this assistance (and other global public goods) on a more sustained level, free from the vagaries of domestic politics in the United States or elsewhere. Several proposals have been put forward. When the IMF was established, it was given the right to create Special Drawing Rights (SDRs), a kind of international money. With countries today wisely putting aside billions of dollars into reserves every year to protect themselves against the vicissitudes of international markets, some income is not being translated into aggregate demand. The global economic slowdown of 2001–02 brought these concerns to the fore. Issuing SDRs to finance global public goods—including financing development assistance—could help maintain the strength of the global economy at the same time that it helped some of the poorest countries in the world. A second proposal entails using the revenues from global economic resources—the minerals in the seabed and fishing rights in the oceans—to help finance development assistance.

Recently, attention has focused on debt forgiveness, and for good reason. Without the forgiveness of debt, many of the developing countries simply cannot grow. Huge proportions of their current exports go to repaying loans to the developed countries.[19] The Jubilee 2000 movement mobilized enormous international support for debt forgiveness. The movement gained the backing of churches throughout the developed world. To them, it seemed a moral imperative, a reflection of basic principles of economic justice.

The issue of the moral responsibility of the creditors was particularly apparent in the case of Cold War loans.[20] When the IMF and World Bank lent money to the Democratic Republic of the Congo's notorious ruler Mobutu, they knew (or should have known) that most of the money would not go to help that country's poor people, but rather would be used to enrich Mobutu. It was money paid to ensure that this corrupt leader would keep his country aligned with the West. To many, it doesn't seem fair for ordinary taxpayers in countries with corrupt governments to have to repay loans that were made to leaders who did not represent them.

The Jubilee movement was successful in getting much larger commitments to debt forgiveness. Whereas before 2000 there had been a debt relief program for the highly indebted countries, few met the criteria that the IMF had erected. By the end of 2000, as a result of international pressure, twenty-four countries had passed the threshold.

But debt relief needs to go further: as it stands now, the agreements touch only the poorest of the countries. Countries like Indonesia, devastated by the East Asia crisis and the failures of the IMF policies there, are still too well off to be brought in under the umbrella.

REFORMING THE WTO AND BALANCING THE TRADE AGENDA

The global protests over globalization began at the WTO meetings in Seattle, Washington, because it was the most obvious symbol of the global inequities and the hypocrisy of the advanced industrial countries. While these countries had preached—and forced—the opening of the markets in the developing countries to their industrial products, they had continued to keep their markets closed to the products of the developing countries, such as textiles and agriculture. While they preached that developing countries should not subsidize their industries, they continued to provide billions in subsidies to their own farmers, making it impossible for the developing countries to compete. While they preached the virtues of competitive markets, the United States was quick to push for global cartels in steel and aluminum when its domestic industries seemed threatened by imports. The United States pushed for liberalization of financial services, but resisted liberalization of the service sectors in which the developing countries have strength, construction and maritime services. As we have noted, so unfair has the trade agenda been that not only have the poorer countries not received a fair share of the benefits; the poorest region in the world, Sub-Saharan Africa, was actually made worse off as a result of the last round of trade negotiations.

These inequities have increasingly been recognized, and that, combined with the resolve of some of the developing countries, resulted in the Doha "development" round of trade negotiations (November 2001), which put on its agenda the redressing of some of these past imbalances. But there is a long way to go: the United States and the other advanced industrial countries only agreed to discussions; just to discuss redressing some of these imbalances was viewed as a concession!

One of the areas that was of particular concern at Doha was intellectual property rights. These are important, if innovators are to have incentives to innovate—though much of the most crucial research, such as that in basic science and mathematics, is not patentable. No one denies the importance of intellectual property rights. But these rights need to balance out the rights and interests of producers with those of users—not only users in developing countries but researchers in developed countries. In the final stages of the Uruguay negotiations, both the Office of Science and Technology and the Council of Economic Advisers worried that we had not got the balance right—the agreement put producers interests over users. We worried that in doing so, the rate of progress and innovation might actually be impeded; after all, knowledge is the most important input into research, and stronger intellectual property rights can increase the price of this input. We were also concerned about the consequences of the denial of life-saving medicines to the poor. This issue subsequently gained international attention in the context of the provision of AIDS medicines in South Africa. The international outrage forced the drug companies to back down—and it appears that, going forward, the most adverse consequences will be circumscribed. But it is worth noting that initially even the Democratic U.S. administration supported the pharmaceutical companies. What we were not fully aware of was another danger, what has come to be termed *bio-piracy*, international companies patenting traditional medicines or foods; it is not only that they seek to make money from "resources" and knowledge that rightfully belong to the developing countries, but in so doing, they squelch domestic firms that have long provided the products. While it is not clear whether these patents would hold up in court if they were effectively challenged, it is clear that the less developed countries may not have the legal and financial resources required to challenge the patent. This issue has become a source of enormous emotional, and potentially economic, concern all around the developing world. I was recently in an Andean village in Ecuador, where the indigenous mayor railed against how globalization had led to bio-piracy.

Reforming the WTO will require thinking further about a more balanced trade agenda—more balanced in treating the interests of the developing countries, more balanced in treating concerns, like environment, that go beyond trade.

But redressing the current imbalances does not require that the world wait until the end of a new round of trade negotiations. International economic justice requires that the developed countries take actions to open themselves up to fair trade and equitable relationships with developing countries without recourse to the bargaining table or attempts to extract concessions in exchange for doing so. The European Union has already taken steps in this direction, with its "Everything But Arms" initiative to allow the free importing of all goods, other than arms, from the poorest countries into Europe. It does not solve all the complaints of the developing countries: they still will not be able to compete against highly subsidized European agriculture. But it is a big step in the right direction. The challenge now is to get the United States and Japan to participate. Such a move would be of enormous benefit to the developing world and would even benefit the developed countries, whose consumers would be able to obtain goods at lower prices.

TOWARD A GLOBALIZATION WITH A MORE HUMAN FACE

The reforms I have outlined would help make globalization fairer, and more effective in raising living standards, especially of the poor. It is not just a question of changing institutional structures. The mind-set around globalization itself must change. Finance and trade ministers view globalization as largely an economic phenomenon; but to many in the developing world, it is far more than that.

One of the reasons globalization is being attacked is that it seems to undermine traditional values. The conflicts are real, and to some extent unavoidable. Economic growth—including that induced by globalization—will result in urbanization, undermining traditional rural societies. Unfortunately, so far, those responsible for managing globalization, while praising these positive benefits, all too often have shown an insufficient appreciation of this adverse side, the threat to cultural identity and values.[21] This is surprising, given the awareness of the issues within the developed countries themselves: Europe defends its agricultural policies not just in terms of those special interests, but to preserve rural traditions. People in small towns everywhere complain that large national retailers and shopping malls have killed their small businesses and their communities.

The pace of global integration matters: a more gradual process means that traditional institutions and norms, rather than being overwhelmed, can adapt and respond to the new challenges.

Of equal concern is what globalization does to democracy. Globalization, as it has been advocated, often seems to replace the old dictatorships of national elites with new dictatorships of international finance. Countries are effectively told that if they don't follow certain conditions, the capital markets or the IMF will refuse to lend them money. They are basically forced to give up part of their sovereignty, to let capricious capital markets, including the speculators whose only concerns are short-term rather than the long-term growth of the country and the improvement of living standards, "discipline" them, telling them what they should and should not do.

But countries do have choices, and among those choices is the extent to which they wish to subject themselves to international capital markets. Those, such as in East Asia, that have avoided the strictures of the IMF have grown faster, with greater equality and poverty reduction, than those who have obeyed its commandments. Because alternative policies affect different groups differently, it is the role of the political process—not international bureaucrats—to sort out the choices. Even if growth *were* adversely affected, it is a cost many developing countries may be willing to pay to achieve a more democratic and equitable society, just as many societies today are saying it is worth sacrificing some growth for a better environment. So long as globalization is presented in the way that it has been, it represents a disenfranchisement. No wonder then that it will be resisted, especially by those who are being disenfranchised.

TODAY, GLOBALIZATION IS being challenged around the world. There is discontent with globalization, and rightfully so. Globalization can be a force for good: the globalization of ideas about democracy and of civil society have changed the way people think, while global political movements have led to debt relief and the treaty on land mines. Globalization has helped hundreds of millions of people attain higher standards of living, beyond what they, or most economists, thought imaginable but a short while ago. The globalization of the economy has benefited countries that took advantage of it by seeking new markets for their exports and by welcoming foreign investment. Even so, the countries that have benefited the most have been those that took charge of their own destiny and recognized the role government can play in development rather than relying on the notion of a self-regulated market that would fix its own problems.

But for millions of people globalization has not worked. Many have actually been made worse off, as they have seen their jobs destroyed and their lives become more insecure. They have felt increasingly powerless against forces beyond their control. They have seen their democracies undermined, their cultures eroded.

If globalization continues to be conducted in the way that it has been in the past, if we continue to fail to learn from our mistakes, globalization will not only not succeed in promoting development but will continue to create poverty and instability. Without reform, the backlash that has already started will mount and discontent with globalization will grow.

This will be a tragedy for all of us, and especially for the billions who might otherwise have benefited. While those in the developing world stand to lose the most economically, there will be broader political ramifications that will affect the developed world too.

If the reforms outlined in this last chapter are taken seriously, then there is hope that a more humane process of globalization can be a powerful force for the good, with the vast majority of those living in the developing countries benefiting from it and welcoming it. If this is done, the discontent with globalization would have served us all well.

The current situation reminds me of the world some seventy years ago. As the world plummeted into the Great Depression, advocates of the free market said, "Not to worry; markets are self-regulating, and given time, economic prosperity will resume." Never mind the misery of those whose lives are destroyed waiting for this so-called eventuality. Keynes argued that markets were not self-correcting, or not at least in a relevant time frame. (As he famously put it, "In the long run, we are all dead.")* Unemployment could persist for years, and government intervention was required. Keynes was pilloried—attacked as a Socialist, a critic of the market. Yet in a sense, Keynes was intensely conservative. He had a fundamental belief in the markets: if only government could correct this one failure, the economy would be able to function reasonably efficiently. He did not want a wholesale replacement of the market system; but he knew that unless these fundamental problems were addressed, there would be enormous popular pressures. And Keynes's medicine worked: since World War II, countries like the United States, following Keynesian prescriptions, have had fewer and shorter-lived downturns, and longer expansions than previously.

Today, the system of capitalism is at a crossroads just as it was during the Great Depression. In the 1930s, capitalism was saved by Keynes, who thought of policies to create jobs and rescue those suffering from the collapse of the global economy. Now, millions of people around the world are waiting to see whether globalization can be reformed so that its benefits can be more widely shared.

Thankfully, there is a growing recognition of these problems and increasing political will to do something. Almost everyone involved in development, even those in the Washington establishment, now agrees that rapid capital market liberalization without accompanying regulation can be dangerous. They agree too that the excessive tightness in fiscal policy in the Asian crisis of 1997 was a mistake. As Bolivia moved into a recession in 2001, caused in part by the global economic slowdown, there were some intimations that that country would not be forced to follow the traditional path of austerity and have to cut governmental spending. Instead, as of January 2002, it looks like Bolivia will be allowed to stimulate its economy, helping it to overcome the recession, using revenues that it is about to receive from its newly discovered natural gas reserves to tide it over until the economy starts to grow again. In the aftermath of the Argentina debacle, the IMF has recognized the failings of the big-bailout strategy and is beginning to discuss the use of standstills and restructuring through bankruptcy, the kinds of alternatives that I and others have been advocating for years. Debt forgiveness

---

* J. M. Keynes, *A Tract on Monetary Reform* (London: Macmillan, 1924).

brought about by the work of the Jubilee movement and the concessions made to initiate a new development round of trade negotiations at Doha represent two more victories.

Despite these gains, there is still more to be done to bridge the gap between rhetoric and reality. At Doha, the developed countries only agreed to begin discussing a fairer trade agenda; the imbalances of the past have yet to be redressed. Bankruptcy and standstills are now on the agenda; but there is no assurance that there will be an appropriate balance of creditor and debtor interests. There is a lot more participation by those in developing countries in discussions concerning economic strategy, but there is little evidence yet of changes in policies that reflect greater participation. There need to be changes in institutions and in mind-sets. The free-market ideology should be replaced with analyses based on economic science, with a more balanced view of the role of government drawn from an understanding of both market and government failures. There should be more sensitivity about the role of outside advisers, so they support democratic decision making by clarifying the consequences of different policies, including impacts on different groups, especially the poor, rather than undermining it by pushing particular policies on reluctant countries.

It is clear that there must be a *multipronged* strategy of reform. One should be concerned with reform of the international economic arrangements. But such reforms will be a long time coming. Thus, the second prong should be directed at encouraging reforms that each country can take upon itself. The developed countries have a special responsibility, for instance, to eliminate their trade barriers, to practice what they preach. But while the developed countries' responsibility may be great, their incentives are weak: after all, offshore banking centers and hedge funds serve interests in the developed countries, and the developed countries can withstand well the instability that a failure to reform might bring to the developing world. Indeed, the United States arguably benefited in several ways from the East Asia crisis.

Hence, the developing countries must assume responsibility for their well-being themselves. They can manage their budgets so that they live within their means, meager though that might be, and eliminate the protectionist barriers which, while they may generate large profits for a few, force consumers to pay higher prices. They can put in place strong regulations to protect themselves from speculators from the outside or corporate misbehavior from the inside. Most important, developing countries need effective governments, with strong and independent judiciaries, democratic accountability, openness and transparency and freedom from the corruption that has stifled the effectiveness of the public sector and the growth of the private.

What they should ask of the international community is only this: the acceptance of their need, and right, to make their own choices, in ways which reflect their own political judgments about who, for instance, should bear what risks. They should be encouraged to adopt bankruptcy laws and regulatory structures adapted to their own situation, not to accept templates designed by and for the more developed countries.[22]

What is needed are policies for sustainable, equitable, and democratic growth. This is the reason for development. Development is not about helping a few people get rich or creating a handful of pointless protected industries that only benefit the country's elite; it is not about bringing in Prada and Benetton, Ralph Lauren or Louis Vuitton, for the urban rich and leaving the rural poor in their misery. Being able to buy Gucci handbags in Moscow department stores did not mean that country had become a market economy. Development is about transforming societies, improving the lives of the poor, enabling everyone to have a chance at success and access to health care and education.

This sort of development won't happen if only a few people dictate the policies a country must follow. Making sure that democratic decisions are made means ensuring that a broad range of economists, officials, and experts from developing countries are actively involved in the debate. It also means that there must be broad participation that goes well beyond the experts and politicians. Developing countries must take charge of their own futures. But we in the West cannot escape our responsibilities.

It's not easy to change how things are done. Bureaucracies, like people, fall into bad habits, and adapting to change can be painful. But the international institutions must undertake the perhaps painful changes that will enable them to play the role they *should* be playing to make globalization work, and work not just for the well off and the industrial countries, but for the poor and the developing nations.

The developed world needs to do its part to reform the international institutions that govern globalization. We set up these institutions and we need to work to fix them. If we are to address the legitimate concerns of those who have expressed a discontent with globalization, if we are to make globalization work for the billions of people for whom it has not, if we are to make globalization with a human face succeed, then our voices must be raised. We cannot, we should not, stand idly by.

Afterword to the 2017 Edition

GLOBALIZATION IS DYNAMIC—it is ever-changing. Trump, the global financial crisis, the East Asia crisis, the rise of China and other emerging markets—these are among the things that have happened in the last two decades that have changed globalization forever. Globalization in 2020 is different from globalization in 2000. In Part I, I described the New Discontents. Twenty years ago, the complaint of the developing countries was that the developed countries were the winners from globalization—they were setting the rules for their own benefit. The simple but big insight, noted in *Globalization and Its Discontents* (*GAID*), is that it wasn't the United States, or the advanced countries as a group, that was setting the rules, but corporate and financial interests within the United States. *They* were the big winners—larger markets and lower costs meant higher profit. As it turned out, the emerging markets as a whole were also among the winners. The countries in Africa were pulled by two opposing forces: China's growth was increasing the demand for their resources, and China became an enormous provider of assistance. From this they benefited. But European and U.S. agricultural policies—maintaining massive subsidies in spite of all the free-market rhetoric—were depressing global agricultural prices, and from this the poorest people in the poorest countries, the farmers in Sub-Saharan Africa, suffered enormously.

I wrote *GAID* in the belief that the rules and institutions of the international order were biased against ordinary individuals in the developing countries and emerging markets. I also deeply believed, however, in the importance of an international rule of law and in international institutions to promote development and coordinate economic policy. Globalization meant that we were interconnected, that what one country did affected others, and that, therefore, the countries of the world had to work together. I wrote the book in the belief that we could construct a better globalization, a better, fairer set of rules and institutions, which would promote growth, development, and stability with equity. Trump has been working to destroy the international rule of law and the international institutions that are so important in making our global system work well. While he garnered a significant number of votes in the United States (though far less than a majority), globally his views are derided and despised.[1] The ugly American—a feature of the global landscape for decades—has just gotten much uglier. And the distance between the views of the global economy of Americans, at least those in power, and the rest of the world has just gotten much greater.

In the original *GAID*, reprinted in Part II of this volume, I wrote about the East Asia crisis, the transition from communism to a market economy, and development—the big issues during the period I had served as chief economist of the World Bank (1997–2000). Since then, we've had more and bigger crises. How should we now look back at what seemed terrible crises at the time but were dwarfed by what happened in 2008? How have the central battles over policies and institutions that I described in *GAID*, so essential to the prosperity of the developing countries and the transition economies, played out?

In the introduction and chapters 1 to 4, I explain how *GAID* provides a lens through which we can better understand the New Discontents, those in the developed world. Here, I take a global view of globalization, on its effects on the developing countries and emerging markets which were at the center of *GAID* as well as on the advanced countries.

Fears More Than Realized

In 2002, I felt strongly that the deficiencies in the way globalization was being managed, guided in particular by the Washington Consensus policies, would eventually become evident. The policies would lead to low growth and more instability for those who followed them, in stark contrast with what was happening elsewhere, in for instance the East Asian countries that did not follow those policies.

In *GAID,* I also wrote much about the governance of globalization, about how the rules are made. With the share of global GDP in the developed countries decreasing, it was inconceivable that they continue to dominate global governance as they had for more than half a century after World War II. I worried, however, that before the deficiencies in the Washington Consensus became evident, enormous damage could and would have been done—there could and likely would be enormous suffering of the kind that I had seen wrought by these policies, as I described in *GAID.* I was particularly fearful of the consequences of unbridled financial market deregulation. I had spent much of my time in the Clinton administration trying to stop it there,[2] only to find the battles even more intense at my next job as chief economist of the World Bank.

So too, while it might be inevitable that emerging markets would eventually play a role in globalization commensurate with their growing economic power, there was a danger that before that happened, dissatisfaction with current arrangements would grow to the point that the emerging markets would go their own way. For a well-managed globalization, one needed global institutions. This kind of fragmentation would be bad, both for the developed and developing countries. But would the advanced countries like the United States recognize the dangers quickly enough? Or would they, fretting about their loss of power, stand in the way of the creation of a better-balanced globalization? Worryingly, during the East Asia crisis, the United States had stood in the way of the creation of the Asian Monetary Fund, which Japan was willing to support (described in chapter 8): so fearful was America about its potential loss of hegemony that it was willing to sacrifice the well-being of the countries in crisis—offering, instead of money, lectures on good policies and institutions, lectures which in the aftermath of the U.S. 2008 financial crisis looked increasingly misplaced. To use the old aphorism, it seemed that the pot was calling the kettle black.

I worried too that these failures, both in policies and governance, would give rise to a backlash against globalization, one in which there would be a wholesale retreat from globalization. To counter that, I repeatedly said, the problem was not with globalization, but with the way we managed it. There was a risk that years of failing to manage it well would lead to a widespread sentiment that globalization *could not* be managed well; globalization could not be tempered and tamed; one could not get the benefits without bearing at the same time the over-whelming harms.

What happened was worse than I ever could have anticipated—and the problems would become evident where least expected. The worst crisis in seventy-five years would originate in the United States, as a result of excessive financial sector deregulation,[3] but globalization enabled the crisis and its aftershocks to spread quickly around the world. The crisis itself did more to discredit the Washington Consensus policies and those who had pushed them than anything I or anyone else could have written or done. In the aftermath, the disparity in growth between the United States and China increased even more (reaching 12 percentage points in 2009[4]), the share of America and Europe in the global economy diminished (to 32 percent in 2016, from 37 percent in 2009), and China and India (whose growth rate rose to 9.2 percent and 8.5 percent, respectively, in 2009) attained new confidence in themselves and their economic policies. And globalization began to be redefined: especially as China attained new prominence, dominating public investment in Africa, and exceeding trade with several countries in America's backyard, Latin America, when compared to the United States.[5] Yet, not surprisingly, America and Europe were slow to give up the power they exercised in global governance. And, again not surprisingly, the emerging markets began to develop their own institutions.

With the election of Trump, America's soft power has, as I just argued, taken a big hit, as the United States has moved from the position of leadership in the creation of a rules-based international system to a position of leadership in its destruction and the creation of global protectionism. The best that can be said is that (as this book goes to press), America's institutions have proven strong enough to at least temper the effects of a bigoted and severely uninformed president with autocratic leanings and no respect for the truth. The silver lining on this very dark cloud is that, at last, the world is likely to move toward multipolarity. Having excessive power in the hands of one country meant the fate of the world was too dependent on what happened there. This is now only too evident. The diminished economic role of the United States in the global economy meant that, eventually, political power too would have to become more dispersed and the world would become multipolar. Trump accelerated the inevitable.

What then is the future of globalization? This afterword provides some answers. The good news is that the institutions that have been created globally are working, in some ways much better than seemed to be the case twenty years ago when I wrote *GAID*. The IMF has reformed. The WTO prevented an outbreak of beggar-thy-neighbor policies in the Great Recession. Trump arrived on the scene as other fundamental forces were inevitably changing globalization. Trump, however, is pushing for an even more "unbalanced" globalization. He will fail. The world will be much the worse for his attempts. But before turning to globalization's future, we need to look more carefully at what has happened to globalization in the years since *GAID* was published.

GLOBALIZATION THEN

Begin by recalling the world almost two decades ago, just a few years after the fall of the Iron Curtain.

World War II had set in motion the process of decolonization, which was almost completed by the mid-1960s. By the latter part of the twentieth century, old-style colonial domination was universally viewed as unacceptable. Besides, as I note earlier in this book, the United States and the former colonial masters discovered that they could get much of what they wanted—resources and economic gain—in more subtle ways. Having been stripped of much of their wealth, without receiving reinvestment in human capital or infrastructure, the former colonies were always on the brink. They became dependent on money from Western banks, and when they couldn't repay, there was a bailout—called a bailout of the country, but really, a bailout of the Western banks that had recklessly lent to them. But then, as a condition of getting this money, the countries experienced a form of Western domination as bitter as the old colonialism—conditions would be imposed to get the loans, which typically included fire sale privatizations of the country's assets, turning them over to Western companies at bargain prices. Seemingly, one didn't need guns and armies to engage in massive exploitation: all one needed was clever bankers, gullible and sometimes corrupt domestic officials, and an international financial regime spearheaded by the IMF and the World Bank, acting as the lenders' collection agency.

Of course, the policies foisted on these developing countries were described to be in the country's own interests, and sometimes more than a little ideology got mixed up with the economic interests of the advanced countries. Often, the policies didn't work. Africa experienced a lost quarter century. Latin America grew, but its growth was marked by huge volatility, and what growth occurred was not shared—it went mainly to the top. Of course, the IMF and the World Bank did everything they could to blame the victims—arguing that if only these countries had really done what they were told to do, the outcomes would have been totally different. Like medieval bloodletters, rather than questioning the efficacy of their prescriptions as their patients languished, they doubled down on their policies.

GAID showed what was already obvious to many of those in the developing world—what they knew but could not themselves say to their former colonial masters: the Washington Consensus policies were not only not working, they *could* not work. *GAID* showed that "the emperor had no clothes." The policies were a far departure from what at least the center-left argued for in their own countries. Having moved directly from being chairman of the Council of Economic Advisers in the United States to the World Bank, I was keenly sensitive to these discrepancies.

For instance, the Clinton administration strongly opposed any form of privatization of Social Security (the public retirement program), and yet the World Bank was advising countries to have a retirement scheme in which the private sector played a central role even for middle-income individuals. The Clinton administration also strongly opposed a value-added tax (VAT), since it was regressive (with poor people paying a larger fraction of their income in taxes than the rich), and yet the IMF was recommending the VAT to countries around the world.

While the IMF claimed that its recommendations were based on the best of economics, a combination of research and experience, in reality that was not the case. The policies being sold as being in the developing countries' and emerging markets' best interests were often nothing but the perpetuation of the pursuit of Western interests and Western ideologies.

But while much of what I said may have seemed self-evident, especially to those in the developing world, it mattered who was saying it: these countries were given a new sense of confidence in themselves and their leaders, new confidence in the alternative policies that they were pushing.

A Less Enthusiastic Response to GAID from the IMF

Not surprisingly, the very factors that made the book so well received in the Third World resulted in an almost unprecedentedly hostile reception from the IMF. The chief economist of the IMF at the time the book came out, Ken Rogoff, engaged in a vitriolic ad hominem attack, accusing me of selling snake oil when I advocated capital controls (restrictions on the free movement of capital across borders). Just a few years later, the IMF itself started supporting capital controls.[6]

The consequences of the attack illustrated the great divide in globalization at that moment: it helped propel the book to be a global bestseller, with forty official translations and two pirated editions, and over a million copies sold worldwide. The fact that the attack contained more venom than analysis—and that the IMF responded with such force—was telling: it reinforced the message of the book. The IMF realized that I had seriously undermined their credibility and, more important, that of the set of policies which they were foisting around the world and the ideology on which those policies rested.

Love That One Could Do Without

One of the most disturbing aspects of the response to GAID was how some of the arguments were picked up *selectively* by those opposed to globalization, by protectionists, old and new. Donald Trump had his antecedents. Ross Perot was another billionaire presidential candidate. He ran for president of the United States in 1992 as an independent and the centerpiece of his campaign was to claim that jobs would go to Mexico because of NAFTA. Lou Dobbs, an anti-Mexican CNN anchor (whose antipathies, though, look mild in comparison to those of Trump), would frequently invite me on his show. He picked up that I was critical of NAFTA. But I was critical because I thought it wrong and hypocritical that the United States had kept its corn subsidies, hurting the incomes of some of the poorest people in North America. And I used the platform he gave me to get this message out more broadly.

There is a moral dilemma that academics often face. The defenders of globalization have suggested that I keep my critique to myself, lest my arguments be abused. But they use that argument in a one-sided way: they never say to be silent about the virtues of globalization, lest praise of globalization lead to ignoring the downsides, leading in turn to policies that would leave large segments of the population worse off.

The only response is to be as transparent and clear as one can: I am criticizing globalization with the belief that we can make it work better for all. I have been equally critical of the special interests that take advantage of protectionism and those (like the financial sector) which seek to gain from mismanaged globalization and deregulation.

NEW THEORIES FOR A NEW WORLD

I approached globalization from perspectives that were often markedly different from others engaged in these discussions in two important ways. The first l have already noted: I came from being President Clinton's chief economic adviser (as chairman of the Council of Economic Advisers)[7]—which was committed to putting into place progressive policies, often distinctively different from those the World Bank and IMF were advocating for developing countries. The second was my background as an economic theorist. Economic theory involves examining the logical conclusions from certain assumptions. It tests for robustness: will small changes in assumptions lead to large changes in conclusions? It looks for hidden assumptions, things we take for granted which may or may not be correct. It is grounded in empirics, in looking at the world; but sometimes, in detailed statistical studies, the forest is lost because of the focus on the trees. Thus, one doesn't need complex statistical studies to see that most firms and households pay a higher interest rate than the U.S. government, presumably because there is a risk of default; or that in many circumstances, individuals or firms cannot borrow as much as they would like at the "market" rate of interest—sometimes even at any interest rate.

My theoretical research focused on the consequences of imperfect information and the inability of firms and households to fully insure themselves against important risks they faced. Standard economics, as it had developed from Adam Smith on, while not denying the importance of risk and information, had proceeded by assuming that a world in which, for instance, information imperfections were not too large would be well described by one in which information was imperfect. My work (together with that of a large number of other scholars working in this area)[8] had shown that that assumption was false: even small amounts of information imperfection could have very large effects. Most importantly, the old theories assumed that normally there was full employment, that there was no credit rationing (no liquidity constraints, no constraints on borrowing), and that the outcome of competitive markets was efficient.[9] These assumptions too were shown to be false.

My criticism of the Washington Consensus policies was in part that they were based on discredited economic theories. In its supporters' minds was a clear view of what an economy should look like, the perfect market economy of elementary textbooks. They realized that all economies—and especially of developing countries—deviated from this ideal, but their policy agenda was to make actual markets as close to the competitive ideal as possible.

As chief economist of the World Bank, my main critique of this approach was pragmatic: it was essentially not working anywhere; and the countries that were successful were following a markedly different model. But my background as a theorist had led me to anticipate the failures of the Washington Consensus, as well as the successes of the development strategies of East Asia. There were two critical failings of the Washington Consensus policies. The first was that the "ideal" for which they were striving was bogus: no economy, ever, would have perfect information, so markets were inherently imperfect. The objective should have been to construct as well-performing an economy as one could, given limitations in information, the costs of setting up markets, the persistent irrationalities of individuals, etc.

The second critique went deeper, and was based on the Theory of the Second Best. Even before my work, it had been shown that even if it were true that an ideal perfect competition model led to efficiency, moving *toward* that might not make matters better. I illustrated this in chapter 1 with an example attacking standard presumptions in favor of trade liberalization: with imperfect risk markets, opening up trade could so increase risk that, to avoid the risk, firms would shift investments toward lower-productivity, safer investments, so much so that everyone could be worse off than they were before trade liberalization.[10]

Globalization and the set of problems that I confronted as chief economist of the World Bank, though, posed a set of new analytic challenges—situations that had not been confronted before. Countries had not before faced the daunting task of moving from communism to a market economy. Perhaps not since the Great Depression had there been a crisis of the magnitude of the East Asia crisis—with half or more of the firms in the region on the verge of bankruptcy. The best one could do in thinking about what were the right policies—to facilitate the transition or to combat the East Asia crisis—was to draw upon economic theory and what one could learn from similar experiences. That, in turn, required having a view about how the economic system as a whole behaves, and particularly how it behaves out of "equilibrium," out of a normal state of affairs. Nothing could have been more exciting to an economic theorist than being confronted with hard, unsolved problems. And nothing could have been more frustrating than to have much of the policy debate dominated by those holding on to models which were clearly inappropriate to the situation.

Consider, for instance, the subject of short-term capital flows. The standard models in economics on which the Washington Consensus was based were clearly wrong: they predicted that these flows would be stabilizing, so that when a country had troubles, money would rush in to help it out. The evidence was to the contrary: when a problem was detected, money rushed out, exacerbating the downturn. (As I jokingly explained to my students, the first principle of banking is never to lend to anybody who really needs your money.)

New theories were required, and in *GAID* I tried to extend the standard theory, suggesting what such models might look like. A few years later, I published some of the underlying mathematics.[11]

The events I confronted led to the development of new areas of research, with results that often modified, and sometimes contradicted, longstanding policy dictums derived from the old models. Later in this afterword, I note a couple other examples.

THE BATTLES OVER POLICY

GAID describes a fundamental fight over economic theory and policy, played out in three battlefields: economies in transition, East Asian countries, and poor countries striving to develop.

The Washington Consensus

The Washington Consensus policies that I was arguing against[12]—focusing on privatization, deregulation, liberalization, and macrostability centered around fighting inflation—were, as I have suggested, predicated on a view that markets worked well and there was a limited role for government. Standard theory, dating back to Adam Smith,[13] had argued that in perfect markets, the pursuit of self-interest by firms and households would lead, as if by an invisible hand, to the well-being of society. My theoretical research[14] had explained why Adam Smith's invisible hand was invisible—it wasn't there. Whenever there was imperfect information or incomplete markets—as is always the case—there is a presumption that markets are inefficient and selective intervention can improve well-being. And my experience in developing countries, crisis countries, and countries in transition confirmed these theoretical insights.

Different economic views naturally translate into important differences in policy. Because my research had shown so clearly the limitations of markets, I was far more reluctant to rely *just* on markets, far more aware of the need for appropriately designed government policies.

By 2016, there was a growing consensus that the Washington Consensus policies were wrong—they often had the opposite effect from that intended. Rather than accelerating growth, they retarded development; rather than enhancing stability, they had helped usher in an era of unprecedented instability. There was a need for a new consensus.

A group of thirteen economists, including four former chief economists of the World Bank (including me), put together what we called the Stockholm Consensus, laying out ten principles of development policy, which included the need to make development inclusive, to attend to inequality, to make development environmentally sustainable, and to get the right balance between the market, the state, and civil society.[15] The new consensus emphasized too that one-size-fits-all policies don't work: there are large differences not only between developed and developing countries, but also among the developing countries, calling for nuanced and tailored policies.

In *GAID,* I criticize each of the central pillars of the Washington Consensus policy framework. The Washington Consensus argued for deregulation, including of the financial sector. I argued that such liberalization could lead to very costly economic volatility. In the aftermath of the 2008 crisis, few doubt that.

The Washington Consensus argued for privatization. I explained in *GAID* why privatizations often fail, in both developed[16] and developing countries—and experiences since *GAID* in both developed countries (e.g., UK railroads) and developing countries (e.g., Chile's pension funds and Mexico's roads) have provided new examples of failed privatizations. In Mexico, the government had to spend nearly $8 billion to renationalize just part of the privatized highway system.[17]

And last, the Washington Consensus argued for trade liberalization. I argued that poorly managed trade liberalization would not lead to more growth and there could be many losers; now, the New Discontents in the advanced countries have made this conclusion abundantly clear.

Capital Controls

One of the fiercest battles *GAID* describes was over a particular aspect of financial deregulation: capital flows across borders, when firms or individuals from one country invest in or lend to another. At the time, the elimination of restrictions on these flows was at the heart of IMF ideology: they wanted to be able to force other countries to open up their capital markets (what is called capital market liberalization), to allow money to move freely in and out. In *GAID,* I expressed skepticism. By 2009—with a crisis in Europe (Iceland)—the IMF began to change its mind. It allowed Iceland to impose capital controls. By 2010 it was in a full-scale retreat, eventually endorsing the idea of capital controls (or as they are now more euphemistically referred to, capital account management measures).

America's ultralow interest rates proved to cause a strain on the global economy. We have a globally interconnected economy—a trend pushed by the United States—but in the conduct of its own policies, it steadfastly refused to consider the consequences of its actions (just as it seems to be doing now, after Trump assumed the presidency). In the 1980s, unprecedented high interest rates in the United States precipitated the Latin American debt crisis. In the aftermath of the 2008 crisis, unprecedented low interest rates led to a rush of money into developing countries, leading in turn to increases in their exchange rate and a loss of competitiveness of their export industries. The strains on their economies were palpable. Around the world, countries did what they could to restrain the flow of money into their countries—to stabilize their economies. These interventions included capital controls, and some countries sought the blessing of the IMF as it undertook unorthodox policies. The IMF reached a new "institutional" consensus in support of these policies.[18]

Risk, the Washington Consensus, Modern Economic Analysis, and Politics

The Washington Consensus position on capital market liberalization reflected an unquestioning belief in markets. Markets are the best way of managing risk, and liberalization allows them to do what they do best, the Washington argument went. Thus, advocates of liberalization believed that with liberalization, markets would be more stable. The historical evidence, as well as a growing body of theory, overwhelmingly refute this claim, and the 2008 crisis is simply one more example demonstrating that unfettered markets actually *create* risk, even if well-managed and well-regulated markets can help manage risk.

How then could so many have ignored the theory and evidence? The central message of *GAID* was that it was a combination of interests and ideology, each reinforcing the other. What has happened in the last fifteen years is consistent with this diagnosis. The responses to the global financial crisis were shaped by interests—the banks, long enamored of free-market ideology, easily put that aside as they clamored for a massive bailout of hundreds of billions of dollars. Interests and ideology resulted in not just the banks being saved, but also the bondholders and shareholders. When President Obama was asked why the United States had not followed what economic theory (and in some respects even U.S. law) suggested—following standard bankruptcy procedures, where depositors and institutions are protected, but shareholders and bondholders bear the costs before U.S. taxpayers—he responded with an appeal to ideology: that was the way of socialism. Of course, he was wrong: what the United States did was a violation of the basic rules of capitalism.[19]

Even though globalization was not the subject on the table, this episode, especially when combined with the failure to adequately help those losing their homes and jobs, has had a profound effect on attitudes toward government and globalization. For it reinforced the view that government and established elites could not be trusted and that the system was rigged, attitudes which opened up the way for demagogues like Trump preaching protectionism and inward-looking policies.

Macromanagement: The Hypocrisy Exposed by the Financial Crisis

The global financial crisis of 2008 not only undermined confidence in unfettered markets and established elites, it also exposed Western hypocrisy: in addressing the crisis, the United States and Europe pursued policies diametrically different to what they had imposed in East Asia and elsewhere—and the cast of characters even included some of the same individuals.[20] For instance, in the East Asia crisis (as described in *GAID*), the IMF and the U.S. Treasury insisted that the countries raise interest rates, cut back spending, and not bail out the banks. (In Indonesia, the IMF's poor management of the no-bailout policy caused a bank run that deepened the downturn in that country.)[21]

In the 2008 crisis, Europe and America instead brought interest rates down to zero rather than raise them to the exorbitant levels demanded of Korea and Indonesia. They vastly expanded government spending—causing unprecedented deficits. And they engaged in one of the most massive bailouts in the history of mankind—even though critics like me had pointed out that such bailouts were not necessary to resuscitate the economy.[22]

Even the diagnosis of the causes of the East Asia crisis by the West suggested hypocrisy: during the East Asia crisis, American lectures about transparency and good corporate governance flowed freely. Blame for the crisis was put on failures in these realms. Yet the 2008 crisis was caused by lack of transparency in the United States, including on the part of the very banks and bankers that had lectured them. The real culprit for the crisis was the Washington Consensus policies—especially the premature push for capital market liberalization. In the other dimensions which the Washington consensus had emphasized—low fiscal deficits, high national savings, and low inflation—East Asia received a grade of A+. Doing well in these areas was supposed to inoculate one against a crisis. It obviously didn't.

Not surprisingly, all of this has left a bitter aftertaste for many who experienced the hardship unnecessarily imposed on Asia. And the fact that the West could be hard on small and less powerful states in the West, like Greece and Portugal, demanding unremitting austerity of them, while equally unjustifiable, provided cold comfort to those in East Asia who had suffered a decade earlier. It only reinforced the view of duplicity: one set of rules for the rich and powerful, another for the rest.

The Aftermath of Crisis

Even by the time I wrote *GAID,* it was clear that the East Asian countries were well on the road to recovery. The critics who had castigated them, pointing to deep flaws in their economic and political systems, were proven wrong. The countries would not have been able to recover so quickly if that had been the case. While they experienced growth at rates somewhat lower than the torrid numbers that had characterized the heyday of the East Asian miracle, they were still impressive—beyond what most thought was even possible a half century earlier: Korea's economy in 2016 was some 84 percent larger than in 2000, Thailand's, some 87 percent, Indonesia's some 132 percent, and Malaysia's, 111 percent.

The crisis showed the dangers of capital and financial market liberalization, even in relatively well-managed economies: money could flow in, then rapidly flow out, leaving havoc in its wake.

Among the most important consequences of the IMF/U.S. Treasury mismanagement of the East Asia crisis was the buildup of massive reserves by developing countries and emerging markets, as I noted in the introduction. The crisis had shown the dangers of not having enough reserves. A country could lose its economic sovereignty—and have economic conditions imposed on it that, however they might help the Western banks who had helped create the crisis, were devastating for the population.[23]

The buildup of reserves weakened global aggregate demand—money that could have been spent was put aside into reserves—and even contributed to the weakness of the American economy. It made it easier for the United States to be debt-dependent. And the inflow of money (the flip side of the buildup of reserves) led to a stronger dollar, hurting manufacturing and contributing to the New Discontents described in chapter 1.

Development—Ethiopia: A Case Study

When I went to the World Bank, I had expected to focus on the development of poor countries, not a crisis in East Asia. Ethiopia was the first country I visited after becoming chief economist of the World Bank—and the last I visited before leaving my position. It set up a tradition that was subsequently followed by my successors.

The end of the Cold War changed the landscape in Africa. In Ethiopia, Meles Zenawi, leader of the Tigrayan People's Liberation Front, quickly grasped the political implications and in 1991 pushed his forces to reach an end to the seventeen-year conflict that they waged against the regime of despot Mengistu Haile Mariam, one of the bloodiest and most ruthless in the world. Less than five years later, the country was trying to go beyond reconstruction to create a dynamic economy based on rural development. But it ran into the ideological taskmasters at the IMF, who didn't like that the country was forging its way forward without obeying IMF ideology.

As I explain in *GAID,* when I visited the country, in early 1997, and again in 1998, I was impressed: they had a clear grasp of the economics of their situation, and in most of the key issues under dispute between the IMF and the government of Ethiopia, I thought Ethiopia was in the right. The IMF was sufficiently critical that it curtailed its program in Ethiopia; and normally, that's the kiss of death: other multilateral institutions won't lend to a country that doesn't have an IMF program in good standing. They worry that the money they give or lend the country will simply "go down the drain." But I thought otherwise, and persuaded the World Bank—in a major break with precedent—to triple its lending.

What happened subsequently showed that my confidence in Ethiopia was fully justified. Over the period from 2000 to 2016, Ethiopia was one of the fastest-growing countries in the world, growing at a rate of 9 percent annually,[24] better than most of the East Asian countries in their heyday. It studied carefully the development model of East Asia in which the government played a central role, so important that it was sometimes referred to as a "development state." It used industrial policies and, using those policies, developed some vibrant new export industries, such as shoes. Other countries, such as Rwanda, looked toward the success of East Asia and the development state, to get similar results. It appeared that the East Asian model—a very different model than the Washington Consensus model—actually worked even in a quite different context.[25]

Most other African countries didn't do quite so well, but with the abandonment, or at least weakening, of the Washington Consensus "structural adjustment" policies, Sub-Saharan Africa as a whole finally started to grow—an average of 4.9 percent from 2000 to 2016[26]—and the long period of deindustrialization under the Washington Consensus policies was halted. Still, many worry that with the decline in global manufacturing employment and the bulge in the population of Africa (expected to be 2.5 billion by 2050),[27] the export-led growth model will be insufficient to propel Africa out of poverty.

The Battles over Transition

The transition from communism to market economies in several countries turned out to be far more difficult and problematic than almost anyone thought, certainly at the beginning of that transition.

The key policy controversy was between Washington Consensus policies typically implemented through shock therapy—rapid change at any cost—and a more gradual approach which begins by building the foundations of a market economy, what I called the institutional infrastructure, including the legal framework.

At the time I wrote *GAID*, with a little more than a decade of data, the economies of transition provided another arena in which Washington Consensus policies seemed to be failing. The evidence strongly favored the gradualists, with their broader approach to economics. The shock therapists claimed that the jury was still out.

It has always been a question of the tortoise versus the hare: shock therapy might seem to do better in the short run, but that is not what really matters. What matters is the long run. The gradualists believed that the best way to build a market economy was by constructing it slowly and carefully. These investments, while costly in the short run and requiring patience, would pay off in the long run. Those favoring the more gradualist approach included those, like myself, who believed that the success of a market economy depended on having the right legal framework—for instance, good corporate governance laws to ensure that the managers don't steal the assets of the firm for their own benefit. Those calling for rapid transition thought that one could skip these "details." The shock therapists argued that one had to quickly destroy the vestiges of the past, and kick-start the market economy through rapid privatization. With clear owners, there would be incentives to create the necessary institutional infrastructure. On the contrary, I worried that those who were engaged in stealing would have every incentive to ensure that they could continue stealing; those who were making their money by monopoly power would fight against good competition laws.

Now, a quarter of a century after the beginning of the transition, the answer is clear: shock therapy and the Washington Consensus policies were an even greater failure than they appeared to be at the time that *GAID* was published, and gradualism even more of a success, as seen in countries such as China and Vietnam.[28]

China and Vietnam continue their remarkable growth—China averaging more than 10 percent growth during the first thirty years of its transition, moving almost 800 million people out of poverty. Vietnam has averaged growth of 6.9 percent since 1990.[29] Meanwhile, the shallow roots of the economies whose transition was based on shock therapy were exposed. Many of those that seemed to be doing well did so because of the real estate sector—there was no real economy underneath—and with the 2008 crisis showing real estate bubbles for what they were, those economies collapsed. Latvia, at one time heralded as a success story for shock therapy, illustrates: it has had an average growth rate of 1 percent over the last quarter century (1991–2016). Russia has deindustrialized, with its fortunes depending on movements in resource prices, especially oil. With the collapse of oil prices in 2014, Russia went into recession.

As I note in *GAID*, communism was an inefficient way of organizing production. Moving from an inefficient system to an efficient dynamic market system should have led unambiguously to higher incomes. The countries that fell behind during the reign of communism should have been able to catch up—the transition should thus have been marked by extremely high growth rates. Of course, there might be some bumps along the way—like the transition recessions seen in so many countries immediately following the fall of the Berlin Wall—but after a quarter century, those bumps should have been a thing of the past. On the twenty-fifth anniversary of the fall of the wall, Branko Milanović, with whom I had worked closely at the World Bank, conducted a reckoning: Seven countries, with a combined population of 80 million—a fifth of all transition countries—have yet to reach the level of real income that they had in 1990. "Basically, they are countries with at least three to four wasted generations. At current rates of growth, it might take them some 50 to 60 years—longer than they were under Communism!—to get back to the income levels they had at the fall of Communism."[30] Forty percent live in countries whose GDP per capita under capitalism continues to fall further behind that of the OECD. This includes, most importantly, Russia. Only a third live in countries that are actually catching up. These include countries that have the good fortune of having an abundance of natural resources (Azerbaijan and Kazakhstan), some that are undemocratic (Belarus), and strong reformers.

The one large country that did well by most accounts, Poland, grew at an average annual rate of 3.2 percent over the period 1989 to 2016.[31] The shock therapists and gradualists both claim its victory as theirs. Leszek Balcerowicz, an early "reformer" in Poland, imposed macroshock therapy—tight monetary and fiscal policies that pushed Poland into deep recession, with a decline in GDP of close to 14 percent from 1989 to 1991. But then Gregory Kolodko, as the deputy prime minister and finance minister, helped structure a gradual privatization, a more gradual transition of the economy toward a market economy. To me, it is clear that Poland's success was due to

Kolodko's gradualism. Poland would have been even more successful had it not been forced to go through the painful macroshock therapy.

Beyond the fact that in almost none of the countries treated with shock therapy was there the burst of growth that so many had anticipated at the beginning of transition, there were three big disappointments, two of which are foreshadowed in *GAID*. The first was an increase in inequality: the way the IMF and the U.S. Treasury managed the transition in Russia and elsewhere helped create the oligarchs. In a short span of time, Russia, Georgia, Estonia, Latvia, and Lithuania managed to increase the Gini coefficient by an astonishing 10 points (by most accounts, twice the increase experienced in the United States since Reagan, an era of almost unprecedented growth of inequality in America).

Second, there was hope that there would be a political transition to democracy as well as an economic transition. In many ways, the former was more important than the latter. Successful democratization would inevitably lead to a move to the market. But I worried that an unsuccessful economic transition would undermine support for democracy. In particular, I worried that the way the IMF, the World Bank, and the U.S. Treasury pushed privatization and the transition more generally in Russia would undermine democratic development there, and that is indeed what happened. As Russian interference in the U.S. election of 2016 showed, an authoritarian Russia is still a global threat to democracy. There is no way of being sure whether a more successful economic transition would have paved the way for a more democratic Russia; but clearly, the failures of economic transition described in *GAID* played some role in the disappointing political evolution of the country.

Similarly, Hungary, after growing at a meager 1.2 percent annual rate from 1991 to 2009, elected Viktor Orbán as prime minister in 2010—and he quickly showed his authoritarian tendencies, working, for instance, to constrain the press. All the EU states are supposed to be committed to democracy: he challenged the rules and the willingness of the others to enforce them.[32]

And then there was the big and unanticipated disappointment: I had expected that the countries in transition that joined the EU would do better in both economic and political transition than they have. Their long-term growth has been a disappointment, their commitment to democracy with transparent and accountable institutions often even more so. The EU helped provide the institutional infrastructure that was necessary for success on both fronts. On both accounts, those countries did better than those who were not so lucky as to get into the EU. Being near the EU's powerhouse, Germany, helps. German firms often located factories in Poland and the Czech Republic to take advantage of their much lower wages, especially given their relatively high levels of education and skills.

In short, neither the political nor the economic transition from Communism to the market economy and democracy has gone smoothly. Some of the forebodings I had as I wrote *GAID* have materialized. In the end, of course, the countries themselves must bear responsibility for what happens there. Still, the way the international community "helped"—including the IMF, the World Bank, and the U.S. government—turned out to be unhelpful.

THE BATTLE OVER GLOBAL GOVERNANCE

A central message of *GAID* is the importance of governance—who makes the decisions matters. Globalization has long been governed by the developed countries for their interest—and most especially for the financial and corporate interests within those countries. In the years since the publication of *GAID*, dissatisfaction with global governance has spread. The disparity between the economic realities of the twenty-first century and governance structures created in 1944 for the World Bank and the IMF have become increasingly evident, even more so after 2008. During the East Asia crisis, the U.S. secretary of the Treasury said, when the countries complained about the conditions imposed upon them, that he who pays the piper calls the tune. With the onset of the 2008 crisis, the money was in Asia. Given that, the Asian countries now felt that it was their turn to call the tune. The old governance structure was increasingly unacceptable.

And yet, since *GAID*, progress has been strikingly slow. The G-20, the group of twenty of the major countries, representing some two thirds of the world's population and 80 percent of global GDP, has replaced the G-7,[33] the small group of seven advanced countries that were trying to "run" the global economy. That's an improvement; but still, the twenty countries of the G-20 were not chosen according to any set of global principles. They are unrepresentative and lack legitimacy. Small countries have almost no voice. Africa, a continent with 1.2 billion people in 2016, is massively underrepresented.[34] Indeed, in terms of governance, in these respects, even the IMF is better.

Financing for Development and Global Taxation

The UN has recognized some of these limitations. In March 2002, it organized a global meeting on finance for development at Monterrey, Mexico. Its view, correct in my judgment, was that finance for development was too important to be left to finance ministers, who are simply too linked to their own financial markets.

What happened in the third Finance for Development meeting, held in Addis Ababa in July 2015, illustrates the persistent problems in global governance. The developing countries had long since given up on the promises of financial assistance (aid) from the developed countries.[35] They knew they had to develop their own sources of finance. Under the urging of the advanced countries, they opened up their markets to multinationals from the advanced countries. Now, the concern was the ability of those companies to avoid taxation—they came to the developing countries demanding and using infrastructure and other public services, but they refused to pay their fair share of taxes. The multinationals' clever lawyers used the international system of taxation to avoid paying taxes both in the developed and the developing countries. The companies had no compunction about being free riders.

There was a real need for reform to the tax regime for multinational corporations. As chairman of the Council of Economic Advisers in the 1990s, I had argued for this reform, but matters have only grown worse. Apple became emblematic, paying a tax in the United States that was far, far below the 35 percent of its income that is the official tax rate by taking advantage of loopholes in the United States tax code and routing much of its profits through Irish subsidiaries. So arrogant was its CEO that he said that he would pay taxes in the United States if the United States lowered the tax rate to (what he judged to be) a reasonable level:[36] some read this to mean "only if."

At Addis Ababa, the debate was over the venue for discussions on global tax reform—a matter of global governance. The United States, home of some of the biggest and best tax avoiders and evaders, wanted it to be the OECD, the "club" of the advanced countries—a venue in which it had enormous influence. The developing world, led by India, said that the appropriate forum was the UN, where all countries have a voice. Power matters: the United States got its way.[37]

United States Blocks Vital Reforms in the Global Economic Architecture
The United States has blocked other important reforms in the global economic architecture—and the fact that it has the power to do so reflects deficiencies in global governance.[38] These much-needed reforms include the following:

- The replacement of the G-20 with a more representative and legitimate Global Economic Coordination Council (GECC). The G-20 was, as I noted, far more globally representative than the G-7, which included small countries like Canada, but excluded large countries like China and India. Still, the G-20 is missing representation from the poorer countries, and even among the richer countries, there is a certain randomness—it was just the list of people President George W. Bush invited to the initial meeting.

  The G-20 played an important role in designing the response to the global financial crisis of 2008–9. It was important for every country to stimulate its economy. As each expanded its economy, others benefited from the resulting increase in trade. But since then, the G-20 has been relatively ineffective in garnering the kinds of cooperation needed to make the global economy work well.

  A GECC reflects the obvious need for more global economic cooperation in our highly integrated global economy. At the UN, there are too many voices—we need a smaller group than 193 members to move the conversation forward. The IMF is distorted: it has traditionally been an institution in which creditor interests and views are disproportionately represented; and with the United States being the only country with the veto power, its perspectives are inevitably strongly influenced by the United States. A GECC can be designed to provide a forum with greater legitimacy and representativeness to address the world's economic problems. The hope is that common understandings could be developed, and in the areas where global cooperation is most needed, unified actions could be taken.

- The establishment of a framework for debt restructuring for countries that have borrowed more than they can repay. While the need for such a framework had long been evident, following the Argentina crisis of 2001–2, U.S. court decisions undermining long-standing principles of international law provided urgency to the matter. Among the principles attacked was that of "sovereign immunity"—the idea that countries could not, in general, be sued without their consent. The U.S. court went so far as to make debt restructuring almost impossible. In 2015 the UN overwhelmingly adopted a set of principles for debt restructuring—by a vote of 136 to 6, with 41 abstentions. The strongest opponent was the United States, where the government seemed beholden to a few hedge funds that had bought Argentinean bonds *after* Argentina defaulted, paying cents on the dollar, and were now trying to collect *as if* they had been the ones who originally lent to Argentina. (Worse, they then took advantage of a quirk in the law to try to get interest on what they had not been paid at rates far, far in excess of the market rate.) In short, the U.S. government sided with those trying to exploit the suffering of countries in crises.[39]

Of course, when global growth is strong and stable, few countries face the extreme situation in which they cannot pay back what they owe. The 2008 global financial crisis racheted up the importance of this issue further, as several countries looked like they would not be able to make their debt commitments. (There were debt restructurings for Cyprus, Greece, and the Seychelles.)

- The establishment of a global reserve system to replace the U.S. dollar as the de facto global reserve currency. We have already described the inequities in the dollar-based system—involving large transfers of money from developing countries and emerging markets to the United States—and how the buildup of reserves depresses global demand, resulting in an overall poorer performance for the global economy. The dollar-based system can also contribute to global instability. Yet the American government refuses to entertain serious discussion of reforming the global reserve system in any venue.[40]

Governance of the IMF and the World Bank

Global financial markets have grown enormously since *GAID* was published,[41] and for the World Bank and the IMF to continue to play the critical role they played in the past, they must have more resources. When the 2008–9 crisis hit, the IMF succeeded in getting substantial additional funding. The World Bank was slow to act, and now, as the deficiencies in its resources become increasingly evident, it appears impossible to get enough funds. The problem is partly that the U.S. Congress won't provide the funds (and, with the Trump presidency, it is not likely to even be asked for them). But the obvious source of money is Asia and the Middle East. It is inevitable that there will be a linkage between funds and governance: naturally, these countries want more of a voice if they give more money. But the United States and other advanced countries are unwilling to allow this. The United States would rather see these institutions lose their influence than lose its own influence within these institutions.

The United States' priority in maintaining influence is most evident in the debate over who should head the Bretton Woods institutions. One of the reforms that the G-20 called for was that the head of the World Bank and that of the IMF be appointed on the basis of merit only—hardly a remarkable recommendation in this day and age. However, it was a recommendation that flew in the face of the narrow U.S. interest that the Bank president be someone that the American president could unduly influence. Historically—since the beginning of the IMF and the World Bank—the United States has always appointed the head of the World Bank and Europe that of the IMF. Disappointingly, the United States decided to pay no attention to the new G-20 reform— even under Obama. Obama first planned to appoint the former U.S. secretary of the Treasury and head of the National Economic Council who played such a big role in some of the stories of *GAID* and whose great achievement as secretary of the Treasury was the bill ensuring that derivatives (those risky products that contributed so much to the global financial crisis) would not be regulated. Reportedly, many of the other countries around the world made it clear that they would have none of that—they were willing to show some, but limited, deference toward the United States. Hurriedly, the Obama administration found an alternative, Dr. Jim Yong Kim, whose background was in health, not economics or finance. The power of the United States was again shown: Dr. Kim got the nod over two extraordinarily well-qualified candidates from the developing world.

CHANGES IN OLD INSTITUTIONS

GAID criticized the central global institutions managing globalization in the hope of eliciting change. There have been marked changes—more in some areas that I could have conceived of, less in others than I had anticipated. There is a common thread: when the international institutions seem willing to strike out on their own, becoming less dependent on the United States, there is some success; where an institution cannot or will not, there is disappointment.

The IMF

A theme of *GAID* is that the IMF paid too little attention to the effects of its programs on inequality in general and the poor in particular—not withstanding its rhetoric. But beginning with the stewardship of Dominique Strauss-Kahn, and continuing under his successor Christine Lagarde, things have changed. When Strauss-Kahn's research staff presented findings showing that inequality can be bad for economic performance, he not only endorsed them, but put this focus at the center of the IMF's programs. He defended this action, saying that IMF's mandate was promoting growth and stability—and inequality was inimical to both.

Since then, the IMF has been a tireless crusader—attacking not just inequality in general, but particular manifestations of it, such as gender inequalities. It has helped convince people all over the world of the central message of my book *The Price of Inequality*: our society pays a high economic, social, and political price for the high level of inequality—in all of its dimensions—that we are experiencing today.

The IMF has undergone other changes as well. Following the crisis, the IMF actively asked where its thinking had gone wrong. Two conferences at the IMF highlighted the change in thinking.[42] While in *GAID* I discussed the excessive focus on inflation, in the years after *GAID* was published, matters became worse as central bankers around the world increasingly adopted an "inflation target." However, inflation hadn't been the central problem of most countries for years, in some places for a decade and a half or more. The IMF has begun to recognize that too much attention was focused on inflation, too little on financial stability.

The Financial Stability Board

In the aftermath of the East Asia crisis, it was recognized that there was a need for better regulation. Indeed, as I note in *GAID*, some of the global regulations almost surely contributed to that crisis. Banks were, in effect, encouraged to lend short-term—making it easier for money to flow in and out of countries. The global rules (called Basel I) were designed to protect the safety and soundness of individual banks in the developed world—with little or no attention to their systemic consequences, especially in developing countries.

The response was to create what was called the Financial Stability Forum (FSF)—and that was what it was; a forum, a place for the central bankers to talk. Since the bankers didn't have a "*systemic* mindset," however, what emerged was, in some ways, even worse than Basel I. The new framework asked banks to self-regulate—and that meant not only having them focus on their *own* risk (and not on systemic risk), but also allowing them to use their own models to make judgments. Almost by definition, self-regulation is an oxymoron. Our regulators—from the "Maestro" himself, Alan Greenspan, on down—didn't seem to realize the contradiction. Each individual bank, in assessing its actions, does not fully take into account its effects on the economic system. Greenspan and other regulators of that era didn't even seem to understand why we have regulations—to prevent banks from imposing costs on *others,* which occurs when taxpayers have to bail out the bank or when a systemic bank failure such as that of 2008 leads to an economic meltdown, with millions losing their jobs and homes.[43] As I have noted, these effects are called externalities, and whenever there are important externalities, markets do not result in efficient outcomes.[44] I had expected the system of self-regulation to fail, and it did—though I did not fully anticipate the magnitude of the failure.[45]

It goes without saying that the Financial Stability Forum did not save the world from the global financial crisis. One of the responses was to *change the name* of the Financial Stability Forum to the Financial Stability Board. I was understandably skeptical that this change would make any real difference. As it turned out, however, the name change was accompanied by a broadening of its mandate, and together with the wake-up call of the 2008 crisis, the Financial Stability Board has advanced a rethinking of the factors that contribute to systemic fragility and instability.[46]

The 2008 crisis made clear that in a globally connected system, weaknesses in any part could have global consequences. The global community has been working to establish standards, such as minimal capital requirements, to make crises less likely, and make it less likely that taxpayers are left footing the bill for banks' mistakes. Still, the banks, especially in the United States, are pushing back. They have been arguing for the repeal of the Dodd-Frank Act, the financial reform bill passed in 2010, even though that act didn't go far enough to ensure that another large crisis would not occur. The banks have done everything they can to undermine Dodd-Frank, to impede its implementation, and to get key provisions repealed. With Trump as president, they have found an ally.[47]

The World Bank

The IMF has changed dramatically, but so have other international institutions. The World Bank entered hard times after James Wolfensohn, who was the president from 1995 to 2005, during the period I served as chief economist, left the bank. His successor was Paul Wolfowitz, who was previously the American deputy defense secretary and is often credited as being the "intellectual godfather" of the Iraq War and the mistaken neoconservative theories that contributed to it.

The way that President Bush reportedly "solved" the problem of how to get Wolfowitz out of the administration was to foist him on the rest of the world. Wolfowitz tried to make the World Bank serve America's foreign policy interests—and did so perhaps more transparently than had been done before. Three years after his appointment, in the midst of massive dissatisfaction from both staff and member countries, he was forced to resign over a corruption scandal. The Bank never (in my judgment) fully recovered the influence and acceptance it had under

Wolfensohn, and the discrediting of the Washington Consensus discredited much of its policy advice.

WTO and the Development Round

The global institution which has perhaps seen the greatest rise and fall is the World Trade Organization. The original ideas for the construction of a post–World War II economic order had three institutions at the apex—the World Bank, the IMF, and a third to regulate trade (referred to at the time as the International Trade Organization). Conservatives in the United States, worried about the loss of national sovereignty, blocked the formation of the trade institution for decades—until it was reborn in a round of negotiations that began in Montevideo, Uruguay, in 1986. These negotiations culminated in the creation of the World Trade Organization in 1995, with a clear judicial system to adjudicate disputes over noncompliance by any one of the signatories. A major deficiency, however, was the limited punishment for noncompliance, which was restricted simply to the right to impose retaliatory tariffs. That discipline has proven effective when one large country sues another, but when a small state—say an island microstate in the Caribbean—sues the United States and wins, there is no effective redress. For example, retaliating by imposing a tariff, say, on the importation of food from the United States only leads to an increase in the cost of living. The injured country is hurt more than the United States.

The provisions of the Uruguay Round were unbalanced. The developed countries got most of what they wanted. And while one of the great achievements of the Round was bringing the developing countries and emerging markets into the fold, these countries were told to be patient: what they wanted—for instance, a reduction of the West's distortionary agricultural policies, which lowered the prices of the goods they produced—could only be delivered gradually over time.

And so, the developing countries imposed as a condition for starting a new round of trade negotiations that any such round be a *development round,* centering on instituting rules that would most promote development.[48] Many of the rules, tariffs, and regulations, inherited from the colonial era, were designed to ensure that the former colonies remain focused on producing raw materials which would then be processed in the developed countries. It should be no surprise that those in the developing world viewed these provisions as unconscionable.

The moment of global unity after September 11, 2001 allowed for the initiation of the new "Development Round," but that moment of unity didn't last long. The developed countries lost sight of the bigger picture, of the inequities that were built into the Uruguay Round, and the promises made to get the Development Round started were quickly broken. Rapid turnover of governments made this especially easy. Meetings in Cancún (2003) and Hong Kong (2005) led to little progress. Finally, in December 2015, the WTO gave up on the Development Round. By then, it was clear that the United States would not make the concessions necessary to create a fairer globalization. The United States would not give up on its cotton subsidies—even though they were declared noncompliant with the WTO under previous trade agreements. Indeed, when Brazil brought a case against the United States and won (and won again, and again, as America tried to circumvent the WTO rulings), the United States simply paid off Brazil. It compensated Brazil for the damage it did to the country, but kept the cotton subsidies in place, harming millions and millions of poor farmers in India and Sub-Saharan Africa.

The United States and Europe have abandoned the global multilateral process, hoping that in bilateral or regional agreements they can throw their weight around more effectively and get agreements more in their favor. China, India, and Brazil have proven to be effective negotiators, and the hope was that with them out of the room, the United States and Europe would set "standards" which served their interests—forcing in the end the large emerging countries to adhere. Trump, while not fully realizing what he is doing, is pushing this approach even further, focusing on bilateral trade agreements and bargaining. The likelihood is that this approach will lead to a global trading regime that is even more biased than the current one—biased in favor of corporate interests in the developed countries. If that happens, the discontent with globalization, both in the developed and developing world, will only grow.

Still, while the WTO won't be at the center of new trade agreements—indeed, the prospect of significant global agreements in the immediate future is low—it is playing a truly critical role. It is partly, perhaps even largely, because of the WTO that Trump has been tamed:

It is too costly for America to act unilaterally. As this book goes to press, he hasn't imposed the across-the-board tariffs, for instance on China and Mexico, that he promised. The "concessions" made in trade negotiations so far have been truly minor—China has, for instance, opened its market to American beef. No one expects these changes to have any significant effect on the U.S. trade deficit with China.[49]

CREATING NEW INSTITUTIONS

With the world changing so rapidly, it was natural that new institutions be created to respond to the evolution. The importance of global warming has only been recognized for the last quarter century. This was a global problem, and had to be dealt with globally; but it was a problem that was not on the agenda when the international institutions like the IMF and the World Bank were created. The United Nations took on the responsibility for negotiating a shared response. The agreement made in Paris in December 2015 was a major step forward—smaller than one would have liked and too small, on its own, to prevent a dangerous increase in temperature—but still, a real commitment to reduce the emissions of greenhouse gases. As I noted in the introduction, the strength of that agreement was demonstrated by the resolve of the rest of the world—and many within the United States—to continue with their commitments in reducing greenhouse gas emissions, even as Trump announced the United States would be leaving the accord in 2020. The World Bank and a special financial fund within the Bank, the Global Environment Fund (GEF), are helping developing countries reduce their emissions. With the government of Donald Trump still denying the reality of climate change and withdrawing from the Paris Agreement (joining only two countries around the world, Nicaragua and Syria, who are not part of the agreement), there will have to be an effective enforcement system. No country can be allowed to put the entire planet in jeopardy. The countries of the world will have to impose a high carbon tax on cross-border trade from countries, like America, that do not reduce their emissions. Such a tax simultaneously "corrects" for an important global externality (by making the United States pay for the costs that it imposes on the entire world) and provides an incentive for the United

States to do something about climate change, for instance, to impose a tax on its carbon emissions.[50]

The need for additional funds to help developing countries respond to the challenge of global warming was one of the motivations for the creation of two new global financial institutions described later, but there were others. The existing institutions (in particular the World Bank and some of the regional development banks) simply hadn't responded as quickly as they should have to the changing world. The huge increases in infrastructure needs in the developing world and emerging markets were beyond what these institutions could have provided; they needed an increase in their capital—but the sentiment among some Republicans in the United States made that impossible.[51] I described earlier the deficiencies in governance of these institutions—there was a need to make it more reflective of the economic realities of the twenty-first century; and though the G-20 recognized this, again, the U.S. Republicans made it clear that changes in governance would be difficult. And with these impediments, adapting the institutions to the fast-changing nature of global financial markets and responding to the deficiencies in these markets *was* difficult.

There was a potential large supply of long-term funds for investment—pension funds and sovereign wealth funds (oil-rich countries had accumulated trillions of dollars in savings; Norway, with a population of 5 million, had almost a trillion dollars alone). There were at the same time huge needs for long-term investment. But standing between the two were short-term financial markets, which paid little attention even to the most pressing global problems, like global warming.

Thus, early into the second decade of this century, the need for new development banks was apparent. And it made sense for the global South—the developing countries—to do this on their own. They had already shown that they could: One of their longstanding development banks, Corporación Andina de Fomento (CAF), or Banco de Desarrollo de América Latina; the Andean Development Corporation—Development Bank of Latin America), has long been flourishing. It has been so successful that it has expanded from its original mission of serving the Andean region (Colombia, Venezuela, Ecuador, Peru, and Chile) to serving the entire Latin American region.

The New Development Bank

With the limitations in the established development banks in mind, and with the gap in "climate finance" especially deep, Meles Zenawi, prime minister of Ethiopia, approached me and my successor as chief economist of the World Bank, Nicholas Stern, in January 2011, to see if we could help in the creation of a new development bank. Though the developed countries had promised help in financing spending to reduce emissions and adapt to climate change, the effects of which were expected to be particularly devastating in Africa, there was a big disparity between promise and delivery, just as there had been in their earlier promise to devote 0.7 percent of their gross national income to helping poor countries.

Five key emerging market countries—Brazil, Russia, India, China, and South Africa—started meeting annually in 2009. The group, called BRICS, even then had a GDP as large as that of the advanced countries at the time of the founding of the Bretton Woods institutions (the IMF and the World Bank). They embrace more than 40 percent of the world's population and almost a quarter of global GDP. It made sense for them to found their own development bank. The idea that a new development bank could be a common project, solidifying their cooperation, quickly caught on, and at the sixth BRICS summit, in Fortaleza, Brazil, in July 2014, the agreement to create the bank was signed. The BRICS Bank, more formally called the New Development Bank, has broader mandates (focusing especially on climate change), better governance, and new instruments, more suited to twenty-first-century financial markets than the old multilateral development institutions.[52]

The Asian Infrastructure Investment Bank

Perhaps the most dramatic development was the founding in 2016 of the Asian Infrastructure Investment Bank (AIIB) under the leadership of China. As of May 2017, AIIB had fifty-seven members and twenty prospective members, and was expanding. The Americans strongly (and foolishly) opposed the founding of the AIIB, worried about the increased influence that it might give China—especially with the lack of willingness of the United States to recapitalize the World Bank so that it could keep growing in tandem with the needs of the developing countries and emerging markets. One lesson of geopolitics is simple: don't oppose something that is inevitable, and don't make a big deal of something that you are going to lose, unless a matter of principle is at stake. Here, the principles were on the other side: surely the countries in Asia should decide for themselves. And the United States had nothing to offer in return. It was reminiscent of what happened during the East Asia crisis when the U.S. Treasury opposed Japan's generous offer to help the crisis countries by providing the funds for the creation of an Asian Monetary Fund.

In both cases, America was so worried about the possible diminution of its own influence that it was willing to let the countries suffer rather than get help from elsewhere. It was selfish and shortsighted. In the case of the AIIB, even the United States' longstanding ally, the United Kingdom, broke ranks. The result, in the end, was what the Obama administration feared—the marginalization of American diplomacy. The bank benefits from China's resources. In 2016, the first full year of its operation, it made $1.73 billion in loans.[53]

New Trading Arrangements

Trump has made it clear that, if he has his way, he will move away from the multilateral system to a bilateral one. He's right that in these bilateral negotiations, the United States may have more power. But he's wrong that such a system is better from a global perspective, or even an American one. As I explained earlier, what matters is the multilateral trade deficit. Bilateral deficits—for example, the deficit between China and America—do not matter. Money was created to avoid the necessity of barter—to avoid the necessity of having trade between any two countries (or people) being balanced.

Moreover, in a globalized world, bilateral agreements can get horribly complex. For example, is a good still Mexican if a fraction of it is made in Asia? What is the critical fraction? And what happens if part of what comes from Asia is itself made in Mexico? Or in the United States? Such agreements distort the global economy and lead to a lowering of standards of living.

As America threatens to withdraw into itself in its protectionism, China is already stepping into the void. Not only is it the convener and largest contributor to the AIIB, it is, for instance, also successfully pushing the Regional Comprehensive Economic Partnership as an alternative to the Trans-Pacific Partnership (TPP),[54] from which China was excluded. China won't put the same emphasis on human rights, labor rights, or perhaps even the environment as Democratic administrations have in the United States; nor will it push the interests of Big Pharma or attempt to circumscribe regulation. It's more likely to stick to its view that trade agreements should be about trade, and countries should be allowed in other areas to do as they please.

But with China the largest economy (in terms of purchasing power parity), the largest saver, the largest trading economy, and the largest manufacturing economy, it is inevitable that the world will move to a more multipolar system, and that China will have a large voice in the global system of the future. No single country will be writing the rules. No single country will be dominant.

Elsewhere, the countries of Latin America are also likely to be advancing new agreements and strengthening old ones, especially with Trump openly expressing such bigotry and hostility toward America's neighbors to the South. There are already moves afoot to strengthen the Pacific Alliance, a trade bloc that brings together Chile, Colombia, Mexico, and Peru. With the United States absent, a new Free Trade Agreement of the Americas might actually occur.

The irony is that Trump's simplistic, shortsighted protectionism, with its focus on bilateral agreements, will have just the opposite of its intended effect. As he tries to pursue an "America First" policy, America's influence in the world—including the world of trade—will only wane. And he will fail in his seemingly[55] most immediate objective, reducing the trade deficit and improving the plight of those in U.S. manufacturing. As I explain in chapter 3, the multilateral trade deficit is set to increase under his policies, and jobs in manufacturing exports to decrease.

GLOBALIZATION IN THE AFTERMATH OF TRUMP

Even as I finished *GAID* at the very beginning of this century, it was clear that globalization would change, and so too would the way globalization is managed and governed. There are five underlying drivers of this change: (a) the demographic shift, with Africa having, by 2050, 26 percent of the world's population;[56] (b) the power shift, with the share of global GDP in the advanced countries shrinking markedly, as I have already noted;[57] (c) the structural transformation of the economy, specifically the move from manufacturing to a service sector economy that has already occurred in most advanced countries and will be part of the future in the rest of the world in coming decades; (d) the change, especially in the manufacturing sector, but in other sectors as well, to a "winner take all" model, where the winner (with globalization) is more likely than not to be in one of the rich advanced countries; (e) ideological shifts and divides—in particular, the weakening of a common belief in the virtues of a rules-based global system, and the growth of nationalism and nativism.

These changes are, of course interrelated: the growth of nationalism and nativism in America can be directly related to the weakening of U.S. global economic power and the economic well-being of large fractions of its population, itself a consequence of the structural transformation in the United States, the decline in manufacturing (as we saw in chapter 1).

In this final section, I want to trace out the major implications, both direct and indirect, of these changes in globalization of the future.

Shifting Power

America and Europe have to cede power to the fast-growing emerging markets. I had hoped that the United States would do it more gracefully and constructively than it had under Clinton; but Obama was little, if any, better. (Their actions were, of course far better than the imperial attempts to extend U.S. power through the threat of military might that marked Bush and the neocons.)[58] I had not expected the "America First" policy, the flight to the past, of Trump—though I worried that if the extremes of inequality, related in part to the mismanagement of globalization, were not addressed, America would be prey to a Trump-like demagogue. But Trump's arrival on the scene could not have come at a worse time. For even before the 2016 election, America was on the defensive, fruitlessly pushing back against

China's efforts at expanding its influence by trying to persuade others not to join AIIB and establishing its own corporate-driven trade agreement across the Pacific that excluded the major player, China, an effort that was one of the first acts to be scuttled by Trump.

Post-Trump Globalization

Whatever happens during the Trump administration, globalization after Trump will be different. America has lost its position of leadership as well as its status as a source of aspiration and inspiration: if the failures of Bush showed the limits of "hard" (military) power, Trump has eviscerated America's soft power—its influence arising out of admiration or respect, though sometimes out of fear of its economic power.

Trump was brazen in his call for American selfishness. His stand on protectionism made it clear: if the United States didn't get what it wanted, it would (to use that old metaphor) take its marbles and go home. But to ensure that it got the good deal—the America First deal—that Trump demanded, he would not bargain with the developing countries and emerging countries as a group, but one by one, bilaterally, in which case it was clear where the balance of power lay, especially in the case of the poorer countries. And yet, as our earlier discussion made clear, what the United States most cared about, its overall trade deficit, would be unaffected by these power plays. The trade deficit, determined by the country's macroeconomics, including its budget deficit, was set to get worse.

Still, America had held itself up as a model of good governance; but here was a president who would announce that there was no such thing as a conflict of interest within the presidency. The conflicts of interest in his plutocratic cabinet were obvious—but the country did nothing about them.

Around the world, Trump has served as a source of humor and media entertainment. In Italy, I hear, "Trump has made Berlusconi look good." In Africa, "Trump has made even our dictators look good." Leadership matters. We would not have the rules-based global system that we have, that for the most part has worked so well to maintain peace and prosperity, were it not for American leadership. But for any country to exercise that leadership, it has to be seen as not just serving its own interests, but also as having a vision that sees the benefits of cooperation, without the use or threat of force.

An International Rule of Law

America's role in the world will have changed as a result of Trump: the damage done will be long-lasting. The United States will no longer be seen as the trusted partner that it has been. But there are long-term consequences for the world too. Earlier, I described how important the rule of law was for any economy—and how important a rule of law was for the global economy. Trump has announced that he would not even honor past deals—he would ignore WTO rulings. The United States publicly announced that it was, in effect, walking away from the rule of law, so important for the functioning of society, but especially for the protection of the weak. It was going to use its military and economic power to get what it wanted. What good was a rules-based international system—that America was pivotal in creating—if the strongest country announces: by the way, the rules are for you, but not for us. If and only if the rules are working for us will we obey them. Whether his "bark is worse than his bite" is not yet clear: as this book goes to press, in some areas, he has been as bad as he promised he would be in his campaign for the presidency, or worse, while in others he has backed off from some of his extreme positions.

Borders Matter

Trump too has reminded us that, in a highly interdependent world, without global government, borders still matter. America (or any other country) can elect an aberrant leader, and there are many things short of war that one country can do to another. The more the interdependence, the more the harm that can be inflicted. And governments can be led by *irrational* leaders who can cause the country itself to be hurt by the policies undertaken.

As I noted earlier in this book, the world has been proceeding with economic globalization as if borders didn't matter. Global supply chains were constructed, with goods moving back and forth across borders. Countries were told not to worry about energy and food security, the ability to produce these essentials within one's borders; one shouldn't strive for that. That's inefficient. It ignores the principles of comparative advantage. But that critique of policies aimed at energy or food security ignored risk, as countries are now learning.

But Perhaps Trump Matters Less

We should not, however, ascribe too much importance to Trump. The world was headed for multipolarization, and Trump may have only accelerated the process. It is likely that the developing countries and emerging markets will do better in this multipolar globalization than they did in the past, as some of the inequities are reduced. Still, the advanced countries will be slow to reduce the agricultural subsidies which hurt the poorest in the developing countries, and they may figure out ways of extending the life of some of their struggling manufacturing sectors.

So too, everyone has always recognized that borders matter, and that in a moment of crisis or conflict, the United States will do as it pleases, little constrained by the agreements it signed. Still, it is also true that the rules matter, as we have seen during Trump's time in office. The WTO rules almost surely circumscribed him from implementing the extremist protectionist policies he advocated during the campaign.

A New Geography

While the United States announced an inward-looking, America First strategy, China was creating a "new silk road initiative," also called "One Belt, One Road," encompassing some sixty countries in Asia, linking them to China. It is as grandiose in scale as the Great Wall of China, an attempt this time not to protect it from "outsiders," but to tie the rest of the world to China. It seeks to overcome economic geography with man-made infrastructure that will lower the economic distance of all to China. Meanwhile, the construction projects are providing an economic boon to the previously moribund regions—a Marshall plan on steroids. China has understood what Western economists have been saying for decades: a world with zero percent interest rates is ripe for a massive infrastructure program. China will benefit, both from the increased influence, already palpable, and the increased demand for its steel and cement, which otherwise would be in excess supply. Rather than selling these products in the United States at low prices, which elicits condemnations of dumping, it sells or gives them to its neighbors, who extend profuse thanks.

The Attractiveness of China's Rhetoric

In much of the world, China's rhetoric resounds far better than either Trump's America First or the "conditionality" which preceded it, in which we sign trade agreements with those who give in to our corporate interests, and we help very poor countries that follow the precepts of good government and market economics that we dictate through the IMF and the World Bank. Knowing the resentment that these stances had engendered, at the first assemblage of the leaders of twenty-nine of the countries on May 14, 2016, China's President Xi talked about a world based on friendship and partnership, in contrast to the divisive alliances (like NATO). He repeated China's call for each country to "respect each other's sovereignty, dignity and territorial integrity, each other's development paths and social systems, and each other's core interests and major concerns."[59]

How Would a China-Led Globalization Differ?

In diplomatic terms, these words take on certain meanings. China and developing countries have been highly critical of the conditionality that has accompanied Western assistance, with China being especially sensitive to those concerning human rights. Echoing back to the Cold War, China suggests that the massive inequalities built into the American economic system represents an abuse of human rights, and it believes that it is hypocritical for the United States to constantly criticize China's human rights violations when there is such massive racial discrimination in America.

This then is one of the critical ways that a China-led globalization would differ: there would be less pressure put on countries around the world to maintain political systems that guarantee human rights. The current system is admittedly weak: for instance, there have been few, if any, repercussions to Turkey as Erdoğan took measures undermining basic freedoms. Still, the fact that the West constantly raises the issue has been a markedly positive force, and this is true even if the West is far from pure itself. The good news is that these ideas have been globalized in the decades after World War II, taking root around the world.

Labor and environmental standards are also likely to take a less prominent place, though China's population is demanding stronger environmental protection itself, and with the rise of incomes, labor standards have increased there too. Critics say that in any case, the weak standards included in recent agreements have never been enforced. In the important issues for American workers—like overtime pay—there is backsliding under Trump in the United States; an American Republican administration may thus be as much a threat to the creation of high global standards as China.[60] Western boycotts of goods produced in substandard conditions—for instance, garments—will still have to be employed.

With China committed to the Paris climate change agreement, there is hope that the standards that will eventually be evolving for carbon emissions might be put into trade agreements they sign—they have an incentive to do so. And again, a Republican administration in the United States represents as much of a threat to this agenda as China does.

These examples are illustrative of a general principle. Obama was right to say that who writes the rules matters. That's why it's important who is at the table. The very way the trade negotiations were structured gave little scope for civil society and representatives of any groups other than corporations to be at the table. The results reflected this.

I noted how trade agreements have gone beyond trade to include investment protections—encouraging American firms to create jobs abroad by making investments more secure there and taking away one of America's biggest comparative advantages, the rule of law affecting how disputes get settled, and replacing it with an adjudication process biased toward corporations. In chapter 2, I showed that the investment agreements could have been written in ways that would have provided the important protections that the United States says it sought, against discrimination, without threatening suits by corporations against governments over regulations to protect the environment, health, safety, and the stability of the economy. The resistance to this straightforward change by the business community showed that what they really wanted was to impair regulations. That was their agenda. It was only cloaked in language about fairness and nondiscrimination. (Indeed, as I note in chapter 2, these provisions gave foreign firms *more* rights than domestic firms. They had tilted the balance the other way.)

But this is an arena in which changes were especially inevitable, with or without Trump: tens of thousands of protestors in Europe and America, demonstrating against these seemingly arcane provisions, had shown that the hidden corporate agenda had at last been exposed. In May 2017, the European Court of Justice ruled that at least certain key provisions of investment agreements had to be passed by the parliaments of each of the members of the EU—unlike trade provisions, where the parliament of no single country had the veto power.[61]

Geopolitical Implications

The one thing that the United States and China agree upon is that the structure of economic globalization—the flow of goods and capital, under investment and trade agreements—has geopolitical implications. For Obama, the TPP was part of the "pivot to Asia," a reassertion of the role of America in that part of the world. So too, China is hoping to get support for its positions— from Tibet, to the South China Sea, to human rights—from those it is helping in the One Belt, One Road initiative.

If globalization is going to work, there has to be a way to resolve disputes and, in some cases there is: an international court of justice was set up in the Hague by the UN Charter in 1945, and it has ruled on a large number of cases involving cross-country disputes, including boundary disputes. Countries' affections for this judicial system depend closely on whether they think they will win.[62]

THE CHANGING GLOBAL ECONOMIC STRUCTURE

While a disproportionate fraction of attention in the globalization debates may be paid to industries of the past—agriculture and manufacturing—some of the *most* difficult issues will arise in sectors of the future, for instance in high tech.

The Digital Economy

Already there is a concern that five American firms (Apple, Google, Facebook, Amazon, and Twitter) dominate globally—except in China—their part of the industrial landscape. The fact that in so many sectors of the economy a single firm dominates is an example of a "winner take all economy," sometimes referred to as the "superstar economy." In the context of ordinary manufactured goods, not everyone will agree on what is the best—products have many characteristics, and what suits one person may not suit another. There has been an important change, however, especially as we move to a digital economy. Upfront costs, most importantly research, represent an increasingly large fraction of overall costs. Competition in these circumstances, where production constraints are typically of secondary importance, focuses on price. When there is intense competition, competitors successively undercut each other, until price is driven down to that of the firm with the lowest marginal cost. That firm becomes the dominant firm. Over time, that firm is able to extend its advantage over others, as it continues to do research, as it gathers data to make it possible to better meet the needs of particular customers, and as it uses sophisticated marketing and product strategies to "lock in" the customer.

What is emerging is a far-from-competitive marketplace. The dominant firm can have strong and ever-increasing market power.[63] Actions by authorities in Europe and elsewhere to circumscribe their market power—or even make them pay taxes—are greeted with charges of anti-Americanism.

So too for rightful concerns about privacy and the ownership of data (and the longer-run issue of the market power to which a concentration of data ownership could give rise). Many in Europe are concerned with privacy; many economists are concerned that control over data could increase even further the market power of certain firms. But the U.S. government, reflecting the interests of America's technology giants, wants the rules for data and data ownership that serve the interests of those firms. In trade negotiations, governments trade off various *producer* interests. So Europe might be willing to give in to American demands on data if it got something in return, say for its auto industry. But what is sacrificed in this grand bargain are matters of principle and the interests of ordinary citizens. This is the way trade agreements have been done since time immemorial. But globalization with rules made in this way will not only lack legitimacy; they will lack the support of the citizens. They provide fodder for the anti-globalization movement.

The problem is that with these enterprises exerting undue influence in the United States—and with politics in America taking the tilt that it has—the government has done little to ensure competition or to address issues of privacy. Given the size of these enterprises (Apple's cash reserves in 2017 exceeded the reserves of Canada and the UK combined), only the governments of the major countries can take them on. If they don't, the problems of inequality and the broader discontent with globalization will only grow deeper. Not surprisingly, the United States government (in the form of the USTR) has, by and large, represented the interests of American producers here, as they have in other arenas, so the American trade agenda (as they put it, setting the standards for the digital economy) is a monopoly-corporate agenda, paying not only little attention to privacy, but to the dangers of the accumulation of market power that may follow from data ownership.

Fortunately, in Europe, a combination of economic interests (the dominating American firms and their monopoly practices disadvantage European rivals and entrants)[64] and social values (so far, Europeans seem far more concerned about privacy and the inherent dangers of monopolies, at least in this area, than do Americans) means that their trade negotiators have been under enormous pressure not to give in to American demands and, at the very least, to give Europe scope to pursue its own "digital standards."

The Gig and Sharing Economy
Another important development is that of the gig economy, of enterprises like Uber and Airbnb. This has posed difficult regulatory issues all over the world. To some extent, their success is based on innovation, providing services that were not previously available. But they are also successful because they take advantage of their ability to avoid regulation and taxes facing conventional producers of similar services (economists refer to this as regulatory and tax arbitrage). There need to be new regulations (for instance, in the case of Uber, to ensure against excessive congestion, and to ensure rider safety and adequate insurance

to compensate in the case of an accident) and new forms of taxation to even the playing field. With investment agreements in place, in principle, these companies could sue for the loss of profits from any such new regulations—an illustration of the rigidity of investment agreements in allowing tax and regulatory regimes to adapt to changing circumstances.

Broader Implications of Moving to a Service Economy
The most important structural transformation is the move from manufacturing to a service sector economy, a shift we have often noted in this book. The stresses being expressed by the New Discontents are often as much a result of this shift as they are of globalization itself. Globalization in a service sector economy *is* different. Most of the growing services are location-specific: for the most part, education and health services are provided where individuals live. Those who manage the provision of services will perform their duties locally, where the services are provided. Of course, some of these services will be globalized: data processing may occur in India, students will come to the United States to get higher education, and medical tourism is likely to continue to grow. But these will be a small fraction of global GDP.

There are several important implications, one of which I have already noted. The manufacturing export–led growth model, the model that had such phenomenal results in narrowing the gap between Asia and the West, won't play the same role in coming decades. Asia, though, has learned how to learn, and will continue to close the gap in productivity. It is in Africa, not as far along in its development, that the problems will arise. As I noted, even if all the manufacturing jobs in China were to shift to Africa—which won't happen—it would not create enough jobs for its burgeoning population, and probably not enough to kick-start the structural transformation that the continent needs. And if the disparity in income levels persists, migration pressures will persist.

This then is the second implication: a manufacturing-dominated globalization, I noted, provides a strong downward pressure on wages in advanced countries. That force will lessen in coming years. Indeed, since services are labor-intensive, there is the possibility that wages in the advanced country (as a share of GDP) may increase. But that will depend heavily on public policy. Some of the most important growing sectors are health and education, the funds for which understandably come disproportionately from the public. If we prioritize quality care and education for citizens of all ages, we will create more higher-paying jobs. But if we starve these new sectors of funds, the structural transformation will be harder, globalization will more likely be blamed for the lack of jobs, and inequality will be higher.

There is another reason that inequality may be greater in the "new economy" to which the world is moving. Services are provided locally, and in many areas, that local provision is dominated by a few firms: two or three providers of health insurance in each area in the United States, one firm servicing each brand of car or tractor, one or two Internet providers, one or two cable TV companies, a few providers of finance to small businesses. This means that there may be a higher level of monopoly power than in the manufacturing-dominated economy, unless the government engages in hard-to-manage antitrust policies at the local level—and that in turn implies more inequality, again, unless the government undertakes countervailing measures.

Yet another implication is that growth, at least as we conventionally measure it, is likely to slow down, especially in the advanced countries. Of course, there may be particular sectors that will do well—while innovation in U.S. tech is celebrated, overall GDP growth has slowed (in 2016, to just 1.6 percent). Historically, the service sectors have experienced low increases in productivity, a phenomenon related to what is referred to as Baumol's disease.[65] It's partly a measurement problem—our metrics don't, for instance, take into account the fact that twenty years ago, a heart surgery had a high probability of death and a low probability of long-term recovery, quite different from today. But even then, there's simply not the innovation we see in manufacturing.[66] A barber may be slightly faster with modern clippers, but only slightly so. New technologies have had only minor effects in education.[67] We needn't bemoan this too much. The effect of further increases in income (beyond that of, say, upper-middle-income Americans) on well-being is likely to be limited.[68] What should matter now is how the wealth of a country is shared. The possibility, or even likelihood, that inequality will continue to grow, even as the extent of globalization declines, means that stronger government actions, along the lines discussed in chapter 4, are needed.

The emerging markets will still have ample opportunities for catching up: with, for instance, China's GDP about one-fifth that of the United States, there is enormous scope for it to increase GDP. But even the process of catching up in the service sector may be harder. A new manufacturing factory in China using advanced technology may be able to achieve close to the same productivity as one in America or Europe. But disseminating knowledge about both technology and business practices to the myriad of small service sector businesses is a far more difficult task.

The final implication is that the growth in trade relative to GDP will slow down, and again, we needn't bemoan this. Some have seen recent statistics showing that this has already been happening as suggesting that the retreat from globalization is already under way. Some seeing a correlation between trade and growth will worry that this decline in trade will imply a decrease in growth. This decline will happen, as I have argued, but it's not because of the slowdown in trade, an important lesson in confused causality. Both the decline in growth in incomes and the decline in the ratio of trade to incomes are caused by the increased role of the service sector in the economy.

GLOBALIZATION, INEQUALITY, AND MARKET POWER

This book is about the discontents with globalization in both the developing world and advanced countries, and how that discontent is linked with the growth of inequality. I believe the focus of the debate over globalization in coming years will continue to be over the well-being of workers, both in developed and developing countries, and the effects of globalization on them. As I explained in chapter 1, even if globalization is not the major cause of the growth of inequality and the evisceration of the middle class in the advanced countries, even if the loss of jobs has more to do with technology than globalization, globalization will bear the brunt of the anger: those who suffer see globalization as the one thing that they can do something about. That's why anyone who believes in keeping markets open should be asking, what can we do to help those at the bottom and middle? While I touched on this in chapter

4, and a full answer would require a more extensive discussion than I can give here, looking at the matter from a global economic perspective may be useful.

Globally, there seems, at least at the moment, to be a surplus of labor and capital,[69] with high unemployment and safe assets (U.S. Treasury bills) yielding a real return close to zero. A natural question is, how can that be? Where is the money going? Part of the answer is that the global economy is not being run well: there is a global deficiency in aggregate demand. This book has been largely about the *microeconomics* of globalization, about how opening up markets, even if it increases the level of income, can so change the distribution of income as to make large groups worse off. But there is a macroeconomics of globalization. If countries like Germany insist on exporting more than they import, on running a trade surplus, their actions may cause a deficiency of global aggregate demand—imposing a large cost on the rest of the world, because with an insufficiency of global aggregate demand, somewhere in the world there will be unemployment. Some country may protect its jobs, but only by causing jobs elsewhere to be scarce. That is why Keynes suggested that there should be a tax on trade surpluses.[70] Taxes are used to discourage countries and individuals from doing things that impose costs on others. The weakening of global aggregate demand caused by surplus countries in the past was offset by other countries (often in the developing world) running unbridled fiscal deficits. But countries have learned the high long-run costs of doing so, and so today there is nothing countervailing to stimulate global aggregate demand. On the contrary, the current wave of austerity has reinforced the weakness in global aggregate demand. It is hard to tell if and when the fads and fashions which have given rise to global austerity will fade: more reasonable minds would have long ago concluded that the current moment of low interest rates is the time government should borrow for long-needed investments in infrastructure, education, and technology.

Inequality too plays a big role. Those at the top spend a much smaller portion of their income than those down below, so when inequality increases, demand decreases. There is a vicious circle at work: a weak economy leads to lower wages and more inequality, which weakens the economy further. If government responds by stimulating the economy, it can offset these untoward results; but the weaker economy typically leads to lower wages and bigger fiscal deficits. If the government responds by another dose of austerity, the economy is pushed down further.

But this is only part of the explanation of today's growing inequality and weak economy: There is a growing consensus that a larger share of the global income pie is being appropriated in monopoly rents, or more broadly, through the exercise of market power.[71] This increase in market power diminishes demand in two ways. More of the money goes to the owners of the monopolies. These individuals, typically among the wealthiest of our society, spend less than ordinary citizens, and so aggregate demand is decreased. At the same time, the firms curtail output (from the level that it would be with competition), since they know that increasing output will lead to lower prices and profits. The result is large, highly profitable corporations that sit on hoards of cash, with little incentive to reinvest the money—precisely the situation that has been observed in recent years.

Alternative Course of Multipolar Globalization

I want to return to a central theme of this book: globalization has the *potential* of increasing standards of living. The insights of Smith and Ricardo that global efficiency could be increased through specialization (taking advantage of economies of scale) and comparative advantage still hold true. Thus, everyone in society could be made better off. But the outcome of unfettered globalization can be just the opposite: a reduction in standards of living for at least large segments of the population.

There is the possibility that twenty-first-century multipolar globalization will create a more competitive global landscape, circumscribing the market power, for instance, of the multinational corporations of the advanced countries. There is the more remote possibility that domestic political forces in the United States and Europe circumscribe market power. There is the possibility too that with a better managed globalization there will not be extended periods of deficiencies in aggregate demand.

But there is also the possibility that twenty-first-century multipolar globalization will not work much better for ordinary citizens than it has been working in recent years. True, the China-led rebalancing of globalization will increase overall incomes in many of the countries of the developing world. And multipolarity—the very presence of China in the global landscape—*may* circumscribe the abuse of market power by the advanced countries and their companies. But it is at least as likely that China's large companies, as they become more established, will see their interests coincident with those of their compatriots from the West. Profits are higher and life is more comfortable without excessive competition; it is more fun, and more profitable, to find ways of cooperating (a more accurate word might be "colluding.") The multinational oil companies will be forced to let into their club new members from China, and so too will companies in other areas. But competition will remain limited and prices will remain high. Profits of Western companies will be somewhat lower, but, overall, globalization may look little different under multipolar globalization than it did under American-led globalization.

The Political Response

The anti-globalization voters are right about one thing: while technology—lower transport and communications costs—may have provided the conditions that led to the growth of globalization during the past third of a century, globalization is shaped by policies and politics. One might hope that the discontent with globalization, in both the developed and developing countries, would lead to a rethinking of globalization, a resolve to manage it better, and to ensure that the potential fruits are shared equitably. That may well happen.

It will not, however, be easy. The simple strategy, widely supported by globalization's advocates, is "globalization with compensation," that is, we need to recognize that without appropriate government policies, globalization can create losers, and we have to make sure that the vulnerable are helped at least enough that that doesn't happen. Everyone needs to be a winner. There are two problems with this strategy. First, on its own, it is unlikely to have support from those who have been on the losing side of globalization. Why would they have confidence that the elites who in the past promised them that globalization would benefit them would now deliver—not just this year, but permanently? When politicians argue simultaneously for weakening of the social protections and for new trade and investment agreements and the expansion of globalization, it is understandable that voters will be especially skeptical about promises of "globalization with compensation." A new trade agreement commits them to openness, but any future administration can easily take away the promised "compensation." Even were the promises somehow made within the agreement itself, would they be enforced? There has been a loss of trust that will not be easily restored. Only deep structural change might make such compensation credible—the construction of a twenty-first-century welfare state described in chapter 4.

Moreover, some, perhaps much of the support for globalization comes from corporations that have benefited from a weakening of workers' bargaining rights. Good systems of social protection actually enhance the ability of workers to bargain for their rights. Almost surely, they would lead to higher market wages. It is not clear that these corporate interests would really support this kind of globalization. The losers from globalization, of course, sense this—one of the reasons that they will be skeptical about promises of compensation.

More than "compensation," however, confidence in globalization needs to be restored. The advocates of globalization rightly point out the key role of the creation of an international rule of law—the rules-based system of globalization, so challenged by Trump, is especially important in curbing unbridled power. This book has argued strongly for the benefits, even to a powerful country like the United States, of such a rules-based system. But the rules themselves matter. They have to have legitimacy, but they can only have legitimacy if they are derived in what is seen as an open, fair, and transparent way—not in the way, for example, that recent trade agreements were negotiated.

There is thus a narrow path forward for achieving the potential benefits of globalization. It requires a deep commitment to shared prosperity, reflected in permanent institutions and policies described in chapter 4, and a deep commitment to more democratic, open, and transparent processes for making trade agreements and for running the global institutions responsible for global governance.

There is another scenario, though, in which politicians like Trump take advantage of the discontent to blame the dysfunctions of globalization on the misconduct ("unfairness") of others, and attempt to redefine the rules of globalization to their own advantage. This is the direction the world is now headed, in which the world will deglobalize and the potential fruits of globalization will be lost.

Perhaps the most likely scenario is muddling through, a continuation of badly managed globalization, with much discontent. With the contours of globalization being redrawn by China, the multinationals in the West will not be quite the cheerleaders for globalization that they were in the past. Indeed, they will continue their hypocritical stance—a belief in free markets, with rules set so that they can win, and urge their governments to take forceful actions on their behalf. But the threats of the West will ring more hollow, and its ability to get what it wants will be more limited. While the global influence of Western multinationals may decline, the global economy will continue in its current course, with large western multinationals—now joined by those from the rest of the world—reaping a disproportionate share of the gains, and ordinary citizens, especially in the advanced countries, left wondering, when will the promised benefits of globalization arrive? If this happens, the discontent with globalization will continue, and it will be a tough political battle to preserve an open global system.

There can be no sustained globalization without sustained shared prosperity, and muddling through doesn't get us there. Without a belief in *sustained* globalization, the full benefits of globalization can't be achieved—one can't construct efficient global supply chains if there is a threat at any moment of deglobalization. Moderate political leaders, always striving to achieve balance and compromise, can't and won't get us there. They won't get us to sustained *shared* prosperity, and so won't get us to sustained globalization. Ironically, only the political leaders committed to the construction of the twenty-first-century welfare state can get us to a twenty-first-century sustained globalization.

CONCLUDING COMMENTS

Over the past three-quarters of a century, the world has created a rules-based system for governing globalization. It was not easy creating this system, and it is an imperfect system. There were many in America, and in other countries, who objected that any system of international law meant giving up some sovereignty. The WTO could—and did—declare some of America's trade practices to be in violation of the WTO, and the United States changed its policies or provided compensation to those who brought the complaint. But America also gained enormously because when others broke their commitments, the United States could bring suit. There didn't have to be a trade war to resolve the dispute. And both sides gained by avoiding a trade war.

In *GAID,* I criticize the system of globalization that had been created because it was unfairly tilted toward the United States and other developed countries. What I saw offended basic notions of social justice. I believed that we could create a system of globalization that was both fairer and worked better—that even the United States would benefit in the long run from this system of fairer and better-managed globalization. As an American, I believed it was in our enlightened self-interest to do what we could to create this better system. In *GAID* and even more in my subsequent writings, such as *Making Globalization Work,* I laid out what could and should be done. I was working to make globalization work better *for all.* I believed an alternative world was possible, one in which the United States was vitally engaged. I was not arguing for a withdrawal.

Trump's election, the Brexit vote, and the rise of protectionist politics elsewhere have upended all of this. Trump in particular has pushed quickly for a new protectionism, for the United States to pursue an America First policy, ignoring international commitments when it is inconvenient to honor them.

Like it or not, we are all linked together by sharing the same planet. One country's actions can—and do—have large effects on others. The international economy is linked in myriad and very complex ways. Rare minerals that are needed for modern technology are located in only a few countries: a world without trade is inconceivable. Terrorists and viruses move quietly across borders. Climate change is real: the emission of greenhouse gases by the United States, China, and others has enormous consequences for people living thousands of miles away. In Africa and India, desertification is throwing people off the land that they have long occupied. Pacific island states will sink beneath the sea, and the citizens of these states will become involuntary migrants. Globalization is thus a reality with which we will have to deal. But how we deal with globalization matters a great deal. If we deal with it in the right way, the world of the future can be marked by shared prosperity.

We don't know where all of this will end, but this much is clear:

if Trump has his way, the United States will lose its global influence, standards of living of Americans will decrease, including for those who supported him, and the world will not be safer, more secure, or more prosperous.

The hope is that the United States and the world will emerge from this episode with a greater resolve to create a fairer and better globalization—the kind of globalization I had in mind as I wrote *Globalization and Its Discontents* at the beginning of this century.

NOTES

INTRODUCTION TO
GLOBALIZATION AND ITS DISCONTENTS REVISITED

1 Source: IMF, World Economic Outlook database (WEO), April 2017, using GDP (in current U.S. dollars) and population data for the year 2016 and the IMF's definition of "emerging and developing economies."

2 GDP per capita (current U.S. dollars) in 2016. Source: World Bank, World Development Indicators database.

3 Of course, Smith and Ricardo didn't call it "globalization." That term emerged in the middle of the twentieth century, and didn't become widely used until the 1980s.

4 More sophisticated analysts quarrel with the way we measure GDP and income, and in particular price deflators, the adjustments used for inflation. While our metrics are imperfect, and do underestimate some of the benefits of technological change, they also underestimate the reductions in well-being as a result of increased insecurity. On net, my judgment is that matters may be worse than the most commonly cited numbers suggest. I chaired the international Commission on the Measurement of Economic Performance and Social Progress, which investigated these matters. See, for instance, its 2010 report: *Mismeasuring Our Lives: Why GDP Doesn't Add Up*, with J. Fitoussi and A. Sen (New York: New Press, 2010).

5 A. Case and A. Deaton, "Rising Morbidity and Mortality in Midlife Among White Non-Hispanic Americans in the 21st Century," *Proceedings of the National Academy of Sciences* 112 (49) (2015), pp. 15078–83. They subsequently updated their findings in "Mortality and Morbidity in the 21st Century," prepared for the Brookings Panel on Economic Activity, March 23-24, 2017.

6 National Center for Health Statistics (2016), *Mortality in the United States, 2015*, NCHS Data Brief 267.

7 Milanović ranks people in the world from the bottom to the top in terms of income. Those around the global 50th percentile represent the new middle classes in the emerging markets, and they've seen an increase in incomes of some 100 percent between 1988 and 2011. See Branko Milanović, *Global Inequality: A New Approach for the Age of Globalization* (Cambridge, MA: Harvard University Press, 2016).

8 Source: The World Bank China Overview, available at http://www .worldbank.org/en/country/china/overview.

9 Comparison based on IMF World Economic Outlook (WEO) and World Bank data available as of August 2017. This comparison deflates the nominal value of the trade increase using the producer price index. Using the consumer price index—which is the more common way of looking at inflation, but less appropriate for gauging trade increases—a somewhat lower figure is arrived at. However, the point stands that trade has grown dramatically faster than the size of the global economy.

10 Sources: IMF World Economic Outlook (WEO) and International Financial Statistics (IFS), April 2017.

11 There is a large literature showing how excessively strong and poorly designed intellectual property regimes can impede innovation. The most telling example is provided by what happened when the U.S. Supreme Court decided that one couldn't patent genes. An American company, Myriad, had the patent on two genes, the presence of which dramatically increased the likelihood of breast cancer. The company would not allow others to provide tests for the presence of the gene, and its own tests were not as accurate as those developed by others. After the Court's decision, there was a rash of innovations, bringing down the cost and improving the quality of the tests. Elsewhere, I have explained how tighter intellectual property rights reduce the size of the pool of knowledge for others to draw upon, thereby impeding innovation. See "Intellectual Property Rights, the Pool of Knowledge, and Innovation," NBER working paper 20014, March 2014, available at http://www.nber.org/papers/ w20014.pdf?new_window=1. For a broader explanation of how innovation can and has been hurt, see C. Henry and J. E. Stiglitz, "Intellectual Property, Dissemination of Innovation, and Sustainable Development," *Global Policy* 1(1), pp. 237–51.

12 The top marginal tax rate has fallen dramatically in the globalization era, going from 70 percent in 1980 to as low as 28 percent in 1988, and to 39.6 percent in 2017. In 1997, taxes on capital gains—a major form of income of the very rich—was markedly reduced, with further reductions under

President George W. Bush, eventually reaching just 15 percent. This contributed to the regressive nature of U.S. taxation, in which those at the top pay a smaller percentage of their income in taxes than those lower down.

13 While some inequality may be useful in providing incentives, there is now a general consensus—including among such mainstream institutions as the IMF and the OECD (the "think tank" of the advanced countries) that excessive inequality leads to poorer economic performance, undermines democracies, and leads to a divided society. See, for example, Joseph E. Stiglitz, *The Price of Inequality: How Today's Divided Society Endangers Our Future* (New York: W. W. Norton, 2012).

14 Of course, this was not always the case, but it was true for many of the better-managed firms, and was the "story" depicted by the advocates of capitalism.

15 Sean F. Reardon and Kendra Bischoff, "Income Inequality and Income Segregation," *American Journal of Sociology* 116 (4) (January 2011), pp. 1092–153; Richard Fry and Paul Taylor, "The Rise of Residential Segregation by Income," *Pew Research Center*, August 1, 2012, available at http://www.pewsocialtrends.org/2012/08/01/the-rise-of-residential-segregation-by-income/.

16 Unlike German steel producers, America hadn't competed by producing high-quality specialty steels, which require highly skilled workers and involve advanced technology. The country didn't make the investments in people and technology that that required. It was trying to compete in the mass-produced steel in which China had quickly learned to excel.

17 A Google image search yields many haunting photos (http://bit.ly/2hmTJ3B). A picture of what has happened to the school and community surrounding it can be vividly seen in a film I did after publishing *GAID*, to graphically show the impact of globalization on various parts of the world: *Around the World with Joseph Stiglitz*, directed by Jacques Sarasin (Les Productions 100 Faire Bleu, Swan Productions, ARTE France, with the participation of Île-de-France), available at https://vimeo.com/153222282.

18 For instance, at the time that I wrote *GAID*, many of the critical decisions were made by the G-7, a group of the richest advanced countries (United States, Germany, France, Canada, Italy, Japan, and the UK). China and India were excluded, even though they had 40 percent of the world's population. There have been some significant changes in global governance since the publication of *GAID*.

19 I emphasize "for the most part" because, for instance, the standard economic models underestimated the dangers of capital market liberalization

and overestimated the benefits. See Joseph E. Stiglitz, "Capital Market Liberalization, Globalization, and the IMF," in Joseph E. Stiglitz and José Antonio Ocampo, eds., *Capital Market Liberalization and Development* (New York: Oxford University Press, 2008), pp. 76–100. (Revised and updated version of an article with the same title originally published in *Oxford Review of Economic Policy* 20 [1] [2004], pp. 57–71.) So too for certain other aspects of globalization, as I emphasize in chapters 1 and 2.

20 I elaborate on this idea in my paper by the same name: "Social Protection Without Protectionism," in Mary Kaldor and Joseph E. Stiglitz, eds., *The Quest for Security: Protection Without Protectionism and the Challenge of Global Governance* (New York: Columbia University Press, 2013), pp. 24–47.

21 A commonly used indicator is the inequality-adjusted Human Development Index (HDI) put out annually by the UNDP, in which the Scandinavian countries Norway, Denmark, Iceland, and Sweden ranked 1, 5, 9, and 14, respectively, in 2015. (Source: *Human Development Report 2016: Human Development for Everyone*, UNDP, March 2017, available online at http://hdr.undp.org/sites/default/files/2016_human_development_report.pdf.)

22 This is a main theme in my recent books *The Great Divide: Unequal Societies and What We Can Do about Them* (New York: W. W. Norton, 2015) and *The Price of Inequality: How Today's Divided Society Endangers Our Future*, op. cit.

23 The idea of a Washington consensus was originally formulated by John Williamson in 1989. The term evolved to incorporate all of the central tenets of IMF/World Bank orthodoxy, even when they were not included in Williamson's original formulation. Thus, capital account liberalization became part of the Washington Consensus, even though Williamson himself was critical of it. For a broader discussion of the evolution of the term, see Joseph E. Stiglitz, "Is There a Post-Washington Consensus Consensus?" in Narcis Serra and Joseph E. Stiglitz, eds., *The Washington Consensus Reconsidered: Towards a New Global Governance* (New York: Oxford University Press, 2008), pp. 41–56; and John Williamson, "A Short History of the Washington Consensus" in the same volume, pp. 14–30.

24 This term is used even when the policies apply outside of the industrial sector, for instance, in agriculture.

25 As I explain in the afterword, many of these ideas are being questioned today, even within the IMF and the World Bank—a shift that began some twenty years ago. For instance, the 1998 World Development Report, *Knowledge for Development,* recognized the importance of secondary and university education, as well as primary education, if the knowledge gap separating advanced countries and developing countries was to be addressed. In the afterword, I also explain how in the past quarter century the Wash-

ington Consensus has become discredited. A new consensus has emerged, called the Stockholm Consensus. (For a summary, see https://www.sida.se/globalassets/sida/eng/press/stockholm-statement.pdf.)

26 These were called "escalating tariffs," with higher tariffs on the higher value-added products. See Joseph E. Stiglitz and Andrew Charlton, *Fair Trade for All* (New York: Oxford University Press, 2005).

27 There is now a large branch of economics called behavioral economics, exploring the systematic ways in which individuals act "irrationally." More recent developments have emphasized that the economic system shapes individual preferences and behavior (in contrast to standard theory, which assumes preferences as given), for instance, making individuals more selfish or more shortsighted than they might be otherwise. See, for instance, bestselling books such as Daniel Kahneman, *Thinking, Fast and Slow* (New York: Farrar, Straus & Giroux, 2011); Michael J. Sandel, *What Money Can't Buy: The Moral Limits of Markets* (New York: Farrar, Straus & Giroux, 2012); and Richard H. Thaler, *The Winner's Curse: Paradoxes and Anomalies of Economic Life* (Princeton, NJ: Princeton University Press, 1992). For a discussion of how preferences are shaped, see Karla Hoff and Joseph E. Stiglitz, "Striving for Balance in Economics: Towards a Theory of the Social Determination of Behavior," *Journal of Economic Behavior and Organization* 126(B) (2016), pp. 25–57.

28 Of course, in a short book, I could not really go far back into history: globalization has been with us in fact for a very long time, evidenced, for instance, by the foods we eat, which originate in many different parts of the world. A key driver of economic activity in the last few centuries has been the creation of new trade routes and new colonies.

29 Fortunately, there seems to be a large gap between Trump's campaign rhetoric and what his administration has done. Later in the book, I explain why this should not come as a surprise.

30 Indeed, the evidence is that such agreements would have had a negligible effect on growth. See the discussion in chapter 1.

31 This has historically been the case, though in recent years developing countries and emerging markets have had larger emissions of greenhouse gases. Still, the United States has the highest level of emissions per capita.

32 See J. E. Stiglitz, "Sharing the Burden of Saving the Planet: Global Social Justice for Sustainable Development," in Mary Kaldor and Joseph E. Stiglitz, eds., *The Quest for Security: Protection Without Protectionism and the Challenge of Global Governance* (New York: Columbia University Press), pp. 161–90.

33 UN Conference on the World Financial and Economic Crisis and Its

Impact on Development, June 2009. Outcome of the conference available at http://www.un.org/esa/ffd/documents/Outcome_2009.pdf.

34　The United States has, however, paid a high price for this advantage. As foreign countries buy more U.S. bonds, the value of the exchange rate increases, depressing exports and increasing imports—part of the cause of the trade deficit that Trump excoriates.

I had been active in promoting a global reserve system, and an international commission which I chaired, whose key recommendations were endorsed by the UN General Assembly, came out strongly in support of such a system. When I discussed the matter with President Obama, he seemed to understand the costs to the U.S. economy of the current reserve arrangement, but he saw too the advantages, the ability to borrow at a low interest rate, and those advantages seemed particularly relevant at a time when the United States was running large deficits in its attempt to emerge from the 2008 crisis. Besides, a change in the global reserve system was a radical change, something too radical for Obama's natural conservatism. See *The Stiglitz Report: Reforming the International Monetary and Financial Systems in the Wake of the Global Crisis,* with Members of the Commission of Experts on Reforms of the International Monetary and Financial System appointed by the president of the United Nations General Assembly (New York: New Press, 2010); Bruce Greenwald and Joseph E. Stiglitz, "A Modest Proposal for International Monetary Reform," in Stephany Griffith-Jones, José Antonio Ocampo, and Joseph E. Stiglitz, eds., *Time for a Visible Hand: Lessons from the 2008 World Financial Crisis* (Oxford: Oxford University Press, 2010), pp. 314–44; and Bruce Greenwald and Joseph E. Stiglitz, "Towards a New Global Reserve System," *Journal of Globalization and Development* 1 (2) (2010), article 10.

35　In 2015, China's urban manufacturing employment was around 80 million, while Sub-Saharan Africa's population between twenty-five and sixty-four years old is projected to increase by 581 million by 2050. Sources: China Statistical Yearbook and United Nations (World Population Prospects, median fertility variant).

36　Which, in any case, will only be effective in 2020, just as his term comes to an end.

37　According to the Department of Homeland Security report, the number of successful illegal entries—including people making multiple attempts—between ports of entry along the entire southern border with Mexico plummeted from 1.7 million in 2005 to 170,000 in 2015. Source: "Barely Half of Illegal Border Crossers from Mexico Caught," Associated Press,

October 6, 2016, http://www.latimes.com/local/lanow/la-me-border-cross-20161006-snap-story.html.

38 See Joseph E. Stiglitz, *Freefall: America, Free Markets, and the Sinking of the World Economy* (New York: W. W. Norton, 2010).

39 Some economists like Nobel Prize winner Gary Becker argued that there was no discrimination—income differences just reflected differences in productivities. See Gary Becker, *The Economics of Discrimination, Second Edition* (Chicago: University of Chicago Press, 1971). Not surprisingly, there was a large subsequent literature explaining what was wrong with Becker's theory. See, for instance, J. E. Stiglitz, "Approaches to the Economics of Discrimination," *American Economic Review* 62 (2) (May 1973), pp. 287–95.

40 See David Autor et al., "A Note on the Effect of Rising Trade Exposure on the 2016 Presidential Election," MIT working paper, 2016; Betsy Cooper et al., "The Divide over America's Future: 1950 or 2050? Findings from the 2016 American Values Survey," Public Religion Research Institute Report, 2016; and Brian F. Schaffner, Matthew MacWilliams, and Tatishe Nteta, "Explaining White Polarization in the 2016 Vote for President: The Sobering Role of Racism and Sexism," University of Massachusetts Amherst working paper, 2017.

41 I noted earlier that China moved some 800 million out of poverty. Standard economic theory predicted that unskilled workers in the less developed world would benefit from globalization. It did not predict that the more educated, skilled workers would benefit as well. That they have done so is in part a tribute to how these countries managed globalization.

42 It would be tempting to focus just on the mortgage originators, who engaged in predatory lending. But the lying and deceit that was necessary to make the whole corrupt system "work" brought into the vortex the rating agencies, most of the investment banks, and a host of others. See Joseph E. Stiglitz, *Freefall: America, Free Markets, and the Sinking of the World Economy*, op. cit., and the studies cited there; and *The Financial Crisis Inquiry Report: Final Report of the National Commission of the Causes of the Financial and Economic Crisis in the United States,* submitted by the Financial Crisis Inquiry Commission, February 25, 2011, available at https://www.gpo.gov/fdsys/pkg/GPO-FCIC/pdf/GPO-FCIC.pdf.

43 The ideas in this section are elaborated upon in Joseph E. Stiglitz with Nell Abernathy, Adam Hersh, Susan Holmberg, and Mike Konczal, *Rewriting the Rules of the American Economy*, A Roosevelt Institute Book (New York: W. W. Norton, 2015), available at http://www.rewritetherules.org.

44 Since *GAID*, I have written extensively on various aspects of globalization,

most notably *Making Globalization Work* (New York: W. W. Norton, 2006); *Fair Trade for All*, with Andrew Charlton (New York: Oxford University Press, 2005); and *An Agenda for the Development Round of Trade Negotiations in the Aftermath of Cancún*, with Andrew Charlton, prepared for the Commonwealth Secretariat, 2004. My book on the euro deals with one aspect of globalization—the attempt by a group of countries to share a common currency. See my book *The Euro: How a Common Currency Threatens the Future of Europe* (New York: W. W. Norton, 2016).

Acknowledgments to *Globalization and Its Discontents Revisited*

1 The report of the commission, as well as a list of the commissioners, is available on the UN Web site (http://www.un.org/ga/econcrisissummit/docs/FinalReport_CoE.pdf) and has been published as *The Stiglitz Report: Reforming the International Monetary and Financial Systems in the Wake of the Global Crisis* (New York: New Press, 2010). The central recommendations of the commission were endorsed by the UN Conference on the World Financial and Economic Crisis and Its Impact on Development (June 24–30, 2009, in New York)—"Outcome of the Conference on the World Financial and Economic Crisis and Its Impact on Development," available at http://www.un.org/esa/ffd/documents/Outcome_2009.pdf. The report was endorsed by the General Assembly in its resolution 63/303 of July 9, 2009.

2 Even before the crisis had brought out how interconnectedness could lead to a spread of risk ("contagion"), we had begun working on the subject, though our most important work was published later. See, for instance, "Credit Chains and Bankruptcy Propagation in Production Networks" (also coauthored with D. Delli Gatti, and B. Greenwald), *Journal of Economic Dynamics and Control* 31 (6) (June 2007), pp. 2061–84; "Default Cascades: When Does Risk Diversification Increase Stability?" *Journal of Financial Stability* 8(3), pp. 138–49; and "Liaisons Dangereuses: Increasing Connectivity, Risk Sharing, and Systemic Risk," *Journal of Economic Dynamics and Control*, 36 (8), pp. 1121–41. (The last two papers are coauthored also with Delli Gatti, Greenwald, and Mauro Gallegati.) The East Asia crisis, with large fractions of firms going bankrupt, had brought out some of the complexities arising from interconnectedness, especially important in understanding financial globalization, since globalization increases interconnectedness. We have finally begun to understand more fully the consequences of this interconnectedness. See "Interconnectedness as a

Source of Uncertainty in Systemic Risk" (coauthored also with Tarik Roukny and Stefano Battiston), in *Journal of Financial Stability* (2017).

3   Oxford University Press, 2010.

4   The report of the commission, *A Fair Globalization: Creating Opportunities for All* (Switzerland: ILO Publications, 2004), with a list of commissioners, is available online at http://www.ilo.org/fairglobalization/report/lang--en/index.htm.

5   The report of the commission is available online (http://ec.europa.eu/eurostat/documents/118025/118123/Fitoussi+Commission+report), and has also been published as *Mismeasuring Our Lives: Why GDP Doesn't Add Up* (New York: New Press, 2010).

6   The report of the commission is available online at https://www.carbonpricingleadership.org/report-of-the-highlevel-commission-on-carbon-prices/.

7   "Overcoming the Shadow Economy," with Mark Pieth, Friedrich Ebert Stiftung International Policy Analysis Paper, November 2016, available online at http://library.fes.de/pdf-files/iez/12922.pdf.

8   *In the Wake of the Crisis,* Olivier Blanchard et al., eds. (Cambridge, MA: MIT Press, 2012); and *What Have We Learned? Macroeconomic Policy after the Crisis*, George Akerlof et al., eds. (Cambridge, MA, and London: MIT Press, 2014).

9   New York: Oxford University Press, 2005. We also wrote several other papers together on both trade and aid.

10   With whom I wrote "Intellecutal Property, Dissemination of Innovation, and Sustainable Development," *Global Policy* 1(1) (2010), pp. 237–51.

11   I coedited a volume with Giovanni Dosi, Keith E. Maskus, Ruth L. Okediji, and Jerome H. Reichman detailing impacts on developing countries (*Intellectual Property Rights: Legal and Economic Challenges for Development* [Oxford: Oxford University Press, 2014]), including a paper with Dosi on the subject. With Dean Baker and Arjun Jayadev, more recently, I wrote a paper spelling out implications for the design of their IPR regimes (Dean Baker, Arjun Jayadev, and Joseph Stiglitz. "Innovation, Intellectual Property and Development: A Better Set of Approaches for the 21st Century" (2017), published on behalf of the Access IBSA project, by the Azim Premji University, the University of Cape Town, and the Oswaldo Cruz Foundation and available at http://cepr.net/images/stories/reports/baker-jayadev-stiglitz-innovation-ip-development-2017-07.pdf). Jayadev and I have written several papers proposing reforms to the global system of testing for medicines ("Two Ideas to Increase Innovation and

Pharmaceutical Costs and Prices," *Health Affairs*, 28 [1] [January–February 2009], pp. 165–68; and "Medicine for Tomorrow: Some Alternative Proposals to Promote Socially Beneficial Research and Development in Pharmaceuticals," *Journal of Generic Medicine* 7 (3) (2010), pp. 217–26).

12 *Too Little, Too Late: The Quest to Resolve Sovereign Debt Crises,* with Martin Guzman and José Antonio Ocampo, eds., Initiative for Policy Dialogue at Columbia (New York: Columbia University Press, 2016).

13 With whom I coedited a book, *The Industrial Policy Revolution II: Africa in the 21st Century* (coedited also with Justin Yifu Lin) (Houndmills, UK, and New York: Palgrave Macmillan, 2014).

14 With whom I coedited several books on Africa (including *Good Growth and Global Governance in Africa*, also coedited by Kwesi Botchwey and Howard Stein (New York: Oxford University Press); *Efficiency, Finance, and Varieties of Industrial Policy: Guiding Resources, Learning, and Technology for Sustained Growth* (New York: Columbia University Press) and have written several papers, including "African Development Prospects and Possibilities," in Ernest Aryeetey et al., eds., *The Oxford Companion to the Economics of Africa* (Oxford: Oxford University Press), pp. 33–40; "Economics and Policy: Some Lessons from Africa's Experience," in *The Oxford Handbook of Africa and Economics, Volume II: Policies and Practices*, Célestin Monga and Justin Yifu Lin, eds. (Oxford and New York: Oxford University Press), pp. 830–48.

15 *The Washington Consensus Reconsidered: Towards a New Global Governance* (New York: Oxford University Press, 2008).

16 Published as *The Quest for Security: Protection Without Protectionism and the Challenge of Global Governance*, Mary Kaldor and Joseph E. Stiglitz, eds. (New York: Columbia University Press, 2013).

PART I

1 Done for the Roosevelt Institute: S. Greenberg and N. Zdunkewicsz, "The Unheard Winning and Bold Economic Agenda," *Democracy Corps Memorandum,* 2016.

2 Though the outcome was the result of America's peculiar electoral system. Trump got 2.9 million fewer votes than Clinton.

3 The United States, representing the interests of producers of GMO seeds, has for instance argued that such disclosures are an unfair trade practice, because consumers in Europe will steer clear of products containing GMO

products. The United States has thus been arguing not only against restrictions on GMOs, but for restrictions on access to information that individuals value.

CHAPTER 1

1 P. A. Samuelson, "Welfare Economics and International Trade," *American Economic Review* 28 (2) (1938), pp. 261–66.

2 See David Ricardo, *On the Principles of Political Economy and Taxation,* 1817, and Adam Smith, *The Wealth of Nations,* 1776. It is worth noting that trade policy has been the subject of contention in public policy for more than two and a half centuries.

3 This is not their only responsibility: they have to balance this against other objectives—most important, ensuring price stability. The central bank of the eurozone, the European Central Bank, has been criticized for having a mandate focusing just on inflation (see, e.g., Joseph E. Stiglitz, *The Euro: How a Common Currency Threatens the Future of Europe,* op. cit.), though more recently, under the leadership of Mario Draghi, it has interpreted that mandate more broadly.

4 Any theory is only as good as the assumptions which go into it—as the expression goes, garbage in—garbage out. If the assumptions are unrealistic, the conclusions are likely to be false or at least misleading.

5 See D. Autor, D. Dorn, and G. H. Hanson, "The China Syndrome: Local Labor Market Effects of Import Competition in the United States," *American Economic Review* 103 (6) (2013), pp. 2121–68.

6 Economists distinguish between traded goods and services—like cars and TVs—that are made in one country and can be purchased in another, and nontraded goods. Some services, like university education, are traded—many students study abroad. The sale of these services to foreigners creates jobs, just like the sale of manufactured goods does. As I note later, Trump and some of his advisers have become obsessed with *goods,* ignoring the high-paying services that are part of America's comparative advantage.

7 The Washington Consensus policies that I discuss briefly in the introduction, and which are the center of my critique of globalization in *GAID,* are based on such models. I often referred to these policies as *market fundamentalism* because they were predicated on an almost religious faith in markets. Adam Smith had talked about the virtues of markets, but he realized, as well, their limitations. Since then, major advances in economics have cen-

tered around deepening our understanding of the limits of markets, for instance showing that whenever there were imperfections of information (that is, *always*), markets are not, in general, efficient. My work in this area was the basis of the Nobel Memorial Prize that was awarded in 2001. (See, in particular, Bruce C. Greenwald and Joseph E. Stiglitz, "Externalities in Economies with Imperfect Information and Incomplete Markets," *Quarterly Journal of Economics* 101 (2) (May 1986), pp. 229–64.) It used to be the presumption that markets were efficient; there were limited circumstances, such as unemployment or pollution, requiring government intervention. Now, the presumption is reversed: markets are typically inefficient. The task of government is to identify those instances where the inefficiencies are the greatest and where selective intervention is most likely to improve matters.

8 This is a result I showed with Professor David Newbery of Cambridge University more than a third of a century ago. See "Pareto Inferior Trade," *Review of Economic Studies* 51 (1) (1984), pp. 1–12. Professor Partha Dasgupta (also of Cambridge University) and I were able to show that quotas—restrictions on the absolute amount that could be imported—might be better than tariffs, upending a key pillar of trade policy of the last half century, which has been to convert quotas into tariffs. See "Tariffs vs. Quotas as Revenue Raising Devices Under Uncertainty," *American Economic Review* 67 (5) (1977), pp. 975–81.

9 I warned about these issues in *Making Globalization Work,* op. cit., the book on globalization that I wrote following *GAID. GAID* had explained what had gone wrong with globalization. In *Making Globalization Work,* I sought to explain what could be done to make it work right. Chapter 4 in this book can be viewed as an extension of that work.

10 This was a concern in South Africa, which took measures to protect small African producers, insisting that Walmart incorporate them into its supply chain. For full disclosure: I was an expert witness appointed by the South African government in its case against Walmart.

11 In these cases, trade can originate based not on relative competence, as in the standard theory, but on relative market power. In Mexico, Walmart demonstrated another strength which need not contribute to societal well-being: greater willingness and ability to engage in corruption. For the story that broke the scandal, see David Barstow, "Vast Mexico Bribery Case Hushed Up by Wal-Mart after Top-Level Struggle," *New York Times,* April 21, 2012.

12 That is, they worry that small producers will *always* claim that a large firm from abroad has market power, and that is why it can undersell.

13 This is one of the central points in Bruce C. Greenwald and Joseph E. Stiglitz, *Creating a Learning Society: A New Approach to Growth, Development, and Social Progress* (New York: Columbia University Press, 2014; Reader's Edition, 2015).

14 Some point to Germany and its success in retaining manufacturing jobs, suggesting that if the United States would only follow Germany's example, it could recover its manufacturing jobs. This is wrong, for several reasons. As I discuss later (chapter 3), total global manufacturing jobs will be in decline, and it will be even difficult for the United States to retain its current share. Germany did so in part by having an undervalued exchange rate, the result of its being part of the euro. But Germany did so in part by having a well-tuned apprenticeship and education system, which would take years for the United States to create—if it could do so. Besides, Germany was "lucky" in focusing on niches within manufacturing, like complex machine tools, that China has yet to enter. As China moves up the "value chain," producing increasingly complex goods, Germany may find it increasingly difficult to retain its share in global manufacturing employment.

15 Indeed, the success the United States has had in retaining jobs in, say, manufacturing has necessitated massive cuts in wages—in some cases by two-thirds. One of the arguments for focusing on manufacturing was that those jobs were "good," high-paying jobs. But that argument is obviously weakened if, to retain manufacturing, those jobs are converted into low-paying jobs.

16 When government revenues exceed spending, government has a surplus, i.e., it is saving. Conversely, when spending exceeds revenues, there is a deficit. National savings is the sum of private savings plus government savings. When the government runs a deficit, the government has negative savings, obviously diminishing national savings. Funds are fungible, so it doesn't matter much whether the government borrows from abroad to finance its deficit, or the government borrows from America's private sector, but the private sector borrows from abroad to finance its investment.

17 In note 6, I noted that exports of services—like sales to tourists or to students—are just as much exports as the exports of manufactured goods. Exports of services create jobs just as exports of goods do.

18 It was not until the Clinton administration that the huge fiscal deficits were reversed. But as this happened, America went through an investment boom—the tech bubble. With limited private savings, the corporate sector had to borrow abroad, so even as the fiscal deficit was eliminated, the trade deficit persisted. Bush returned to fiscal deficits with his tax cuts

of 2001 and 2003, and during his tenure we had both fiscal deficits and a housing boom. Finally, Obama inherited the Great Recession, leading to massive fiscal deficits even as investment contracted. Thus, the gap between domestic investment and domestic savings persisted.

19 Though the United States did restrict some exports of high-technology products to China. China argues that U.S. complaints about China not buying enough American goods are unfair: the United States refuses to sell it some of the key goods in which the United States has a comparative advantage.

20 The lower interest rate made it less attractive to buy U.S. Treasury bills. Money shifted from the United States to, say, Europe, lowering the value of the dollar relative to the euro. The defense of the United States was that this fall in the exchange rate was an *incidental* side effect. In reality, of course, the adjustment of the exchange rate is one of the main mechanisms by which interest rates have a macroeconomic effect. These benefits would not have occurred if other countries had lowered interest rates in tandem. But in April and again in July 2011, the European Central Bank, then headed by Jean-Claude Trichet, actually increased interest rates; it was worried about incipient inflation, and saw its mandate narrowly as fighting inflation. Later, Europe did lower its interest rates to levels close to that of the United States, eliminating this advantage.

21 This amounts to a decline of 25 percent. Source: Bloomberg.

22 As in the case of his complaint about Mexican immigrants, Trump's timing was badly off.

23 What determines comparative advantage in a modern economy is complex. In the simple agricultural economy analyzed by David Ricardo, it's weather: Portugal has a comparative advantage compared to the UK in producing wine, relative to wool, because its weather is more suited to wine. But with capital, and even skilled labor, relatively mobile, and even knowledge that resides within a corporation moving easily across borders, comparative advantage resides in those aspects of production which are not mobile, such as the legal institutions.

24 These expenditures could, however, affect the sectors in which a country has comparative advantage.

25 See Joseph E. Stiglitz, *Making Globalization Work,* op. cit., chapter 6.

26 Trade agreements have not dealt with the problems posed by market power, but some countries have used their own competition laws. For instance, when Walmart entered South Africa, competition authorities required it to take certain actions (including making certain payments) to ensure that small South African producers were not adversely affected.

27 This was called the factor price equalization theorem. Trade in goods was (under the stipulated conditions) a *perfect* substitute for movement of people. If one worried about the consequences for unskilled wages of a large immigration of unskilled workers from developing countries, one should have been equally worried about free trade with developing countries. See Paul Samuelson, "International Trade and the Equalisation of Factor Prices," *Economic Journal* 58 (230) (1948), pp. 163–84.

28 Wolfgang Stolper and Paul Samuelson showed that trade liberalization—reducing tariffs—would lower unskilled wages in the country with relatively high unskilled wages. See W. Stolper and P. A. Samuelson, "Protection and Real Wages," *Review of Economic Studies* 9 (1) (1941), pp. 58–73.

29 This is an aphorism attributed to John F. Kennedy in various speeches, most notably in 1963. See "Remarks in Heber Springs, Arkansas, at the Dedication of Greers Ferry Dam," October 3, 1963.

30 See Joseph E. Stiglitz, *The Price of Inequality*, op. cit.

31 See Joseph E. Stiglitz et al., *Rewriting the Rules of the American Economy*, op. cit.

32 Later, Warren Buffett would say: "There's class warfare, all right, but it's my class, the rich class, that's making war, and we're winning." As quoted by Ben Stein, "In Class Warfare, Guess Which Class Is Winning," *New York Times*, November 26, 2006, available at http://www.nytimes.com/2006/11/26/business/yourmoney/26every.html.

33 While *GAID* focuses on the consequences of globalization for the poor in developing countries, in *Making Globalization Work*, op. cit., I explain how unskilled workers in advanced countries would be hurt. But the underlying ideas, as I explain, could be traced by to the work of Stolper and Samuelson cited earlier.

34 This particular president was a doctor, and when he asked me whether he should sign the proposed trade agreement, I replied by asking him whether he had taken the Hippocratic Oath (required of all doctors) which includes: do no harm. He said he had. I replied that he then *couldn't* sign the trade agreement, especially since the proposed agreement would have reduced access to life-saving medicines. Whether because of these arguments, or more likely domestic politics, he decided not to push for an agreement with the United States.

35 As I've explained here and elsewhere, perhaps even more important was the fact that over the past third of a century, the rules of the market economy have been rewritten in ways which have weakened unions' and workers' bargaining position. This is one of the central themes of Joseph E. Stiglitz et al., *Rewriting the Rules of the American Economy*, op. cit.

Changes in technology have combined with changes in the structure of the economy and in the rules and their enforcement leading to an increase in market concentration in many sectors. The resulting increase in prices leads, in turn, to lower standards of living for workers.

Some argue too that there is greater dispersion of wages within the service sector than in manufacturing, and as the economy moves to a service sector economy, there will be more wage inequality. This, however, does not account for the decline in the share of labor overall, and the fact that workers' compensation has not kept pace with productivity. See Josh Bivens and Lawrence Mishel, "Understanding the Historic Divergence Between Productivity and a Typical Worker's Pay: Why It Matters and Why It's Real," Economic Policy Institute Briefing Paper #406, 2015, http://www.epi.org/publication/understanding-the-historic-divergence-between-productivity-and-a-typical-workers-pay-why-it-matters-and-why-its-real/.

36 See Bruce Greenwald and Judd Kahn, *globalization: n. the irrational fear that someone in China will take your job* (Hoboken, NJ: Wiley, 2009).

37 Perhaps that's because he believes in American exceptionalism—that because of U.S. economic power, it can get away with doing what others can't. But while this might have been true at one time, it isn't true today, at least when other large economies, like China and the EU, are affected.

38 Globalization's rules have had an ambiguous effect on the disparity between developed and developing countries in knowledge. What separates developing and developed countries is a disparity in knowledge even more than a disparity in resources (See Stiglitz and Greenwald, *Creating a Learning Society*, op. cit., and World Bank, *Knowledge for Development*, World Development Report, 1998.) Those in the advanced countries enjoyed enormous "knowledge rents," extra income that they receive because of the advantage of knowledge that they have that is not universal. While globalization facilitated the movement of technology across borders—thus reducing this advantage—an important part of modern globalization, discussed below, are global intellectual property rights, designed to impede the movement of knowledge across borders and to ensure that those in the advanced countries maintain their knowledge rents.

Still, the location of production matters for learning associated with production, learning by doing. And there are important spillovers from such learning for the entire economy. This learning has played an important role in the success of China and some of the other countries of East Asia.

39 Trump, of course, never explains how he calculates this; indeed, through-

out the campaign and months after the election, he refused to even specify
what he would like changed.

40 From 1994 to 2013, Mexican corn production was reduced from 8.0 million hectares to 6.8 million, while that in the United States increased from
29.3 million to 35.5 million. American subsidies take many forms, some of
which are more distorting than others. The U.S. mandate for cars to use
ethanol and subsidies for U.S. ethanol production played an important role
in the expansion of U.S. production. See G. C. Hufbauer, C. Cimino-Isaacs,
and T. Moran, "NAFTA at 20: Misleading Charges and Positive Achievements," *Peterson Institute for International Economics, PB14-13* (2014).

41 A 2016 study by the Wilson Center put Mexico-dependent jobs at 4.9
million, while a 2012 report by the U.S. Chamber of Commerce esti-
mating 6 million jobs is also frequently cited. See Christopher Wilson,
"Growing Together: Economic Ties Between the United States and
Mexico," Mexico Institute at the Wilson Center, November 2016, and
"Enhancing the US-Mexico Economic Partnership," U.S. Chamber of
Commerce, April 2012.

42 Source: United States Census Bureau's 2016 Foreign Trade statistics,
retrieved from https://www.census.gov/foreign-trade/index.html.

43 In 2016, for instance, the United States had a goods trade deficit with
Canada of $12 billion, but a services trade surplus of $25 billion. Source:
United States Trade Representative, retrieved from https://ustr.gov/
countries-regions/americas/canada.

44 The international system, in which there are reciprocal agreements about
how each country behaves with respect to exports and imports and how disputes about compliance with such rules are to be resolved is often referred
to as the "global rules-based system." Respect for such agreements—
actually complying with the agreement—is part of the respect for the
international rule of law.

Some might argue that since countries can always withdraw from
such agreements, they have not really given up any sovereignty. (The
contrast is between the states of the United States, which cannot withdraw from the union, and the members of the EU, which can.) *De facto,*
however, there is a weakening of sovereignty (and that is certainly how
signing the WTO agreement was perceived, especially by conservatives,
in the United States). The United States has respected most of the adverse
WTO decisions, either changing its action or providing compensation to
the offended party to induce it to withdraw the complaint. In no instance
has there been retaliation against a country that has been authorized by the

WTO to impose trade sanctions in response to what has been judged to be a WTO-noncompliant action. Thus, the WTO has avoided trade wars.

45 For a popular account, see Daron Acemoglu and James A. Robinson, *Why Nations Fail: The Origins of Power, Prosperity, and Poverty* (New York: Crown Business, 2013).

46 See, e.g., President Xi's speech in Davos, January 17, 2017, available at https://www.weforum.org/agenda/2017/01/full-text-of-xi-jinping-keynote-at-the-world-economic-forum.

47 This principle is long-standing and was embodied in international agreements that preceded the WTO, in GATT, the General Agreement on Tariffs and Trade, which went into effect in 1948.

48 See, for instance, *The Stiglitz Report: Reforming the International Monetary and Financial Systems in the Wake of the Global Crisis,* Report of the Commission of Experts on Reforms of the International Monetary and Financial System appointed by the President of the United Nations General Assembly (New York: New Press, 2010).

49 Thus, TPP was seen as part of the "pivot to Asia." In fact, as I will note later, the economic benefits were estimated to be negligible.

50 Obama not only overestimated the trade benefits of TPP, but also the foreign policy benefits. China already had multiple trade agreements around the region, and with most countries in the region, its trade was far larger than the trade with the United States. Many believe that the United States should have been focused on encouraging cooperation with China, not the kind of confrontation that TPP represented. Earlier, the Clinton administration had switched from a policy of containment and confrontation to one of engagement and cooperation. In other arenas, such as climate change, the Obama administration did engage in cooperation, and without this cooperation, the Paris global deal on climate change would not have been possible.

51 The U.S. recession also played a role in discouraging migration.

52 I discuss how they do this in greater detail later.

53 Source: "Trans-Pacific Partnership: Likely Impact on the U.S. Economy and on Specific Industry Sectors," United States International Trade Commission, 2016, available at https://www.usitc.gov/publications/332/pub4607.pdf.

54 J. Capaldo, A. Izurieta, and J. K. Sundaram, "Trading Down: Unemployment, Inequality, and Other Risks of the Trans-Pacific Partnership Agreement," GDAE Working Paper 16-01, Tufts University, 2016.

55 Consistent with there not being significant externalities to other jurisdictions. Unfortunately, the European Commission often seems to have forgotten this principle in its quest for regulatory uniformity.

Chapter 2

1 The Riegle-Neal Interstate Banking and Branching Efficiency Act eliminated previous restrictions. The restrictions were originally motivated out of a worry that the big money center banks would drain money out of the rest of the country toward them. It was thought that such restrictions would encourage the development of different regions of the country, and there is some evidence that that is in fact the case. (See, e.g., Bruce Greenwald and Joseph E. Stiglitz, *Towards a New Paradigm in Monetary Economics* [Cambridge: Cambridge University Press, 2003].) One of the arguments for the act was that the banks had found many ways of circumventing the restrictions.

2 See, e.g., Stiglitz and Greenwald, *Creating a Learning Society*, op. cit.

3 Smith's most famous book, *The Wealth of Nations,* was published in the year of U.S. independence, 1776.

4 Almost a half century ago, I showed that when the tax code provides for deductibility of interest (as the U.S. code does), the corporate income tax has no effect on investment when depreciation rates correspond to "true" economic depreciation. In fact, most tax codes (including that of the United States) provide for faster depreciation, so that the effect of the corporate income tax is actually to encourage investment, with the tax reducing marginal returns by less than it reduces marginal costs. See "Taxation, Corporate Financial Policy and the Cost of Capital," *Journal of Public Economics* 2 (February 1973), pp. 1–34.

5 Source: Data from the Bureau of Economic Analysis, U.S. Department of Commerce.

6 The full analysis is slightly more complicated because of exchange rate effects.

7 These are called macroeconomic externalities. Bruce Greenwald and I (in our 1986 paper, "Externalities in Economies with Imperfect Information and Incomplete Markets," op. cit.) showed that whenever there was imperfect information or incomplete risk markets—that is, essentially always—markets are not fully efficient; there are always government interventions that could make some individuals better off without harming others. Subsequently, a host of economists showed that these effects can manifest themselves in a significant way at a macroeconomic level, with firms, for instance, borrowing excessively in foreign-denominated debt (see, for example, Markus Brunnermeier and Yuliy Sannikov, "International Credit Flows and Pecuniary Externalities," *American Economic Journal: Macroeconomics* 7 [1] [January 2015], pp. 297–338).

8 Matters are even worse: the compensation schemes provide incentives to distort accounting systems to make it seem as if profits are higher than they really are. For a fuller account, see my book, written in the aftermath of the scandals of the early years of this century: *The Roaring Nineties: A New History of the World's Most Prosperous Decade* (New York: W. W. Norton, 2003), and especially the discussion of creative accounting (chapter 5). For a discussion of some of the changes in the rules of the American economy that led to the changes in compensation schemes, see Joseph E. Stiglitz et al., *Rewriting the Rules of the American Economy,* op. cit.

9 In democratic societies, governments turn over frequently, and this also gives rise to "short-termism," a focus on the short-term consequences of policies, with insufficient attention given to the long run. But while there is thus clearly a tendency for short-termism, it can and has been combated—but that can only happen once the problem has been recognized. Thus, Norway has put almost a trillion dollars of its oil revenues away for the future in its sovereign wealth fund. In short, there are institutional mechanisms for addressing short-termism.

10 The first such agreement, between Pakistan and Germany, was signed in 1959. In recent years, they have proliferated—and the world began to understand the problems that they brought. See my paper, "Regulating Multinational Corporations: Towards Principles of Cross-Border Legal Frameworks in a Globalized World Balancing Rights with Responsibilities," *American University International Law Review* 23 (3) (2007), pp. 451–558, Grotius Lecture presented at the 101st Annual Meeting of the American Society for International Law, Washington, DC, March 28, 2007.

11 Trump has necessitated a reexamination of the vocabulary used to describe falsehoods. A lie conveys a malicious intent to deceive.

12 The branch of the World Bank Group that does this is called MIGA (Multilateral Investment Guarantee Agency). The U.S. government has an agency called OPIC (Overseas Private Investment Corporation).

13 Source: Duff Wilson, "Cigarette Giants in Global Fight on Tighter Rules," *New York Times,* November 13, 2010.

14 International Center for Settlement of Investment Disputes. 2013. Philip Morris v. Uruguay: Award, ICSID Case No. ARB/10/7, http:// icsidfiles.worldbank.org/icsid/ICSIDBLOBS/OnlineAwards/C1000/DC9012_En.pdf. Had Uruguay lost, it might have had to pay as much as $2 billion to Philip Morris, an enormous amount for this small country. ("Uruguay vs. Philip Morris," Center for Public Integrity, available at https://www.publicintegrity.org/2010/11/15/4036/part-iii-uruguay-vs-philip-morris.)

15 The provisions of the investment agreements restricting regulations are sometimes called "regulatory takings" provisions. The argument is that regulations take away property rights; in this way, they are similar to confiscation, except the owner is only deprived partially of his use of the asset. Courts in the United States, and Congress, have repeatedly affirmed that owners do not have to be compensated for the effects of regulations on the value of their assets, for the obvious reason that doing so would totally impair the ability of government to regulate. Indeed, that is the intent of the anti-environmentalists who are the strongest advocates of these provisions.

16 Thus, imagine what would have happened had these provisions been in place when the health consequences of asbestos were discovered and, as a result, asbestos was forbidden in construction. Rather than the asbestos manufacturers compensating those hurt, the government would have had to compensate the asbestos manufacturers for their lost profits. Critics of tobacco suggest that Philip Morris, in the suit against Uruguay, was effectively asserting its "right to kill." Though eventually Philip Morris lost, the fact that it was a 2-to-1 decision makes clear that in some other case, the ruling might go the other way.

17 I was asked by the government of Panama to head a commission to advise them on what reforms were required to enable them to be a good global citizen. When they refused to commit to making our report transparent, Mark Pieth—another non-Panamanian Commissioner and a devoted anti-corruption expert from Basel—and I felt we had no choice but to resign. Subsequently, we wrote a report describing what Panama and other fiscal paradises needed to do. See "Overcoming the Shadow Economy," Friedrich Ebert Stiftung International Policy Analysis Paper, November 2016. For other discussions of the fiscal paradises, see N. Shaxson (2011), *Treasure Islands: Uncovering the Damage of Offshore Banking and Tax Havens* (New York: Macmillan, 2011); and G. Zucman, *The Hidden Wealth of Nations: The Scourge of Tax Havens* (Chicago: University of Chicago Press, 2015).

18 U.S. Senate, Hearings of the Permanent Subcommittee on Investigations, "Offshore Profit Shifting and the U.S. Tax Code—Part 2 (Apple Inc.)," May 21, 2013, available at https://www.hsgac.senate.gov/subcommittees/investigations/hearings/offshore-profit-shifting-and-the-us-tax-code_-part-2. European Commission, August 30, 2016, press release, http://europa.eu/rapid/press-release_IP-16-2923_en.htm.

19 The distinction between tax avoidance and tax evasion is that the latter entails not paying taxes that are legally due, while the former entails

taking advantage of loopholes and differences in tax rates and provisions across different jurisdictions to lower one's tax obligations. The boundary between the two may be thin.

20 One of the few things on which Democrats and Republicans in the United States agree is that these arrangements need to change, but they differ in the view of how they should be changed. They all agree that the pile of profits stashed abroad should be taxed now—this gives a one-time bonus that can be used to finance infrastructure investments, or more tax cuts for corporations (in the case of Republicans) or for the middle class (in the case of Democrats). The repatriated money would be taxed at a lower rate than the current 35 percent, but, as this book goes to press, Republicans are talking about a much lower rate than what the Democrats are proposing. Republicans (by and large) believe in a territorial income tax system, where money earned abroad would not be taxed at all by the United States. The Democrats believe that American companies making money abroad should be taxed at the same rate as they would be taxed for production in the United States—otherwise we would be encouraging firms to locate abroad to lower-taxed jurisdictions.

21 These were called tax inversions. The Obama administration issued regulations to stymie these attempts at tax avoidance. As this book goes to press, Trump appears to be making efforts to undo these restrictions.

22 I noted earlier (in the introduction) the large reduction in the revenues raised in the United States by corporate taxation (as a percentage of GDP). In Europe, individuals can easily move between countries, choosing a low-tax residence, making it difficult to impose very progressive income taxes. By contrast, U.S. citizens are taxed on their income, regardless of where they live. For a fuller discussion, see Joseph E. Stiglitz, *The Euro,* op. cit.

23 Source: David Riker, "Intellectual Property Rights and International Receipts of Royalties and Licensing Fees," Office of Economics Working Paper, U.S. International Trade Commission, August 2014.

24 The true cost to developing countries of IPR is much greater than this amount, for the IPR gets leveraged into monopoly, and those in the developing countries thus have to pay much higher prices for goods which fall under the protection of IPR. In the absence of this monopoly, firms in developing countries could enter and the country would benefit not just from the lower prices but from the learning that resulted. India had a thriving generic drugs industry before stronger IPR laws restricted its scope. See Stiglitz and Greenwald, *Creating a Learning Society,* op. cit.

25 Economists distinguish between two kinds of compensation: what one receives for the exertion of effort (wages), and what one receives from the

ownership of an asset (land), which has nothing to do with one's exertions, also called "rents." Rents also include the returns one gets from the ownership of a monopoly. Economists have broadened the concept: rent-seeking is any attempt to increase one's income in a way unrelated to one's exertions directed at increasing the size of the national pie. For an elaboration, see Joseph E. Stiglitz, *The Price of Inequality*, op. cit.

26 As I have noted elsewhere, what separates developing and developed countries is a disparity in knowledge that is even greater than the disparity in resources. Excessively strong IPR impede the closing of the knowledge gap and force a flow of resources from developing countries to the developed.

27 Association for Molecular Pathology et al. v. Myriad Genetics, Inc., et al. Case No. 12-398. Argued April 15, 2013-Decided June 13, 2013. I was pleased to have written an Amicus brief, in support of the ACLU (Case 1:09-cv-04515-RWS, Document 224, Filed 01/20/2010).

28 There was a net outflow of Mexican immigrants of 140,000 from 2009 to 2014. "More Mexicans Leaving Than Coming to the U.S.," Pew Research Center, November 19, 2015, available at http://www.pewhispanic.org/2015/11/19/more-mexicans-leaving-than-coming-to-the-u-s/.

29 Trade in goods would be a nearly perfect substitute for movement of labor. In such a world, if we imported more unskilled-labor-intensive goods from China, the demand for unskilled labor in China would increase, while in the United States it would decrease, thereby increasing unskilled wages in the former and decreasing them in the latter. This back-and-forth would continue until the wages for unskilled labor would be the same in both countries. This was the central message of our earlier discussion on trade liberalization.

30 There are some "limiting" cases where full-factor price equalization might not occur, for instance, a country with much unskilled labor totally specialized in producing goods intensive in unskilled labor.

31 Branko Milanović, *Global Inequality: A New Approach for the Age of Globalization* (Cambridge, MA: Harvard University Press, 2016).

32 In particular, of public services, like defense, in which there is no increase in costs when another person moves into the country. Moreover, an increase in the supply of unskilled workers could increase the productivity and wages of skilled workers. (Technically, economists would say that that happens if unskilled and skilled workers are *complements*. It is usually assumed that they are.) Of course, if the direct public services used by the immigrant are greater than his total tax contributions (direct and indirect), then there will be a burden on those already living in the country.

33 This discussion has focused on the effects of immigration on the "receiving"

country. There are similarly benefits and costs to the sending country. A large literature has analyzed the benefits that arise from the remittances that are sent back. Some have argued that there are also "cultural remittances": returnees bring back skills that they have learned abroad. There can also be negative effects on the sending country: when the most talented young people leave, leading to a "hollowing out" of their society, it may impede the growth and development of the sending country. Developing countries rightly complain that after spending large sums in providing education, some of the most talented emigrate to developed countries, which receive the benefits but provide no compensation to the developing countries. Malaysia's former prime minister described this as the theft of the country's intellectual property. (See Joseph E. Stiglitz, *Making Globalization Work,* op. cit.) Some have suggested there can be other adverse effects—for instance, that workers returning from the Middle East to Bangladesh, Pakistan, and some other countries have been radicalized.

34 Boeing also is helped by loans through the U.S. government's Export-Import Bank (sometimes called "Boeing's Bank"). To be fair, Europe also subsidizes its producer, but in a different form. Indeed, the entire industry is rife with subsidies.

The construction of an assembly plant by Airbus, the main European aircraft manufacturer, in Mobile, Alabama, illustrates the secondary role played by standard comparative advantage. The parts were shipped into Alabama largely from Europe. The workers there had no relevant skills that Airbus was taking advantage of. Indeed, the mentality of American workers—don't worry about getting things right the first time; we can fix it later—was seen as a problem. Rather, having a plant in the United States was seen as helping promote sales to the American government, and possibly other purchasers. Assistance from the state government—it picked up much of the tab for training workers—mattered, as did the absence of unions, which resulted in wages topping up at $23 an hour. Binyamin Appelbaum, "Politics Rives Epic Assembly Line Project," *New York Times International Edition,* May 9, 2017, p. 1.

35 See M. Mazzucato, *The Entrepreneurial State: Debunking Public vs. Private Myths* (London: Anthem Press, 2013).

36 Source: 2015 National Health Expenditure Accounts, United States Government Centers for Medicare and Medicaid Services.

37 Indeed, in the TPP negotiations, the USTR was asking for stronger protection for Big Pharma than the president had argued for in other contexts.

38 Indeed, when the USTR compromised on a technical provision (the length

of data exclusivity for certain products)—in a way that even the president had advocated—one of the key senators threatened to torpedo the entire agreement and send it back for renegotiation.

The industry justifies its demands in terms of ensuring that American firms get a fair return on their investments in R&D. The battle between access to medicines and ensuring returns to innovation was settled within the United States by the Hatch-Waxman Act of 1984, which enabled Big Pharma to maintain very high profit levels, while generics grabbed more than 80 percent of the market. Without generics, as I have noted, drug prices would be much higher than they are today. Big Pharma has tried to reopen the matter, behind closed doors, through trade agreements—trying to get a far better deal for themselves than under Hatch-Waxman.

39 There were two arguments of modest validity: Why, they said, should those who lose their jobs from globalization be singled out? Weren't those who lost their jobs due to technology equally deserving of help? The answer, of course, was yes, and we as a society should have helped both. But the Republican stance was to help neither.

The other argument was that these job assistance programs sometimes don't work. And that was true, especially when the economy was far from full employment. We can't retrain people for jobs that don't exist. But here again, the right answer was to change macroeconomic policies to ensure that the economy operated with a tight labor market—even if it meant mild inflation; and to learn, from countries like Sweden, how to make job retraining programs work well.

40 Economics plays an important role in these political trends, but there are other forces at play. Those who supported nativist policies, which include many who have suffered as a result of globalization or changes in technology, also include disproportionately those with less education, and at least the United States and Europe each have their own history of such inward-looking politics.

Chapter 3

1 There are profound consequences of just being able to pick one's "alternative facts." In a Trumpian world, what is one to make of "due process," or many of the other terms that constitute our system of jurisprudence? Presumably, the president could just make up his alternative facts, concluding that he had done what the law requires.

2 For an elaboration of these ideas, see J. Mokyr, *The Gifts of Athena: Historical*

Origins of the Knowledge Economy (Princeton, NJ: Princeton University Press, 2002); J. Mokyr, *The Enlightened Economy: An Economic History of Britain, 1700–1850* (New Haven, CT: Yale University Press, 2009); and Joseph E. Stiglitz and Bruce C. Greenwald, *Creating a Learning Society,* op.cit.

3 Even when they are defeated, as Le Pen was in France in the 2017 election, the size of their vote—about a third of those voting chose Le Pen—is disturbing.

4 For a more extensive account of the crisis and its aftermath, see my book *Freefall,* op. cit.

5 Source: E. Saez, "Striking it Richer: The Evolution of Top Incomes in the United States (Updated with 2015 preliminary estimates)," UC Berkeley, June 30, 2016, available at https://eml.berkekey.edu/~saez/saez-USStopincomes-2015.pdf.

6 Of course, some businessmen have engaged in the serious study of economics, and their practical experience has no doubt been of some value. The point here is simple: knowing how to buy and sell real estate itself teaches very little about how our global economic system works. Worse, there is a danger that it narrows the lens through which one sees the world. A real estate developer will naturally assign a great deal of value to real estate, and think that lowering capital gains taxes on land is a good thing, because it makes his business do better; in fact, a tax on land has long been established as one of the most efficient taxes, because it has zero effect on land supply. This is but one of many examples of how understanding the economy through the lens of a particular industry can be dangerous.

7 Since becoming president, he seems to have backed off from these extreme threats, but as this book goes to press, he continues with his strongly protectionist rhetoric.

8 See World Bank, *The East Asian Miracle: Economic Growth and Public Policy* (Oxford: Oxford University Press, 1993).

9 In standardized tests, among the thirty-five countries in the OECD, the United States performed around average in science. Its performance was also around average in reading, but below average in mathematics. Source: OECD 2015 Programme for International Student Assessment (PISA) findings.

10 Source: 2014 data (most recent) from the Bureau of Labor Statistics.

11 "U.S. Energy and Employment Report," U.S. Department of Energy, January 2017. The Department of Energy has acknowledged that the data it collects on solar industry is imperfectly comparable to some other industries. But regardless, the figures support a picture of an industry in ascendancy, whereas investment and employment in coal are in marked decline.

This also suggests the foolishness of the imposition of duties on solar panels from China during the Obama administration—pushed by U.S. solar manufacturers. Lower panel costs induce more use of solar panels—a boon to the environment as well as to job creation. The new jobs created there almost surely outweigh the limited number of jobs that would have been created in manufacturing solar panels.

12 These ideas are developed at greater length in two papers I wrote with D. Delli Gatti, M. Gallegati, B.C. Greenwald and A. Russo: "Sectoral Imbalances and Long-Run Crises," in Franklin Allen et al., eds., *The Global Macro Economy and Finance*, IEA Conference Volume No. 150-III (Houndmills, UK, and New York: Palgrave, 2012), pp. 61–97 (originally presented to World Congress of the International Economic Association, Jordan, June 2014); and "Mobility Constraints, Productivity Trends, and Extended Crises," *Journal of Economic Behavior and Organization* 83 (3), pp. 375–93.

For a more popular and accessible account, see Part VIII in Joseph E. Stiglitz, *The Great Divide,* op. cit.

13 The most egregious example was the demand of the Western powers that China keep its markets open to opium, which was having a devastating effect on the country. From the perspective of the West, this was important to correct a trade imbalance. When China refused, the Opium Wars (1839–60) ensued. As I have already noted, tariff structures (called escalating tariffs) designed to encourage developing countries to produce raw materials, with value-added activities occurring in the more advanced countries, remain a part of today's rules-based trade regime. See Andrew Charlton and Joseph E. Stiglitz, *Fair Trade for All,* op. cit.

14 In 2016, $3.7 trillion, higher than $3.6 trillion for the United States, according to the IMF.

15 In 2016, $5.2 trillion, compared to the United States' $3.3 trillion, according to the IMF.

16 Much of *GAID* (Part II of this volume) was devoted to explaining the Washington Consensus and why it failed.

17 For an overview, see, for instance, A. Noman and J. E. Stiglitz, "Economics and Policy: Some Lessons from Africa's Experience," in Célestin Monga and Justin Yifu Lin, eds., *The Oxford Handbook of Africa and Economics, Volume II: Policies and Practices* (Oxford and New York: Oxford University Press, 2015), pp. 830–48; and Akbar Noman and Joseph E. Stiglitz, eds., *Efficiency, Finance, and Varieties of Industrial Policy: Guiding Resources, Learning, and Technology for Sustained Growth* (New York:

Columbia University Press, 2016), and especially the "Overview," pp. 1–20. For the cases of Tanzania or Mozambique, see "Learning to Compete: Industrialization in Africa and Emerging Asia," Brookings Institution, 2014, https://www.brookings.edu/research/learning-to-compete-industrialization-in-africa-and-emerging-asia.

18 See World Bank, *The East Asian Miracle: Economic Growth and Public Policy* (New York: Oxford University Press, 1993); and J. E. Stiglitz, "Some Lessons from the East Asian Miracle," *World Bank Research Observer* 11 (2) (August 1996), pp. 151–77.

19 Indeed, just before this time, Nobel Prize–winning economist Gunnar Myrdal had predicted that Asia would be condemned to continue the life of poverty in which they had been mired for centuries. See G. Myrdal, *Asian Drama: An Inquiry into the Poverty of Nations* (New York: Twentieth Century Fund, 1968).

20 In the introduction, I describe other aspects of this nostalgia which may have played an especially important role in the United States and some other countries: a nostalgia for a world in which certain groups (white males) had a more dominant role than they do today. That world too will not be coming back.

21 I explain how it works in chapter 1. In brief: when a country saves less than it invests, it has to borrow the difference from abroad (or in some other way get the difference through capital inflows). But capital inflows, in turn, are just equal to the difference between a country's imports and exports. Hence, an increase in the gap between domestic investment and savings leads to more capital inflows, which must mean an increase in the trade deficit. So in the end, to analyze changes in the trade deficit, one has to go back to analyze changes in domestic savings and investment. If there are no changes in domestic savings and investment, then there can't be a change in the trade deficit.

22 Higher prices might induce households to save less (until they can adjust their living standards), and if so, that would lead to a still higher trade deficit.

23 See J. Furman, K. Russ and J. Shambaugh, "US Tariffs Are an Arbitrary and Regressive Tax," VOX Column, January 12, 2017, http://voxeu.org/article/us-tariffs-are-arbitrary-and-regressive-tax.

24 Indeed, as I note in the introduction, the rules-based system prevented an outbreak of beggar-thy-neighbor protectionism as the world sank into the Great Recession.

25 As I note earlier, his administration has already announced that it will not honor adverse rulings from the WTO.

26 Source: IMF World Economic Outlook, April 2017. This is the source of GDP data in Part I and the afterword, unless otherwise noted.

27 Source: People's Bank of China, see "Template on International Reserves and Foreign Currency Liquidity (as at July 31 2017)" at http://www.safe .gov.cn/wps/portal/english/Data.

28 For instance, if a country provides "illegal" subsidies, one can levy what are called countervailing duties. The U.S. has claimed that China has subsidized solar panels—even though having inexpensive solar panels is of enormous benefit to the world in the fight against climate change. Ironically, though the rationale for the suit was that China was stealing American manufacturing jobs (without China's subsidies, allegedly there would have been more manufacturing jobs), China indirectly helped create more U.S. jobs. There are far more jobs associated with the installation of solar panels than with manufacturing them, and lower solar panel prices encouraged the development of this new industry.

    There are provisions in U.S. law that allow the imposition of duties when imports threaten U.S. security. As this book goes to press, Trump is threatening to use this little-used provision in steel, even though America's current steel capacity seems more than adequate to meet any security needs.

29 This is true even in the case of long-term friendly trading partners—like Canada—when we start acting in a hostile manner. Trump has threatened to impose duties on Canadian lumber, claiming that the way the government allocates logging rights effectively subsidizes it. Canada denies it. (The U.S. has been accused of subsidizing the lumber industries, though in different ways.) One response, broached by the premier of one of Canada's provinces, was to forbid dirty American coal from its ports—a measure long sought by environmentalists. See Sunny Dhillon and Wendy Stuek, "Christy Clark Calls on Ottawa to Ban Coal Exports After Softwood Lumber Duties," *Globe and Mail*, April 26, 2017, available at http://www.theglobeandmail.com/news/british-columbia/christy-clark-calls-on-ottawa-to-ban-coal-exports-after-softwood-lumber-duties/ article34822276/.

30 M. Angeles Villareal, "U.S.-Mexico Economic Relations: Trends, Issues, and Implications," *Congressional Research Service*, 2017, https://fas.org/sgp/ crs/row/RL32934.pdf. Data source is the Global Trade Atlas.

Chapter 4

1 This point has been forcefully made in a recent book by two Nobel Prize winners, George Akerlof and Rob Shiller, entitled *Phishing for Phools: The Economics of Manipulation and Deception* (Princeton, NJ: Princeton University Press, 2015).

2 As we discuss in the afterword, one of the marked changes in globalization since *GAID* was first published is the position taken by the IMF towards capital controls or other measures designed to stabilize short-term capital flows. While among the major battles I had with the IMF was over their adamant opposition to such measures, their official "institutional" view now is that at least in certain situations, such measures are desirable.

3 That excessive faith in markets—combined with special interests—fed the zeal for privatization that I describe in *GAID*. Failures in privatization in the years since *GAID*, in both developed and developing countries, reinforce this conclusion. In *GAID*, I describe the story of America's privatization of USEC, the public company making enriched uranium. The privatized company was very unsuccessful and filed for Chapter 11 bankruptcy in the first quarter of 2014. Among the most criticized privatizations in the United States has been the privatization of its prisons, which proved to be the training grounds for many of those engaged in human rights abuses in the Iraq War. Other privatizations that are widely viewed as failures include UK's railroads and road privatizations in Mexico.

4 The drug companies' retort that these high prices are necessary to finance their research has little validity. Indeed, I note in chapter 2 that intellectual property protection was stripped away from naturally occurring genes in the United States. The result was not just lower prices, but an increased pace of innovation—better, and lower-cost tests for the presence of the relevant genes.

5 In Europe, the Troika (the IMF, the European Central Bank, and the European Commission, which together managed the bailouts and rescue packages) has consistently and massively underestimated the effects of their programs—which induced a 25 percent collapse in Greece's GDP between 2009 and 2013. One might think that after missing the mark once or twice they would have come to question their models. But no, they held on to them with even more vigor, and doubled down on the policies which brought so many countries in Europe into depression.

6 A fuller description of these changes is given in Joseph E. Stiglitz et al., *Rewriting the Rules of the American Economy*, op. cit.

7 This is part of the critique of Thomas Piketty's analysis of the source of the growth of inequality. See his book, *Capital in the Twenty-First Century* (Cambridge, MA: Belknap Press of Harvard University Press, 2014), and my books *The Great Divide,* op. cit., and *The Price of Inequality*, op. cit.

8 See in particular Joseph E. Stiglitz et al., *Rewriting the Rules of the American Economy*, op. cit.

9 See S. F. Reardon and K. Bischoff, "Income Inequality and Income Segregation," *American Journal of Sociology* 116 (4) (2011), pp. 1092–153.

10 With the earned income tax credit, an individual with a low income receives money from the government in proportion to his wage income.

11 There are many details of how this can be done that take us beyond this brief overview. For instance, the United States could impose a global minimum corporate income tax. The underlying problem is what is called the transfer price system, which allows multinationals largely to make up prices—allowing them to pretend that most of their profits originate in low-tax jurisdictions. Apple, discussed in an earlier chapter, provided an example of how this could be done in ways that almost eliminated taxes on profits made in Europe.

12 Data for 2016. For the United States, the figure is the share of manufacturing in total nonfarm employment from the BLS. For Germany, employment in manufacturing is from the OECD and total employment is from Bundesagentur für arbeit. The definition of manufacturing sometimes differs across countries, but the picture is still clear: the share of employment in manufacturing has been declining in the past decades.

13 Recall from our earlier discussion that industrial policies are not limited to policies promoting industry. Any policies by which government promotes a particular sector are called industrial policies—including policies aimed at restructuring the economy from manufacturing to a service sector.

14 See Bruce C. Greenwald and Joseph E. Stiglitz, *Creating a Learning Society: A New Approach to Growth, Development, and Social Progress*, op. cit.

15 Joseph E. Stiglitz and Mary Kaldor, eds., *The Quest for Security: Protection Without Protectionism and the Challenge of Global Governance* (New York: Columbia University Press, 2013).

16 We also need to manage the trade deficit—sudden changes in the trade deficit, such as occurred under Reagan (as a percentage of GDP, the trade deficit increased from 0.5 percent in 1981 to 3.1 percent in 1987) or Bush (increasing from around 3.6 percent in 2000 to 5.5 percent in 2006), put enormous stress on the economy.

17 We can, for instance, backward-engineer what is required to achieve all of these goals. Take the hardest case which the United States confronted after the onset of the Great Recession, where interest rates were set at zero, so there was no further scope for monetary policy. Even at a 0 percent interest rate, there is some level of government expenditure that can support full employment. At this zero interest rate, full employment equilibrium, we can calculate both the trade and fiscal deficits, and the exchange rate which is consistent with that trade deficit. Assume now, worried about the effect of the trade deficit on industrial

workers, the United States wished to lower it. There are again tools at the government's disposal with which it can do this—and simultaneously continue to maintain full employment. It can, for instance, spend more on items, like education, with more "U. S." content. This enables full employment to be maintained with a lower fiscal deficit. The lower fiscal deficit resulting from the changed expenditure policies means a lower trade deficit.

18 That is, if at full employment, domestic savings is increased relative to investment, the exchange rate falls, helping the manufacturing sector.

19 This was one of the key recommendations of the International Commission of Experts on Reforms of the International Monetary and Financial System. See discussion in the afterword, pp. 363–64.

20 Warren Buffett, "Here's How I Would Solve the Trade Problem," *Fortune,* April 29, 2016, available at http://fortune.com/2016/04/29/warren-buffett-foreign-trade/.

21 See the discussion of trade chits in Joseph E. Stiglitz, *The Euro: How a Common Currency Threatens the Future of Europe*, op. cit., and J. E. Stiglitz, "Macro-Economic Management in an Electronic Credit/Financial System," NBER Working Paper 23032, January 2017.

22 As I noted, though, under the rules of globalization—that allow free mobility of short-term money in and out of the country—if those in the financial market believe that deficits will lead to problems, they will pull their money out of the country. The *belief* itself is what creates the problems—whether that belief is grounded in theory or empirical evidence or not.

Some Republicans in the United States have opposed increasing the deficit or, more accurately, have opposed it during Democratic administrations; they've supported it under Republican presidents, such as Reagan, George W. Bush, and most recently Trump. But even then, they support it not for financing the structural transformation described earlier or for addressing the problems of inequality, but for tax cuts for the rich and an expansion of military spending.

23 Poverty head count ratio at national poverty lines, percentage of total population. Source: World Bank.

24 The strictures imposed by the European Union may be even worse. See Joseph E. Stiglitz, *The Euro,* op. cit.

25 See Joseph E. Stiglitz et al., *Rewriting the Rules of the American Economy,* op. cit.

26 See, for instance, Jonathan D. Ostry, Andrew Berg, and Charalambos G. Tsangarides, "Redistribution, Inequality, and Growth," *IMF Staff Discussion Notes*, 2014, available at https://www.imf.org/external/pubs/ft/sdn/2014/sdn1402.pdf.

27 In *The Great Divide,* op. cit., Part I: Big Think, "Of the 1 Percent, by the

1 Percent, for the 1 Percent" (originally published in *Vanity Fair,* May 2011), I describe more fully the dangers of pursuing an unenlightened self-interest. In the introduction to that volume, I describe a dinner party of billionaires, where the conversation turned repeatedly to "remember the guillotine," a reference to the risk of ignoring what is going on with the majority of citizens.

28 See, in particular, Stiglitz, *The Great Divide,* op. cit.

PART II

CHAPTER 5

1. J. Chirac, "The Economy Must Be Made to Serve People," address at the International Labour Conference, June 1996.

2. In 1990, 2.718 billion people were living on less than $2 a day. In 1998, the number of poor living on less than $2 a day is estimated at 2.801 billion—World Bank, *Global Economic Prospects and the Developing Countries 2000* (Washington, DC: World Bank, 2000), p. 29. For additional data, see *World Development Report* and *World Economic Indicators,* annual publications of the World Bank. Health data can be found in UNAIDS/WHO, *Report on the HIV/AIDS Epidemic 1998.* While there has been some controversy concerning these numbers, there is little disputing three facts: There has been little progress eliminating poverty; most of the progress has been in Asia, and especially China; and in much of the rest of the world the plight of the poor has worsened. In Sub-Saharan Africa, 46 percent of the population lives in absolute poverty (on less than a dollar a day), and in Latin America and the former Soviet Union the percentage of the population in poverty (on this very stringent definition) is 16 percent and 15 percent, respectively.

3. See Gerard Caprio, Jr., et al., eds., *Preventing Bank Crises: Lessons from Recent Global Bank Failures. Proceedings of a Conference Co-Sponsored by the Federal Reserve Bank of Chicago and the Economic Development Institute of the World Bank.* EDI Development Studies (Washington, DC: World Bank, 1998).

4. While there have been a host of critiques of the structural adjustment program, even the IMF's review of the program noted its many faults. This review includes three parts: internal review by the IMF staff (IMF Staff, *The ESAF at Ten Years: Economic Adjustment and Reform in Low-Income Countries.* Occasional Papers #156, February 12, 1998); external review by an indepen-

dent reviewer (K. Botchwey, et al., *Report by a Group of Independent Experts Review: External Evaluation of the ESAF* [Washington, DC: IMF, 1998]); and a report from IMF staff to the Board of Directors of the IMF, distilling the lessons from the two reviews (IMF Staff, *Distilling the Lessons from the ESAF Reviews* [Washington, DC: IMF, July 1998]).

CHAPTER 6

1. Mengistu's regime is blamed for killing at least 200,000 persons, according to Human Rights Watch, and for forcing about 750,000 citizens to become refugees.

2. For a more extensive discussion of the Ethiopia episode, see Robert Hunter Wade, "Capital and Revenge: The IMF and Ethiopia," *Challenge* 44 (5) (September 1, 2001), pp. 67–75.

3. T. Lane, A. Ghosh, J. Hamann, S. Phillips, M. Schulze-Ghattas, and T. Tsikata, "IMF-Supported Programs in Indonesia, Korea, and Thailand: A Preliminary Assessment," Occasional Paper 178, International Monetary Fund, January 1999.

4. The list of criticisms of conditionality discussed below is not meant to be comprehensive. See, for instance, M. Goldstein, "IMF Structural Conditionality: How Much Is Too Much," revision of the paper presented at the 2000 NBER conference on "Economic and Financial Crises in Emerging Market Economies," Woodstock, Vermont, October 19–21. The IMF and the World Bank have come to question conditionality, both its effectiveness and the consequences of excessive conditions. See, e.g., IMF, "Strengthening Country Ownership of Fund-Supported Programs," December 5, 2001, and World Bank, *Assessing Aid: What Works, What Doesn't Work, and Why* (Oxford: Oxford University Press, 1998).

5. There is considerable controversy about whether central banks should or should not be more independent. There is some evidence (based on cross-country regressions) that inflation rates may be lower, but there is little evidence that *real variables*, like growth or unemployment, are improved. My point here is not to resolve these disputes, but to emphasize that, given that there is such controversy, a particular view should not be imposed on the country.

CHAPTER 7

1. To take one example, see Peter Waldman and Jay Solomon, "How U.S. Companies and Suharto's Circle Electrified Indonesia—Power Deals That

Cut in First Family and Friends Are Now Under Attack," *Wall Street Journal*, December 23, 1998, p. 1.

2. Adam Smith put forward the idea that markets by themselves lead to efficient outcomes in his classic book, *The Wealth of Nations*, written in 1776, the same year as the Declaration of Independence. The formal mathematical proof—specifying the conditions under which it was true—was provided by two Nobel Prize winners, Gerard Debreu of the University of California at Berkeley (Nobel laureate in 1983) and Kenneth Arrow of Stanford University (Nobel laureate in 1972). The basic result, showing that when information is imperfect or markets are incomplete, competitive equilibrium is not (constrained Pareto) efficient, is due to B. Greenwald and J. E. Stiglitz, "Externalities in Economies with Imperfect Information and Incomplete Markets," *Quarterly Journal of Economics* 101 (2) (May 1986), pp. 229–64.

3. See W. A. Lewis, "Economic Development with Unlimited Supplies of Labor," *Manchester School* 22 (1954), pp. 139–91, and S. Kuznets, "Economic Growth and Income Inequality," *American Economic Review* 45(1) (1955), pp. 1–28.

CHAPTER 8

1. For some contrasting views, see Paul Krugman, "The Myth of Asia's Miracle: A Cautionary Fable," *Foreign Affairs* (November 1994), and J. E. Stiglitz, "From Miracle to Crisis to Recovery: Lessons from Four Decades of East Asian Experience," in J. E. Stiglitz and S. Yusuf, eds., *Rethinking the East Asian Miracle* (Washington, DC, and New York: World Bank and Oxford University Press, 2001), pp. 509–26; or J. E. Stiglitz, "Some Lessons from the East Asian Miracle," *World Bank Research Observer* 11 (2) (August 1996), pp. 151–77. See also World Bank, *The East Asian Miracle: Economic Growth and Public Policy* (New York: Oxford University Press, 1993); Alice Amsden, *The Rise of "the Rest": Challenges to the West from Late-Industrialization Economies* (New York: Oxford University Press, 2001); and, Masahiko Aoki, Hyung-Ki Kim, Okuno Okuno-Fujiwara, and Masahjiro Okuno-Fjujiwara, eds., *The Role of Government in East Asian Economic Development: Comparative Institutional Analysis* (New York: Oxford University Press, 1998). For an extremely readable account of the East Asia crisis, see Paul Blustein, *The Chastening: Inside the Crisis that Rocked the Global Financial System and Humbled the IMF* (New York: Public Affairs, 2001). More technical discussions are provided, e.g., in Morris Goldstein, *The Asian Financial Crisis: Causes, Cures, and Systemic Implications* (Washington,

DC: International Institute for Economics, 1998), and Jason Furman and Joseph E. Stiglitz, *Brookings Papers on Economic Activity*, presented at Brookings Panel on Economic Activity, Washington, DC, September 3, 1998, vol. 2, pp. 1–114.

2. Since the U.S. economy was not affected, the United States did not offer any assistance, in marked contrast to the generous treatment it had given Mexico in its last crisis. This gave rise to enormous resentment in Thailand. Especially after the strong support it had provided the United States during the Vietnam War, Thailand thought it deserved better treatment.

3. See E. Kaplan and D. Rodrik, "Did the Malaysian Capital Controls Work?," working paper no. W8142 National Bureau of Economic Research, Cambridge, Mass., February 2001. It is possible to find this paper at Professor Rodrik's Web site, http://ksghome.harvard.edu/~.drodrik.academic.ksg/papers.html).

4. Korea received $55 billion, Indonesia $33 billion, and Thailand $17 billion.

5. See J. Sachs, "The Wrong Medicine for Asia," *New York Times*, November 3, 1997, and "To Stop the Money Panic: An Interview with Jeffrey Sachs," *Asiaweek*, February 13, 1998.

6. In 1990, foreign direct investment ($ millions) was 24,130; in 1997, it was 170,258, and in 1998, 170,942; portfolio investment in 1990 ($ millions) was 3,935, rising to 79,128 in 1997, and 55,225 in 1998. Bank and trade related investment was 14,541 in 1990, 54,507 in 1997, and 41,534 in 1998. Total private capital flows (in $ millions) 42,606 in 1990, 303,894 in 1997, and 267,700 in 1998. From World Bank, Global Development Finance 2002.

7. On factors involved in financial and banking crises, see, e.g., D. Beim and C. Calomiris, *Emerging Financial Markets* (New York: McGraw-Hill/Irwin, 2001), chapter 7; A. Demirguc-Kunt and E. Detragiache, *The Determinants of Banking Crises: Evidence from Developing and Developed Countries*, IMF Staff Papers, vol. 45, no. 1 (March 1998); G. Caprio and D. Klingebiel, "Episodes of Systemic and Borderline Financial Crises," *World Bank*, October 1999; and World Bank Staff, "Global Economic Prospects and the Developing Countries 1998/99: Beyond Financial Crisis," The World Bank, February 1999.

8. M. Camdessus, "Capital Account Liberalization and the Role of the Fund," remarks at the IMF Seminar on Capital Account Liberalization, Washington, DC, March 9, 1998.

9. The American slowdown of 2000–2001 too has been traced to excessive market exuberance, an overinvestment in Internet and Telecom brought

on in part by soaring stock prices. Marked fluctuations in the economy can arise even in the absence of mismanagement of financial institutions and monetary policy.

10. The debate surrounding Korea was part of a broader debate about capital market liberalization and the bailouts that follow when things go wrong, as they inevitably do—a debate that was held within the IMF and the U.S. government almost completely behind closed doors. It occurred repeatedly, for instance, as we prepared for regional trade agreements and for G-7 meetings. On the one occasion (the Mexican 1995 crisis) when Treasury brought the issue of bailouts to Congress and Congress rejected the proposal, Treasury went back to its usual closed quarters, figured out a way of proceeding with the bailout without congressional approval, and strong-armed other governments to participate (in a manner that engendered large hostility in many European quarters—the full ramifications of the strong-arm tactics of the U.S. Treasury have played out slowly over the ensuing years, as U.S. positions in a variety of contexts have subtly been opposed, e.g., the choice of the head of the IMF). The issues are complicated, but the U.S. Treasury almost seemed to revel in its ability to outsmart Congress.

11. In IMF, *Annual Report of the Executive Board for the Financial Year Ended April 30, 1998* (Washington, DC), p. 25, some IMF directors doubted the need for strict fiscal policies during the Asian crisis because these countries did not experience fiscal imbalance. Interestingly, the IMF in its similar report for 2000 recognized (p. 14) that an expansionary fiscal policy is behind the recovery from the crisis of Korea, Malaysia, and Thailand. See also T. Lane, A. Ghosh, J. Hamann, S. Phillips, M. Schulze-Ghattas, and T. Tsikata, "IMF-Supported Programs in Indonesia, Korea, and Thailand: A Preliminary Assessment," Occasional Paper 178, International Monetary Fund, January 1999.

12. Stanley Fischer, "Comment & Analysis: IMF—The Right Stuff. Bailouts in Asia Are Designed to Restore Confidence and Bolster the Financial System," *Financial Times*, December 16, 1997.

13. Over the years, I have never heard a coherent defense of the IMF's strategy of raising interest rates in countries with highly leveraged firms from any IMF staffers. The only good defense I did hear was from Chase Securities chief economist John Lipsky, who focused explicitly on imperfections of capital markets. He observed that domestic businessmen typically kept large amounts of money abroad but borrowed domestically. The high interest rates on the domestic loans would "force" them to bring back some of their foreign funds in order to pay off the loans and avoid paying such

rates. This hypothesis has not yet been evaluated. Certainly for several of the crisis countries, net capital flow moved in the opposite direction. Many business people assumed that they simply could not be "forced" to pay the high interest rates and that there would have to be renegotiation. In effect, the high interest rates were not credible.

14. The Ministry of Finance official in charge, Eisuke Sakakibara, has subsequently written his own interpretation of the events in E. Sakakibara, "The End of Market Fundamentalism," Speech delivered at Foreign Correspondents Club, Tokyo, January 22, 1999.

15. For further details, see E. Kaplan and D. Rodrik, "Did the Malaysian Capital Controls Work?," op. cit.

16. During this crisis period, foreign direct investment to Malaysia showed a pattern similar to other countries affected by the crisis and in the region. Nonetheless, the evidence is still too preliminary to draw solid conclusions. A deeper econometric study (and more data) is required in order to disentangle the effect of capital controls on foreign direct investment from other factors that affect foreign direct investment.

Chapter 9

1. Much of this and the next two chapters is based on work reported more extensively elsewhere. See the following papers: J. E. Stiglitz, "Whither Reform? Ten Years of the Transition" (Annual World Bank Conference on Development Economics, 1999), in Boris Pleskovic and Joseph E. Stiglitz, eds., The World Bank (Washington, DC, 2000), pp. 27–56; J. E. Stiglitz, "Quis Custodiet Ipsos Custodes? Corporate Governance Failures in the Transition," in Pierre-Alain Muet and J. E. Stiglitz, eds., *Governance, Equity and Global Markets, Proceedings from the Annual Bank Conference on Development Economics in Europe*, June 1999 (Paris: Conseil d'Analyse economique, 2000), pp. 51–84. Also published in *Challenge* 42 (6) (November/December 1999), pp. 26–67. French version: "Quis custodiet ipsos custodes? Les defaillances du gouvernement d'entreprise dans la transition," *Revue d'Economie du Developpement* 0 (1–2) (June 2000), pp. 33–70. In addition, see D. Ellerman and J. E. Stiglitz, "New Bridges Across the Chasm: Macro- and Micro-Strategies for Russia and other Transitional Economies," *Zagreb International Review of Economics and Business* 3(1) (2000), pp 41–72, and A. Hussain, N. Stern, and J. E. Stiglitz, "Chinese Reforms from a Comparative Perspective," in Peter J. Hammond and Gareth D. Myles, eds., *Incentives, Organization, and Public Economics. Papers in Honour of Sir James Mirrlees* (Oxford and New York: Oxford University Press, 2000), pp. 243–77.

For excellent journalistic accounts of the transition in Russia, see Chrystia Freeland, *Sale of the Century* (New York: Crown, 2000); P. Klebnikov, *Godfather of the Kremlin, Boris Berezovsky and the Looting of Russia* (New York: Harcourt, 2000); R. Brady, *Kapitalizm: Russia's Struggle to Free Its Economy* (New Haven: Yale University Press, 1999); and John Lloyd, "Who Lost Russia?," *New York Times Magazine*, August 15, 1999.

A number of political scientists have offered analyses broadly agreeing with the interpretations provided here. See, in particular, A. Cohen, *Russia's Meltdown: Anatomy of the IMF Failure*, Heritage Foundation Backgrounders No. 1228, October 23, 1998; S. F. Cohen, *Failed Crusade* (New York: W. W. Norton, 2000); P. Reddaway, and D. Glinski, *The Tragedy of Russia's Reforms: Market Bolshevism Against Democracy* (Washington, DC: United States Institute of Peace, 2001); Michael McFaul, *Russia's Unfinished Revolution: Political Change from Gorbachev to Putin* (Ithaca, N.Y.: Cornell University Press, 2001); Archie Brown and Liliia Fedorovna Shevtskova, eds., *Gorbachev, Yeltsin and Putin: Political Leadership in Russia's Transition* (Washington, DC: Carnegie Endowment for International Peace, 2000); and Jerry F. Hough and Michael H. Armacost, *The Logic of Economic Reform in Russia* (Washington, DC: Brookings Institution, 2001).

Not surprisingly, a number of reformers have provided accounts that differ markedly from those presented here, though such interpretations were more frequent in the earlier, more hopeful days of the transition, some with titles that seem to jar with subsequent events. See, e.g., Anders Aslund, *How Russia Became a Market Economy* (Washington, DC: Brookings Institution, 1995) or Richard Layard and John Parker, *The Coming Russian Boom: A Guide to New Markets and Politics* (New York: The Free Press, 1996). For more critical perspectives, see Lawrence R. Klein and Marshall Pomer, eds. (with a foreword by Joseph E. Stiglitz), *The New Russia: Transition Gone Awry* (Palo Alto, Calif.: Stanford University Press, 2001).

Data cited in this chapter come largely from the World Bank, *World Development Indicators and Global Development Finance* (various years).

2. Janine R. Wedel, "Aid to Russia," *Foreign Policy in Focus* 3 (25), Interhemispheric Resource Center and Institute Policy Studies, September 1998, pp. 1–4.

3. For further reading, see P. Murrell, "Can Neo-Classical Economics Underpin the Economic Reform of the Centrally Planned Economies?" *Journal of Economic Perspectives* 5(4) (1991), pp 59–76.

4. See International Monetary Fund, "IMF Approves Augmentation of Russia Extended Arrangement and Credit Under CCFF, Activates GAB," Press release no. 98/31, Washington, DC, July 20, 1998.

5. There is an argument that the IMF really did not ignore this. In fact, some believe that the Fund was trying to close the devaluation option by making the cost of devaluation so high that the country would not do it. If this was indeed the argument, the IMF miscalculated badly.

6. There was, of course, more to the Russian government's announcement of August 17, but these were among the central features for our purposes. In addition, the Russian government established temporary controls of capital such as a prohibition on nonresidents investing in short-term ruble assets and a ninety-day moratorium on foreign exchange credit and insurance payments. The Russian government also announced its support to a payment pool set up by the largest Russian banks in order to maintain the payment stability and sent legislation for timely payments to government employees and for the rehabilitation of banks. For details, see the Web site www.bisnis.doc.gov/bisnis/country/980818ru.htm, which provides the original texts of the two public announcements on August 17, 1998.

7. See the Web site of the Institute for the Economy in Transition, at http://www.iet.ru/trend/12-99/3_e.htm.

8. See Chrystia Freeland, op. cit.; Richard Layard and John Parker, op. cit.; and Anders Aslund, op. cit.

9. For the implications and costs that barter imposes on the Russian economy, see C. G. Gaddy and B. W. Ickes, "Russia's Virtual Economy," *Foreign Affairs* 77 (September–October 1998).

10. The transition has not appeared to benefit the poor. For example, the lowest quintile of the population had a share of income equal to 8.6 percent in Russia (in 1998), 8.8 percent in Ukraine (in 1999), 6.7 percent in Kazakhstan (in 1996) (World Bank, *World Development Indicators 2001*).

11. Using a standard measure of inequality (the Ginii coefficient), by 1998 Russia had achieved a level of inequality twice that of Japan, 50 percent greater than UK and other European countries, a level comparable to Venezuela and Panama. Meanwhile, those countries that had undertaken gradualist policies, Poland and Hungary, had been able to keep their level of inequality low—Hungary's was even lower than Japan's and Poland's lower than the UK's. See Angus Maddison, *The World Economy: A Millenial Perspective* (Paris: Organisation for Economic Co-operation and Development, 2001).

12. See Stiglitz, "Quis Custodiet Ipsos Custodes?" op. cit.

13. For instance: If one liberalizes capital markets before an attractive investment climate is created at home—as the IMF recommended—one is inviting capital flight. If one privatizes firms before an efficient capital market is created

at home, in a way that puts ownership and/or control in the hands of those who are nearing retirement, there is no incentive for long-term wealth creation; there are incentives for asset stripping. If one privatizes before creating a regulatory and legal structure for ensuring competition, there are incentives to create monopolies, and there are *political* incentives to prevent the creation of an effective competition regime. If one privatizes in a federal system, but leaves state and local authorities free to impose taxes and regulations at will, one has not eliminated the power, and incentives, of public authorities to extract rents; in a sense, one has not really privatized at all.

14. For the Coase theorem itself, see R. H. Coase, "The Problem of Social Cost," *Journal of Law and Economics* 3 (1960), pp. 1–44. This theorem holds only where there are no transactions costs, and no imperfections of information. Coase himself recognized the force of these limitations. Moreover, it is never possible fully to specify property rights, and this was especially true for the economies in transition. Even in advanced industrialized countries, property rights are circumscribed by concerns for the environment, worker rights, zoning, and so forth. Although the law may try to be as clear on these matters as possible, disputes frequently arise, and have to be settled through legal processes. Fortunately, given the "rule of law," there is general confidence that this is done in a fair and equitable manner. But not so in Russia. See A. Shleifer and R. Vishny, *The Grabbing Hand: Government Pathologies and Their Cures* (Boston: Harvard University Press, 1999) for an articulation of the view that once property rights are granted, there will be strong forces for the creation of the rule of law. For a more extended discussion of Coase's theorem and the role it played in reasoning about appropriate privatization strategies, see J. E. Stiglitz, *Whither Socialism* (Cambridge: MIT Press, 1994); J. E. Stiglitz, "Whither Reform? Ten Years of the Transition," op. cit; J. E. Stiglitz, *Quis Custodiet Pisos Custodes*, op. cit.; and J. Kornai, "Ten Years After 'The Road to a Free Economy', The Author Self-Evaluation," in Boris Pleskovic and Nicholas Stern, eds., *Annual World Bank Conference on Development Economics 2000* (Washington, DC: World Bank, 2001), pp. 49–66.

CHAPTER 10

1. Though this was the *supposed* defense, as we noted earlier, even this defense was questionable. The oligarchs did not use the funds to finance Yeltsin's reelection. But they did give him the organizational basis (and the TV support) he needed.

2. The transition countries governed in 2002 by former Communist parties or

leaders were: Albania, Azerbaijan, Belarus, Croatia, Kazakhstan, Lithuania, Moldova, Poland, Romania, Russia, Slovenia, Tajikistan, Turkmenistan, and Uzbekistan.

3. For details, see M. Du Bois and E. Norton, "Foiled Competition: Don't Call It a Cartel, But World Aluminum Has Forged a New Order," *Wall Street Journal*, June 9, 1994. This article noted the close relation between O'Neill and Bowman Cutter, at that time Clinton's deputy director of the National Economic Council, as instrumental in order to "cook" the deal. The sweetener for the Russians was an equity investment worth $250 million, guaranteed by the OPIC. The American aluminum executives did everything to take care of the appearances in order to avoid antitrust prosecution, and the American government included three antitrust lawyers to draft the agreement, which, according to this article, was carefully vaguely worded in order to satisfy the Justice Department.

In 1995, this cartel started to fall apart with the increase in world demand for aluminum and the difficulties of enforcing the cartel agreement with the Russian producers—see S. Givens, "Stealing an Idea from Aluminum," *The Dismal Scientist*, July 24, 2001. In addition, Alcoa and other American aluminum producers were sued for conspiring to restrain trade; but the case was dismissed in courts—see J. Davidow, "Rules for the Antitrust/Trade Interface," Miller & Chevalier, September 29, 1999, at www.ablondifoster.com/library/article.asp?pubid=143643792001&groupid=12. For an editorial expressing an opinion similar to that here, see *Journal of Commerce*, February 22, 1994.

The story does not end there: in April 2000, news emerged about how two Russian oligarchs (Boris Berezovsky and Roman Abramovich) were successfully forming a private monopoly to control 75–80 percent of the Russian yearly production, creating the second largest aluminum company in the world (after Alcoa). See "Russian Aluminum Czars Joining Forces," *The Sydney Morning Herald*, April 19, 2000, and A. Meier and Y. Zarakhovich, "Promises, Promises," *Time Europe* 155(20), May 22, 2000. See also, R. Behar, "Capitalism in a Cold Climate," *Fortune* (June 2000). Despite accounts to the contrary, Boris Berezovsky vehemently denied any wrongdoing in relation to Russia.

CHAPTER 11

1. In the *New York Times*, Kolodko wrote: "But there was another, equally important facet of our success. Poland did not look to the international

financial community for approval. Instead, we wanted Polish citizens to go along with these reforms. So salaries and pensions were paid and adjusted for inflation. There were unemployment benefits. We respected our own society, while doing tough negotiating with international investors and financial institutions." George W. Kolodko, "Russia Should Put Its People First," *New York Times*, July 7, 1998.

2. Poland also showed that one could maintain state ownership of the assets and not only prevent asset stripping but actually increase productivity. In the West, the largest gains in productivity were associated not with privatization, but with corporatization, i.e., imposing hard budget constraints and commercial practices on enterprises while they still remained state-owned. See J. Vickers and G. Yarrow, *Privatization: An Economic Analysis* (Cambridge, MA: MIT Press, 1988), chapter 2, and J. Vickers and G. Yarrow, "Economic Perspectives on Privatization." *Journal of Economic Perspectives* 5(2) (Spring 1991), pp. 111–32.

3. China's net private capital inflows were $8 billion in 1990. By 1999, China's capital inflows had soared to $41 billion, more than ten times the amount of money attracted by Russia in that same year (World Bank, *World Development Indicators 2001*).

4. See, e.g. World Bank, *World Development Report 1996: From Plan to Market* (London and New York: Oxford University Press, June 1996).

5. The best defense that the radical reformers in Russia have of their failure is this: we do not know the *counterfactual*, what might otherwise have been. The options available in these other countries were simply not available. By the time the radical reformers had taken over, a centrally guided reform like the one in China was no longer possible, because central power in Russia had collapsed. The takeover of the enterprises by the *nomenklatura*, the existing managers, which occurred in many cases anyway, *was* the alternative. On the contrary, I would argue that a recognition of these problems made it even more important not to conduct the privatization and liberalization strategy in the way that it was done. The breakup of central power should have made it easier, and more important, to break up the large national enterprises, especially in natural resources, into competing parts, leading to greater diffusion of economic power. It made it more imperative to ensure that a working tax system was in place before the sources of revenue generation were given away. China's reforms involved enormous devolution of economic decision making. The alternative strategies in the end might not have worked, but it is hard to believe that matters could have turned out worse.

CHAPTER 12

1. See S. Fischer, "On the Need for an International Lender of Last Resort," *Journal of Economic Perspectives* 13 (1999), pp. 85–104. Fischer, like many others advocating the lender of last resort view, makes an analogy between the role of a central bank within a country and the role of the Fund among countries. But the analogy is deceptive. A lender of last resort is required domestically because of the first-come-first-served basis of deposits, which contribute to the possibility of runs—see D. Diamond and P. Dibvig, "Bank Runs, Deposit Insurance, and Liquidity," *Journal of Political Economy* 91 (1983), pp. 401–19. And even then, it does not suffice to avoid runs, as the experience in the United States demonstrates forcefully. Only when accompanied by strong banking regulation and deposit insurance does a lender of last resort suffice to fend off runs. And no one—not even the most ardent supporters of the IMF—has advocated that it provides anything analogous to deposit insurance. Moreover, the rigidity with which the Fund has implemented many policies makes many countries wary of ceding to it much regulatory authority (even if the appropriate domain of regulatory authority could be defined, and even if issues of national sovereignty did not become paramount). It is worth noting that U.S. regulatory authorities have often argued that *well-designed* policies of forbearance are a critical part of macroeconomic management, while the IMF has typically argued against such forbearance. Elsewhere, I have argued that in doing so, the IMF has often failed to take account of the basic fallacy of composition: in the presence of systemic problems, the absence of forbearance may be self-defeating as each bank, unable to raise additional capital, calls in its loans, leading to more widespread defaults, and furthering the economic downturn.

2. What I call a "super-Chapter 11." For details, see M. Miller and J. E. Stiglitz, "Bankruptcy Protection Against Macroeconomic Shocks: The Case for a 'Super Chapter 11,' " World Bank Conference on Capital Flows, Financial Crises, and Policies, April 15, 1999; and J. E. Stiglitz, "Some Elementary Principles of Bankruptcy," in *Governance, Equity and Global Markets: Proceedings from the Annual Bank Conference on Development Economics in Europe*, June 1999 (Paris: Conseil d'Analyse economique, 2000), pp. 605–20.

3. While it is hard to blame the crisis on lack of transparency, lack of transparency did have its cost. Once the crisis had occurred, the lack of information meant that creditors withdrew their funds from all borrowers regardless of quality. Creditors simply did not have the information with which to distinguish between good and bad borrowers.

CHAPTER 13

1. The term *corporate governance* refers to the laws that determine the rights of shareholders, including minority shareholders. With weak corporate governance, management may effectively steal from shareholders, and majority shareholders from minority shareholders.

2. World Bank studies, including those coauthored by my predecessor as chief economist at the World Bank, Michael Bruno, formerly head of Israel's Central Bank, helped provide the empirical validation of this perspective. See Michael Bruno and W. Easterly, "Inflation Crises and Long-run Growth," *Journal of Monetary Economics* 41 (February 1998), pp. 3–26.

3. Economists have analyzed what the attributes of such goods are; they are goods for which the marginal costs of supplying the goods to an additional individual are small or zero, and for which the costs of excluding them from the benefits are large.

4. Economists have analyzed deeply why such markets may not exist, e.g., as a result of problems of information imperfections (information asymmetries), called *adverse selection* and *moral hazard*.

5. It was ironic that the calls for transparency were coming from the IMF, long criticized for its own lack of openness, and the U.S. Treasury, the most secretive agency of the U.S. government (where I saw that even the White House often had trouble extracting information about what they were up to).

6. The perception in some quarters is that those inside the country can decide on such issues as when the school year will begin and end.

7. The IMF's position of institutional infallibility makes these changes in position particularly difficult. In this case, senior people could seemingly claim, trying to keep a straight face, that they had been warning of the risks associated with capital market liberalization for a long time. The assertion is at best disingenuous (and itself undermines the credibility of the institution). If they were aware of these risks, it makes their policy stances even more unforgivable. But to those who were subjected to their pressure, these concerns were at most minor caveats, matters to think about later; what they were told was to proceed, and to proceed rapidly, with liberalization.

8. As we noted in chapter 12, the multiple objectives—and the reluctance to discuss openly the tacit change in the mandate to reflect the interests of the financial community—led to many instances of intellectual incoherence; this in turn made coming up with coherent reforms more difficult.

9. As its name indicates, a contingent credit line provides credit automatically in certain contingencies, those associated with a crisis.

10. There were more profound problems. While a contingent credit line could make sure that some new funds were made available in the presence of a crisis, it could not prevent other short-term loans from not being rolled over; and the amount of exposure that the banks would be willing to take would presumably take into account the new loans that would be made under the contingent credit line facility. Thus there was a concern that the net supply of funds available in the event of a crisis might not be affected that much.

11. These provisions allow a creditor to demand payment under certain circumstances—generally precisely the circumstances in which other creditors are pulling back their money.

12. In Europe, a great deal of attention has focused on one particular tax proposal, the so-called Tobin Tax—on cross-border financial transactions. See, for instance, H. Williamson, "Köhler Says IMF Will Look Again at Tobin Tax," *Financial Times*, September 10, 2001. There is now a large body of literature analyzing the tax theoretically and empirically. For an account of this literature, see the Web site www.ceedweb.org/iirp/biblio.htm. Interestingly, even the former Treasury secretary wrote an article that could be interpreted as supporting the principles underlying the tax—L. H. Summers and V. P. Summers, "When Financial Markets Work Too Well: A Cautious Case for a Securities Transactions Tax," *Journal of Financial Services Research* 3 (1989), pp. 261–86. But there remain significant implementation problems, especially in a world in which the tax is not imposed universally and in which derivatives and other complicated financial instruments have become prevalent. See also J. E. Stiglitz, "Using Tax Policy to Curb Speculative Short-Term Trading," *Journal of Financial Services Research* 3(2/3) (December 1989), pp. 101–15. For the original proposal, see J. Tobin, "A Proposal for International Monetary Reform," *Eastern Economic Journal* 4 (1978), pp. 153–59, and B. Eichengreen, J. Tobin, and C. Wyplosz, "Two Cases for Sand in the Wheels of International Finance," *Economic Journal* 105 (May 1995), pp. 162–72. In addition, see the collection of essays in M. ul Haq, I. Kaul, and I. Grunberg, eds., *The Tobin Tax: Coping with Financial Volatility* (London and New York: Oxford University Press, 1996).

13. Though in the aftermath of the East Asia crisis, these proposals received considerable attention, with the Argentine crisis, which involved public indebtedness, attention was switched to sovereign debt restructuring mechanisms—in spite of the fact that many of the recent crises have involved private not sovereign debt.

14. As we saw, opening up a country to foreign banks may not lead to more

lending, especially to small and medium-sized domestic enterprises. Countries need to impose requirements, similar to those in America's Community Reinvestment Act, to ensure that as they open their markets up, their small businesses are not starved of capital.

15. The debt crisis hit Argentina in 1981, Chile and Mexico in 1982, and Brazil in 1983. Output growth remained very slow throughout the remainder of the decade.

16. The reassessment (as we have noted) actually began earlier, under pressure from the Japanese, and was reflected in the Bank's publication in 1993 of the landmark study, *The East Asian Miracle: Economic Growth and Public Policy*. The changes in thinking were reflected in the annual reports on development, called the World Development Report. For instance, the 1997 report reexamined the role of the state; the 1998 report focused on knowledge (including the importance of technology) and information (including the imperfections of markets associated with imperfect information); the 1999 and 2001 reports emphasized the role of institutions, not just policies; and the 2000 report took a much broader perspective on poverty.

17. Not surprisingly, the Bank still has not taken as seriously as it should the theoretical and empirical critiques of trade liberalization, such as that provided by F. Rodríguez and D. Rodrik, "Trade Policy and Economic Growth: A Skeptic's Guide to the Cross-National Evidence," Ben Bernanke and Kenneth S. Rogoff, eds., in *Macroeconomics Annual 2000* (Cambridge, MA: MIT Press for NBER, 2001). Whatever the intellectual merits of that position, it runs counter to the "official" position of the United States and other G-7 governments that trade is good.

18. There are many dimensions to this transformation—including the acceptance of change (recognizing that things do not have be done in the way they have been done for generations), of the basic tenets of science and the scientific way of thinking, of the willingness to accept the risks that are necessary for entrepreneurship. I am convinced that such changes, under the right circumstances, can occur in a relatively short span of time. For a more extensive articulation of this view of "development as transformation," see J. E. Stiglitz, "Towards a New Paradigm for Development: Strategies, Policies and Processes," 9th Raul Prebisch Lecture delivered at the Palais des Nations, Geneva, UNCTAD, October 19, 1998.

19. In several of the countries, debt service is more than a quarter of exports; in a couple, it is almost half.

20. Such debts are sometimes referred to as "odious debts."

21. An important exception is Jim Wolfensohn, who has pushed cultural initiatives at the World Bank.

22. Recently, developing countries have been increasingly pushed to comply with standards (e.g., of banking) that they have played little part in setting. Indeed, this is often heralded as one of the few "achievements" of the efforts to reform the global economic architecture. Whatever good they may do to improve global economic stability, the way they have been brought about has engendered enormous resentment in the developing world.

AFTERWORD TO THE 2017 EDITION

1 A survey of nearly 50,000 people in 45 countries, conducted by WIN/Gallup International Association, found that Hillary Clinton would beat Donald Trump by a landslide in every country except Russia. "WIN/Gallup International's Global Poll on the American Election" available at http://www.wingia.com/web/files/richeditor/filemanager/WINGIA_Global_Poll_on_US_Election_-_FINALIZED_Revised_Global_Press_Release.pdf.

2 I describe this in my book *The Roaring Nineties,* which was published in 2003, the year after *GAID.* My position on these issues was based, in part, on theoretical work I had done prior to moving to Washington, some of which was itself motivated by financial crises in the United States (the S&L bailout of 1989) and elsewhere. See, e.g., "The Role of the State in Financial Markets," *Proceedings of the World Bank Annual Conference on Development Economics* (Washington, DC: World Bank, 1994), pp. 19–52; "Introduction: S&L Bailout," in J. Barth and R. Brumbaugh, eds., *The Reform of Federal Deposit Insurance: Disciplining the Government and Protecting Taxpayers* (New York: HarperCollins, 1992), pp. 1–12; "Financial Restraint: Toward a New Paradigm," with T. Hellmann and K. Murdock, in M. Aoki, H. Kim, and M. Okuna-Fujiwara, eds., *The Role of Government in East Asian Economic Development* (Oxford: Clarendon Press, 1997), pp. 163–207; and "Liberalization, Moral Hazard in Banking and Prudential Regulation: Are Capital Requirements Enough?" with T. Hellmann and K. Murdock, *American Economic Review* 90 (1) (March 2000), pp. 147–65.

Two papers with Bill Easterly and Roumeen Islam that I wrote while I was at the World Bank showed empirically that financial market deepening (usually associated with deregulation) could lead to more volatility: "Shaken and Stirred: Explaining Growth Volatility," *Annual Bank Conference on Development Economics 2000* (Washington, DC: World Bank, 2001), pp. 191–212; and "Shaken and Stirred: Volatility and Macroeconomic Paradigms for Rich and Poor Countries," in Jacques Drèze, ed., *Advances in Macroeconomic Theory*, IEA Conference Volume 133 (Houndsmill, UK: Palgrave, 2001), pp. 353–72.

3 The story of the financial crisis is told more fully in my book *Freefall* (New York: W. W. Norton, 2010).

4 The figures are 9.2 percent for China, -2.8 percent for the United States.

5 This includes Brazil (U.S. receives 13 percent of Brazil's exports and China 18 percent; and U.S. is 15 percent of Brazil's imports and China is 18 percent); and Argentina (U.S. is 6.1 percent of Argentina's exports and China is 8.9 percent; U.S. is 13 percent of Argentina's imports and China is 20 percent). Source: The Observatory of Economic Complexity from UN COMTRADE data, 2015, available at http://atlas.media.mit.edu/.

6 See discussion "Capital controls" on p. 352.

7 There were, of course, many others that advised the president on economic matters, but typically from the perspective of one part of the economy or the other—Labor Secretary Robert Reich had much to say about what was happening to workers and the inequality which even then was at a worrisome level; Treasury Secretary Robert Rubin reflected the perspectives of financial markets, and particularly, of the large multinational banks like Goldman Sachs, from which he came, and Citibank, to which he went after leaving government service; and Commerce Secretary Ron Brown represented a variety of business interests. The Council of Economic Advisers uniquely took a national, and often a global, perspective. I explained these differences in a speech to the American Economic Association in January 1997, subsequently published as "Looking Out for the National Interest: The Principles of the Council of Economic Advisers," *American Economic Review* 87 (2) (May 1997), pp. 109–13.

8 Including George Akerlof and Michael Spence, with whom I shared the Nobel Memorial Prize in economics; and a large number of coauthors with whom I had worked over the years, including Michael Rothschild, Bruce Greenwald, Andy Weiss, Carl Shapiro, Patrick Rey, Yungyoll Yun, Andrew Kosensko, Thomas Hellman, Kevin Murdoch, Sanford Grossman, Richard Arnott, and Thomas Hellmann.

9 The particular notion of efficiency was called Pareto efficiency, after the great Italian economist, Vilfredo Pareto (1848–1923)—no one could be made better off without making someone else worse off.

10 See D. Newbery and J. E. Stiglitz, "Pareto Inferior Trade," *Review of Economic Studies* 51 (1) (1984), pp. 1–12.

11 See "Capital-Market Liberalization, Globalization, and the IMF," *Oxford Review of Economic Policy* 20 (1) (Spring 2004), pp. 57–71. Later, in response to a subsequent IMF attempt to defend their model, I extended the analysis: see chapter 2 in J. E. Stiglitz and J. A. Ocampo, eds., *Capital Market Liberalization and Development* (New York: Oxford University Press, 2008), pp. 76–100. That volume contains other critiques of capital market liberalization—a view that since the crisis has become mainstream.

12 See the introduction for a discussion of the origins of the Washington Consensus and some of the controversy over what it entailed. *GAID* (Part II of this volume) was, of course, centered on a critique of Washington Consensus policies.

13 As I also explain in *GAID*, Adam Smith was keenly aware of some of the limitations of markets, far more so than modern advocates of free markets.

14 The work for which I received the Nobel Prize in 2001. With Michael Rothschild, I showed that even a little bit of information imperfection could drastically change the nature of the equilibrium ("Equilibrium in Competitive Insurance Markets: An Essay on the Economics of Imperfect Information," *Quarterly Journal of Economics* 90 [4] [November 1976], pp. 629–49); with Carl Shapiro, now at the University of California, Berkeley, I showed that competitive markets could have persistent unemployment—as is evidently the case ("Equilibrium Unemployment as a Worker Discipline Device," *American Economic Review* 74 [3] [June 1984], pp. 433–44). With Andy Weiss, I showed that even in competitive markets there could be credit rationing ("Credit Rationing in Markets with Imperfect Information, *American Economic Review* 71 [3] [June 1981], pp. 393–410). With Bruce Greenwald, now of Columbia University, I showed that with imperfect information and incomplete risk markets, competitive markets were not, in general, efficient ("Externalities in Economies with Imperfect Information and Incomplete Markets," *Quarterly Journal of Economics* 101 [2] [May 1986], pp. 229–64).

15 The consensus was forged at Saltsjöbaden, Sweden, on September 16–17, 2016, at a meeting sponsored by the World Bank and the Swedish Aid Agency. See https://www.wider.unu.edu/news/stockholm-statement-%E2%80%93-towards-new-consensus-principles-policy-making-contemporary-world.

16 E.g., in chapter 10, I describe the U.S. privatization of uranium enrichment. At the time, it seemed set for failure. What happened since confirmed those expectations.

17 Michael Seigel and Elliott Young, "Privatization in Mexico Is a Road to Nowhere," *Quartz*, August 9, 2013, available at qz.com/113017/

privatization-in-mexico-is-a-road-to-nowhere. Foreign Minister Jorge Castañeda is quoted describing the private road project as "a dumb idea that didn't work."

18 See "The Liberalization and Management of Capital Flows—An Institutional View," November 14, 2012 (press summary available at http://www.imf.org/external/pubs/ft/survey/so/2012/POL120312A.htm).

19 Elsewhere in this book (see chapter 1, section "Increased Risk" and the references cited there), we have noted how without a complete set of risk markets, markets are not efficient. The problem with markets is worse than that they don't efficiently manage risk. It is that they sometimes undertake excessive risk, failing to take into account the effects of their actions on others. See note 44 for a discussion of these macroeconomic externalities. Moreover, in the absence of adequate government regulation, they are prone to create credit and asset bubbles. For an historical discussion, see C. P. Kindleberger and R. Z. Aliber, *Manias, Panics, and Crashes: A History of Financial Crises*, 6th ed. (New York: Palgrave Macmillan, 2011). For a broader theoretical analysis, see Joseph E. Stiglitz, *Towards a General Theory of Deep Downturns* (New York: Palgrave Macmillan, 2016), also available, as NBER Working Paper 21444, August 2015, originally presented as Presidential Address to the 17th World Congress of the International Economic Congress, Dead Sea, Jordan, June 2014.

20 In particular, Larry Summers, who was undersecretary of the Treasury and later secretary of the Treasury during the events described in *GAID,* and head of the National Economic Council under President Obama; and Tim Geithner, who was undersecretary of the Treasury under President Clinton, and secretary of the Treasury under Obama. They would, of course, argue that the circumstances were different, and different circumstances require different policies.

21 By announcing that *some* private banks would be closed an the depositors not bailed out—but not disclosing which banks—a run on virtually all of the private banks was induced.

22 See Joseph E. Stiglitz, *Freefall,* op. cit. At the time I wrote *GAID,* bail-ins (forcing depositors to bear part of the cost of a bank restructuring) and bailouts were subjects that had at the time received scant attention, and as a result, much of the policy advice was based on, at best, incomplete analyses that did not take adequate account of how various market participants would respond to whatever policy the government announced.

There has since developed an extensive literature, including Olivier Jeanne and Anton Korinek, "Macroprudential Regulation Versus Mopping Up After the Crash," NBER Working Paper 18675, 2012; Martin Schneider and Aaron Tornell, "Balance Sheet Effects, Bailout Guarantees, and Financial Crisis," *Review of Economic Studies*, 71 (3) (2004), pp. 883–913; Emmanuel Farhi and Jean Tirole, "Collective Moral Hazard, Maturity Mismatch, and Systemic Bailouts," *American Economic Review* 102 (1) (2012), pp. 60–93; and A. Caproni, B. Bernard, and J. E. Stiglitz, "Bail-ins and Bail-outs: Incentives, Connectivity, and Systemic Stability," Columbia University working paper, 2017.

23 As I noted in the introduction, the increase in reserves, in the trillions of dollars, had one very peculiar aspect: because most of the reserves were held in dollars (U.S. Treasury bills), it meant that poor countries were lending money to the United States, at very low interest rates, and often simultaneously borrowing back money at much higher interest rates.

24 Source: IMF World Economic Outlook (WEO), April 2017.

25 Some of the economically successful countries of East Asia have had a hard time making a smooth transition to democracy, and similar worries are being raised in Africa.

26 Source: World Bank, World Development Indicators (WDI), August 2017.

27 Source: UN World Population Prospects. Median estimate.

28 Several years after leaving the World Bank, I undertook a reexamination of the data on the relative performance of the countries undertaking the two different strategies, using the nearly ten years' additional data that was available then. The results reinforced the conclusions reached in *GAID*. See S. Godoy and J. E. Stiglitz, "Growth, Initial Conditions, Law, and Speed of Privatization in Transition Countries: 11 Years Later," in S. Estrin et al., eds., *Transition and Beyond* (Hampshire, UK: Palgrave Macmillan, 2007), pp. 89–117. More recently, with still more data available, I reexamined the matter once again—and the results were if anything still stronger. As I also note later, many of the shock therapy countries never succeeded in constructing a diversified economy, so that they were particularly hard hit by the 2008 financial crisis.

29 Average annual growth rates between 1980 and 2010 for China and between 1990 and 2016 for Vietnam. Sources: IMF World Economic Outlook (WEO), April 2017, and World Bank.

30 See his blogpost, "For Whom the Wall Fell? A Balance-Sheet of Transition to Capitalism," glineq.blogspot.com, November 3, 2014, available at http://glineq.blogspot.com/2014/11/for-whom-wall-fell-balance-sheet-of.html.

31 Source: IMF World Economic Outlook (WEO), April 2017.

32 The fact that even in Poland there is growing concern that the principles of constitutional democracy are being undermined shows that economics is not the only determinant of these political evolutions.

33 The G-7 consisted of the United States, the UK, France, Germany, Canada, Italy, and Japan.

34 The only African country of the G-20 is South Africa. Other countries have participated as "guests."

35 At the Gleneagles G-8 meeting in 2005, the developed countries committed themselves to increasing financial aid to Africa by $50 billion a year, and to spend 0.7 percent of their GDP on aid. Few of the countries have come anywhere near living up to their promise.

36 U.S. Senate, Committee on Homeland Security and Governmental Affairs, "Offshore Profit Shifting and the U.S. Tax Code—Part 2 (Apple Inc.)," May 21, 2013, p. 47, available at https://www.gpo.gov/fdsys/pkg/CHRG-113shrg81657/pdf/CHRG-113shrg81657.pdf. There was no suggestion that Apple was doing anything illegal in the United States. In Europe, however, the European Commission argued that Apple and Ireland had secretly worked together to circumvent European laws, with Apple owing some $14.6 billion (or €13 billion).

37 There is a tax committee within the UN that would have to be "elevated" in order to enable it to address such issues. The OECD has brought emerging markets within its deliberations, but they feel that within the OECD, the advanced countries, and especially the United States, dominate.

38 As noted in the introduction, at a special meeting held on July 9, 2009, the UN General Assembly, following the report of a Commission of Experts on Reforms of the International Monetary and Financial System that had been appointed by its president in the aftermath of the global financial crisis, expressed overwhelming support for the Commission's recommendations. Even the United States supported the resolution, though noting reservations that the subject of global reserves was an area that should be the responsibility of the IMF. The report of the Committee of Experts is available as *The Stiglitz Report: Reforming the International Monetary and Financial Systems in the Wake of the Global Crisis*, with Members of the Commission of Experts on Reforms of the International Monetary and Financial System appointed by the President of the United Nations General Assembly (New York: New Press, 2010).

39 The Obama administration's position was especially peculiar because of concerns that it might lead countries around the world to look askance at borrowing in U.S. markets. It provided another instance of a weakness in governance in the advanced countries, and of the revolving door which I so sharply criticize in *GAID*. Among the lobbyists for the hedge funds was someone who had formerly had a senior position in Obama's National

Security Council. Hedge funds were put ahead not only of the interests of the Argentine people, but of other parts of the financial sector.

In effect, the lobbying worked. After a new government took office in Argentina in December 2015, it settled with the vulture funds, some of which made an enormous return on their investments. The estimated return of NML Capital Ltd., the leading litigant, was 1270 percent. See Martin Guzman, "An Analysis of Argentina's 2001 Default Resolution," Centre for International Governance Innovation (CIGI) Papers No. 110, October 2016.

40 The issue of reform, which I cannot treat adequately here, is so important that I devoted a whole chapter to it in *Making Globalization Work* (chapter 9).

41 World foreign direct investment inflows and portfolio equity net inflows were, respectively, 2.6 and 2.1 times higher over the period from 2002 to 2016 than between 1988 and 2002. Source: World Bank. Portfolio equity includes net inflows from equity securities other than those recorded as direct. Both Portfolio Equity and FDI inflows are highly volatile from one year to the next.

42 See Olivier J. Blanchard et al., eds., *In the Wake of the Crisis* (Cambridge, MA: MIT Press, 2012); and George Akerlof et al., eds., *What Have We Learned? Macroeconomic Policy After the Crisis* (Cambridge, MA, and London: MIT Press, 2014).

43 Alan Greenspan, the chairman of the Federal Reserve from 1987 to 2006, was often given credit for the long period of seeming stability, sometimes referred to as the Great Moderation. The pinnacle of this hagiography was a book by Bob Woodward, called *Maestro: Greenspan's Fed and the American Boom,* published in 2001 just before the breaking of the tech bubble, in response to which Greenspan let loose the real estate bubble that was to bring down the global economy a few years later.

44 Macroeconomic externalities was another area in which, as I wrote *GAID,* I felt the need for more research—the conventional models gave little insight, with sometimes wrong, sometimes contradictory, policy recommendations. Consider the issue of contagion. Everybody, including the IMF, talked about it and about the dangers that it presented: a downturn in one country could quickly spread to others. This is clearly an example of an extreme externality. But contagion occurs when there is financial integration—the kind the IMF had been advocating. Before the crisis, the IMF heralded the virtues of financial diversification and integration; afterward, they worried about the consequences. Their advice was obviously intellectually incoherent—and the models they used before crises occurred focused only on the benefits, not the costs. Indeed, the economics pro-

fession as a whole was weak in that respect. The theory of diversification that they focused on would have meant that if 100 individuals exposed to Ebola arrived in New York, the response would be to send 2 to each state *to diversify the risk.* Work in this area has continued—with the global financial crisis providing a big impetus. Before the crisis, I had begun work with a group of European economists on the question of when does diversification increase risk (through contagion), with most of the results published after the 2008 crisis. See, for example, "Credit Chains and Bankruptcy Propagation in Production Networks," with S. Battiston, D. Delli Gatti, and B. Greenwald, *Journal of Economic Dynamics and Control* 31 (6) (2007), pp. 2061–84; and two papers with S. Battiston, D. Delli Gatti, M. Gallegati, and B. Greenwald: "Default Cascades: When Does Risk Diversification Increase Stability, *Journal of Financial Stability* 8 (3) (2012), pp. 138–49, and "Liaisons Dangereuses: Increasing Connectivity, Risk Sharing, and Systemic Risk," *Journal of Economic Dynamics and Control* 36 (8) (2012), pp. 1121–41. I published two articles on contagion in the immediate aftermath of the 2008 crisis: "Risk and Global Economic Architecture: Why Full Financial Integration May Be Undesirable," *American Economic Review* 100 (2) (2010), pp. 388–92; and "Contagion, Liberalization, and the Optimal Structure of Globalization," *Journal of Globalization and Development* 1 (2) (2010), Article 2.

45 In congressional testimony, Greenspan admitted that there was a "flaw" in his reasoning—a flaw that cost the economy trillions of dollars. He had thought that the banks would be able to manage their risks better. In saying this, he admitted that he had paid insufficient attention to one of the key developments in modern economics emphasizing corporate governance. It should have been obvious that the banks gave their executives incentives to engage in excessive risk taking. Thus, the excessive risk taking was predictable, and predicted. And even then, he seemed not to recognize the key role of externalities. The case of Bernanke is different. He was overly influenced by the models which he and others had constructed—models which typically left out banks and bankruptcy, and simply ignored systemic externalities. That was partly why the Fed seemed so unprepared for the consequences of shutting down Lehman Brothers. The possibility, or even likelihood, of Lehman Brothers going bankrupt had been widely discussed in financial markets for months before the event. With the Fed having even better data on the situation, the failure to be prepared was hard to explain, other than by noting that the Fed, in this period, seems to have been overly influenced by free-market ideology.

46 This is still another area in which, at the time I wrote *GAID,* there was

insufficient research. Indeed, little attention was given even to the concept of systemic fragility and the implications of that for the design of financial structure (or as I referred to it in my 2010 paper on contagion, financial architecture). See, in particular, the work of Franklin Allen and Douglas Gale ("Financial Contagion," *Journal of Political Economy* 108 [1] [2000], pp. 1–33) and my work with Bruce Greenwald, *Towards a New Paradigm in Monetary Economics* (Cambridge: Cambridge University Press, 2003), chapter 7. My work was in part inspired by the East Asia crisis, and the challenge of resolving systemic bankruptcy described in chapter 8—when firms owe money to each other, and the ability of each to repay depends on what it gets repaid. There is obviously a high degree of interdependence, with very non-linear relationships in the presence of bankruptcy costs. A reasonably full analysis has only been achieved recently. See Tarik Roukny, Stefano Battiston, and J. E. Stiglitz, "Interconnectedness as a Source of Uncertainty in Systemic Risk," op. cit.

Most notable of the work after the crisis on systemic risk is that of Andy Haldane and his coauthors—P. Gai, A. Haldane, and S. Kapadia, "Complexity, Concentration and Contagion," *Journal of Monetary Economics* 58 (5) (2011), pp. 453–70; or A. G. Haldane and R. May, "Systemic Risk in Banking Ecosystems," *Nature* 469 (7330) (2011), pp. 351–55. See also S. Battiston, G. Caldarelli, R. Maye, T. Roukny, and J. E. Stiglitz, "The Price of Complexity in Financial Networks," *PNAS (Proceedings of the National Academy of Sciences of the United States of America)* 113 (36) (2016), pp. 10031–36.

47 At a dinner I attended in New York, one of his chief economic advisers waxed poetic about how Trump was quickly going to undo regulations, including and especially in the financial sector, apparently not fully understanding the process by which regulations got adopted and repealed or replaced. Someone asked a rhetorical question which went unanswered: Hadn't there been a major financial crisis in 2008, which had proven enormously costly? What did the Trump administration propose, to avoid a recurrence?

48 President Clinton had hoped that the new round of negotiations would be initiated in a meeting in Seattle in November 1999. Massive street protests—sometimes referred to as the "Battle of Seattle"—led to the scuttling of talks.

49 As we explained in chapter 3, even if the U.S.-China deficit improved, the multilateral trade deficit wouldn't be affected, because that is determined by macroeconomics. Given the low level of trade barriers, the effect on global GDP of the absence of new trade agreements may be limited. As I

noted earlier, what was described as the largest trade agreement ever, TPP (set aside by Trump in one of his first acts as president) was estimated to have a negligible effect on growth.

50 I argue in *Making Globalization Work* that such a cross-border tax would in fact be WTO-compliant. There is increasing support for such actions, especially as firms in countries that are responding to climate change argue that the failure of the United States to do anything gives its firms a competitive advantage; because they don't have to pay this cost of production (the costs of carbon emissions), they are effectively being subsidized, and such subsidies are not compliant with the WTO system. Countries can impose countervailing duties.

51 As I noted earlier, they simultaneously refused to provide the additional funds necessary, or to change the governance rules to allow those that did provide funds to have a say in governance commensurate with their contributions. Others naturally remain unwilling to provide additional funds unless they have a greater share in the governance (in voting rights).

52 I noted earlier the enormous potential supply of funds. Some of these "funders" are reluctant to take on excessive risk, but one of the advances in modern financial markets has been the ability to shift and reallocate risk. The New Development Bank, it is anticipated, will take advantage of these new developments.

53 It officially opened for business on January 16, 2016, and the Articles of Agreement went into force on December 25, 2015.

54 One of Trump's first acts as president was to withdraw from TPP, but the TPP is not quite dead, since the 11 remaining members have said that they will revive it. But many of the provisions of the TPP were put there at the insistence of the United States (such as those concerning intellectual property, and particularly drugs). Without the United States, there would be no reason for them to retain those provisions. If the TPP is revived, it will need to be renegotiated.

55 I say "seemingly" because all of the protectionism may be little more than campaign rhetoric. Though he has continued with some of the same rhetoric, those he has appointed seem more in synch with advancing the interests of America's rent-seeking plutocrats than in helping those who lost their jobs in manufacturing.

56 Source: United Nations, Department of Economic and Social Affairs, Population Division (2017). World Population Prospects: The 2017 Revision, Key Findings and Advance Tables. ESA/P/WP/248. Available at https://esa.un.org/unpd/wpp/Publications/Files/WPP2017_KeyFindings.pdf.

57 In 2016, the United States and the EU accounted for 32 percent of the

World GDP. They are projected to account for 21 percent of the World GDP by 2050. China and India accounted for 25 percent of the World GDP in 2016 and will account for 35 percent of the World GDP by 2050. Source: "The World in 2050," PWC, available at https://www.pwc.com/gx/en/issues/economy/the-world-in-2050.html.

58 As I noted above, these were reflected in policies to reshape the World Bank under Paul Wolfowitz.

59 For China, "core interests" include claims it makes over islands in the South China Sea. "Full text of President Xi's speech at opening of Belt and Road Forum," available online by the Permanent Mission of the People's Republic of China to the UN, http://www.china-un.org/eng/zgyw/t1465819.htm.

60 Poor countries do not pay low wages to take advantage of trade agreements; they pay low wages because they are poor. Differences in the cost of labor are part of comparative advantage. One cannot say one is in favor of free trade, but only if it is fair, and fair trade entails paying workers wages comparable to those in the United States. Labor standards/working conditions are analogous. There are likely to be longer hours of work in poorer countries—just as there was in the United States a hundred years ago. So outside of a few egregious cases—like the use of prison labor—it is hard to determine what "unfair" labor conditions means. Some agreements simply say that governments have to enforce whatever conditions they specify. But this may actually have an adverse effect. In some countries, setting labor conditions in law serves a "norm"-setting function; it defines what firms should aspire to. Large differences from these norms are punished. If they are told to punish even small differences, they will set standards lower.

61 Belgium had held up for a while the Canadian-EU trade agreement in 2016.

62 When the United States lost a case brought by Nicaragua over its covert war against that country, the United States decided to accept the court's jurisdiction only on a case-by-case basis.

63 This form of competition is called "Bertrand competition." With Bertrand competition, small differences in (marginal) costs can result in large differences in market share, in contrast with the more common Cournot competition, where firms with slightly different costs share the market place, and the firm with the lower costs has a slightly larger market share. An important part of the analysis is that firms are able to entrench themselves. Joseph Schumpeter (1883–1950), the great scholar of innovation, argued that one should not be worried that markets where innovation is

important are dominated by a single firm. That monopoly power would be temporary; there would be a succession of monopolists; and competition for the market would replace competition in the market. Research over the past quarter century has shown that he was wrong; the dominant firm has mechanisms to ensure its position becomes entrenched, the resulting equilibrium is inefficient both statistically and dynamically. For globalization, this becomes particularly important when a disproportionate share of the entrenched monopolies is in the United States or other advanced countries, and then the United States and the other advanced countries work to create global rules that, on the one hand, allow the monopoly to remain entrenched, stifling innovation elsewhere and, on the other, allow the monopoly to avoid paying taxes on the economic activities that occur in the developing countries and emerging markets.

64 Microsoft's anticompetitive policies were clever and effective—but ruled to be illegal on three continents. But the legacy of these anticompetitive practices was significant; its market domination continued for years after it discontinued some of its worst practices.

65 Baumol's disease is the rise of real wages in jobs that have not experienced any increase in labor productivity, in response to rising wages in other sectors in which labor productivity has increased. Baumol was the first to make that observation in the performing arts sector (in Theatre, Opera, Music, etc.). Real wages had increased in this sector in the first half of the twentieth century despite no real productivity growth in the sector. See W. Baumol and W. Bowen, *Performing Arts—the Economic Dilemma: A Study of Problems Common to Theatre, Opera, Music and Dance* (New York: Twentieth Century Fund, 1966).

66 In some ways, our metrics overestimate growth; they don't take into account, for instance, the lower quality of service provided in most modern retail stores, where the customer may have to spend more time searching for the right product himself and is provided with less information about the qualities of the products being purchased.

67 For instance, MOOCS, the massive online open courses, have provided valuable access to some of the best teachers in the world, and even while free, the numbers reached remains limited and so too the extent to which they have been integrated into standard instructional programs. This may, of course, change in the future.

68 There is an extensive literature on the relationship between subjective well-being and income suggesting that this is the case.

69 While the United States and Britain have low unemployment rates, glob-

ally, some 200 million remained unemployed in 2016, about 15 percent more than before the 2008 crisis. Source: World Bank (from modeled ILO estimates).

70 See J. M. Keynes, "Proposals for an International Clearing Union," in Seymour E. Harris, ed., *The New Economics: Keynes' Influence on Theory and Public Policy* (London: Dennis Dobson, 1943).

71 I note in chapter 4 the increase in concentration in a large number of important sectors in the United States. Market power can be exercised even when there are two or three firms. Prices will be far higher than costs, and there can be sustained profits, which show up as abnormally high returns to capital.

INDEX

Page numbers beginning with 395 refer to endnotes.